IDENTITY
ISSUES
AND
WORLD
RELIGIONS

Design and Cover Design by Rosemary Aliukonis

Printed by the University Relations Unit, Flinders University.
Distributed by Wakefield Press, 282 Richmond Rd., Netley S.A., Australia 5037.

First Published July 1986

National Library of Australia card number and ISBN

ISBN 0 908083 14 9

TABLE OF CONTENTS

PART A
THE SELECTED PAPERS

Twenty-seven Select Papers Related to the Congress Theme:
Religion and Identity

I What Gives Identity to a Religion or a Morality

II Personal Identity Issues in Various Religions

III The Keynote Address, A Brief Response, and the Major Issue of Lost Identity in the History of Religions

PART B
THE CONGRESS PROCEEDINGS

INTRODUCTION

Victor C. Hayes

South Australian College of Advanced Education

Here is a volume of scholarly conversation for everyone caught up in or concerned with issues of identity and religion in a pluralistic, changing world.

That such a volume of international scholarship in the History of Religions should emerge out of Australia was, until but yesterday, highly improbable. But it happened! For the first time in its 85-year history, the International Association for the History of Religions (IAHR) ventured into the Southern Hemisphere. It held its 15th Congress at the University of Sydney, Australia, from August 18 through 23, 1985. Participants numbered 439 and came from 29 countries. Their theme: Religion and Identity.

Of 281 papers delivered at the Congress, perhaps one quarter were "theme-related". With the invaluable assistance of eighteen Sectional Co-ordinators, 65 of these were selected and considered for publication. All were "of scholarly merit" and most were within the "suggested 6,000 word length-limitation". Responsibility for the final choice of 27 papers (10% of the total) belongs to the editor who has tried to give shape to this anthology while representing fairly the diversity of concerns, academic disciplines, religious traditions, and even world geographic areas, involved in our discussions.

PART A

Perhaps fortunately, most papers do not linger long over definitions of "religion" and "identity". It is enough that a few familiar definitions of "religion" appear as heuristic devices, e.g., "religion is the relationship to the Ultimate, the source of everything" **(Mantovani)**, or "religion is any means towards ultimate transformation" (**Tsui**'s use of Streng), or "religion is the sacralisation of identity" **(Mol).** Most papers accept Western conventions about which traditions and which phenomena are "religious" but a few (e.g. those by **Rule, Bradley, Tsui, Mantovani**) critique the dominance of Western categories as distorting or irrelevant when applied to Eastern or primal traditions.

Nor do authors linger long over definitions of "identity". The word may suggest something static, but in these papers identity is associated with dynamic temporal process. Authors speak of it as being lost, sought, found and maintained; as being stripped away, re-established, reconstructed and transformed. Identities are said to compete, help, threaten, jostle and reinforce one another; they collide, adapt, intersect and become entangled. The boundaries of religions are porous enough, or understood flexibly enough, to make possible much traffic between religions and between religions and the world. In all this the key notion may be not so much identity-sameness as discerned continuity.

The theme "Religion and Identity" may thus appear continuous, if not identical, with the 1980 Winnipeg Congress theme: "Traditions in Contact and Change". Under either rubric most of the important questions can be subsumed (cf. Ninian Smart below). In this volume 27 papers are gathered into seven sections.

I

Papers in the first group focus on what gives identity to a religion or a morality. They raise basic and seemingly straightforward questions: Wherein lies the identity of a religion? **(Hubert Seiwert)** How is it that different religions appear to share common moral ground? **(Peter Donovan)** Why do religions persist in their separateness? **(David Bradley)** All three papers are concerned with "boundaries" and "authority" and the basic identity-conferring functions of myth and tradition.

II

A second group of papers focuses variously on personal identity issues in diverse traditions. **Karl Werner** explores Vedic, Upanisadic and early Buddhist concepts of personal identity, and finds no essential difference between them for, he argues, each holds that the phenomenal personality is a structural unity of constituents held together and/or inwardly controlled by a force which does not itself provide any distinctive marks of one's personal identity. This force is aja ("the Unborn") in the Vedas; or atman (neither this nor that) in the Upanisads; or atta, the transcendent force which early antimetaphysical Buddhism referred to only negatively by denying that khandhas, individually or collectively, comprise it. Werner holds that with some exceptions subsequent Hindu and Buddhist systems can be shown to be variations and elaborations of this pattern. (It is not the case, therefore, that "Hinduism" believes in an indestructible, individual, transmigrating soul while "Buddhism" denies it.)

Turning to an Eastern Christian tradition, **Luther Martin** first reminds us that the Delphic maxim, "Know thyself", was understood by the Greeks from Plato on as the obligation to take care of oneself, the main principle of Greek ethics and a guide to the art of life. However, in the Eastern non-canonical Thomas tradition — which contrasts with the Western tradition of a "doubting Thomas" and which presents the apostle as possessing salvific knowledge, the nature of which is self-knowledge — "taking care of oneself" appears not as an obligation but as an interdiction! Martin explores the implications of this antithesis for an Eastern Christian view of the self.

Noel King then directs our attention to three classic pilgimage accounts from as many great traditions. The *peregrinatio* as a genre cannot be tightly defined, says King, but the search for and the finding of identity may be one of its important features. King concludes that pilgrimage through the centuries has been, among other things, a means of transmitting spiritual and religious genes and that the *peregrinatio* preserves the encoding. As those who know Noel King know, these are not merely armchair speculations. The adventurous risk-filled questings of King and his pilgrims seem far from the pastoral "comfortings" of **Kenneth Dempsey's** Australian rural minister who seems forced to seek a sense of meaning and personal worth in non-church community affairs! Yet, while moving in radically different directions, both pilgrim and pastor are "religious" figures questing in their different ways for personal identity.

In a further contrast, **James Horne** presents John Henry Newman as one whose commitment to the social morality of his religious community was combined with responsible social criticism and self-realization. In Newman's concept of conscience — given by God through Newman's personal experience and his church's scriptures and traditions — a strong sense of individual identity is significantly influenced by social morality. Horne considers this synthesis in terms of "moral luck" (Thomas

Nagel, Bernard Williams) and "destiny" (Paul Tillich, Langdon Gilkey) in order to conclude that "identity achieved without social morality would have a deficient sense of destiny".

III

The third and central section begins with the opening address given to the Congress by **Hans Mol**. Mol suggests that in everyday life the meaning of identity has moved away from abstract idea to the much more concrete notion of "bounded system" or "unit of social organization", such as self, tribe, community, family, ethnic group, class, nation, etc. These "systems" or "identities" attempt to maintain unity, sameness, continuity, or structure within, but do so in the face of many factors frustrating their boundaries. Mol sees them as a jostling configuration of cooperating but also contending units of social organizations displaying the same kind of differentiation-integration or fragmentation-wholeness dialectic that is present in age-old religious traditions.

This dialectic between identity and change is, for Mol, part and parcel of the very being of any surviving religion. Religion, he says, reinforces the various units of social organization ("identities") through transcendental ordering (objectification), emotional anchoring (commitment, faith) and sameness enacting (ritual). It also reconciles the tension between them or redresses imbalances in accordance with its transcendental blueprint. Yet by doing so, it introduces de-sacralizing elements through relativization of existing standards, de-commitment from undesired beliefs and values, and the stripping away of old identities.

It seemed appropriate to present Mol's theoretical considerations — and **Ninian Smart's** response to them — just prior to our fourth and fifth group of papers; and to place this sociological perspective in a position where it could itself contend with the many other perspectives represented by the papers from fifteen other Congress sections. But not only that. We have also placed here **Ursula King**'s paper in order to insist on the centrality of an issue which cuts through all traditions and academic disciplines: the recognition of women in their full humanity and dignity, the welcoming of the distinctive, enriching feminist perspective and experience into the study of religion. Dr King's paper will not permit any of us, men or women, to indulge some traditional androcentric perspective (whether conscious or unconscious) without challenge, as she argues for a major "paradigm shift" in studies in the history of religions.

IV

In the fourth section, several papers recount the efforts made by specific traditions to re-establish or maintain identity in changing contexts. **Alan Williams**, sees Zoroastrians in deep crisis as to their present identity. Today there are but 130,000 members of this, "the world's oldest revealed religion", and they are geographically fragmented across the world. William's study suggests that a religious identity survives when a community values its own theological distinctiveness. The Sikhs, too, as **W.H. McLeod** reports, have been deeply concerned to resolve the identity issue, and this has involved them in a lengthy quest for the definitive "rahit-nama", that is, a manual which would effectively define normative Sikh belief and behavior, modes of personal devotion, corporate ceremonies, etc. McLeod surveys this quest and assesses the success of the 1950 *Sikh Rahit Maryada* in stabilising Sikh religious identity. **M.H. Klaiman**'s paper takes us back to 16th Century Bengal to show how Brahmins used the (pre-existing) popular Krishna cult, Gaudiya Vaishnavism, to re-stabilise a threatened Hindu community and re-establish identity. This is followed by the paper by **Azim Nanji** with its focus on recent issues of tradition, revitalization and identity in the case of Nizari Ismaili Muslims. In illustrating both the unity and diversity of Muslim responses to modernization, Nanji underscores the transformative potential within the religious consciousness.

The two papers which conclude this section are in a different key. They raise the issue of self-definition (or auto-interpretation) vis-a-vis definition by others and in doing so point up the possible limitations of Western approaches to Eastern faiths. Taoism, says **Bartholomew Tsui**, is not to be equated with the order of Nature (Needham is a leading culprit here, he claims), for Taoism is "a way of ultimate transformation", hence a "religion"; and the biographies of Taoist immortals serve as exemplars for the Taoist, providing the latter with religious identity. **Paul Rule**, in his turn, argues that Neo-Confucianism is a "religion". If its true identity cannot be caught by our common Western categories, then these categories need a thoroughgoing revaluation!

V

The fifth section constitutes a recognition of the fact that in our generation, especially in the last fifteen years or so, the religious scene in many countries has been transformed by a new religious pluralism. Australia is a good example of this, but the countries reported on here are Canada (Quebec), Nigeria and Great Britain. These and other countries have experienced an invasion of new religious movements, some drawing inspiration from the West and some from the East.

Roland Chagnon reports an estimated 250 new religious movements in Quebec. He scans the religious and social history of Quebec in an attempt to show that after long having been in search of a collective identity, first in a religious sense and then in a secular sense, Quebeckers are now seeking group and personal identity among these new movements. There is a kind of triumph of individualism here, says the author, and the new cultural mode has made its impact on the established churches. In Nigeria, as **Rosalind Hackett** tells us, there has been, since 1970, an influx and indigenous growth of "the spiritual sciences" — groups specializing in metaphysics, mysticism and occultism, mostly from the U.S.A., Britain or India. There has been an accompanying growth market in magical objects and imported popular literature on magic, astrology, Kabbalism, parapsychology, secret biblical texts, etc. All this has generated new forms of religiosity (as well as some indigenous institutions) which Hackett calls "spiritual technology". It is characterized by a quest for spiritual knowledge, power and development and a direct experience and manipulation of the sacred. The author explores reasons for the popularity of this new, privatized and "self-sufficient" religiosity and considers its consequences for religious behavior and identity.

In Britain, as **Kim Knott** reports, the range of ethnic minority religions has been greatly widened by the recent influx of Muslims, Hindus, Sikhs, Parsees and West Indian and African religious communities. These transplantations of religions from one place to another raise many practical issues associated with the dynamics of identity-maintenance. What happens to the content of the transplanted faith? What happens to collective ritual-practice? to folkways? to the education of children? How does the religion now relate to culture, language, caste, business activity, and to the search for social and political identity? Knott observes, incidentally, that for some groups religious and ethnic identity are co-extensive (e.g., the Punjabi Sikhs), but that more often ethnic enclaves share a common religious identity. **Penelope Johnstone**'s paper considers the specific case of Muslims who, from varied backgrounds, have settled in Britain and now search to make explicit a common Islamic identity. Johnstone asks: Is the preservation of Islam compatible with British nationality? What are the distinctive features of being Muslim in a Western society? Is the concept of Umma relevant?

VI

The sixth section comprises three papers which self-consciously relate religion and culture in the examination of identity. **Richard Pilgrim** considers religio-aesthetic values and cultural identity in Japan by exploring the arts of MA. Ma (aida) indicates any interval or space within the continuity of either things or time — the empty space which is a room, a rest in music, a pause, the state of being "in-between" anything. More deeply, the term takes on philosophic, religious, and aesthetic significance especially as used in the traditional arts of Japan. Pilgrim is able to point to an underlying pan-Japanese religio-aesthetic value system which helps provide and support one form of cultural identity and consistency within the diversity of Japanese history, culture, art and religion. **Ennio Mantovani**, from Papua New Guinea, analyses the Simbu Pig Festival — which he has observed over the past twenty years — in order to arrive at an understanding of the meaning, the substance, of Simbu culture and the roots of Simbu identity. Missionaries, says Mantovani, have hitherto interpreted this festival from the wrong symbolic system, i.e., from a theistic rather than a bio-cosmic point of view. This has prevented them from seeing it as an impressive and authentic religious celebration which creates, expresses and strengthens Simbu identity. In the third paper, **James Tulip** discusses the question of Australian identity in terms of its poetry, religion and culture. Tulip's paper charts some half-dozen positions in modern Australian poetry for the insight they give into how Australians are seeing themselves imaginatively and, arguably, religiously. Differing responses to nature, aboriginal perceptions of reality and their white adaptations, urban parables, feminist criticism and artistic imagination are all represented.

VII

In the seventh and concluding section, three papers examine loyalties or identities of great generality. These are referred to as generational, ecumenical or world identities.

In the first paper, **Dale Bengtson** suggests that personal and cultural identities coalesce in the notion of generational identity. A generation, says Bengtson, is the primary agent of social change, and this generational process is identifiable as a ritual process (with pre-liminal, liminal and post-liminal phases). In terms of this model, the author interprets the religious changes wrought in America by the generation born following the close of the Second World War — a generation which brought about protean transformations in all aspects of American life. **Walter Principe** then directs our attention to the notion of "catholicity", one of the self-identifying traits of the Christian Church, and shows how various historical interpretations of the concept have affected cultural and national identity. Understood as uniformity, this "mark" of the true Church has often threatened national, cultural or personal identities, says the author. On the other hand, immigrant groups, as well as peoples or nations under pressure or persecution, have sometimes had their identities reinforced by the sense of belonging to a "catholic" church extending beyond their immediate situation.

This relationship or tension between universalist teaching and local identity-creating forms is a focus of much interest in the study of religious traditions. **Michael Pye**, in our last paper, describes an unusual and positive instance of this relationship in the modern Japanese religious movement known as Byakkō Shinkōkai (White Light Association). Here a liturgy for world peace dramatically emphasizes the search for a world (even cosmic) identity. Dr Pye, incoming Secretary-General of IAHR, reflects on the significance of this Japanese religious celebration for the overall theme of this Fifteenth Congress.

PART B

All Congress members received a 106 page *Congress Program Book* and a 184 page *Book of Abstracts*. These provided invaluable orientation and a guide to the six days of Congress activities.

The Proceedings incorporated into this volume as Part B do not repeat the material in these two pre-Congress books, with the important exception that the Academic Program *is* re-presented so as to incorporate all cancellations, additions and changes, checked item for item with Section Co-Ordinators. Part B opens with a contextualizing essay by **Eric Sharpe** who places this 15th Congress in the sequence of congresses beginning with Paris 1900 and describes its unique Australian setting. Sharpe's essay is followed by a record of Formal (and some informal) Events, a listing of the 281 papers which made up the Academic Program, a roll-call of the 440 Congress members (with their addresses), and information on IAHR and AASR.

For the record the following statistics are offered. Of the 281 papers given at the Congress, three were presented in Plenary Sessions, six at the Panel session, thirteen at the two Symposia, and 259 at the many sessions convened by the eighteen Sections. With the exception of the Sections on "Judaism" and "Indonesia and Southeast Asia", *all* Sections have at least one paper in this anthology. Some have more, thus: Islam 2, Methodology and Hermeneutics 2, Indian Religions 2, Comparative and Phenomenological Studies 2, East Asian Religions 3, and Anthropology and Sociology 4 (plus the Opening Address and Response). Christianity, the largest Section with 27 papers, has only one paper in this volume. The Congress Theme was suggested by a sociologist. Although the concept of identity has been around for a long time, it has been increasingly prominent in the more recent social science literature.

The authors come from eight countries: England 7, USA 7, Australia 4, Canada 4, New Zealand 2, Papua New Guinea 1, Hong Kong 1 and West Germany 1. Five of the authors are women. Of the 440 registered Congress members, 200 have Australian addresses (and almost half of these are members of AASR which has some 350 members). My best estimate (since gender cannot be read into initials) is that 123 women were members of the Congress and that some two dozen were featured on the Program.

Finally, it might be noted that the 13th Congress, Lancaster 1975, produced a volume of Abstracts and Proceedings but no papers. The 14th Congress, Winnipeg 1980, had 650 persons attending and 440 papers offered, and printed 43 papers (10%) but without a record of other Proceedings. The editor of the present volume, instructed by the experienced editors of these past two volumes has attempted to combine in the following pages both a record of Proceedings and a useful record of contemporary scholarship in the History of Religions.

PART A

THE SELECTED PAPERS

Twenty-seven Select
Papers Related to the
Congress Theme:
Religion and Identity

WHAT CONSTITUTES THE IDENTITY OF A RELIGION?

Hubert Seiwert

University of Hannover

I. THE PROBLEM

The problem I am going to discuss arose out of a historical investigation of Chinese religion in Taiwan. As everyone knows we customarily distinguish in China three religious traditions: Buddhism, Taoism and Confucianism. As a result of my research I came to the conclusion that what is normally called 'popular religion' also has to be regarded as a religious tradition of its own (Seiwert, 1985). The ensuing dispute with a sinological colleague made it obvious that the history of religions (Religionswissenschaft) has no theoretical concept whatsoever to decide on which account the congeries of religious phenomena — religious beliefs, practices and institutions — may be regarded as a religion. To put it differently: What constitutes the identity of a religion, if there is any?

Looking for comparable cases where problems like the one I was facing have already been discussed and were possibly solved I turned my attention to Ceylon. Unfortunately the solutions offered in this case are by no means unanimous. One scholar cites the coexistence of Theravada Buddhism and popular religion, the former clearly exhibiting its own particular identity (Bechert: 220, 224); another detects three religious systems each having its own identity (Evers: 98f), a third comes to the conclusion that there is only one religious system in Ceylon consisting of four different sub-systems (Ames: 27f). No one discusses the problem I am interested in: What makes the identity of a religious system? and Is a religious system the same as a religion?

On further consideration you will find that the problem under discussion has important theoretical dimensions for our discipline. For it becomes obvious that one of the seemingly most self-evident notions of the history of religions, that of 'a religion', is ill-founded. We talk of religions as historical units but find ourselves in difficulties when asked to define the identity of these units. The fact that only very few scholars have actually been puzzled by this problem is doubtless due to the seeming self-evidence of the notion "the religions". This has a long tradition in our discipline.

One of the forefathers of Religionswissenschaft, Friedrich Schleiermacher, took pains to show that religion as something infinite and unfathomable cannot but individualize itself and reveal itself in the so-called positive religions. To him every single 'individuum of religion' had its own marked 'physiognomy' (Schleiermacher: 165, 167, 171). The concept of individual religions, each having its own life and development became widely held during the following one and a half centuries of Religionswissenschaft. Still today most historians of religion would agree that while 'religion' as such is a concept which should be used only with great caution — if used at all — the individual religions are something which are given empirically and historically and therefore represent the genuine objects of the history of religions or Religionswissenschaft (cf. Flasche: 274, 277).

1

As one example I may quote Ninian Smart who has formulated this almost universally held position in very precise words: "... we are not confronted in fact by some monolithic object, namely religion. We are confronted by religions. And each religion has its own style, its own inner dynamic, its own special meanings, its uniqueness. Each religion is an organism, and has to be understood in terms of the interrelation of its different parts" (31f). Here a religion is called not an individuum but an organism; still others prefer to speak of a system. These different terms, of course, do not mean exactly the same but in one regard they are fully congruent: they all presuppose that there is something, called 'a religion', which exists as a historical entity and can as such be identified, in short, that there is something like the identity of a religion.

Only a few scholars have challenged this common view of the religions. One of the most vigorous attacks was launched by Wilfried Cantwell Smith.[1] Smith argues in a very striking way that "the concept of religion and the religions ... ought to be dropped altogether ... For fundamentally one has to do not with religions, but with religious persons" (153). Smith's arguments are certainly not to be taken lightly. Obviously what we call 'a religion', e.g. Buddhism or Christianity, is nothing that can be observed without further ado. What is given empirically are individual human beings, their individual beliefs and practices and a host of other individual facts. All these individual phenomena are said to belong to a larger unit called "a religion". And this religion is said to exist in history expanding over centuries and continents. This being so we are supposed to see the same religion, Buddhism, in the fourth century B.C. in India as well as in the thirteenth century A.D. in Japan. If we look closer, however, we do not see Buddhism but individual phenomena, persons, rites, scriptures and monasteries. In what sense are they part of a historical entity called 'Buddhism' and in what way is Buddhism in Japan and India the same? If they are! These are questions of a wide bearing and you should not expect me to give the final answers right now. What I try to do is to bring to light a problem which lurks in the darkness deep down at the foundations, the methodological foundations, of our discipline. Of course I shall also give a few hints as to where in my view we can possibly look for a solution of this problem.

II. TWO KINDS OF IDENTITY

What do we mean by 'identity'? From the logical point of view the matter is quite simple. 'Identity' here signifies a relation in which a given object is only to itself. Put differently: a is identical with b if a is exactly equal to b, if there is no difference whatsoever between a and b.

Taking this logical meaning of 'identity' as a basis we meet conspicuous difficulties in applying the term in the realm of the history of religions. Obviously one cannot maintain that there is no difference whatsoever between Buddhism in China of the 8th century and Buddhism in Ceylon of the 20th century. This implies that we cannot speak of an identity between these two phenomena. We can even generalize the issue: Every observable phenomenon, i.e. every empirical fact, has as one of its attributes a spatiotemporal specificity. No empirical phenomenon can, therefore, be identical with any other but itself. From this it follows that either there is no identity of Buddhism or that Buddhism is not an empirical phenomenon. If the latter applied, however, then the study of Buddhism or that of any other of the so-called 'religions' would not be empirical research but some kind of metaphysics. Given that alternative most of us would probably prefer to relinquish the claim that Buddhism and the other religions have an identity in history. In principle our inquiry into the identity of a religion could be concluded at this point as there obviously is no such identity. But that would be just one side of the medal.

Historians of religion certainly realize that the logical argument which I have proposed and which leads us to deny the identity of the so-called historical religions, is soundly Buddhist. It suggests that the empirical world consists of congeries of ever-changing elements and what seem to be identities and individuals are in fact nothing but illusory products of our unenlightened minds. From the point of view of the logically analyzing observer, this reasoning is doubtless true. But from the point of view of most participants in history this notion of identity is all but meaningless. Most people do not regard their own religious beliefs and practices, their religious feelings and institutions, as isolated events but consider their own religious life as part of something more comprehensive which exists in history. You may call it 'cumulative religious tradition' instead of 'religion' as Smith (154-168) does but this does not change the fact that people not only identify themselves with a certain religious tradition but regard this tradition or religion as something possessing its own identity. This of course cannot be the kind of logical identity we were dealing with before but is another kind of identity. For sake of convenience I shall name it 'historical identity'.

What constitutes a historical identity? Let us first consider the following example: In the year 1752 the imperial government of China introduced the sacrifices to Xiannong, the 'First Farmer', as obligatory in all counties of the empire. On this occasion the question was discussed whether these sacrifices were the same as those which were offered during the Han dynasty to the local earth-god *she* who was also an agricultural deity (cf. Seiwert, 1985:205). It seems that no final agreement was reached.

The case may serve as an illustration for a discussion of historical identity. The question was whether two things which are separated in time as well as in space can be regarded as the same. Now, an answer to this question cannot be given by us as historians of religion. What we can possibly ascertain are facts such as: the sacrifices to Xiannong in the 18th century and the sacrifices to the local earth-god during the Han-dynasty bear or do not bear strong similarities; there exists or does not exist a historical connection between both. But neither similarity nor historical connections nor both taken together amounts to historical identity. It is only the participants, the objects of our historical interest, who can settle the question. If they regard what they do as identical with what has been done in the past then we have a case of historical identity even if there should happen to be not the slightest historical connection. By the same token we as observers could not assert historical identity of two different phenomena on the grounds of similarity and historical connection if the participants refuse to do so. For historical identity is nothing that can be proved objectively — as indeed it is no real identity at all —but it is a category of subjective meaning. Historical identity is a category by which men interpret history and above all their own place in history. As historians we have to take historical identifications as given facts which cannot be criticized any more than we could criticize other religious beliefs. As the study and understanding of religious beliefs is one central task of our business as historians of religion the study of historical identifications must also be part thereof.[2]

Again we could conclude our investigation of the identity of a religion by stating that historical identity is a category of subjective meaning which as historians we have to understand and to recognize. But understanding other persons' meanings, understanding how they interpret history, cannot be the last word. Otherwise we would find ourselves only with a host of different ways of looking at history not only because the multiple religious traditions have each their own interpretation but also because single individuals within the same tradition do not necessarily share the same view. As historians we, too, interpret history and this means more than just understanding other people's view of it. Our own interpretations of history are, so to speak, on another level than that of the persons and traditions we try to understand in our hermeneutical enterprise. Let me call those which are the object of our understanding and interpretation the 'object-level' contrasting it with our own views of history, our interpretations of it and our theories about it, which I would designate as the 'meta-level'.

Talking about meta-level interpretations of history, there are two points which are important in our present context. First we have to recognize that historians presuppose historical identities as a matter of fact. Historians deal with states, peoples, institutions or religions assuming without hesitation that these entities possess some kind of identity. On this point there is no significant difference between historical identities on the object-level and on the meta-level. Coming to the second point, however, we must admit that historians claim that their own views and interpretations of history are not quite the same as anyone else's. Not that their statements are necessarily more true but that at least they have been arrived at in a methodologically well-founded way. And this is an important point. As historians of religion we are obliged to try to give a methodologically sound foundation if we use concepts signifying historical entities like Buddhism and the other religions — or to stop using these concepts altogether. Since it is not to be expected that we can ban the concept of "the religions" from our vocabulary I keep to the other alternative and try to find a methodological foundation.

III. THE IDENTITY OF RELIGIOUS SYSTEMS (SYSTEMIC IDENTITY)

What is a religion? An ingenious man or woman has answered this perennial question by stating that religion is everything which Religionswissenschaftler investigate. Now we actually study a host of different phenomena, ranging from beliefs about the world including gods and human fate to rituals and ethical practices, social institutions and personal feelings. In view of the diversity of these empirical phenomena it seems no easy task to prove that they normally form unities which we call religions. The task does not become much easier if we replace the term 'religion' by 'religious system' although the latter is less suspected of metaphysical ambiguities — falsely, as I believe.

If we designate the congeries of different religious phenomena "a religious system" we have to proceed on two assumptions: First, that we can prove some kind of unity and closedness. The minimum requirement for something to be called a system is that we can define its boundaries. This is exactly what nobody has yet done for a religious system. The second assumption would be that the system somehow persists in time. If both conditions were met we could fairly conclude that the religious system possessed something like an identity. Let me name this hypothetical identity which would be the outcome of our own historical and theoretical analysis 'systemic identity' to differentiate it terminologically from historical identifications on the object-level.

I begin by turning to this second assumption which supposes the diachronical persistence of a religious system. It is not necessary to explain again that actually there can not be any identity of concrete phenomena at two different points of time. What is happening in the Malvatta Monastery at Kandy in central Ceylon today is certainly not identical with what was happening there last year of fifty years ago. On the other hand it would be foolish to maintain that there was no connection whatever between these different facts. There is an almost unlimited number of possibilities with respect to how people can behave, how they can interpret the world or what they can consider to be their own destiny. Although there are numberless possibilities for acting and believing, however, the members of any given society usually select only a few of them which results in conspicuous similarities in their actual beliefs and practices. What is more, even diachronically we find these similarities pointing at some kind of connection.

What is the connecting element between the beliefs and practices of different people? I think it is the rules or norms which determine the selection out of the in-principle numberless possibilities. Because these norms affect the actual beliefs and practices we find these otherwise astonishing regularities. Is it then the norms which constitute a religious system and define its identity? In a way this is the case. A religious system doubtless can be regarded as a system of norms for selection.[3] But on a closer look we see that the norms can on no account be regarded as defining the identity and the boundaries of a system. For on the one hand we must admit that norms may change. What was taken for the right way to look at history for a Christian in the Medieval Ages is not the same as today. On the other hand it is obvious that we may find substantially the same norms, especially in the realm of ethics, in different religious systems. This proves beyond doubt that it is certainly not the substance of the norms which defines the systemic identity of a religious system.

If we suppose that there really exists some kind of systemic identity then we can proceed on the assumption that however much the substance of the system may change at least the system itself must be able to identify itself. Otherwise it could not maintain its boundaries which is crucial for the persistence of the system as a unity distinguished from its environment. This means we have to look for some sort of self-reference by which the system identifies what belongs to itself and what not.

Turning now to our hypothesized religious system being basically a system of norms we can detect one essential form of self-reference: Each system of norms has to define itself on grounds which it claims to be valid. This is evidently a crucial element since it is essential for a religious system not only to offer norms for selecting ways to act and to understand the world but at the same time also to claim that these are the right rules in contrast to other possibilities. This, however, is a pretension which obviously cannot be founded in any way without referring in the last analysis to a principle which has to be accepted as unquestionable. If you subscribe to this source of authority then you will adopt as valid the normative system which is set up on it. The validity of a system of norms depends on the recognition of the authority which is defined by the system itself.[4]

It is exactly this source of authority which marks the boundaries of a given authority A, e.g. the Buddha, as part of the normative system a, while substantially the same norm, not to kill, would belong to the normative system b if founded with reference to authority B, e.g. the New Testament.

On this basis we can now define the boundaries of a religious system and by the same token its unity rather precisely: they are defined by the recognition of the source or the sources of authority on which the system is founded. On the same ground we can also explain in which sense a religious system persists in time: we are dealing with the same system as long as the same authority is recognized. This is my approach to the problem of systemic identity of a religion.

In fact it is just an approach not yet the final answer. Let me conclude by pointing to a few implications and open problems. Most important: a "religious system" in the defined sense is not altogether the same as a "religion" as this term is commonly understood. On the one hand a religious system may be more than a religion. We may take as an example the religious system of Ceylon which comprises besides Theravada Buddhism also beliefs and practices associated with the so-called popular religion. What defines the religious system as a whole is the recognition of several sources of authority, Buddhist scriptures and institutions as well as popular customs and priestly institutions.

On the other hand a religious system may be less than a religion. The various schools of Mahayana Buddhism are most easily differentiated by pointing to the different sources of authority to which they adhere, be it a particular sutra, or a particular line of patriarchs or teachers. They may, therefore, each be regarded as a particular religious system or sub-system, which belongs to the more comprehensive system called 'Buddhism'. The unity and identity of Buddhism as a whole would be defined by the recognition of the Buddha as the final source of authority.

This leads me to my last point: Buddhism may serve as an illustration for my argument that it is not the content or the substance of the norms, i.e., what is actually believed and practiced, that is decisive for the identity of a religion but the authority referred to. For the contents of a religion may change almost beyond recognition as the substantial differences between the various forms of Buddhism from Ceylon via Tibet to Japan show. It seems difficult if not impossible to define the identity of a religion on such grounds. As the approach just presented overcomes at least this kind of problem I recommend it to your attention.

NOTES

1. Another critic of the notion of 'the religions' using different arguments is Baird (126-142).

2. Of course we can still engage in what Rudolph (1978) has called the 'ideologiekritische Funktion der Religionswissenschaft'. This is, however, a special case and not one of the central tasks of the history of religions.

3. The idea that a religion is to be regarded as a system of norms has already in outline been advanced by Durkheim (22). In contrast to him, however, I do not believe that a religious system is constituted by 'croyances obligatoires' and 'pratiques obligatoires' (19) but by the *rules for selecting* the right beliefs and practices. As a matter of fact most religions have only a few if any obligatory beliefs and practices. They are within a certain range more or less flexible as to which beliefs and practices out of the countless possibilities are to be considered as acceptable. It is this range of what is still regarded as acceptable for members of the religious system which is defined by the rules for selection.

4. The central role which authority plays for the definition of the category 'religious' has been discussed in another article of mine (Seiwert, 1981).

WORKS CONSULTED

Ames, Michael M.
1964 Magical-animism and Buddhism: A Structural Analysis of the Sinhalese Religious System. In: *Conference on Religion in South Asia*, ed. Edward B. Harper. Seattle: Washington University Press, 21-52.
Baird, Robert D.
1971 *Category Formation and the History of Religions*. The Hague/Paris: Mouton (Religion and Reason. 1)
Bechert, Heinz
1978 On the Popular Religion of the Sinhalese. In: *Buddhism in Ceylon and Studies on Religious Syncretism*

in Buddhist Countries, ed. Heinz Bechert. Göttingen (Abh. d. Akad. d. Wissenschaften Göttingen, philos.-hist. Klasse, Folge 3, 108) 217-233.

Durkheim, Emile
1898 De la définition des phénomènes religieux. In: *Année Sociologique* 1, 1-28.

Evers, Hans-Dieter
1972 *Monks, Priests and Peasants. A Study of Buddhism and Social Structure in Central Ceylon*. Leiden: Brill.

Flasche, Rainer
1978 *Die Religionswissenschaft Joachim Wachs*. Berlin/New York: de Gruyter.

Lorenz, K.
1976 Identität (II.). In: *Historisches Wörterbuch der Philosophie*, ed. Joachim Ritter and Karlfried Gründer. Basel/Stuttgart: Schwabe, vol. 4, 144-148.

Rudolph, Kurt
1978 Die 'ideologiekritische' Funktion der Religions-wissenschaft. In: *Numen* 25, 17-39.
1979 Gnosis — Weltreligion oder Sekte. In: *Kairos* 21, 255-261.

Schleiermacher, Friedrich
1967 *Über die Religion. Reden an die Gebildeten unter ihren Verächtern*, ed. Rudolf Otto, 6th edition. Göttingen: Vandenhoeck & Ruprecht.

Seiwert, Hubert
1981 'Religiöse Bedeutung' als wissenschaftliche Kategorie. In: *Annual Review for the Social Sciences of Religion* 5, 57-99.
1985 *Volksreligion und nationale Tradition in Taiwan*. Stuttgart: Steiner (Münchener Ostasiatische Studien. 38).

Smart, Ninian
1971 *The Religious Experience of Mankind*. London: Fontana Library.

Smith, Wilfried Cantwell
1978 *The Meaning and End of Religion*. London: S.P.C.K.

Related works by the author of this paper:

1. "Systematische Religionswissenschaft: Theoriebildung und Empiriebezug", in *Zeitschrift für Missionswissenschaft und Religionswissenschaft*, 61 (1977), 1-18.

2. "'Religiöse Bedeutung' als wissenschaftliche Kategorie", in *Annual Review for the Social Sciences of Religion*, 5 (1981), 57-99.

3. "Ausgrenzung der Dämonen — am Beispiel der chinesischen Religionsgeschichte", in *Saeculum*, 34 (1983), 316-333.

DO DIFFERENT RELIGIONS SHARE MORAL COMMON GROUND?

Dr Peter J. Donovan

Massey University, New Zealand

The suggestion is often made that followers of different religions share common ground at the level of their morality, despite their disagreements over doctrine and metaphysical beliefs. This suggestion may seem too vague to be worth serious discussion as it stands. Yet in the form of Natural Law theory it is a view which has an ancestry extending throughout Western philosophy and religious history. The theory maintains that beneath the varying beliefs and practices of different peoples can be glimpsed natural laws concerning moral conduct, laws grounded in basic facts about common human existence.

For the Greeks, while one philosophical school or another might offer its own metaphysics to account for it, the fact that natural law existed was thought to be evident to any who observed and reflected on the human world. 'Those who speak with sense must rely on what is common to all . . .', says Heraclitus (c.500 BCE), one of our earliest sources on the subject; 'For all the laws of men are nourished by one law, the divine law'.[1]

When natural law enters Christian thought the appeal to 'common knowledge' remains present to some extent. It is justified by reference in particular to the Apostle Paul's words in *Romans* which imply that there is available to all humankind evidence of God's existence and nature, and of a basic moral law written on the hearts of those to whom no special revelation has been given, yet who 'do by nature what the law requires'.[2]

In Aquinas's classic discussion of the sharing by intelligent creatures in the Eternal Law of God, it is admitted that not everyone is found to recognize natural law. Nonetheless the exceptions which an inspection of human practice reveals do not contradict the theory but are simply to be accepted as anomalies such as occur even at times with physical laws.

> 'As for particular specific points, which are like conclusions drawn from common principles, here also natural law is the same for most people in their feeling for and awareness of what is right. Nevertheless in fewer cases either the desire or the information may be wanting. The desire to do right may be blocked by particular factors — so also with physical things that come to be and die away there are occasional anomalies and failures due to some obstruction — and the knowledge also of what is right may be distorted by passion or bad custom or even by racial proclivity; for instance, as Julius Caesar narrates, the Germans did not consider robbery wicked, though it is expressly against natural law.'[3]

The possibility implicit in Aquinas, of an empirically-discoverable natural law free from theological assumptions, is made explicit by Grotius who offers natural law as a basis for international codes to govern the dealings, one with another, of different nations. And by the 18th century, a body of general principles of natural morality has come to be viewed, by Deists and Rationalists at least, as the chief good to be salvaged from the otherwise superstitious and partisan religious orthodoxies of the time. Thus Voltaire writes:

'Let us discard all subjects of dispute which divide nations, and discern the common bonds which may unite them. Submission to God, resignation, justice, goodwill, compassion, tolerance, these are the great principles. May all the theologians of the earth live together like the merchants who, without questioning in what country they were born, in what tradition they were schooled, follow among them the inviolable rules of equity, fidelity and reciprocal confidence.'[4]

Nineteenth century evolutionisms add an emphasis on morality as advancing, by natural laws of development, beyond religious attachments and thus as fit to be studied by a science of ethics — while admitting, with Herbert Spencer, that 'originally ethics has no existence apart from religion, which holds it in solution'.[5] Thus emerges a way of thinking by which secular moralists can display a measure of charity towards the religiously-based moralities of the past, while being no longer bound by their supernaturalist assumptions. It is a formula which Basil Mitchell, in reference to Kant, has called the 'matrix theory' of relations between religion and ethics; a religious metaphysic providing a matrix 'within which ethical conceptions develop as a matter of social and cultural history, but of which they are logically independent; so that in due time the matrix can decay leaving the ethic to live its own life'.[6]

C.D. Broad, for instance, has paralleled the rise of rational morality out of its religious antecedents with the rise of modern science out of magic and alchemy, holding that in each there have been persons of genius who have introduced new concepts and beliefs which have won wide acceptance. 'It does seem somewhat arbitrary', Broad states, 'to count this process as a continual approximation to true knowledge of the material aspect of the world in the case of science, and to refuse to regard it as at all similar in the case of religion'.[7]

The suggestion is, then, that a fund of moral knowledge — not necessarily static, but developing through human history — is there to be discovered; reliable recommendations for human conduct preserved amongst the diverse components of otherwise obsolescent religious traditions. As Mary Midgley puts it:

'The great religions have combined innumerable elements, many of them essential to life. These cannot be abandoned just because of the way people have misused them in the past.'[8]

There are, at the same time, religious voices to be heard nowadays, asserting on their own theories 'the essential unity of all religions', at least in their moral dimension. A typical statement is that made recently by the Dalai Lama.

'I maintain that every major religion of the world — Buddhism, Christianity, Confucianism, Hinduism, Islam, Jainism, Judaism, Sikhism, Taoism, Zoroastrianism —has similar ideals of love, the same goal of benefiting humanity through spiritual practice, and the same effect of making their followers into better human beings. All religions teach moral precepts for perfecting the functions of mind, body, and speech. All teach us not to lie or steal or take others' lives, and so on.'

'All religions agree upon the necessity to control the undisciplined mind that harbours selfishness and other roots of trouble, and each teaches a path leading to a spiritual state that is peaceful, disciplined, ethical, and wide. It is in this sense that I believe all religions have essentially the same message. Differences of dogma may be ascribed to differences of time and circumstance as well as cultural influences; indeed, there is no end to scholastic argument when we consider the purely metaphysical side of religion. However, it is much more beneficial to try to implement in daily life the shared precepts for goodness taught by all religions rather than to argue about minor differences in approach.'[9]

What kind of investigation is appropriate, for putting to the test such a claim or exploring such a possibility? Present-day seekers of common ground, concerned as they generally are about international peace and security and the pursuit of a global civilized society, have a right to expect some guidance from Religious Studies where there is, presumably, expertise to be found in this area. How is the comparative religionist to respond? And what guidance can the philosopher give, in making sense of the question being posed?

The obvious place to begin is where the moral dimension of religions becomes most explicit, i.e., in the form of teachings or precepts. Here we find lists of rules, commandments, laws, codes of conduct, models and paradigms, by which ideals and principles are illustrated and virtues and vices exemplified. Sayings, maxims, proverbs teach these principles, and when filled out with narrative they form myths, parables, allegories and legends, all aiming to reinforce certain kinds of behaviour and discourage others, by cultivating appropriate attitudes and emotions.

The discovery of a number of shared moral precepts (e.g. versions of the Golden Rule) amongst different religions seems to offer *prima facie* evidence, at least, for moral common ground as a reality. Moreover the modern history of religions shows that the sharing of similar material is often not accidental. Religious moralities appear to draw on an international pool of resources, including law-codes, heroic legends, moralistic fables and wisdom literature, gathered throughout history amongst a variety of races and cultures. Wilfred Cantwell Smith has recently illustrated his view of a 'world process of religious convergence' with a moral tale which can be shown to have passed through several Indian traditions, as well as Manichaeism and Islam, before entering Christian folklore as the Baalam and Josaphet legend and reaching modern thought through its influence on Tolstoy and Gandhi.[10]

The demonstration that moral codes and precepts are common property in religious history might well be taken to support the contention that a universal morality is there to be seen, at least in an emerging form, by the unprejudiced observer who takes a broad, cross-cultural view.

It is clearly too simple, however, to think that because followers of different religions assent, on occasion, to similar sets of moral precepts, they therefore must share moral common ground in some significant way. What is important in comparing moralities is not merely the rules people assent to in principle, but why and to what extent they follow them in particular cases, especially in cases of moral conflict or dilemma. Only when these details are appreciated can an observer be said to understand the moralities in question and be in a position to make reliable comparisons between them. To assume that once differing religious beliefs are down-played a common moral code will emerge is to ignore the fact that similar rules and precepts may be adopted as means to different ends. The nature of those ends will determine the sense in which the precepts are understood and applied by those who follow them.

Stewart Sutherland, in a recent paper, argues against the view that holders of different beliefs can be said to 'share an ethic' whenever they are observed to be following similar moral precepts.[11] Sutherland does not deny that there is *prima facie* common ground across the frontiers of religious belief. But genuine sameness of action cannot be established, as in the case of physical objects, by mere observation or comparison. Moral actions have to be individuated with reference to the intentions of those who do them. And as intentions entail beliefs, we are not entitled simply to assume that people 'may agree about what ought to be done without necessarily agreeing about the way the world is'.[12]

In Sutherland's example two men, Barry (a Marxist) and Brendan (a Christian) do appear, superficially, to be carrying out the same moral action — in this case driving lorryloads of food to a refugee camp. But when fuller descriptions of their intentions are given, involving on the one hand Marxist world-view, goals and values, and on the other hand Christian ones, it becomes apparent that what they are each doing is not in fact the same action in a moral sense, at all, and so they cannot be said to 'share an ethic' at that point.

From this it would seem to follow that adherents of different faiths — say, a Buddhist, a Christian, and a traditional Maori — may not in a moral sense be doing the same action at all when each, for instance, gives food to a starving enemy or, for that matter, kills a brother or robs a neighbour. For it will be according to quite different systems of belief, involving such diverse concepts as *karma, sin* and *tapu* respectively, that the parties will explain their motives, characterize their intentions, or lament their misdoings.

Such common maxims, then, as may be found in various religions (Tell the truth, do not kill, respect the property of others, feed the starving) do not necessarily reveal any underlying commonality. Like shared items of devotional practice (rosaries, candles, bodily postures) or like architecturally-similar buildings (temples, synagogues, churches, mosques) what they reflect may not be any essential common factor, but only a coincidental similarity of means to quite different moral ends.

Sutherland's argument, extended along these lines, throws considerable doubt on the likely success of any attempt to demonstrate the existence of natural moral laws, or a shared basic morality, by appealing to similarities in teaching or practice amongst followers of different religions.

The problem lies not only with the notion of an action, but with the word *moral* itself. As Sutherland uses the word (and here he reflects modern philosophical usage) morality is necessarily associated with a certain kind of intentionality. The identifying and characterizing of actions as moral involves reference to aims and intentions, beliefs and explanations, on the part of the agents in question. A rule, precept or law becomes a *moral* action-guide for a particular piece of conduct only when it is adopted with the appropriate kind of intention in mind.

Just what intentions are to be counted as necessary for morality is a matter of considerable dispute in contemporary ethics. The point for our purposes, however, is a simple one. Comparisons of rule or precept-following in order to discover moral common ground will of necessity involve comparisons of intentionality. A demonstration of shared rules or precepts, or even of similar behaviour, will not be sufficient for it fails to take account of the variety of differing intentions which may accompany those regularities. This is even more true of the attempt to demonstrate common ground simply by selecting from religious moralities the shared precepts and practices, and deliberately discarding 'differences at the theoretical level', as Voltaire and modern rationalists have recommended.

For all that, it is undoubtedly the case that from time to time people who hold different and conflicting religious beliefs do nonetheless find themselves, like Sutherland's Barry and Brendan, disposed to act according to similar maxims and to involve themselves in common patterns of behaviour. Is this to be considered as morally of no significance at all — a matter of sheer coincidence? Sutherland admits that his argument does not preclude what he calls 'partial overlap' in descriptions of the actions of holders of different ultimate beliefs. But the overlap, he says, 'may turn out to be very limited indeed both in extent and significance'.[13]

It is here that Sutherland's argument, cogent though it is in theory, may well be felt by the historian of religions to do less than justice to the phenomena of religions themselves and of morality in religious contexts. It is remarkable, for instance, that while emphasising the need for adequate criteria to individuate and describe actions, Sutherland says so little about how to identify, and distinguish between, the systems of belief in terms of which, on his argument, the moral intentions of different agents are to be defined. He refers variously to 'different theological or metaphysical positions', 'patterns of belief', 'view-points', views about 'the way the world is', 'habits and rules of thinking', and so on. But no clear way is offered for aligning these abstractions with the living world of religious belief and action.

At one point, Sutherland says his thesis does not commit one to the view that there are as many 'ethics' as there are thinking human beings, and admits that 'an elucidation of the reasons for this would be instructive'.[14] But he gives no hint of what those reasons might be. Yet if we are going to give the sense which he suggests to the notion of 'sharing an ethic', we must have criteria for estimating appropriate degrees of sameness (i.e. similarity) between two or more belief-systems.

Reliance on commonly-used names or labels is obviously inadequate, given the reality of religious diversity. Do all Hindus share a common ethic; or only Shaivite with Shaivite, Vaishnavite with Vaishnavite? Do the trinitarian beliefs of Catholic, Lutheran, and Kimbanguist Christians unite them on a moral common ground, while excluding Unitarians and Latter-day Saints? No doubt some theological beliefs will be more relevant than others to the moral outlook of adherents. Does the traditionalist Christian who expects a 'literal Day of Judgement' adhere to the same belief-system, for moral purposes, as the modernist who does not? Or might the traditional Christian in fact have more in common, on this score, with the orthodox Muslim, who similarly undergirds his conduct with a belief in 'That Which Is To Come'? Questions like these reflect the growing awareness in modern religious studies of the inadequacy of thinking of religious faiths as clearly distinguishable by reference to static, named systems of belief with clear boundaries.[15]

Studies of religious change and interaction show that when followers of theoretically quite distinct faiths are thrown together in situations of practical necessity, implicit adjustments are made, priorities reassembled, compromises accepted, in the interests of common well-being. Thus over a period of time basic doctrines can come to be related in quite different ways to the moral outcomes and sensitivities they are believed to entail. Even religious belief-systems containing such diverse concepts as *karma, sin,* and *tapu,* which earlier were given as instances of distinctly different beliefs, may turn out to be capable of undergoing mutual influence through the pressure of a moral concern for dialogue, cultural interaction and the like.[16] The existence, nowadays, of a vigorous Christian/Marxist dialogue may even raise the question whether the two systems Sutherland takes to be obviously incompatible must necessarily be so under all possible interpretations.

It would, of course, be quite unjustified to conclude from the evidence of inter-religious dialogue, that all differences of religious belief can in the end be adjusted to meet common moral interests. But to rule out any significant or substantial common ground because of incompatibility of beliefs at the most general or ultimate level seems to remove moral theorizing too far from the experience of moral agents in practice.

People holding divergent ultimate beliefs about 'the way the world is' do commonly, nowadays, in multi-cultural societies especially, find themselves acting side-by-side in situations of common concern.[17] Discoveries like this are part of the experience of life by which one's ultimate beliefs themselves are put to the test.

Religious ideologies which down-grade immediate personal and communal concerns in the interests of some long-term or supposedly ultimate ideal seem likely, sooner or later, to arouse a sense of their own moral inadequacy. It is to this sense that reformers of religions commonly appeal; as is illustrated, for instance, by Jesus's story of the Good Samaritan, by Muhammad's denunciation of the Meccan cult, or by Mahatma Gandhi's rejection of the caste system.

Common ground sought between different peoples today, moreover, is likely to be related to issues on which long-established religious belief-systems have little specific to say. The uses of nuclear energy, the control of environmental pollution, genetic engineering, information storeage, and so on, raise questions about human life and the world itself which are not easily answered from within any of the existing ideologies. There may well be situations, then, in which divergent ultimate beliefs are neither determinate enough, nor play an immediate enough part in the thinking of the people in question, to stand in the way of their genuinely sharing concerns at the moral level. The here-and-now benefits of arriving at similar moral convictions, in other words, may carry greater conviction and be a truer expression of religious commitment than is loyalty to some more remote interpretation of an ultimate theology or ideology.

This possibility is well illustrated from the situation in which world religions have found themselves, in recent years, with the emergence of international agreements regarding human rights. In its Universal Declaration of Human Rights, the General Assembly of the United Nations in December 1948 proclaimed as 'a common standard of achievement for all peoples and all nations' a number of rights and fundamental freedoms. These include the right to life, liberty and the security of person; freedom from slavery, torture, cruel, inhuman or degrading treatment or punishment; equal and fair treatment before the law; freedom of movement; rights to nationality, family life, ownership of property; freedom of thought, conscience and religion, expression, peaceful assembly and association, and a variety of others. The Declaration has served as a model for subsequently international conventions, and for numerous Bills of Rights entrenched in constitutions of many countries.

While 'human rights' have legal and political implications as well as moral ones, the U.N. Declaration may nonetheless be viewed as a global affirmation of moral common ground. It is offered without theological or ideological justification, yet it reflects ethical norms defined by common consent amongst nations whose members include the widest possible range of religious affiliations. Can these adherents of different religious faiths genuinely affirm an intention to be bound by the Declaration, as a set of common moral precepts, despite the differences and incompatibilities amongst their ultimate beliefs?

In a recently-published discussion of human rights by representatives of world religions, there is a clear concern that the resources of religious belief should be drawn upon, in a combined effort to make the U.N. Declaration universally effective. As one contributor puts it:

'In this new world of intercultural bonds and international communications, there is splendid opportunity to stimulate common effort for the support of human rights. Not only is there an opportunity through theology as a discipline to take an expanded role in fostering intellectual support for these rights . . . but religiously formed persons also have a greatly expanded opportunity to insist upon and campaign for the strengthening of the supportive social processes and institutions which shape cultural mores with respect to rights.'[18]

There is also frank admission that in certain respects the world religions themselves, in their own histories and institutions, do not meet the moral standards proclaimed in the Declaration. For instance, in areas such as sexual equality, freedom of speech and conscience, and religious toleration, it is admitted that, even with their various ultimate belief-systems in place, the religions left to themselves have failed both in theory and in practice to attain to anything like the universality of scope which the Declaration proclaims. Some serious reinterpretation of belief-systems will be needed, it is recognised, to make genuine assent to the Declaration possible. As the Hindu contributor comments:

> 'It is evident that the establishment of human rights among Hindus demands not only social reform movements, but also exploration, investigation, and reinterpretation of the theoretical foundations underlying the social hierarchy of Hinduism.'[19]

Other writers (e.g. Buddhist and Jewish) seem more confident that human rights as defined by the Declaration are already encompassed, implicity or explicit, by their ultimate beliefs, and that in their affirming these common moral principles, only practice, not ultimate ideology, will need to be brought into line.

There is a clear impression created, of theologians casting about in their respective traditions for concepts and arguments by which to justify and reinforce commitment to a common morality the content of which, in today's world, they find compelling in itself. A Catholic scholar, for instance, appears to have little doubt about the primacy of shared moral commitment over ultimate theoretical justification. He writes,

> 'A very good case can be made that the appeal of human rights norms themselves is really far broader than the appeal of any philosophical or theological foundation which may be offered for them.'[20]

In describing the process of justifying this prior moral conviction as 'casting about for concepts and arguments' I do not wish to imply that such rationalization is a spurious activity, intended only to save the appearances. Rather, it is an indication of the open texture even of ultimate belief-systems, and the two-way relation between them and the immediate moral and religious experiences of adherents. Were this not the case, it would be difficult to account for the change and reform of religious ideologies which takes place continually, in the light of wider encounters at the moral and social levels.

There are reasons for thinking, then, that Sutherland's argument too lightly dismisses the significance of common moral intentions, shared by followers of different religions at a level less than that of ultimate beliefs about 'what the world is like'. In practice, when asked to give reasons for their moral actions, representatives of a religion may well express themselves in the concepts of the official ideology, with reference to its ultimate goal and world-view. yet this may not be the best guide as to what for them personally, in a particular situation, are the most relevant moral considerations. (This must be still more true for adherents who are inarticulate or barely aware of the official world-view. Suppose, for instance, Sutherland's 'Brendan' is a convert from a freshly-evangelized hill tribe, and 'Barry' a peasant newly-recruited into the Vietnamese army. Neither will have much grasp of the ultimate ideals of their new-found belief-systems. Yet both, following the example and instruction of those in whose ideology they are placing their faith, have accepted 'serving one's fellows when in need' as an approved moral principle and, so far as they are aware, are morally in agreement in doing so.)

There will, undoubtedly, also be situations such as those Sutherland envisages, in which the apparent similarity of behaviour and even of precepts will in no way count as a genuine moral sharing, because the ultimate beliefs and intentions on the part of one or more of the parties will explicitly exclude that interpretation. (Christians holding firmly to a Calvinist theology, for instance, may reject 'universal human rights' as an unscriptural product of secular thought. They may still, however, find themselves able to affirm many of the same principles as those of the U.N. Declaration, on the basis of a belief in Divine covenants of grace.[21]) Given the difficulty of individuating belief-systems, and of determining which, in the minds of the moral agents themselves, are incompatible with which, confidently identifying situations where moral common ground is excluded will not be as straight-forward a task as Sutherland's argument suggests.

According to the argument so far, then, moral teachings found by inspection to be shared by many religions will not in themselves count as evidence for a common morality existing by some natural necessity, in the way that natural law theories supposed. What inspection can reveal will be contingent, though perhaps quite widely-occurring, similarities in recommended moral conduct, resulting from commitment to similar principles and ideals. This can be said to amount to a genuinely shared ethic when, for the parties concerned, the intention to regard those principles as matters of moral agreement is not consciously excluded through adherence to incompatible ultimate beliefs.

Among the factors which open the way for such inclusive intentions may, of course, be the presence of beliefs about universal moral principles, carried in the scriptures of religious traditions or enshrined in their dogmas. (It is clear, for instance, that the availability of scholastic natural law theory assisted in Pope John XXIII's endorsement of the U.N. declaration of human rights in the encyclical *Pacem in Terris.*)

From the fact that representatives of different religions may proclaim 'Despite our theological differences we all acknowledge the same basic moral precepts' it does not follow that they do. What may follow, however, is that through proclaiming that belief, they increase the likelihood that their followers will, in situations of potential common moral concern, adjust their own intentions so as to identify them with those of others holding different ultimate beliefs.

Pronouncements like that of the Dalai Lama ('All religions teach common moral precepts') are not to be taken, then, as descriptions of an actual state of affairs. They are, rather, pleas for religions to make common cause (in the interests, in this case, of world peace), interpreting and adjusting their traditions of belief so as to be able to intentionally affirm such common concerns as moral. What is offered, in other words, is encouragement for a creative theological enterprise; not a description of an already-existing universal moral bedrock, there to be uncovered once religious differences are set aside. Whether or not the proposal is capable of being implemented, by whom, for how long, at what cost to other beliefs, and so on, are different matters entirely.

In reply, then, to the question Do different religions share moral common ground, the answer must be: Yes, from time to time they do, when their belief-systems are found to be sufficiently flexible of interpretation to permit believers to have inclusive moral intentions in situations involving common action. But this is no evidence that universal moral laws, independent of culturally-borne religious beliefs and intentions, are waiting to be discovered at the level of common human nature. Whatever else they might be, such laws could not in themselves, by present definitions, count as moral at all.

ENDNOTES

1. *Fragment 114.* From *The Presocratic Philosophers,* by G.S. Kirk and J.E. Raven, Cambridge Univ. Press, 1969, p.213.

2. *Romans* chapter 2 verse 14.

3. *Summa Theologiae* la2ae.94,4. In the Blackfriars edn., Eyre & Spottiswoode, vol.28, pp.89-90.

4. *Third Homily.* In *Voltaire on Religion: Selected Writings* translated and introduced by Kenneth W. Applegate, Frederick Ungar Publishing Co., 1974, pp.75-6.

5. *The Principles of Ethics,* 1892 edition, reprinted by Otto Zeller, 1966, p.307.

6. *Morality: Religious and Secular,* Clarendon Press, 1980, p.123.

7. 'Arguments for the Existence of God', reprinted in *Religion, Philosophy and Psychical Research,* Humanities Press, 1969, p.200.

8. *Beast and Man: The Roots of Human Nature,* Harvester Press, 1979, p.362.

9. *A Human Approach to World Peace,* by His Holiness Tensin Gyatso, The Fourteenth Dalai Lama, Wisdom Publications, 1984, p.13.

10. *Towards a World Theology,* Macmillan, 1981, pp.7-11.

11. 'Religion, Ethics and Action', in *The Philosophical Frontiers of Christian Theology,* Cambridge Univ. Press, 1982, p.153.

12. *Ibid.,* p.164.

13. *Ibid.*

14. *Ibid.,* p.166.

15. See W. Cantwell Smith, *The Meaning and End of Religion,* first published in 1962. On the limitations of the concept 'religious system' see Trevor Ling, 'Communalism and the Social Structure of Religion', in *Truth and Dialogue,* edited by John Hick, Sheldon Press, 1974.

16. In the contemporary theology of Melanesian, Maori and Pacific Island Christianity, indigenous concepts such as *mana* and *tapu* are freely used to help interpret Biblical morality and soteriology. On compatibilities between Hindu and Christian moralities see *Christian and Hindu Ethics,* by Shivesh Thakur, George Allen and Unwin, 1969.

17. For an introduction to the range of inter-religious activities in modern Britain, see appendix to *God Has Many Names,* by John Hick, Macmillan, 1980. See also *Religious Co-operation in the Pacific,* edited by Emiliana Afeaki and others, University of the South Pacific, 1983.

18. 'Human Rights in Religious Traditions', in *Journal of Ecumenical Studies,* vol. xix, no.3, Summer 1982, p.86.

19. *Ibid.,* p.84.

20. *Ibid.,* p.26-7.

21. *Ibid.,* p.11-12.

Related works by the author of this paper:

1. *Interpreting Religious Experience.* London: Sheldon Press, 1979.
2. *Religion in New Zealand Society* edited by Brian Colless and Peter Donovan. Palmerston North: Dunmore Press, 2nd Edition, 1985.

"PROPHET, GURU, SAGE:
Three Paradigms of the Hierophant"

David G. Bradley

Duke University, U.S.A.

This paper focuses on the perennial question of why it is that with so many similarities discernable among the world's religions these same traditions remain separate, each claiming to possess unique truth with no signs of a merging into a universal, all embracing faith. Our Congress theme is "Religion and Identity", and it raises for consideration the question of how it is that traditions endure for millenia with singular strength and continuity. This section of the Congress carries the label of Comparative and Phenomenological Studies.

In recent decades the comparative method has been is disrepute for at least two main reasons. The first of these is that the comparative method which was dominant in the study of religions at the turn of the twentieth century led to the propagation of numerous methodological errors which tended to discredit any use of this approach. Both Christian missionaries and secular scholars from Europe and America made the comparison of religions possible by producing excellent translations of Asian scriptures. At the same time they also, all too often, superimposed their own western interpretations on them. The writings of Max Weber, Albert Schweitzer, Rudolf Otto and James Legge typify both the high level of scholarship represented as well as the sorts of errors which can result from searching Asian scriptures with biblical and western questions in mind. For instance, Max Weber sought to find the equivalent of the Hebrew prophet in Indian and Chinese traditions, and failing this pronounced them inferior or lacking in the highest religiosity. Albert Schweitzer, in *Christianity and the Religions of the World*, applied the test of an ethical standard with the Christian ethic as the norm and concluded that Asian religions such as Hinduism, Buddhism and Confucianism did not measure up to Christianity.

The second reason involves the reductionism currently dominant in the social sciences wherein considerations which include belief in supernatural aspects of religion are bracketted out or even ignored as unimportant to understanding a culture or tradition. This is no doubt due, at least in part, to reactions against European colonialism, usually linked with Christian claims to final truth, which have pushed anthropologists and other social scientists towards neutrality on matters of religious belief. One purpose of this paper is to make a modest attempt to reinstate the comparative method as both possible and necessary in the field of History of Religions, including a stress on the importance of religious belief in our discipline.

Today the dominant method in history of religions is phenomenology with its emphasis on the historical, sociological and other such measureable time-space aspects of religion. While Christian missionaries were proclaiming their unique faith, western anthropologists, linguists, mythologists, social theorists and psychologists were hard at work demonstrating that all religious traditions have many things in common and that patterns of religious behaviour are quite similar through the centuries and across the world. Every religious tradition honors sacred places and times, has its myths, rituals, pilgrimages and festivals. Each also has its human functionaries who preserve and perpetuate the tradition and its ceremonies. These persons variously are called shamans, priests/priestesses, witch doctors, teachers, sages, gurus, prophets, etc. In various ways these sacred persons are concerned with the basic *raison d'être* of every religion, the desire to appropriate supernatural power and meaning for living from the realm of the gods. For this paper I have chosen to delineate and compare three representatives of a type of religious leader found in all traditions. This type is the hierophant who manifests the divine world to his or her disciples by teaching and example, not as a priest in charge of ritual, but rather as a spiritual guide who shows or proclaims the way to salvation for others to follow. These three paradigms are the *prophet* of the biblical religions, sc., Judaism, Zoroastrianism, Christianity and Islam; the *guru* of the Indian traditions — Hinduism, Jainism, Buddhism and the Sikhs; and the *sage* of East Asia as evidenced especially in Taoism and Confucianism.

Now as one who began his scholarly career as a New Testament "form critic", I would like to stress that I have every respect for the contribution of phenomenologists, linguists and all the other anthropological and sociological contributions to the comparative study of religion, and attest that my own work would be impossible without it. But as I have just stated it is my position that this historical, time-space study of religious phenomena all too frequently fails to include the supernatural — the religious dimension — as integral to any truly comparative study. For instance, in preparing this presentation I read a recent excellent monograph, *Prophecy and Society in Ancient Israel*,[1] by Professor Robert R Wilson of Yale, and also a competent essay by the Dutch scholar, Jan Gonda titled "The guru".[2] Each of these studies relates its subject — prophet or guru — to the phenomenon of religious leaders found in past and present tribal societies. Wilson shows how the Hebrew prophets fit the pattern of the prophet as found in other ancient near-Eastern, African and other tribal societies. In all these contexts, biblical and non-biblical, the prophet operates either as part of the inner, ruling group or else on the fringe, as protestor and as leader of a dissident group which is striving to replace the central leaders in power. Gonda traces the guru figure from Vedic times through successive stages of development in Indian religious history. He reminds us that the word 'guru' is related to the Latin 'gravis', heavy or important, and states that "the sanskrit term *guru* in itself is an illustration of the widespread belief that mighty, divine, or holy persons are held to be characterized by an uncommon weight."[3] He then proceeds to delineate the attributes, functions and duties of the guru and to adduce pre-historical antecedents and parallels in Persian, Greek and other early cultures.

But neither of these scholars focuses attention on what both the Indian and the biblical community would consider most significant — why it is that the guru or the prophet has special access to supernatural knowledge, or how it is that he is able to transmit divine wisdom and power to the believer and the community. If it seems to be the case that the Christian missionary places too much emphasis on ultimate truth which must be taken on faith, the phenomenologist, at his scholarly peril, ignores or suppresses any vital consideration of the supernatural world as a necessary factor in describing his subject.

I have said "at his scholarly peril" deliberately because it is my conviction that it is not unscientific or unscholarly to concern oneself with the metaphysical and epistemological views of the supernatural world among various religions. It is one thing to find parallels to prophet, guru or sage among various cultures, especially when the linguistic evidence supports one's views about the significance of those parallels. But to relate such an important figure to the faith of the community requires that his function in turn be related to the thematic myths of that tradition.

This assertion requires, on my part, a brief statement of what I intend by such terms as supernatural, the divine dimension, or the infinite and eternal. It amounts to a truism to state that the supernatural is unknowable as well as unprovable. One cannot prove the existence of God, any more than the reality of the doctrine of rebirth. Thus the opening line of the *Tao Teh Ching* states: "The Tao that can be named is not the eternal Tao". The Hindu World-Soul is unknowable, and beyond all proof or measure, so that the proper response to any question or affirmation about the Paramatman is *neti, neti,* not this, not any thing, and so on. The notion of the nature of a supreme being, or any concept of the supernatural must remain a great question mark, or else be merely a profession of unprovable faith. But in studying the myths of the various religious traditions I discern certain affirmations about the supernatural which all religions include, and I find also that because of significant differences in these affirmations it is possible to compare and contrast the role and function of the prophet, guru and sage as hierophants — revealers of the sacred, or supernatural.

The first of these common elements is that the world of the supernatural is a world of power. Though expressed in various ways, and with no discernable unity or agreement on the nature of this power, each tradition does assert this claim. The second point of agreement is that the supernatural dimension contains, or is the source of, timeless wisdom, eternal meaning or truth sufficient to provide solutions for all the problems of mankind. And finally, all religions teach that this power and this meaning can be made available both to the individual and to the entire community of believers offering hope for living.

THREE GREAT SYSTEMS OF BELIEF

It is my contention that there are three main patterns of myths about man and his relation to the supernatural to be discerned among the great religious traditions. Since living religions have their roots in the prehistoric, pre-literate age of mankind many of the obvious similarities to be found probably are due to this common origin along with the high survival value of certain prehistoric patterns of religious life — such as rites of passage, symbolic terminology for the supernatural, and so on. What is surprising is that there are so few major patterns which have survived and became dominant.

In the so-called "fertile crescent" of biblical lands which produced one of the important early human cultures, and where the Semitic language gained prominence, there developed a pattern of myth which became basic to Jewish, Zoroastrian, Christian and Muslim traditions. The myth common to these religions stresses a single deity who is ultimate ruler of all things. This is because he has created our time-space world in which he has placed human beings, commanding them to obey his will in order that their existence might be meaningful and harmonious, and that they be deserving of his saving power. Judaism, Zoroastrianism, Christianity and Islam are known as revealed religions because the deity in each case reveals to his creatures what his will for them is — what they are to believe and do in order to merit his guidance and saving power. The tradition itself was shaped, kept strong and passed on to succeeding generations by persons called "prophets". The deity of this myth reveals his will through these chosen spokesmen — Moses, Zoroaster, Jesus, Muhammad, as well as many others — who in turn have proclaimed the will of their god to their fellow believers. In this myth each person is a unique creature who has but one life in which to obey and conform to the deity's will, a belief of crucial importance since one's final destiny is completely in the control of the creator deity, so that, of necessity, one must heed the teachings of the prophets. Where the Jew, Parsi, Christian and Muslim differ is not about this basic myth of a deity who is creator, judge and savior but about which prophetic tradition is the true one, that of Moses, Zoroaster, Jesus or Muhammad.

In the Indus Valley of Northwest India another great tradition became dominant, even absorbing and redirecting the intrusive tradition of the invading Aryans. Its emphasis is not on creation and obedience but on the fact of rebirth — the *samsaric* fate of each individual who is born again and again into various finite and temporary forms of existence. In Hinduism, Jainism and Buddhism, as well as in the tradition of the Sikhs, it is not a creator deity and his revelation which is normative. Instead, in this myth it is taught that each person has generated and shaped his own rebirth cycle out of ignorance, and powered it by *karma* — the results of one's thoughts, words and deeds through many previous existences — leading to one's present life. Here also there is no tradition of prophets who are called by a creator to proclaim the way of obedience to the revealed will of the all powerful deity. Instead help is available from heroic beings who already, by extreme diligence and sacrifice in countless previous lives among gods and among men have achieved a level of wisdom and insight sufficient to guide others in the right path to deliverance from the round of rebirth. Such self perfected beings are called "gurus" or guides, such as Gautama, the Buddha; Mahavira, the Jina; Lord Krishna and Guru Nanak. These and many other gurus in the context of the myth of rebirth teach that the goal of religion is to achieve eventual, final escape (*moksha*) from life's relentless cycle. They also teach others how to gain the supernatural wisdom and power necessary for the attainment of this goal by thoughts and actions which they have found efficacious in their own agelong pilgrimage from life to life. The metaphysical systems as well as the doctrine of the nature of man and his miserable condition differ markedly among these traditions. But they also agree on the all-important need for the disciple to have a guru to teach the cause and cure of entrapment in the rebirth cycle, while stressing as well the necessity for each person to work out his own salvation.

In the religious traditions of China — Taoism and Confucianism — a third mythological pattern prevails on how it is that mankind learns to overcome the barrier which separates the time-space and infinite-eternal dimensions of existence. The barrier between the two modes of existence is neither breached by a god's revelations nor by the many rebirths of intrepid heroes; instead the Chinese "sage" finds himself to be in total harmony with the infinite and eternal in the here and now. Thus the Book of Tao says:

> "Without leaving his door
> He knows everything under heaven.
> Without looking out of his window
> He knows all the ways of heaven.
> For the further one travels
> The less he knows.
> Therefore the Sage arrives without going.
> Sees all without looking,
> Does nothing, yet achieves everything."[4]

The message and effectiveness of the early Chinese classic, *I Ching (Book of Changes)* is predicated on the conviction that all aspects of existence — worldly or heavenly, measureable or infinite — all exist in continuous harmony. The mysterious Tao, or *Way* of the universe, is everywhere and at all times at work affording meaning and power for man's existence, sustaining all things and causing all things to work in harmony. Chapter XLII of the Tao Teh Ching puts it this way:

"The Tao begot one.
One begot two.
Two begot three.
And three begot the ten thousand things.
The ten thousand things carry yin and embrace yang.
They achieve harmony by combining these forces."

Confucius, for his part, seems to have accepted this basic view of the ideal harmony of the supernatural and natural worlds. He said that he had a mandate from Heaven and that Heaven's truth was in him. It is also reported in his legendary life that three times he wore out the thong on which the bamboo slips were strung forming his copy of I Ching, indicating his conformity to the early myth of Tao and yang-yin as the supernatural forces which energize all existence. His teaching of salvation differed from the Taoist, however, in that he stressed the necessity of harmony in the social world which he found exemplified in an idealized feudal past. Thus we find for these two Chinese traditions not a deity breaching the barrier separating the natural world from the supernatural, nor gurus bringing to this world the message of the eternal and infinite gleaned from their own rebirths in the worlds of gods and men, but a quiet, neutral experience in which the sage finds eternity in the midst of time. The two dimensions of existence are intertwined and merged, and the ideal to be sought by all is harmony in the interaction between the ways of heaven and of earth and mankind. This view I have chosen to call "immanentism."

I do not want, however, to ignore or bypass one very important consideration. If prophet, guru and sage serve as hierophants for three different kinds of supernatural worlds the question naturally arises, does this mean that they really are three different divine realms? My answer is that no one knows for sure, nor can one prove whether there even is such a dimension to human existence, and it must always remain a huge question mark. But every tradition has its counterpart of the shaman — prophet, guru, or sage — to whom the followers of a tradition assign special powers and wisdom and to whom the members of the tradition turn for access to such meaning and power for their lives.

Prof. D. Howard Smith says of the Chinese world-view that from early times is found "the belief that the main purpose of religion was to maintain a harmonious relationship between heaven, earth and man."[5] He also states of the Confucian ideal of sagehood (shêng jên) that "the perfect sage not only attained to harmony, serenity, peace and joy in his own inner nature, but functioned as heaven itself functions, so that his 'virtue' outflowed and pervaded the environment in which he lives, and exercised an influence throughout the whole sphere in which he ruled."[6]

When one turns to the Taoist views on sagehood one is struck by the apparently passive views of the nature of the true sage. This is in sharp contrast to the biblical prophet who speaks boldly in the name of his deity, or the Indian guru, such as Siddharta Gautama, who after 10,000 lives announced at his final birth: "The chief am I in all the world."

Thus in chapter XV of the Tao Teh Ching we read what is regarded as a description of the sage:

"Of old those that were the best officers of Court
Had inner natures subtle, abstruse, mysterious, penetrating,
Too deep to be understood.
And because such men could not be understood
I can but tell of them as they appeared to the world;

Circumspect they seemed, like one who in winter crosses a stream,
Watchful, as one who must meet danger on every side.
Ceremonious, as one who pays a visit;
Yet yielding, as ice when it begins to melt.
Blank, as a piece of uncarved wood;
Yet receptive as a hollow in the hills.
Murky, as a troubled stream —
Which of you can assume such murkiness, to become in the end still and clear?
Which of you can make yourself inert, to become in the end full of life and stir?
Those who possess this Tao do not try to fill themselves to the brim,
And because they do not try to fill themselves to the brim
They are like a garment that endures all wear and need never be renewed.

In this passage the self-effacing conduct of the sage stresses the ideal of the total harmony of the universe — heaven, earth and mankind wherein it is shameful to call attention to oneself and thereby to break the harmony of life. This shame is, of course, in contrast to the guilt which characterizes biblical religions, or the pollution dominant in the Indian religions which follow the doctrines of rebirth and of karma.

Now one difficulty encountered in using the comparative method is the necessity of developing the background and context for two or more traditions so as to afford a basis for true comparison. To this end I would like to save time by comparing and contrasting two brief stories, one Confucian and one Christian.

In the Lun Yü of Confucius there is a well-known episode recounted in Book XIII, chapter 18:

"The 'Duke' of She addressed Master K'ung saying, In my country there was a man called Upright Kung. His father appropriated a sheep, and Kung bore witness against him. Master K'ung said, In my country the upright men are of quite another sort. A father will screen his son, and a son his father — which incidentally does involve a sort of uprightness."[7]

This story has been used to offer the Christian an example of the failure of Confucius to measure up to the "high morality" of Jesus who stressed obedience to God and reverence for truthfulness. Yet to the Confucian it is a perfect example of how the virtue of *hsiao*, of filial duty, undergirds the harmony of heaven, earth and mankind.

But when a would-be disciple of Jesus said that he would follow Jesus wherever he led, except that he first had to go and bury his father, Jesus rebuked him quite rudely when he said: "Let the dead bury their dead, but as for you, go and preach the Kingdom of God."[8] This would offend the Confucian as well as the Hindu, for burial of one's father is for them — as it was for the Jew whom Jesus rebuked — a necessary deed which takes first priority. But for Jesus, the prophet, the intended meaning was to stress to the man that nothing — not any excuse whatsoever — could come ahead of total obedience and service to his God, the Creator and Lord of the universe.

Turning back to our three paradigms of the hierophant — prophet, guru and sage — we find that each of them represents the ideal person in their respective traditions. Thus in the biblical religions the perfect Jew, or Christian, or Muslim would be that person who obeys his God, the Creator, completely. For the Jew, Moses is the hierophant who ideally served his God; for the Christian, the dogma of Jesus' sinlessness is due to his perfect obedience, even unto death, to his God — not because he was known to live a blameless life free of mistakes or bad thoughts; while for the Muslim, Muhammad was the seal of the Prophets because of his total submission to Allah. Among Indian religions the perfect guru is characterized by the naked ascetic who has severed all ties with the world, and is *jivamukti*, or free spirit, or perhaps *Tathagata* as was the Buddha. Such ideal persons are no longer bound by the rules of society, or any other space-time considerations.

As for the sage, the ideal man is described in the fourth appendix of the *I Ching* thus:

> "The Great man is he who is in harmony in his attributes with heaven and earth; in his brightness, with the sun and moon; in his orderly procedure, with the four seasons; and in his relation to the good and bad issues, in harmony with the spiritual agents. He may precede Heaven, and Heaven will not act in opposition to him; he may follow Heaven, but will only act as Heaven at that time would do. If Heaven will not act in opposition to him, how much less will man! how much less will spiritual beings!"[9]

Were there time it might be worthwhile to apply other comparative tests to demonstrate the important distinctions between prophet, guru and sage. Not only can one see perhaps more clearly the origins of guilt, pollution and shame cultures, but such questions as the nature and cause of evil, the ideal of the perfect person in a perfect society, or the meaning of death could be explored in the context of each of these three great traditions. Phenomenology is most necessary to the comparison of religions, but each religion must be view and interpreted in the Context of its own basic myth and tradition.

ENDNOTES

1. (Philadelphia: Fortress Press, 1980).

2. J. Gonda, *Change and Continuity in Indian Religion* (The Hague: Mouton & Co., 1965), Chapter VIII.

3. P.237.

4. Waley's translation here and in following quotes.

5. D. Harold Smith, *Chinese Religions* (London: Weidenfeld & Nicholson, 1968), p.11.

6. P.45.

7. Waley's translation.

8. Luke 11:20 (ASV).

9. I:34, Legge's translation.

Related works by the author of this paper:

1. *Circles of Faith: A Preface to the Study of the World's Religions.* Nashville: Abingdon Press, 1966.

2. "Is Mysticism a Common Denominator among the World's Religions" (Paper given at IAHR Congress, Winnipeg, 1980).

PERSONAL IDENTITY IN THE UPANIṢADS AND BUDDHISM

Dr. Karel Werner

University of Durham.

Important issues in philosophical and religious thought often enter popular awareness in a simplified if not simplistic form and sometimes they petrify into *clichés* which do not serve any informative purpose and may even distort the picture and create confusion. One such *cliché* is the often repeated view that Hinduism believes in a transmigrating soul while Buddhism denies it.[1]

In Western thinking there is a deeply ingrained notion of soul which stems from Christianity and survives also in secular thinking. Therefore the doctrines of soul and no-soul are often demonstrated using Christianity and Buddism as two contrasting systems. In John Hick's formulation " . . . whereas Christianity has traditionally taught the existence and the immortal life of the individual soul, Buddhism has traditionally taught that there is no permanent soul."[2]

As a result of wrongly identifying the Christian notion of soul or at least closely relating it with the Upaniṣadic concept of *ātman*, the apparent dichotomy between the Hindu and Buddhist conceptions of personality has been overemphasized and largely distorted. The use of the term "soul" for *ātman* in translating the Upaniṣads (R.H. Hume, Radhakrishnan, and others before and after them) has spread this distortion widely and resulted in confused interpretations of the Hindu understanding of the transmigrating personality. The situation has not been helped by further importation of Christian type notions, such as Parrinder's "indestructible souls".[3]

We should be acutely aware that there is no Indian equivalent of the Western notion of "soul" as an immortal part of man as a person. The notion of man as a combination of an immortal soul and a mortal body is, in any event, a simplistic concept within religious thought. It was widespread in 19th century Europe and its application to the Indian situation was wrong and should not be perpetuated.

It is the purpose of this paper to examine the early understanding of the human personality as it was developed in the early Upaniṣads and early Buddhism, since all subsequent elaborations of the problem depend on these early conceptions.

The history of the Indian understanding of human personality can be traced back to the Vedas and as with most other crucial issues of Indian philosophical and religious thought it is necessary to state that even the problem of human personality and personal identity was implicitly, if not quite explicitly, solved already in the Vedas and bits of information concerning this solution are scattered throughout the hymns, particularly in the Ṛg Veda and also the Atharva Veda.

In the first place we can say that there is no expression in the Vedas which would lend itself to the interpretation which the Upaniṣadic *ātman* was subjected to, namely an individual soul. The atman of the Ṛg Veda is still quite clearly a universal force of life whose presence in living beings is manifested in breathing and as such it is comparable to other universal forces of which beings are composed.

What is quite clear from the Vedic texts is that the Vedic man experienced himself as a rather complex being. He felt that he was a collection of elemental and dynamic forces of the universe (endowed with intrinsic intelligence) which somehow combined to produce his individual being. This is, in a way, a very modern conception. We can easily see that our physiological organism is composed of elements and forces — biological, chemical and physical — which temporarily form a structural functioning unit. The intrinsic intelligence is represented by our notion of self-regulatory systems within our organism controlled and coordinated by our central nervous system, the brain. And even as our organism as a structural functioning unit functions, its universal components are being constantly rebuilt by materials and energies (or dynamic forces) entering it from outside while spent materials are constantly leaving it in order to join the "universal pool". The constant interchange between the individual and the universal and the dependence of the individual on the universal is thus clearly illustrated.

The big question, of course, is: what makes the universal elements combine into an individual structure? This is probably a perennial problem of philosophy. The platonic type of philosophy is one attempt at an answer found also in India, in the Vijñānavāda system. A German psychologist of the 1930s, Hans Driesch, borrowed the Aristotelian term *entelekheia* in his attempt to account for the fact of a structural unity of the human psychophysical organism.

Though not offering clear answers, the Vedic texts provide some interesting hints which were hardly ever improved upon by subsequent developments.

The elemental and dynamic forces of the universe which make up a person are called *devatās* in the Vedas. (The term implies their intrinsic dimension of intelligence.) They seem to operate on two distinct levels, one subtle and one gross. Then there is a force behind the scene which is mysterious and transcendent and is probably responsible for keeping it all going.

We in our objectively impartial way have to admit that we simply do not know why and how we exist in the way we do, namely as self-regulating or self-regulated structural units of impersonal constituent elements and forces making up a bodily organism and a mental personality which feels one with it while using it as its tool and being, at the same time, self-conscious and on occasions unconscious, yet surviving it, or even ecstatically superconscious and surviving even that.

The explanation the Vedas afford is philosophical and mystical as are all the subsequent Indian explanations. There are three tiers to the personality structure:

1. *The transcendental tier* is the unborn (*aja*) which is the creative and supporting force of the universe or of reality as a whole (RV 10, 16, 4; 10, 82, 6; 1, 67, 5; 1, 164, 6; 8, 41, 10) and as such corresponds to the later Upaniṣadic concept *brahman*, although it appears under this name also in the Atharva Veda (11, 8, 32). The unborn, being the supporting force of reality, supports also individual things and beings and is therefore the inner essence of man like the Upaniṣadic ātman. This unborn force holds together the elements and forces which make up the human personality, but remains totally hidden or transcendental even though, being the inner essence, it has to be regarded as immanent to man, to all individual things and to reality as a whole.

Although the unborn is responsible for holding together individual personality structures and is their indwelling inner core, it cannot be regarded as their personal soul, or indeed, as the universal soul. It remains totally outside any conceptual grasp and any spacio-temporal configuration. It has, however, to be viewed as harbouring intrinsic intelligence like all other universal forces.

2. *The subtle tier* is represented by the specifically Vedic concept *tanū*. It is often translated as "body" and in some instances it is an adequate rendering. On many occasions, however, it is inadequate. Gods as well as deceased humans possess

tanū. It corresponds more to the expression rūpa rather then śarīra. Its true meaning, however, is more accurately expressed by the word "likeness" rather than form. According to the Vedas it exists, for an infinitesimal fraction of time, on its own when a person dies, having left the material organism behind and lost all its mental faculties as well, since on death they dissolve and return into their cosmic abodes (mind to the moon, hearing into space, seeing into the sun etc. RV10, 16, 3).

In this disembodied and "disensouled" or "dementalised" form it is just an empty structure or shadow of a person (comparable to the Cheshire cat's smile left behind in the sky on the disappearance of the cat in Alice's *Adventures in Wonderland*). In that state it is presumably supported by, and linked to, the unborn alone and so it should be possible to encounter the unborn directly; hence perhaps the later speculations on the possibility of instant enlightenment immediately after death if someone manages to take advantage of this extremely brief moment (Cf. *The Tibetan Book of the Dead*).

This shadow is, however, immediately filled again by the cosmic elements and forces which make up a reconstituted or reborn personality. This virtually accomplishes the reconstitution of his *tanū* in the new surroundings. I think that *tanū* corresponds, on the mental level, to what we call man's character or to the popular meaning given to the word "personality" (he's got "personality"). It gives the specific individual imprint to the universal forces which constitute the subtle tier of a person and which are: mentality (*manas*), animating power (*asu*), life-force (*prāṇa*) and various mental faculties, such as understanding, hearing, seeing etc. I think that we can regard *tanū* simply as the "phenomenal self" which passes from life to life, not as an unchanging soul, but as a structural continuum of ever changing configurations of elements and forces (mental characteristics, faculties, talents and capacities). As such it is superior to the third tier.

3. *The third tier* is clearly, in our context, our physical body called *śarīra*, our physiological organism made up of the four elemental forces (*māhabhūtas* in later terminology) which combine into its organs and are given structural unity and outward shape and likeness by *tanū*.

No doubt, *tanū* is the most important concept for our understanding of man and his personal identity. It is that which is at all times unmistakably perceptible and identifiable as one particular person despite the fact that all the factors involved are never the same and are constantly in flux. When we say that we know a person, we mean his *tanū* or the way it has imprinted itself on his mental structure, known to us as his character, and on his bodily likeness in which, of course, his character is also in a way reflected.[4]

When we now turn to the Upaniṣadic view of human personality, we face first the problem of *ātman*, frequently translated as soul and therefore regarded as indestructible and somehow assigned by many Western interpretations the role of the transmigrating core of the individual, even though it is usually recognised that *ātman* is also the inmost essence of man linked to or identical with the cosmic source of all reality, *brahman*, with which it is therefore in a mysterious way one.[5]

This is certainly not the correct interpretation of the Upaniṣadic experience of *ātman*. Ātman is indeed the ultimate reality identical with *brahman* and the way to it is indeed through the inner recesses of man's mind. But once the inner core is reached, there is no trace of the individual in it, even though the mystical experience itself of the hidden *ātman* is an individual experience accessible at the moment of its duration just to that one particular person. The knowledge of the ultimate reality, *ātman*, is not the same as the knowledge of the self, *ātmajñāna*, a later expression, although it is through self-knowledge that one penetrates beyond onself to the ultimate experience.

When exploring the nature of *ātman* in the ultimate sense, we have to leave aside the usages of the word on the phenomenal level — as a reflexive pronoun and as referring to the phenomenal self as a whole or to its parts like the body or the mind. When the true nature of *ātman* is being explored in the Upaniṣads it is found to be "not this and not that" (*neti . . . neti*), ungraspable (*agṛhya*), unattached (*asaṅga* — see BU 3, 9, 26). The true relation of *ātman* to the things of the phenomenal world, including human personalities, is described in the Upaniṣad by the word *antaryami*, the inner controller (BU 3, 7, 1-23) of all things and beings. Thus the *ātman* controls and holds together the elements and forces which make up individual things and beings in the same way as the Vedic *aja*, without himself being these individual things and beings and without being subject to the changes they have to undergo in space and time. Therefore the *ātman* himself does not transmigrate from life to life and is not the bearer of personal identity through a person's progress from one life into another.

Even when the Upaniṣad says: "just as a goldsmith, having taken a piece of gold, produces another, newer, more beautiful shape, so, verily, this *ātman*, having discarded this body, removed ignorance, makes another, newer, more beautiful shape, like one of fathers, spirits, gods, Prajāpati or Brahmā or of other beings" (BU 4, 4, 4), it does not mean that the *ātman* migrates into the new form, just as it does not mean that the goldsmith migrates from one statue into another. The *ātman* remains the supreme transcendent as well as immanent subject on whom all the changing forms depend, but who is unaffected by their transitoriness and changeability. The *ātman*, like the Vedic *aja* (*ātman*, of course, is unborn anyway) holds together but does not himself provide any distinctive marks for the phenomenal personality even though he dwells within it.

The personal identity of an individual is preserved by the continuity of the distinctive marks of his personality, i.e. by the specific configuration of the functional constituents filling his structure. This configuration is what was called *tanū* in the Vedas and what the Upaniṣad refers to as savijñāna, "that which has consciousness", perhaps "mentality" (or dare we translate "linking consciousness"?), the mental framework which is made out of constituents which form the person, namely the degree of his knowledge (*vidyā*), his actions or volitional tendencies (karmāṇi) and the sum-total of his previous experiences (pūrva prajña) which thus becomes a kind of inborn intelligence for him (BU 4, 4, 2).[6]

The driving force of this phenomenal personality is desire (kāma) on which depend his volitions (kratu) and actions (karma — BU 4, 4, 5). These determine his future abodes. The expression used a little further on for the transmigrating personality, perhaps for the first time in Indian sources, is the word *liṅga* (BU 4, 4, 6), "mark", which in later Vedantic philosophy became the *terminus technicus* for the subtle body (*liṅga śarīra*) which survives the physical body and carries within itself the personal characteristics and future destiny shaped by past deeds of the deceased individual. In popular literature it is often called the causal or karmic body. It certainly cannot be regarded as the equivalent of the Western notion of soul, because it is compound and undergoes changes. But it sufficiently demonstrates the thesis that it is not the *ātman* in the absolute sense, but a lower order entity that represents and preserves personal identity, or perhaps better to say, personal continuity, throughout successive lives.

The terminology did not, of course, develop any degree of consistency or unification in the time of the early Upaniṣads. Sometimes it seems to be the mind (*manas*) which denotes the personal configuration or represents the identity of the person within the structure of *liṅga* (as in BU 4, 4, 6), but often it is also *nāma* (BU 3, 2, 12), a word which is linguistically identical with the English word "name", but clearly designates the whole character structure of man, perhaps because in ancient and archaic thought the name of a person magically incorporated its bearer's personality. In older times in our history names often did express some characteristic of their bearers and in our time some nicknames still fulfil this function. So when Yājñavalkya answers the question about what stays with the person after death by saying: "Name, for name is without end, without end are all the gods", he means the character or the personality of the individual which is, as previously described, all composed of universal elements and forces (*devas, devatās*). Therefore its duration, albeit not in unchangeable or unchanging form, is as unlimited within the confines of the manifested world as are all its other entities or forces and intelligences all of which are, in some way, dependent upon the unborn or transcendental *ātman*.

It should not be difficult to see, even without detailed analysis, that subsequent Hindu systems are only elaborations and variations of the Upaniṣadic conception of the phenomenal transmigrating personality structure whose controlling core does not represent its personal identity. Advaita Vedānta is the most obvious case in point, since it regards phenomenal personality and its self identity as illusory and ascribes reality only to the universal *brahman-ātman*. On the phenomenal (or "illusory") level, however, it presents an elaborate teaching of personality as a complex structure of layers or sheaths (*kośas*) forming various bodies of which the subtle body (*sūkṣma śarīra*, also called the *linga śarīra* and made of three sheaths, namely *prāṇa-, mano-* and *vijñānamaya kośas*) is the one which transmigrates and preserves personal identity from life to life.

But it might, perhaps, be regarded as understandable if the Sāṅkhya system with its plurality of *puruṣas* were to be seen as providing a theory of individual souls which preserve the personal identity in the full sense of the word (not just continuity) in successive incarnations. And yet this is not so.

Leaving aside the problem of popular Sāṅkhya trends which use Sāṅkhya terminology but twist its meaning in a Vedāntic way, in classical Sāṅkhya *puruṣa* is a pure transcendental spirit whose nature is pure consciousness and he does not carry within himself any distinctive marks of the phenomenal personality. All the constituents which form the empirical personality are evolutes of *prakṛti* or "nature" via its principle of individuation (*ahaṅkāra*). These constituents are of dual nature. The sattvic set comprises the mind (*manas*), cognitive capacities (*budhindriyas*) and capacities for action (*karma-indriyas*), while the tamasic set furnishes the material framework.

There is nothing one can say about the *puruṣa* except that it is his "illuminating power" which gives the individual phenomenal or prakṛtic personality structure the capacity to function and to be conscious of things and of itself. So the *puruṣa* acts practically in the same way as *ātman* does in controlling the changing temporary configuration of elements and forces which form the transmigrating personality.

It is possibly only Rāmānuja's Viśiṣṭādvaita and Madhva's Dvaita which might be seen as positing the existence of something that might lend itself to the interpretation of an indestructible individual soul. In Rāmānuja's system individual souls are attributes of God, although also beings in their own right, and in Madhva's system they are thought to be separate individual selves entirely different from, though totally dependent on, God. Since the positions of these two teachers are based more or less on authoritative assertions derived from a religious attitude of faith, they are largely outside the scope of philosophical analysis proper. In the general context of Hinduism their specific views have made little impact.

The early Buddhist approach to the problem of personality is highly pragmatic serving, as virtually all other expositions of topics in the Pali Canon, the primary purpose of final liberation from the round of births and deaths. In keeping with this aim the Buddha undertook an analysis of the human personality into constituents which are readily accessible to everybody's immediate experience through self-examination. They are the five groups or "bundles" (khandhas), namely (1) the bundle of form (rūpa khandha) representing corporeality, though nothing is said about its actual nature — whether it does or does not have a material substratum, (2) the bundle of feelings (vedanā khandha) classified as pleasant, unpleasant and neutral, (3) the bundle of perceptions (saññā khandha) of sixfold kind (seeing, hearing, smelling, tasting, touching and "mentating"), (4) the bundle of volitional processes (saṅkhāra khandha) and (5) the bundle of consciousness (viññāna khandha).

It is no more possible to speak about these constituents in terms of cosmic elements and forces as in the Vedic tradition, but it may be nevertheless regarded as quite obvious that individually they are impersonal phenomena which are, broadly speaking, the same in everybody's experience: a pleasant feeling, a heard sound, a desire to eat — these are generally occurring processes which are individualised as personal experiences only as a result of a willed conscious act of self-observation either at the time of the experience or in retrospect. We are so used to self-awareness and self-observation that we automatically regard all processes within ourselves as personal or even unique experiences.

But this again raises the question of personality as a coherent self-regulatory structure and, naturally, of the way in which it is referred to in early Buddhism.

The most obvious expression which covers the notion of the whole mental framework of the personality is nāma, frequently occurring in the compound nāmarūpa (sometimes also nāmakāya), and therefore regarded as standing for the four mental bundles (arūpino khandhā)[7]. This quite clearly testifies to the acceptance, by the Buddha or the early Buddhism of the Sutta Piṭaka, of the existence of the individual as a personality structure as a fact of experience on the phenomenal level of reality, i.e. within saṁsāra.

On specific occasions one has the impression that other terms are used when a special coordinating factor is indicated which circumvents all mental processes, gives them structured character and thereby presents them all together as a personality. It happens when the texts mention the mind (manas, mano, or mana). Manas is the sixth sense within the bundle of perceptions and as such it is called the mind-organ (manindriya), the mind-sphere (manāyatana) or mind-element (manodhātu). Its objects are conceptual cognizables (dhammā) which are derived by mental abstraction from the perceptions of the other five senses. Thus, as the PTS Dictionary puts it, "manas is the sensus communis which recognises the world as a mundus sensibilis (dhammā)". The other senses being subordinate to it, manas appears to be the personal controlling factor.[8]

Sometimes the term viññāna, normally designating consciousness or cognition, appears to have a wider meaning synonymous to that of manas (S, PTS ed. II, 95). Also, being the necessary condition of nāmarūpa in the chain of dependent origination (paṭiccasamuppāda), it appears to be the underlying factor of the personality structure, permeating all the other five senses (S, PTS ed. II, 4; III, 61). It is in turn conditioned by saṅkhāras, the configuration of volitional tendencies, and thus it becomes the carrier of the individuality of a person.

This is where citta comes in, too. The terminology of the Sutta Piṭaka is by no means fully systematic and consistent and citta appears to be sometimes synonymous with viññāna or manas. But mostly it refers to the inner make up of a person which we sometimes figuratively call the heart. Indeed, it is often used in connection with the word hadaya, the heart. The best clue to its meaning and function in the texts of the Sutta Piṭaka is the maxim: "Whatever one ponders and reflects on much, that way turns the inclination of his heart." (M 19; PTS ed. I, 115). This is the way inclinations, habits and features of character (saṅkhāras) are formed and ingrained. Citta thus appears to be the sum-total of a person's characteristics, in fact his "personality" or character (again like tanū in the Vedas) as it is in varying degrees known to those who know that person more or less closely. It goes without saying that citta, a person's heart or character, is not immutable, but changes by shedding old and developing new characteristics, strengthening some and weakening others, however slowly such changes may be occurring.

Thus the combination of expressions nāma, manas, viññāna and citta leave us in no doubt that there is, in early Buddhist understanding, a well-developed notion of a personality structure whose concrete contents may not be entirely identical in two consecutive moments, but whose identity is preserved by its continuity which carries on beyond physical death, i.e. the loss of a particular rūpa, to appear as a discarnate spirit ready to get hold of another rūpa in the physical world (provided it does not reappear as a deva or some other being in a different existential sphere), in which case he is referred to also as a gandhabba. Three conditions are mentioned as necessary for a birth in our world to take place: (1) a couple engaged in sexual intercourse, (2) the woman must have "her time" and (3) a gandhabba seeking rebirth must be around (M 38; PTS ed. I. 266).

The expression gandhabba is apparently a convenient conventional term used to avoid conceptual complications or confusion if a more technical expression like those discussed above were employed, but it serves us well to illustrate and confirm, in the early Buddhist context, our thesis that there is a transmigrating structural unit which, it is true, is not granted any ultimate status but has the capacity to carry on as a configuration, albeit a changing one, through successive lives.[9]

Technically speaking, the gandhabba must carry the whole mental equipment of a particular person from his previous life, namely viññāna, since Paṭisambhidāmagga called "linking consciousness" (patisandhi viññāna — PTS ed. I. 52), the accompanying force of past actions (kamma) and the sum-total of his volitional drives, inclinations and tendencies (saṅkhāras) which was also expressed by the term citta and which we have often called character.

One cannot escape the feeling that there should be one particular expression available which would suitably designate the mental being undergoing all those changes, transformations and rebirths. Citta would appear a good candidate, particularly because it figures in the early texts also in connection with a person who has acquired a highly purified state of citta (Dh 42, 43; also M 7). We also find the expression cittekaggata, the unified heart or mind. And it is even said that the Buddha has a cultivated and liberated heart/mind samādhi-subhāvitam cittam ca vimuttam, S 1, 38; PTS ed. 1, 28). Johansson tried to make a case for citta in this sense, though not very successfully.[10]

Historically, the Pudgalavāda school attempted to give expression to the desire to pinpoint the carrier of personal identity and posited the existence of a pudgala/ puggala, a person, not only as a phenomenal, saṃsāric being, but also in the ultimate sense. It seems thus that the Pudgalavādins asserted the full reality of the structural unity called the person which was not fully defined by the five khandhas, but could not be described as existing outside them either. It was undefinable and fully known only to the Buddhas.

This was, of course, heresy in that it went too obviously beyond the accepted authentic pronouncements of the Buddha on the topic. No other subsequent school dared to take it up again and the sources on Pudgalavāda are very meagre.[11]

It is most unlikely that any other attempt to formulate a fully fledged philosophical theory of personality within Buddhism can ever succeed. Neither can any Hindu theory be regarded as such, for that matter. Have we one in the West?

This brings us back to the comparison of the teachings on personality in the two main Indian traditions, the Hindu and the Buddhist. We have seen that there is no essential difference between the Upaniṣadic and the subsequent Hindu systems' conceptions of the transmigrating personality on the one hand and the Buddhist ones on the other. In both traditions there is a notion of a personality structure whose constituents, variously termed but basically referring to the same or similar functions such as consciousness, sensory perceptions, volitional processes and a physiological organism, vary as a result of changes in volitional drives and in accordance with the law of karmic causation, both during the person's present lifetime and in the course of the long sequence of his lives.

The most conspicuous difference between the two traditions is the assertion of the Upaniṣadic *ātman* (which is, in its peculiar way, parallelled by *puruṣa* in Sāṅkhya) as the transcendental agent, presumably of universal nature, who is responsible for the structural unity of the phenomenal personalities as their inner controller, while the Buddhist tradition keeps silent about any such transcendental influence. It does not, however, expressly deny it, contrary to the assertions advocated by the Theravāda interpreters. The so called doctrine of *anattā* is a postcanonical elaboration or, in any event, is not contained in the texts of Sutta Piṭaka, which is our main source of the early Buddhist teachings whose formulations may be regarded as predating sectarian developments, while many passages of Vinaya Piṭaka and the whole of Abhidhamma Piṭaka originated within Theravāda after the onset of sectarian splits.

The Sutta Piṭaka uses the concept of *attā* in connection with the analysis of the phenomenal personality into the five groups of constituents each of which is denied the status of *attā* on account of being impermanent and subject to suffering. This implies the tacit maxim that if there is an *attā* it must be free from those impediments which obtain in saṁsāra only. This is also how *ātman* is viewed in the Upaniṣads. But there is no statement in the Sutta Piṭaka about the ultimate existence or non-existence of *atta*, completely in keeping with the exclusion of metaphysical propositions which cannot be verified by everybody's experience from the practical set of instructions aiming at the final or ultimate experience of liberation which is what the doctrine of early Buddhism is all about.[12]

But since, as we have seen, the *ātman* of the Upaniṣads (and the puruṣa of the Sāṅkhya system) is not the individual transmigrating kernel of the human personality, his inclusion in or omission from the theory of personality does not make any difference whatsoever to the notion of personal identity or continuity from life to life. Neither Hinduism nor Buddhism posits an abiding, unchanging, purely individual soul inhabiting the personality structure and therefore the Upaniṣadic assertion of the *ātman* and the Buddhist arguable negation of the *attā* do not justify or substantiate the often repeated view that Hinduism believes in a transmigrating soul while Buddhism denies it.

END NOTES

1. This point is more often made by protagonists of Buddhism than by Hindus, e.g. in the booklets of the Buddhist Publication Society, Kandy: "... the personality, in which other systems of thought imagine the presence of a permanent spiritual principle, a self or soul (*attā*), is, from the point of view of the Buddha, only a bundle of elements or forces (*saṅkhāra*) ... The individual is entirely phenomenal ... without any extra-phenomenal self or soul within him." G.P. Malalasekera, *The Truth of Anattā*, BPS Kandy 1966 (Wheel 94), p.16.

V.C. Mutsuddi speaks in his lecture *Outlines of Buddhism and how it differs from Hinduism*, delivered at a meeting of the East and West Fraternity, Chittagong, on 25.8.1945, of "transmigration of souls, regarded by Hindu thinkers as the necessary complement of a belief in the essential sameness of all souls ... and in their ultimate reunion with the Parameshvara, the Supreme Soul ...", while "According to Buddhism there is no permanent Ego, and the soul is not transmigrating from body to body." See pp.18 and 22 of the published version of his talk, BPS Kandy (no date of publication given).

2. See the Foreword to: Lynn A. de Silva, *The Problem of the Self in Buddhism and Christianity*, Macmillan, London 1979 (first Colombo 1975), p.IX.

3. Geoffrey Parrinder, *The Indestructible Soul. The Nature of Man and Life after Death in Indian Thought*, Allen & Unwin, London 1973. This book summarises views of several Indian systems, but fails to clarify the issue of soul, basically because it does not attempt to define it while using the term throughout with different shades of meaning and in different contexts and because it does not analyse sufficiently the individual and universal connotations in which both the core and the phenomenal components of the personality structure appear.

4. More details and references are available in my article "The Vedic Concept of the Human Personality and its Destiny", *Journal of Indian Philosophy*, vol. 5, (The Hague 1978), pp.275-289.

5. Cf. Radhakrishnan, Introduction to *The Principal Upanisads*, Allen & Unwin, London 1953, pp.73-75.

6. When a person dies, i.e. when *ātman* departs from him in the sense that it stops controlling his organism, and life (*prāna*) and all other vital forces depart too, "he becomes (*bhavati*) (a being) with consciousness (*savijñano* — a masculine adjectival form standing for a noun); that which is with consciousness (*savijñānam* — a noun, neuter) or that which is of mental nature follows; knowledge, actions and previous experience envelop him (*tam samanvārabhete*). All this suggests the idea of a mental body, further down referred to as *liṅga*. There is another expression used later to designate the individual personality while still preserving the connotation of universality from which it stems, viz. *jīvātman*. Its, perhaps first, appearance is in ChU (6, 3, 2-3) is in the context of the creation of individual beings (*nāmārupe*) by the deity with the help of the living self (*jīvenā'tmanā*). To pursue this line would be outside the scope of this paper and would not change its basic thesis, but it would be an interesting topic in itself, particularly also in connection with the use of the term *jīva* in Buddhist texts.

7. Sometimes *nāmakāya* does not appear to be the equivalent of *nāmarūpa*, i.e. of the whole psychophysical structure, but seems to mean what is sometimes called the "mental body" corresponding to the four *arūpino khandhā*. Its counterpart then is *rūpakāya*, the material body. See D 15. Alex Wayman wrote an exhaustive paper on the theme of *nāmarūpa*: "A Study of the Vedāntic and Buddhist Theory of Nāma-rūpa", *Indological and Buddhist Studies. Volume in Honour of Professor J.W. de Jong on his Sixtieth Birthday*. Ed. I.A. Hercus, F.B.J. Kuiper, T. Rajapatirana, E.R. Skrzypczak. Faculty of Asian Studies (The Australian National University), Canberra 1982, pp. 617-642. He concludes that *nāma* came to indicate individuality in the human case, and individual things in the case of external entities (p. 617). For *rūpa*, which he says is matter or its appearance, he suggests the rendering "formation" (p.620) when it occurs as a part of the compound *nāmarūpa*. He also lists later definitions of the two terms in contrast (*nāmakāya* as against *rūpakāya* p.621). In connection with his discussion of what he calls "two kinds of *nāmarūpa*" Wayman makes a speculative suggestion when he says at the end of his paper: "A rather exciting outcome of these researches is that in the Brahmanical as well as in the Buddhist portrayal of *nāmarūpa*, this constitutes a kind of dividing line between our commonplace world and the superior world of the gods or of yoga-success." (p.634) I confess that it is not entirely clear to me what Wayman means by this remark, since it seems too vague. But I do accept that there is likely to be an issue behind it which would merit a careful philosophical analysis.

8. See PTS Dictionary where references can be found.

9. There is a precedent for the term *gandhabba* meaning a spirit departed from the human world in the Upanisads. TU (2, 8, 1) mentions, among other categories of beings enumerated in an ascending hierarchical order, human spirits (*mānusya gandharvas*) and divine spirits (*deva gandharvas*), followed by fathers in their "long enduring worlds" and several categories of gods above them etc. In a similar enumeration in BU (4, 3, 33) both the categories of *gandharvas* are missing. One can regard human and divine *gandharvas* as spirits of those who have departed from the human and the *deva* world, respectively, now living in a kind of intermediary existence before proceeding further into another world.

10. R. Johansson, *The Psychology of Nirvana*, Allen & Unwin, London 1963.

11. Cf. E. Conze, *Buddhist Thought in India*, Allen & Unwin, London 1962, pp.122-132.

12. The problem of the status of *atta* in the teachings of early Buddhism as it can be ascertained mainly in the Sutta Piṭaka has not been fully and properly researched yet. The existing expositions of the so called *anattā* doctrine are based on the interpretation of the *sutta* passages in the light of Abhidhamma materials, Theravāda commentaries and postcanonical Theravāda works such as Milinda Pañha and Visuddhi Magga. Thus Lynn A. de Silva, *op. cit.* (see note 2) or S. Collins, *Selfless Persons*, Cambridge U. P. 1982.

Nyanaponika Thera in his booklet *Anattā and Nibbāna*, Wheel Publications 11, BPS Kandy 1952 (p. 20), tried to show that there is a direct denial of *attā* in M 22 (PTS ed. M I, 138) in a passage which I.B. Horner translated in a way that asserts the existence of *atta* (*The Middle Length Sayings*, PTS I, 77). Both are wrong. The passage goes as follows:

Attani vā bhikkave sati attaniyam-me ti assāta. — Evam-bhante. — Attaniye vā bhikkhave sati attā me ti assāti. — Evam-bhante. — Attani ca bhikkhave attaniye ca saccato thetato anupalabbhamāne yam-p' idam ditthitthanam: so loko so attā, so pecca bhavissāmi nicco dhuvo sassato aviparināmadhammo, sassatisamam tath' eva thassāmiti, nanāyam bhikkhave kevalo paripūro bāladhammo ti. —

Nyanaponika translates: "If, bhikkhus, there is a self, will there also be something belonging to a self?" —"Certainly, Lord". — "If there is something belonging to a self, will there also be (the view) 'My self'?" —"Certainly, Lord". — "But since, bhikkhus, a self and anything belonging to a self cannot truly and really be found, is it not a perfectly foolish doctrine to hold the point of view 'This is the world. This is the self. Impermanent (*sic!* It should read *permanent*), abiding, eternal and immutable shall I be after death, in eternal identity shall I persist'?"

I.B. Horner translates: "If monks, there were Self, could it be said: 'It belongs to my self'?" "Yes, Lord." "Or, monks, if there were what belongs to Self, could it be said: 'It is my self'?" "Yes, Lord." "But if Self, monks, and what belongs to Self, although actually existing, are incomprehensible, is not the view and the causal relation that: 'This is the world, this is the self, after dying I will become permanent, lasting, eternal, not liable to change, I will stand fast like unto the eternal' — is not this, monks, absolute complete folly?"

I would translate: "Were there, monks, a self, could one say: 'There is something selflike in me.'?" — "Just so, Lord." — "Were there something selflike in me, could one say: 'My self.'?" — "Just so Lord." — "As self and something selflike cannot be truly and reliably made out, is not the point of view: 'This is the world, this is the self: that, having passed away, I shall be, permanent, stable, eternal, a changeless entity; I shall stand the same in eternity', monks, a wholly and completely foolish doctrine?" The passage is to be understood in relation to the well known analysis of the personality into five *khandhas*, none of which can be pinpointed as being the self, my self or selflike or belonging to self or to my self. Therefore the self (*attā*) and what belongs to self or is self-like (*attaniya*) cannot be made out, got at, found or known (*anupalabbhamāna*). One cannot draw the conclusion from the passage that self (*attā*) does not exist since that would amount to an ontological proposition about the ultimate existence or non-existence which the Buddha in the Sutta Pitaka never does. He similarly refuses to make such a statement about the *tathāgata*. Nyānaponika himself quotes such a passage later on (p.22): ". . . the Perfect One, Anurādha, cannot truly and really be found . . . " (*tathāgate anupalabbhyamāne* — S, PTS IV, 384; similarly in III, 118).

All that it amounts to is that ontological questions of ultimate significance cannot be "truly and really" made out from man's everyday, limited (i.e. samsāric) position and any belief or view about them is futile or foolish, i.e. unprofitable or detrimental with respect to the actual attainment of the ultimate goal. The problem of the existence of the *ātman/attā* in the Upanisads and the early Buddhism may be, after all, only a question of semantics. It can certainly be regarded as an important or at least interesting philosophical question worthy of a thorough re-examination. Here, however, I can only state again that it does not have any bearing on the thesis advocated in this paper.

Abbreviations:

BPS Buddhist Publication Society

BU Brhadāranyaka Upanisad

ChU Chāndogya Upanisad

M Majjhima Nikāya

PTS Pali Text Society

RV Rg Veda

S Samyutta Nikāya

TU Taittirīya Upanisad

IDENTITY AND SELF-KNOWLEDGE IN THE SYRIAN THOMAS TRADITION[1]

Luther H. Martin

The University of Vermont, U.S.A.

I

In studying both the most admired and the most detested figures in any society, we can see, as seldom through other evidence, the nature of the average man's expectations and hopes for himself. — Peter Brown[2]

The understanding of a Hellenistic period of history, since its first delineation by J.G. Droysen in the mid-nineteenth century as the result of Alexander's challenge to Persian hegemony, has resulted in a tendency to understand Hellenistic culture as a syncretistic homology. Although common systemic structures are indeed identifiable as defining a Hellenistic culture,[3] we must take care not to lose sight of such cultural differences as exist, for example between views of self-identity, within this system.

The emergence of individualism in the Hellenistic world did not signal the promise of potential which characterized Renaissance humanism, but presented rather a problematic to be solved in response to those transformations which characterized the Hellenistic period. A locative image of the cosmos had been replaced by the exploded topography of what came to be termed the Ptolemaic system. The ascent of Alexander's Greco-Macedonian empire had challenged the traditional social conventions of political identity with its imposed but often unrealized cosmopolitan ideals. The collective piety of political allegiance or that of antiestablishment Dionysian *orgia* as portrayed in Euripides' *The Bacchae* gave way to the labyrinthian wanderings of Apuleius' Lucius. And the classical speculations of Plato and Aristotle about a metaphysical and cosmological order of things were replaced by the ethical concerns of Hellenistic philosophy. These Hellenistic transformations all generated the question asked of Jesus by the anonymous everyman: "What must I do . . . ?" (Mk. 10, 17).

Stoic and gnostic ethics represented alternative responses to the new exigencies of existence represented by the Hellenistic world. Both accepted *heimarmene*, or a natural fate, as the normalizing principle of the cosmos, more than the power of any sovereign, whether emperor or god. And both knew the disastrous effects of the passions, of the sensuous world, for self-knowledge. Neither responded, however, in terms of fixed systems of thought, but represented, rather, antithetical strategies of existence within a contiguous cultural and historical context.

The Stoics applied traditional philosophical values to the new individualism and taught the taming of human passions by self-examination in order to effect a harmonious relation with the external order of things. True freedom was the moral freedom of a philosophical self-knowledge which recognized and conformed to an assumed orderly principle of the cosmos.

Gnostics, on the other hand, represented a Hellenistic strategy of individual existence *par excellence*. They were rarely organized into autonomous institutional forms, if ever, but articulated their perspective through existing religious and philosophical alternatives.[4] They repudiated this world, along with its ruling powers, altogether. This anti-cosmic rebellion was based upon their absolute certainty of a knowledge which they believed was revealed from beyond the normalizing cosmic limits of what, hitherto, had been considered possible.[5]

To the new exigencies of existence represented by the Hellenistic world, gnostic thought responded, "know yourself, and you will possess," in the well-known words of the second century Valentinian Gnostic, Theodotus:

> knowledge of who we were, and what we have become, where we were or where we were placed, whither we hasten, from what we are redeemed, what birth is and what rebirth. Ex. Theod. 78, 2[6]

Or again, in the words of his contemporary, the gnostic Christian theologian, Clement of Alexandria:

> It is then ... the greatest of all lessons to know one's self. For if one knows himself, he will know God. — Paedagogus, III, 1.[7]

An eastern "gnostic" Thomas tradition, probably centered in Edessa, presents this apostle, contrary to the western canonical tradition of a "doubting" Thomas (Jn. 20, 24-29), as the exemplum of individual self-knowledge.[8] This tradition can be traced from the *Gospel of Thomas* through a *Book of Thomas*, both from the second codex of the Nag Hammadi library, to the *Acts of Thomas*.[9]

II

> Simply saying 'Look towards God' is of no avail without teaching how to look.
> — Plotinus[10]

The Delphic maxim concerning self-knowledge was widely cited in Greek and Hellenistic literature generally,[11] and in gnostic literature specifically.[12] Since the *Alcibiades I*, attributed to Plato, self-knowledge had been at the center of western ethical thought. When the young Alcibiades wishes to begin his public life (123 D), Socrates intervenes, and with reference to the Delphic inscription, seeks to lead Alcibiades to a knowledge of himself (124 A-B), for, by knowing oneself, the political leader knows the proper affairs of others and thereby the affairs of state (133 D — 134 A).

To Alcibiades' query about how he might achieve this self-knowledge (124 B), Socrates responds that he would come to know himself if he takes care of himself (*epimelesthai sautou*) (127 E, 132 C). Thus, for the western tradition, self-knowledge was the function of certain obligations associated with taking care of the self.[13] The association of taking care of oneself with the Delphic maxim concerning self-knowledge which was characteristic of Greco-Roman ethical literature since Plato, is characteristic of the eastern Thomas tradition as well, but as an interdiction rather than obligation.

The Syrian *Acts of Thomas*, dated in the early third century CE,[14] belongs to an eastern collection of apocryphal *Acts of the Apostles* attributed, since the fifth century, to Leucius Charinus, a supposed companion of the apostle John.[15] The *Acts of Thomas* is generally considered to belong to a genre of Hellenistic-Oriental romances, a somewhat loosely defined genre of literature characterized primarily by the adventurous travels of a hero to exotic foreign places and by his erotic encounters.[16] This "romance" of Thomas elaborates earlier themes of the Thomas tradition in terms of the apostle's supposed missionary activities in India.

The *Acts of Thomas* begins with the disciples of Jesus conducting a lottery to determine which region of the world each would evangelize. Thomas draws India, but, as a Hebrew, is reluctant to travel to so foreign a region. Jesus forces the issue by selling him as a slave to the Indian merchant, Abban, who soon sets sail with Thomas in tow. They arrive first in Andrapolis during a city-wide festival celebrating the marriage of the local king's only daughter.

During the celebrations, a cup-bearer unexpectedly slaps Thomas, presumably because of the attention shown him by one of the entertainers, a Hebrew flute-girl. Responding to this unwarranted attack, Thomas promises that:

> My God will forgive this injury in the world to come, but in this world he will show forth his wonders, and I shall even now see that hand that smote me dragged by dogs.

> —AcTh. 6

— a somewhat uncharitable response by canonical standards. And indeed, according to the *Acts*, when the cup-bearer goes out to the well for water, he is slain and dismembered by a lion and a black dog picks up the right hand which had struck Thomas, and carries it back to the party.

Having now attracted the attention not only of the flute-girl, but of the entire gathering, Thomas is conscripted by the anxious King to pray for the marriage of his daughter. After praying that Jesus might do "the things that help and are useful and profitable" for these newlyweds, Thomas blesses the couple and departs.

When everyone finally leaves, the bridegroom anxiously approaches his bride, but is amazed to find Jesus, in the likeness of his twin, Thomas, chatting with his new wife in the bedroom. As the three of them sit down together to discuss the situation, Jesus counsels the newlyweds to abandon the "filthy intercourse" they obviously had been anticipating and

> become holy temples, pure and free from afflictions and pains both manifest and hidden, and you will not be girt about with care for life (*phrontidas biou*) and children, the end of which is destruction ... But if you obey and keep your souls pure unto God, you shall have living children ... .and shall be without care (*amerimnoi*).

> —AcTh. 12

Unexpectedly for the modern reader, and likely for Thomas's non-Christian contemporary as well, the bridegroom thanks Jesus for this unsolicited but timely advice and for revealing his corrupt and morally sick condition by directing him to seek himself and to know (*gnonai*) who he was and who and how he now is (AcTh.15).

The *Acts of Thomas* presents a self-knowledge constituted by secret teachings (*gnosis*) which Thomas has received from Jesus (AcTh. 39) and which are now recorded in this account of his missionary activities. Contrary to the western ethical tradition, this self-knowledge results in a freedom from care (*aphrontis, amerimnos*) (AcTh. 12; 35). This antithetical relationship between self-knowledge and taking care of oneself is soteriological. In her rejection of "filthy intercourse" (see also AcTh. 43.), the bride did not become yoked to a "short-lived" husband but to the "true man" (AcTh. 14); the bridegroom came to know his true self (AcTh. 15; see also 43 and 144); and even the flute-girl found soteriological rest (*anapausis*) as a result of these events.[17] Similarly, in the third act of Thomas, a young man who had been killed by a giant serpent but resuscitated through the intercession of Thomas concludes that: "I have become free from care (*phrontidos*) ... from the care (*phrontidos*) of night, and I am at rest (*anapaen*) from the toil of day" (AcTh. 34)

In the Socratic obligation to take care of oneself, two points of view intersect, the political and the erotic. When the young Alcibiades wishes to enter political life, he submits to Socrates, the first of his lovers (103 A, 104 E). According to Socrates, to know oneself one must know both one's body, one's sexuality, and how to participate in the socio-political world. This positive relationship between techniques of self and that which is not-self — teachers, the city (or the socio-political realm), and the cosmos — is a persistent theme of western philosophizing.

Similarly, in the *Acts of Thomas*, a political context is established when Thomas attends the wedding celebration of the princess at the court of the king, and then participates in this royal celebration by blessing the union. However, this participation in public life is required of Thomas against his will, whereas Alcibiades aspired to political life. An erotic context is also established in the *Acts of Thomas* when the groom approaches his new bride for the first time. However, the new wife does not submit physically to her husband, but spiritually to the "true man", Jesus.

Jesus shows the bride and groom, even as Socrates taught Alcibiades, that self-knowledge is not of the body, but of the soul (Alc. 130 E; 132 B-C). However, and here the two traditions diverge, in the Platonic and later Stoic traditions, self-knowledge requires practices of taking care of one's self characterized by a network of obligations and services, whereas in the eastern Thomas tradition, self-knowledge results in a carefreeness characterized by a network of interdictions.

The Coptic *Book of Thomas*, from the same Nag Hammadi codex as the *Gospel of Thomas*, is dated earlier in the second century CE than the Acts of Thomas.[18] It introduces the same interdiction as does the *Acts*, but in the context of a revelatory dialogue. This form is revealed as pseudo-dialogical, however, when Thomas tell Jesus that, "It is you Lord whom it benefits to speak, and me to listen" (BkTh. 142, 9).

Although Jesus points out that the secret teachings are already known to and have been pondered by Thomas, he invites Thomas to examine himself in order to know who he is in light of this revelation. Jesus does not consider it seemly that his twin brother should be ignorant of himself (BkTh. 138, 10-12): "for he who has not known himself has known nothing, but he who has known himself has at the same time already achieved knowledge about the Depth of the All" (BkTh. 138, 16-18).

The relation between self-knowledge and rejection of the world is clearly summarized by Jesus in a concluding section of the *Book of Thomas*.[19] Those who have not received the revealed doctrine are ignorant and, thus, are renounced. Their soul has been corrupted by the body and by the world. The Blessed, on the other hand, are those who, like Thomas, have prior knowledge of these things.

The general rejection of the world by the *Book of Thomas* (143, 13f.) does not explicitly refer to political involvement as does the *Acts of Thomas*, but it is explicit concerning rejection of the body.[20] The body is transitory (BkTh. 139, 4), it decays and perishes (BkTh. 139, 5). This cycle of fleshly life derives finally from "intimacy with women and polluted intercourse" (BkTh. 144. 9f.; and 139, 8-10), the fire of lust "that scorches the spirits of men" (BkTh. 140, 3f.), "the bitter bond of lust for those visible things that will decay and change" (BkTh. 140, 33f.).

The rejection of world by Jesus is summarized in the *Book of Thomas* by the interdiction against *prooush bios* (BkTh. 141, 12-14; 38f.). The Coptic word *rooush* translates not only *phrontis* and *merimna*, the words for "care" used in the Greek version of the *Acts of Thomas*, but also *epimeleia*, the technical term for "care" in the Western ethical tradition.[21] This interdiction against any concern or care for this life seems to include the practice of care itself. When Thomas shows care (*merimna*) for those deprived of the kingdom (BkTh. 142, 3-5), he is persuaded by the savior not to care for them, for their depravation is the lot of the ignorant (BkTh. 142, 11-19).

The obligation to know oneself is central also to the teachings of the *Gospel of Thomas*. One of the first things Jesus tells his disciples in this *Gospel* is that:

> When you come to know yourselves, then you will become known, and you will realize that it is you who are the sons of the living Father. But if you will not know yourselves, you dwell in poverty and it is you who are that poverty.— GosTh. 3

Consequently, they are repeatedly exhorted to seek this knowledge until it is found (GosTh. 2; 92; 94). This is a difficult task, however, for the knowledge which is to be sought has already come and the disciples have not recognized it (GosTh. 51). As Jesus says in another passage, "That which you have will save you if you bring it forth from yourselves" (GosTh. 70).

Dated from the second half of the first century CE to the first half of the second century CE,[22] the opening lines of the *Gospel of Thomas* differ significantly from the *Book of Thomas* only in that Thomas himself is represented as recording "the secret sayings which the living (or resurrected) Jesus spoke" (GosTh. incip.), rather than the secretary, Mathias (BkTh. 138-1-3). Thomas, however, is not simply the secretary for Jesus and the other disciples in the *Gospel*, for Jesus takes him aside and reveals to him knowledge not shared with the other disciples (GosTh. 13). In other words, the knowledge which saves and is revealed by Jesus only to Thomas (GosTh. 13) is an inner knowledge (GosTh. 108) which Thomas has written down (GosTh. incip.) for whoever has ears to hear (GosTh. 8, 21, 63, 65, 96), or, for his reader's eyes to see.

For the *Gospel of Thomas*, self-knowledge seems to result in a negative stance towards the external world: "Whoever finds himself is superior to the world" (GosTh. 111). However, this priority of knowledge to action is not so clear as it comes to be in the *Book of Thomas*. Other sayings of Jesus in this Gospel seem to suggest that self-knowledge is the result of certain practices of world-rejection: "Be on your guard against the world," Jesus warns (GosTh. 21), for "If you do not fast as regards the world, you will not find the Kingdom" (GosTh. 27). In either case, the self-knowledge is clearly understood by the Gospel of Thomas to be inner, apart from and other than the external world: "Whoever has come to understand the world has found (only) a corpse." (GosTh. 56).

Although a specific interdiction against care does not appear in the *Gospel of Thomas*, the earliest of the Thomas texts, its sense is clearly present. Like the *Acts of Thomas*, the *Gospel* not only rejects the external "world" generally but also the sexual and political activities of this world specifically. "Blessed are the womb which has not conceived and the breasts which have not given milk," Jesus tells an adoring woman (GosTh. 79), for only those who "make the male and the female one and the same, so that the male not be male nor the female female" will enter the Kingdom (GosTh. 22). And again Jesus commands his disciples:

> Give Caesar what belongs to Caesar, give God what belongs to God, and give Me what is Mine.—GosTh. 100; see also 81 and 110

Self knowledge for the Gospel of Thomas, therefore, is other than the social relationships required by sexual and political activity. "Many are standing at the door," Jesus says, "but it is the solitary who will enter the bridal chamber" (GosTh. 75; see also 49).[23]

The rejection of socio-political obligations in the eastern Thomas tradition stands in marked contrast to their necessary inclusion within practices of self-identity in the western tradition. In the Platonic and later Stoic traditions, self-knowledge is the result of "caring for the self," characterized by a network of external obligations and practices, whereas in the Thomas tradition self-knowledge is a revealed or prior knowledge, resulting in a carefreeness characterized by inner discipline within a network of interdictions. This revealed "prior" knowledge is the subject of the "gnostic" Thomas literature.

III

There is a dialogue between the author and the model reader ... He wants to reveal the reader to himself.—Umberto Eco[24]

Asked by Alcibiades what he must do to take care of himself and thereby come to know himself, Socrates responds that he must engage in dialogue (127 E), a technique which ensures social relationships. Socratic dialogue, however, was literary dialogue, the fictive device of Plato. This technique of dialogically writing the self was perfected by the Stoics whereby they remembered the day's activities in letters written to others.[25] By contrast, the self-emphasis by the Thomas tradition on the writing of revelation suggests rather a solitary, inner, technique of reading the self.

The Thomas tradition consists of the secret teachings of Jesus "received" by "listening" to the revelations of Jesus (GosTh. *incip.*; BkTh. 138, 1-4; 142, 9f.; AcTh. 39),[26] which, according to the *Gospel of Thomas*, Thomas wrote down, while according to the *Book of Thomas*, they were written down by a secretary. Whatever the historical origin of these pseudo-dialogues, they claim to reveal a prior *gnosis* in writing. They do not recommend dialogic activity, for which the questioning Thomas of the western canon might have served as model, but instead record a particular content to be read and known.

The practice of reading as a technique for knowing self is described in the *Acts of Thomas* itself, in the "Hymn of the Pearl," which was sung by Thomas while in prison to encourage his fellow inmates (AcTh. 108-113). In this famous hymn, a king's son, the first person author of the song, is sent forth to seek a precious pearl, an allegorical destination for his true self,[27] which is guarded by a ferocious serpent in Egypt. But the son soon forgets his task, and himself, as he takes up a foreign way of life.

The royal parents write their lost son a letter, identical to what is already "written" in his heart, recalling him to its contents so that he might know who he really is. When the son reads this letter, he is awakened to his true self and is able successfully to complete his quest for the pearl and return home.

In this hymn, the son's knowledge of himself is arrived at by reading a text. This text reveals a prior knowledge of his true self already written within, but forgotten. In other words, this eastern tradition represents a practice of reading the self in which the reader is disclosed to himself.

This technique of "reading of the self" recalls the thesis advanced by Richard Reitzenstein early in this century of a genre of *Lese-Mysteria*, or literary-mysteries.[28] This genre, he argued, preserved the outward form of a Hellenistic mystery religion through a series of discursive and doctrinal writings. If the reader of such a literary mystery were one who had turned away from the world, the literary presentation would affect him just as if he had actually participated in a mystery ritual.[29] Festugiere has also described the enigmatic Orphic literature as such a literary-mystery,[30] following the lead of Pausanias who equated a reading of Orphic writings with the witnessing of initiation at the Eleusinian Mysteries (I, 37, 4).

Reinhold Merkelbach also has argued that the Hellenistic romances were written in the service of the Hellenistic mystery cults.[31] While his view has been challenged,[32] it is generally agreed to hold true for two late romances, Apuleius' *The Golden Ass*, and the *Acts of Thomas*.[33] Apuleius' romance is clearly propaganda for the Hellenistic cult of Isis, while the *Acts of Thomas* present a Christian-Gnostic mystery of redemption.[34] As such, their point is not to recommend dialogic — or social — activity, but like the *Gospel* and the *Book of Thomas*, to present a particular content through the written word. The reading of such texts constituted a hermeneutics of the self.

In conclusion, two differently situated technologies of the Hellenistic self may be identified. The first, which is characteristic of the western ethical tradition, might be termed an epistemological technology of self. This tradition emphasizes the activity of self-disclosure always in terms of an other. By disclosing oneself in dialogue, self was constituted. The second, exemplified by the eastern Thomas tradition, might be termed an ontological technology of self. This tradition emphasizes the discernment or deciphering of what the self already is. This knowledge is reclaimed by passive listening and later, through the solitary activity of reading. The first, dialogic activity, is social. The second, contemplative activity, was more conducive to the Syrian encratitic technology of self generally considered to have been introduced to Western Christianity by John Cassian only at the end of the Hellenistic period in the early fourth century.[35]

NOTES

1. A first draft of this paper was read at Professor Michel Foucault's seminar at The University of Vermont in 1982, and is dedicated to his memory.

2. "The Rise and Function of the Holy Man in Late Antiquity," 1972. *Society and The Holy in Late Antiquity* (Berkeley: U California Press, 1982, 103-152) 106.

3. Luther H. Martin, "Why Cecropian Minerva?: Hellenistic Religious Syncretism as System," *Numen*, (1983) XXX: 131-145.

4. Kurt Rudolf, *Gnosis: The Nature and History of Gnosticism*, 2nd rev. ed., trans. ed. Robert McLachlan Wilson (San Francisco: Harper & Row, 1983) 54-5.

5. The ascetic rejection of the ethical in its conventional sense suggests the basis for representing gnostic ethic as "licentious." Based upon accusations by Christian apologists, it has been argued, at least since the end of the 19th century, that the ascetic renunciation of the sensuous nature of the self had a counterpart in a libertine indifference towards the sensuous, (Adolf Harnack, *History of Dogma*, 1885, trans. from 3rd German ed. Neil Buchanan, 7 vols. (New York: Russell and Russell, 1958) I: 263), and even a "positive obligation" to violate this-worldly ethical standards (Hans Jonas, *The Gnostic Religion*, 2nd ed., rev. (Boston: Beacon Press, 1963) 273).

6. *The Excerpta ex Theodoto of Clement of Alexandria*, ed. and trans. Robert P. Casey, (London: Christophers, 1934).

7. Trans. *The Ante-Nicene Fathers*, Alexander Roberts and James Donaldson, ed. Vol. II (Buffalo: The Christian Literature Publishing House, 1885).

8. On the identity of the eastern with the western Thomas, see Helmut Koester, "GNOMAI DIAPHOROI: The Origin and Nature of Diversification in the History of Early Christianity," *Trajectories through Early Christianity*, James M. Robinson and Helmut Koester (Philadelphia, Fortress Press, 1971) 127-8 and 133-4. On the origins of Christianity in Syria, see A.F.J. Klijn, *The Acts of Thomas*, Supplement to Novum Testamentum V (Leiden: E.J. Brill, 1962) 30-33; Arthur Voeoebus, *History of Asceticism in the Syrian Orient*, 2 vols. (Louvain: CSCO, 1958-1960); and Han J.W. Drijvers, "Facts and Problems in Early Syriac-Speaking Christianity," *The Second Century* (1982) 2: 157-175.

9. Robinson and Koester 126-143; see also John D. Turner, *The Book of Thomas the Contender* (Missoula, Montana; Scholars Press, 1975), 233-239; and Drijvers 157-175.

10. Ennead II, 9, 15.

11. Eliza Gregory Wilkins, *"Know Thyself" in Greek and Latin Literature* (1917; rpt. Chicago: Ares Publishers, 1980, especially the compilation of passages in which the maxim either is explicitly cited, or indirectly expressed (100-104).

12. Rudolf, 113; and Hans Dieter Betz, "The Delphic Maxim GNOTHI SAUTON in Hermetic Interpretation," *Harvard Theological Review* 63 (1970): 465-484.

13. Foucault, *supra* and *Histoire de la Sexualité*, Vol. III: *Le Souci de Soi* (Paris: Gallimard, 1984), esp. Ch. 2: "La Culture de Soi", 53-85; Wilkins, 60f.

14. Syriac text with English trans. W. Wright, in *Apocryphal Acts of the Apostles*, 2 vols. (London: Williams and Norgate, 1871); Greek text, ed. R.A. Lipsius and M. Bonnet, *Acta Apostolorum Apocrypha* (1903. Darmstadt: Wissenschaftliche Buchgesellschaft, 1959; Intro. and trans. Gunther Bornkamm in *New Testament Apocrypha*, ed. E. Hennecke and W. Schneemelcher, trans. ed. R. Mcl. Wilson, 2 Vols. (Philadelphia: Westminster Press, 1965) 2: 442-531.

15. Bornkamm 427; W. Schneemelcher and K. Schaeferdiek, in *New Testament Apocrypha* 178-188.

16. Albin Lesky, *A History of Greek Literature*, trans. James Willis and Cornelis de Heer, (New York: Thomas Y. Crowell, 1966) 857-879; Ben Edwin Perry, *The Ancient Romances: A Literary-Historical Account of Their Origins* (Berkeley: U of California P. 1967); and P.G. Walsh, *The Roman Novel: The 'Satyricon' of Petronius and the 'Metamorphoses' of Apuleius* (Cambridge UP, 1970).

17. See AcTh. 142 where carefreeness (*aphrontis*) is equated with "rest."

18. Trans. John D. Turner, in Robinson, *the Nag Hammadi Library* 188-194.

19. This section originally may have been a separate work (Turner, *The Book of Thomas the Contender* 164-199, 215-225).

20. Turner, *The Book of Thomas the Contender* 235.

21. W.E. Crum, *A Coptic Dictionary* (Oxford UP. 1939) 307b.

22. But see, for example, Drijvers 173.

23. For "solitary" the Coptic text uses the Greek work "monachos" — "monk."

24. *Postscript to The Name of the Rose*, trans. William Weaver (New York: Harcourt Brace Jovanovich, 1984) 47-49. See also *The Role of the Reader* (Bloomington: Indiana University Press, 1979).

25. For example, the correspondence between Fronto and his student, Marcus Aurelius.

26. In the *Acts of Thomas*, The Greek word used for "receive," (*dechomai*) also means "to listen."

27. Richard Reitzenstein, *Hellenistic Mystery-Religions: Their Basic Ideas and Significance*, 3rd ed. 1927, trans. John E. Steely (Pittsburgh: The Pickwick Press, 1978) 58: Jonas 125-6.

28. Reitzenstein 51-52, 62.

29. Reitzenstein 51-2.

30. A.J. Festugiere, *L'ideal religieux des grecs et l'evangiel* (Paris: Lecoffre, 1932; "Les mysteres de Dionysos," *Revue biblique* (1935) 44: 192-211, 366-96.

31. *Roman und Mysterium in der Antike* (Munich and Berlin: C.H. Beck, 1962).

32. E.g., Perry.

33. Helmut Koester, *Introduction to the New Testament*, Vol I: *History, Culture, and Religion of the Hellenistic Age*, trans. Helmut Koester (Philadelphia: Fortress Press and Berlin and New York: Walter de Gruyter, 1982) 139.

34. Bornkamm 429.

35. *Oxford Dictionary of the Christian Church*, ed. F.L. Cross (Oxford UP, 1958) 243. On Cassian, see Owen Chadwick, *John Cassian: A Study in Primitive Monasticism*, 2nd ed. (Cambridge UP, 1968).

Related works by the author of this paper:

"Why Cecropian Minerva? Hellenistic Religious Syncretism as System", *Numen* XXX (1983).
"Artemidorus: Dream Theory in Late Antiquity", *The Second Century*, forthcoming, 1985.
"Those Elusive Eleusinian Mystery Shows", *Helios*: Special issue on Greco-Roman Religions, forthcoming, 1986.

EGERIA, FA HSIEN AND IBN BATTUTA:
Search for Identity through Pilgrimage?

Noel Q. King

University of California
Santa Cruz

In the Pirates of Penzance, we find the Major General meditating among the ruins of his ancestors. In the subsequent dialogue, it transpires he had taken over the ancestors with the ruins of the Chapel in the estate he had bought.[1] Is pilgrimage a means of taking over ancestors, part of the process by which a new religion vests itself in trappings from an older, just as 'Christian' boys and girls in America, Africa, the Philipines come to be blessed with Jewish names 'since the Church is the new Israel?' Is it 'whether in the local congregation or on the wider stage of ecclesiastical politics ... a qualification for influence?'[2] Is it a rite of passage?[3] Many other possibilities can be suggested.[4] The whole concept is multi-faceted and the symbols multi-valent, even the word itself is slippery. 'The Pilgrimage narative' is hardly a real genre of literature. *Peregrinatio* may have a distinct meaning, but with *riḥla* and *hajj, yatra* and *tirtha*, the larger word often subsumes the more specific. 'The search for identity' is as useful a thread for argument and study as any, so it is the purpose of this paper to examine three well known examples of the species chosen from an enormous literature, using the search for identity as the leitmotif of our study and glancing at some of the other possibilities as well as a participant-observer interpretation.

The *Peregrinatio* of Egeria is a late fourth century account in Latin of a pilgrimage to the area of the Exodus, to Mount Sinai and to Jerusalem, with many details of the liturgical year developing at the latter, and of visits to holy places along the route to Palestine, Syria, Mesopotamia and on the road to Constantinople.[5] It is written by a lady of imperial rank. Everywhere officials and soldiers turn out to escort her; clergy, monks and laity treat her with great diffidence; clearly, she is used to wealth, respect and obedience. She is writing to a group of noble ladies dedicated to a religious life back in her homeland which is in the far west, perhaps in Spain or southern Gaul. The ruling Theodosian house was from that area, and its women were of no mean piety and power, but the attempt to identify the writer with a major figure we know about from other sources has failed. Of course, Egeria stands close to St Helena, Constantine's mother, in her interest in the Palestinian holy places. One of the best known accounts of the Invention of the Holy Cross (after which towns from Madras Airport to California are named) by Helena comes to us from the *de obitu Theodosiani* of St Ambrose which is but a couple of years older than the *Peregrinatio*.[6] Again, Egeria reminds one of her contemporaties, the holy women aristocrats of fabulous riches who gathered round St Jerome and Rufinus.

As one reads Egeria's writing one becomes aware of a strong woman who knows who she is, a leading member of a rich and powerful ruling class. But this ruling class had lost its sheet anchors. Symmachus, its great spokesman, had been routed (not defeated) by St. Ambrose and the imperial *coercitio* which was now on the Christian side. Its members were deserting the old Graeco-Roman "paganism" and the old methods of defending the Empire. If we see them from the old point of view, they have lost their identity as upholders and defenders of the Roman *patria*. They are base deserters, treacherous Quislings, treasonous betrayers, lily-livered paltroons, as well as incapable of enjoying life and the delights of being human and aristocratic. These are not my accusations against them. One may cull examples of all these in Rutilius Namatianus' *de reditu suo* or Libanius' *pro Templis*.[8] Edward Gibbon of *Decline and Fall* fame took much the same point of view of the triumph of barbarism and Christianity. On the other hand, if one can enter into the mind of St. Augustine's *Civitas dei* and of the people who held out in Constantine's Christian Rome until 1453, one can perceive how Egeria and her ilk saw themselves as defenders, upbuilders and protectors of the new Christian Empire and strengtheners of its defenders and militia.

For Egeria then and many other west Europeans ever since, pilgrimage to the Holy Land and Jerusalem has been a filling out of their baptismal identity. They have remained Europeans and the pilgrimage enables them to take over the Biblical ancestors from Jesus and Paul back to Adam. Earlier in Christian history, before the Roman Emperors and the Church came together, pilgrimage to Jerusalem had not apparently mattered so much. After the idea behind *Romanitas* and the Holy Roman Empire had faded, we find this pilgrimage for the moment less popular. Then as the journey to Jerusalem becomes easy, we find many going again. Then the flood starts. But by this stage it is not easy to tell the difference between a tourist and a pilgrim. But still today's pilgrim goes not so much to find herself or himself as an upholder of *Regnum Christi* but as someone trying to walk where those feet trod.

Our second example of a pilgrimage narrative is the *Self-account of the Indian Travel of the Monk Fa-Hsien* which took place during 399-414 C.E.[9] Buddhism had entered China some centuries before and though the exact date is not easy to specify, there is no doubt that the basic features of Buddhism and of Chinese thought had met and indeed in a number of respects clashed.[10] It becomes clear from the first line of the *Self-account* that Fa-Hsien was trying to improve his knowledge as a Buddhist monk. He says at once he "was saddened by the incompleteness of the books of Discipline," so he "set out for India to search for copies." Within China he was treated as a person of high standing, receiving honor and assistance from Chinese officials and Prefects along all the way on the Chinese side of the Gobi. As he travels through Central Asia, apart from the terrors and horrors of the way, his only interest is in the practice of Buddhism. Mainly he is concerned with monasticism and the *Vinaya*, but he describes some fine popular festivals with processions of images on floats as well as the munificence of Kings to various shrines and stupas. He has a great interest in performing pilgrimages to places where the Buddha Sakyamuni's relics are treasured. Even before he reaches India, he visits a spitoon reputed to be the Master's, a footprint, rocks where the Buddha's clothes were dried and a place where the fortunate may see his shadow.

As he enters India proper, the visits to stupas with relics of the Buddha's bones and traditions of visits by the Buddha Sakyamuni become more numerous. The buildings and stupas of major Indian Buddhist Emperors like Asoka and Kanishka do not escape his interest and a reverent visit including no doubt a circumambulation. He comes to places where, as he carefully notes, ceremonies of offerings and other rituals have been passed down since the Buddha's day. The Indians on seeing the Chinese holy men said: "How is it possible for people from the borders to learn to leave home and, for the sake of the way, to travel so far searching for the way of the Buddha" (Chapter XV). Soon after this they reached "the country called the Middle Kingdom." Of course, this is Madhya Pradesh, the middle land of the Indic world. Fa-Hsien accepts that he is from a border, China; to this day Zhong-guo, by definition the Middle Kingdom, to every Chinese, is no longer so for him. In a way his Buddhism has meant he is no longer Chinese, he has become an Indian.

When Fa-hsien reached the original hear-land of the Buddha's ministry, from the Yamuna to the Gompti, Gogra, Rapti, and Gandak, along the Ganges and south to Bodhgaya, the pace of his pilgrimage becomes breathless as he visits place after place where incidents in the Buddha's life took place. Fa-Hsien again and again rejoices in the privilege of being there and regrets he was born so far away. Thus on visiting the Jetavana he says of himself and his sole remaining companion: "they considered how the World-honored One had in time past lived there twenty-five years, they felt sad that they were born in a border area ... as they looked at the place where the Buddha had lived, they were sad down to the heart." (Chapter XX).

Again in the area of Gridhrakuta Mountain he offers his devotions with flowers, incense and lamps at the place where the Buddha performed miracles, lived and taught. His account says: "He felt sad. He tried to keep back his tears and said 'The Buddha in old times lived here and here uttered the *Shuu léng yan* (Surangama Sutra). I, Fa-hsien, in my own life do not live at the same time as the Buddha. I look only at his remains and the place where he lived.' "(XXIX)

After Fa-hsien had visited the holy places and completed the traditional pilgrimage to the major sites, he left Varanasi and Sarnath and returned to Pataliputra, Asoka's capital. As he says, his original purpose, the seeking for the books of the monastic discipline had not been possible in North India because there he found "master-to-master transmission by mouth, no written versions for him to copy" (XXXVI). But at Pataliputra, in a Mahayana monastery, he found a written set of the rules as well as other materials. He remained there three years studying Sanskrit and copying books. His sole surviving companion "remembered sadly how broken and imperfect the discipline was among the assemblies of monks in China and uttered this resolution: 'From this time till I achieve Buddhahood, may I never be born again in a border land.' He therefore ended his days in India (XXXVI). Fa-hsien went on to the great port at the mouth of the Ganges, Tamalipti. He stayed there two years' copying texts and diagrams of icons" (XXXVII). Then he visited the monks of Sri Lanka and Sumatra and finally got back home.

In contrast with Egeria and Fa-hsien who stood at the beginning of a great pilgrimage tradition and could well be considered trail-blazers and pioneers, our third pilgrim, Muhammad ibn Battūta (1325-1358 C.E.), stands late in a well established tradition already seven hundred years old.[11] Indeed his account of the *hajj* is not even original; he has incorporated the account of ibn Jubair from the previous century in his own work. He does not seem in need of an identity, he knows who he is, above all he thinks of himself as an Arab and a Muslim. He is proud to call himself a member of the Luwata tribe, which connects him up with Berber ancestors. We know that his family had fairly recently been turned out of Spain and had re-settled in Morocco. He is proud of the Maghrib and its pure Arabic. We know other details of his self-identity; when he is old and tired and homesick, over against the people of Bilād-as-Sudān he identifies himself as white. Throughout he is dependant on women for company; he confesses he hates to travel without a female companion. He cares immensely for prestige, honor and gifts. We gather that his pretensions to scholarship were not well founded.[12] Yet the main things that strike the reader apart from admiration for the immensity of the man's travels — from Tangier to Canton via West and West Central Asia, India, Sumatra, East Africa to Sofala,

Constantinople, Spain, lastly across the Sahara to Mali and the Niger bend — are the centrality in his narrative of his divine vocation to visit holy places with the *hajj* as central. If in detail we compare his account of the *hajj* with that of ibn Jubair whose outline he has used, we find sufficient evidence to suppose that the effect of his first Meccan-Medinan pilgrimage had a tremendous and lasting effect on him as a young man. It was on his way to his first pilgrimage with mind obsessed by Lubbaika, "I stand to do thy will," that he perceived Allah's will for him. His vocation was to be, as ibn Ḥajar sums it up, "the pre-eminent traveller of the Muslim age." His repeated performances of the *hajj* and his residence at Mecca were undoubtedly central to him and indeed to the prestige which he used as his traveller's checks. (He being an Arab, we must spell it "cheque.")

Comparative Religion has tried to establish herself as a science based on hard objective criteria, and a satisfactory methodology for analyzing and evaluating participant observership has hardly been worked out. This writer has "roamed" and peregrinated over the Buddhist pilgrim ways from Barabudur to Bamian, has participated, so far as respect for others permitted, at Varanasi, Hardwar, Jeddah, Rome and Jerusalem and at sites in Eire and Mexico. Such things are not easy to write about in academic terms. One motive was to re-build a life which had been broken up, to re-find, re-new, ideals and purposes which had been destroyed. In a way, it was like a temporary spell in a mental ward or like an L.S.D. trip. In another way pilgrimage can be an attempt to blackmail the divine, to extort some sort of special experience as theophany. In such cases the divine answer is: "What doest thou here?" In another way it is a de-programming and re-programming, or to adapt the metaphor a little, an attempt to substitute parts of the DNA message so as to become someone else. In another way, it is a form of suicide for it was meritorious to die on the way and the hazards of the journeys and diseases rampant at pilgrimage centers made such merit reasonably attainable. Death apart, if the pilgrimage were really effective, a pilgrim was never quite the same again.

We are bound to conclude that the search for identity is a strong and pervading feature of the pilgrimage phenomenon. There is of course much which mingles with this. Even a cursory examination of Victor Turner's methodology indicates the rites of passage interpretation is highly valuable. So too is the idea that people go on pilgrimage so as to out-class the stay-at-homes. As Wingate told the Chindits: "You will be proud to say: 'I was there'." Again, by analogy with birds, insects and animals, lemmings, sheep, chickens and soldier-ants, once a stream of movement starts, others will by all means join in. Mere curiosity and voyeurism have their part. In one shape or form it will survive as long as human nature exists. At the moment the jet has enabled it to become one of the major industries of the modern world.

Pilgrimage remains one of the most curious and inexplicable ritual dances that *homo* so-called *sapiens* insists on carrying out. Those who study it are even curiouser.

FOOTNOTES

1 Gilbert and Sullivan, *The Pirates of Penzance*, Act 2, Scene 1.

2 E.D. Hunt, "St. Silvia of Aquitaine," *Journal of Theological Studies*, New Series 23, 1972, p. 373.

3 The recently deceased and much lamented Dr. Victor Turner revolutionized the study of pilgrimage by working out along these lines from his studies of African initiation rituals. Of course, there is much more than can be said concerning Turner's treatment. *Image and Pilgrimage in Christian Culture*, New York: Columbia University Press, 1978, written in collaboration with Edith Turner, gives a full statement and refers to and relies upon the earlier work stretching back to 1969.

4 There is a good summary and discussion of a great number of these in the chapter "Theoretical perspectives for pilgrimage" in E. Alan Morinis: *Pilgrimage in the Hindu Tradition, a Case Study of West Bengal*, Delhi: Oxford University Press, 1984.

5 The text is readily available. H. Petre, *Ethérie, Journal de voyage*. Texte latin, introduction et tradution. *Sources chrétiennes*, volume 21, Paris, 1948. See also E. Francheschini et R. Weber: *Itinerarium Egeriae*. (Corpus Christianorum, Series Lat., volume 175), Turnhout, 1965, pages 27-90 (Indices in volume 176). English translations include C.E. Gingras: *Egeria, Diary of a Pilgrimage* (Ancient Christian Writers, Number 38) Westminster, Md., 1970 and John Wilkinson: *Egeria's Travels*, London, SPCK. 1971.

6 Migne's *Patrologia Graeca* XVI col. 1385 ff. Mannix published an edition at Washington in 1925. Theodosius died in 395 C.E.

7 Symmachus: *Relatio* III and Ambrose *Epp* XVII and XVIII.

8 Rutilius Namatianus: *de reditu suo* and Libanius *oratio* XXX, *pro templis*.

9 The Pin yin is Fa-Xian but the well known Wade-Giles spelling is retained for the name. The most readily available text is that given in James Legge's *A Record of Buddhistic Kingdoms being an account by the Chinese monk Fa-Hien of his Travels in India and Ceylon*, London, 1886. That volume also gives a translation (which met with a great deal of criticism) and excellent notes. H.A. Giles published a better translation, *The Travels of Fa Hsien, 399-414 A.D.*, London, 1923.
The Chinese Buddhist Association published a new translation by Li Yung-Hsi at Beijing in 1957. The translation used for this paper is an unpublished one by Ching-Yi Dougherty. The beginning of his visit to India is to be dated to 399 C.E. when India was enjoying the prosperity and security associated with the Guptas. By contrast, China was in turmoil. He returned home in 414 C.E. The route taken by the pilgrim is well mapped in (edited) Joseph E. Schwartzberg: *Historical Atlas of South Asia*, Chicago: University Press, 1978. Details and bibliography of some others who followed in his footsteps will be found in T.O. Ling's Dictionary of Buddhism, New York: Scribner's, 1972. s.v. I Ch'ing and Hsuan Tsang. One should not omit Wu Cheng-en's *Monkey* conveniently available in Arthur Waley's translation (Penguin 1972, first published by Allen and Unwin). See also (translated and edited) Anthony C. Yu: *The Journey to the West*, Chicago, 1977-83 and his article, "Two Literary Examples of Religious Pilgrimage: the *Commedia* and *The Journey to the West*," *History of Religions*, 1982, volume 22:1, pages 202-221.

10 Eric Zuercher: *The Buddhist Conquest of China*, Leiden: E.J. Brill, 1972. Fa-hsien mentions the tradition that Indian missionaries first crossed the Indus in answer to a dream of an Emperor who reigned from 59-75 C.E.

11 A beautiful edition of the text with a serviceable French translation is to be found in C. Defrémery et B.R. Sanguinetti: *Voyages d'Ibn Batoutah*, Paris, four volumes, 1853-1858, reprinted 1968. H.A.R. Gibbs: *Selections from the Travels of Ibn Battuta*, London, 1929, is still very serviceable. Three volumes of his full translation and notes have appeared in the London Hakluyt series from 1958 onwards. The fourth volume has not appeared.

12 See Ibn Ḥajar of Ascalon's *Al-Durar al-Kāmina*, Hyderabad, India, Volume III, 1929, pages 480-481.

Related works by the author of this paper:

African Cosmos, An Introduction to African Religion, Belmont CA.: Wadsworth, 1985.
Editor: *Mtoro bin Mwinyi Bakari's "Customs of the Swahili"*. Los Angeles: University of California Press, 1981.
Ibn Battuta in Black Africa. London: Rex Collings, 1975.

IDENTITY AND THE RURAL MINISTER[1]

Kenneth Dempsey

La Trobe University, Australia

INTRODUCTION

In studies I have made of religion in small Australian country towns I have found that the minister's identity as a minister informed all aspects of his life. Whatever activity he participated in — attendance at a Rotary meeting or playing a game of tennis — he was perceived as a minister. He may have become other things as well to those who got to know him: such as an enthusiastic participant or 'a good bloke for a parson' but no one ever lost sight of his occupational identity and rarely did other people let the minister forget about it for long.

In such ways the minister's work identity became his public identity (Finch, 1983: 70-72) and by so doing helped set him apart, or marginalise him to a significant degree (Mol, 1976: 31-34). Furthermore, this apartness joined with other factors to ensure that the minister's work identity largely controlled his understanding of himself or his self identity. As one minister in my sample put it: 'I find I cannot put my life into compartments in this community. Being a minister seems to affect all I think and do: my family life, my friendships, my activities in the town, even on holidays I find I cannot forget that I am a minister'.

Yet despite work being the basis of his self identity, it appeared that it frequently offered few rewards and a good deal of emotional and mental punishment. So for example, by marginalising him, it interfered with him realising his need to belong (Mol, 1976: 32). Other fundamental needs often went unmet and heartfelt aspirations were denied. Delineating some of the factors responsible for the situation I have outlined, as well as some of its manifestations, are major purposes of this paper. More specifically, I will attempt to answer three questions:

i Why did the minister's work identity become equated with his public identity and the focal point of his self identity?

ii Why did his work often fail to satisfy a number of basic needs and aspirations or allow him to affirm values and use skills which were for him intrinsic elements of his identity?

iii What were some of the effects of these outcomes on the minister's sense of identity, his sense of belonging, and his integration into the parish community?

In dealing with these questions I will assume that a minister's self identity is at the same time, a stable and fragile phenomenon. Stability is emphasised in Bellah's definition of identity. He says it is 'a statement of what a person or group is essentially, and as it were, permanently' (Bellah, 1965: 1973 quoted by Mol, 1978: 2). I am assuming that a minister will attempt to hold onto and express, in a particular parish situation, those understandings of himself that he has distilled from previous roles, group memberships and socialisation experiences with which he most closely identifies. But I am also assuming that there is a certain fragility to a minister's identity, a point that is emphasised by Mol and others (Mol, 1976: Ch. V; Breakwell, 1978). Wrong points out that a stable identity arises from a 'a secure anchorage' in social groups and 'firm attachments to social roles' (1976b: 88).

Such social links and supports may be disrupted when a minister is geographically mobile. If this happens and there are no similar memberships and roles in the new context he may try and create a working environment that is compatible with understanding of himself or is compatible with the self he aspires to be. Such actions may threaten the identities of the lay people and the integration of parish life and will therefore be resisted (Mol, 1976: 32). Finally, I am also assuming that ministers will need evidence that their efforts as ministers are worthwhile if they are going to sustain their identities. Where there are few tangible or objective signs of the worthwhileness of their efforts they will be reliant on the positive evaluation of others (Gergen, 1970: 57). However, these will not be forthcoming if his actions challenge the factors supporting lay identities and the identities themselves (Mol, 1976: 57).

DATA SOURCES

The data I am utilising to deal with the questions I am posing has emerged during the course of research on minister/lay relationships in a number of rural communities in New South Wales and Victoria, Australia (Dempsey, 1983, 1985). Through interviewing and observing laymen and ministers I have obtained information on the beliefs, values and behaviour of twenty Protestant ministers. All of these worked for some period of time during the years between 1950 and 1985 in at least one rural community. Nineteen of these ministers were stationed in towns with populations of only two or three thousand people. The twentieth lived in a provincial city. This city and the towns functioned as service centres for the surrounding farming districts. Their Protestant churches were peopled and led by farming and business families and, to a much lesser extent, by professional families.

WHY DID THE MINISTER'S WORK INFLUENCE SO GREATLY HIS SELF-IDENTITY?

This was partly because the ministry was viewed as a vocation or calling given by God. This calling was formally recognised by the practice of ordination for what was called by church leaders, local lay people and the ministers themselves: 'the full-time work of God'. All but one of them stated that they had no choice but to enter the ministry or priesthood. A number said that they had entered despite feeling that they were not personally suited for or attracted to many of the things ministers had to do such as administering an organisation of considerable size and working for so much of the time with people. Here is the kind of thing a number of them said to me: 'I was very happy in the job I had before I commenced training. I was a carpenter and I think I really preferred to work with tools and materials than with people. There are always results for you to see. But God would not leave me alone. I continually resisted the idea of entering the ministry but in the end I could resist no longer'.

For all but one or possibly two of these ministers, the view they held of their work — at least initially — was similar to the view that most people traditionally held of marriage: it was to be a life-long commitment. Such a commitment helped confirm the centrality of the minister's work to his sense of identity. It also helped set ministers apart from laymen: an apartness which was reinforced by the belief that a minister's calling was to a life of sacrificial and honorific service in which the needs of others were to take precedence over his own needs and even those of his family (in Dempsey, 1985). In the communities in which I have conducted most of my fieldwork I have found that ministers were expected to be more than fair in their dealings with others, to refrain from participating in local gossip, to avoid 'playing favourites' and to be above reproach in their personal behaviour and manners. The small size of the communities and their possession of effective gossip chains added greatly to the pressure these expectations brought to bear on the ministers. For example, they were criticised for drinking and smoking or for doing these things to excess, for losing their temper, for failing to be friendly towards all, for transmitting information about individuals they had been given in confidence and so forth. Such pressure not only set men apart but made it impossible for them to escape their work identity, both socially and psychologically.

The inability of a minister to clearly distinguish his private life and time from his work life and time had a strong influence on his understanding of who he was. This was not a nine to five job. It went on for at least six days of the week and usually invaded many of a minister's evenings and frequently his 'so-called day off'. The scrambling of his work identity with other identities such as those of father and husband was increased by the minister's work activities being conducted in the home or from the home. So, he often worked over lunch and in the evening held church meetings in the lounge-room. All such practices and activities highlighted for the minister the feeling that first and foremost: 'I am a minister'.

The notion 'I am a minister' could be so motivating for members of my sample that they would sometimes ask their wives and families to make considerable sacrifices in its service. For example, one minister's wife told me that her husband had asked her to forego the chance of her and her young children living in a modern well-heated manse on the grounds that he could not reconcile such comfort with his calling as a minister.

Some minister's children recounted incidents during interviews which showed that their fathers related to them primarily as ministers. By so doing the ministers confirmed their work selves as their 'real selves'. Here is what one minister's son said: 'Dad could never forget he was a minister. I was almost terrified to bring home a new playmate because he would ask him almost the moment he met him whether he went to Sunday School and whether his parents went to church'.

Despite the centrality of a minister's work to his life and to his self identity, it often seemed that this work did not yield many intrinsic rewards nor satisfy a range of basic needs such as those for approval, self esteem, a sense of continuity in his identity, for the achievement of meaning from his work and for a sense of belonging. Why was this?

Two of the most important contributing factors were the diffuse and intangible nature of the job.

A DIFFUSE AND INTANGIBLE JOB

The parish ministry in the communities from which I have drawn my sample was a general practitioner type ministry entailing preaching, leading worship, administering the sacraments, presiding at marriages and funerals, counselling, house visitation, a wide range of administrative responsibilities, sometimes responsibility for fund raising and often responsibility for a number of educative functions such as teaching, giving religious instruction in school and 'filling in' as a Sunday School teacher. As I have pointed out, the minister was to be above reproach in his personal behaviour. The most crucial expectations centred on his personality, personal style, and pastoral activity and on his responsibility for the local cause. He was to be approachable, a good mixer and one who took a personal interest in local people. Furthermore, he was usually perceived as being ultimately responsible for the viability of the church at the local level, organisationally and financially. (I will return to the last-mentioned issue later).

No individual could hope to excel in all the things I have just outlined. Furthermore, how could he objectively measure his achievement in many of these areas: for example as a pastoral visitor or counsellor? Obviously he was dependent on the subjective response of his 'clients' and even if they approved of his actions they often failed to let him know. Consequently, for much of the time the minister was left 'in the dark' about the value of his contribution. Such ignorance could generate uncertainty about his worth as a minister. Some laymen said that they were reluctant to praise the minister because they believed he was well-paid for what he was doing. 'Why should he be looking for praise all the time? We don't get praised every time we bring in a good crop. Isn't the minister the man who is supposed to be concerned about what other people are doing and not be so wrapped up in himself?'

Although laymen might be slow to praise they were often quick to complain if things were not done to their satisfaction. In communities with small populations the news of any 'failure' on the part of the minister was quickly communicated to lay leaders and ministers were frequently asked to explain their behaviour. It is true that ministers did not attach the same salience to all activities they were expected to engage in. Accordingly, criticism in some areas was not as likely to have as negative an impact on their identity as criticisms in other areas. But it is also true that in a context where, for much of the time, they did not know how they were going, apparently trivial criticisms could assume monumental significance. Such criticisms not only caused a great deal of emotional pain but could threaten a man's attachment to the ministry or what he regarded as his real self.

The chances of criticism having such an impact were heightened by the fact that laymen often moved from criticising an alleged failure of a minister in a particular area to condemning him as a minister. So I have often heard statements such as the following: "Once Mr. Jones introduced politics into the pulpit I was finished with him. I won't go back to church until he leaves this town".

The threat that such criticism could pose to a minister's identity, especially when it was made in a public context, is borne out by the response of one man who resigned after he was accused of "pulling the Bible to bits" in his preaching. His accusers said that his preaching is causing people to leave the church. The minister said: "I thought to myself, to hell with them! This isn't just this congregation, this is my whole future. In parish after parish I would face the same problems. I could never satisfy such people and if I did, it would only be by selling my soul, so I quit".

INABILITY TO ACHIEVE TANGIBLE SUCCESS AND IDENTITY

The ministers in my sample were no more likely to receive tangible signs of their worth than they were comments of approval from the lay people. All of them were living in communities whose populations were declining, primarily because of the mechanisation of farming. Support for the churches was also eroded by the impact of the process of secularisation that has had a negative influence on church life generally in the Western world. In each of the centres from which my sample has been drawn, there has been a dramatic decline in church attendance, organisational activity and financial buoyancy in recent years. For example, one church was forced to amalgamate with another to avoid bankruptcy. In two other churches, over the last twelve years, attendance at worship has fallen by about two-thirds, the youth clubs have disappeared and the Sunday Schools declined dramatically in size (Dempsey, 1984).

Such developments have particular relevance for the stability of the minister's sense of identity and for his integration into the local group. This is especially because it is often believed that ministers must bear major responsibility for the success or failure of the local cause. Such beliefs are almost always held by local lay people, and often by denominational leaders and ministers themselves. When questioned on this matter, some ministers rejected, with a considerable show of emotion, the idea that "I am the Church". But even these ministers could not rid themselves of the idea that if they were somehow "better ministers" they would be able to "turn the tide" of decline. Guilt feelings of this kind are not surprising, given the strength of the nexus in our culture between responsibility and monetary reward. Many ministers and certainly a majority of lay people whom I have interviewed have pointed out that it is the minister who is paid to do the work of the church and it is therefore his special responsibility that it survives and ideally flourishes.

Laymen hold strongly to the belief that there is a direct relationship between the quality of a minister as a preacher, pastor, and a person who can relate effectively to people and the success or failure of the local cause. These convictions were constantly articulated in the presence of the ministers of my sample. Their articulation made its impact as the following comment illustrates: "I suppose I am in part to blame for the financial problems the church now faces. If they had liked my preaching those people probably would not have left". These words were uttered by a minister whose preaching was being blamed by some lay leaders for people who had been strong financial contributors leaving the church. As Rawls observes: "Our self respect normally depends on the respect of others" (1971: 178; quoted by Rosenberg: 603). This man's self esteem has been affected both by the criticism and the feeling of at least partial responsibility for the financial problems of the church. In fact his sense of identity has been so threatened by his experience in the parish ministry and he now feels so estranged from a number of key leaders that he is trying to find alternative employment.

As far as my sample as a whole is concerned, the constant worry over finances and organisational decline wore most ministers down. It significantly reduced the degree of satisfaction they drew from their jobs, sometimes lowered their self-esteem and sometimes caused them to leave the ministry altogether.

THE MINISTER'S EXEMPLARY BEHAVIOUR, HIS VISIBILITY AND IDENTITY

I have already shown in an earlier section that the expectation that the minister's behaviour would be beyond reproach and that he would put the service of others before his own needs added significantly to the pressure causing him to view his ministerial life as the fulcrum of his self-identity. What I am suggesting in this section is that such expectations — which were quite unrealistic ones — markedly reduced the rewards he got from being a minister; especially when that ministry was being practised in small communities where his behaviour was highly visible. So ministers found small failings were publicly paraded, often causing a loss of respect which in turn dented their self-esteem. Ministers were criticised for: playing golf on their day off when they still had not visited some members of the parish for the first time; singling out some parishioners as "special friends"; neglecting the manse garden; dressing untidily or losing their temper during a debate with lay leaders.

The minister who is working in the provincial city told me that the large nature of the centre has given him some protection from the scrutiny of lay people and therefore reduced the bases for criticising him but the limited nature of this protection is borne out by the fact that he has recently asked his Board of Management to place him on a three-quarter stipend so that he can spend time legitimately on non-parish activities that he finds personally rewarding. He said: "There can be no argument now about me taking time out to do some teaching or writing". That remains to be seen.

The visibility of ministers and the existence of the expectations I have just described combined with the ability of lay people to sanction ministers, sometimes formally and often informally, prevented many ministers from doing things which would have off-set much of the stress of their work or provided alternative sources of recognition and improved self-esteem.

DIVERGING PRIORITIES AND MINISTER'S IDENTITY

The chances of a minister's pursuit of job satisfaction and other rewards being productive was often lessened by a difference between himself and lay people over priorities. When this occurred, approval of some ministers was withheld and others were strongly criticised because they treated as of only limited importance or no importance at all, aspects of their job that had great salience for lay people.

The activities that were most likely to be assigned different priorities were pastoral visitation, discussion group activity and youth work. For example, in all parishes, there were church leaders who gave top priority to youth work, especially if they had children of youth club age themselves. They usually believed that unless the church provided a suitable environment, their children would fall into "bad company" or drift away from the church. So ministers were often put under considerable pressure to lead a youth group. However, in a number of instances the ministers ignored the pressure because they were not particularly interested in doing youth work or because they felt they lacked the skills to do it well. Hence one minister, when asked if he would lead the youth group his predecessor had established said: "I don't feel it is the kind of thing I am best suited to do. My interests lie in other directions. I will be making some changes to the worship and I hope to get a number of house churches going. We're all different you know. We all work in our own special ways".

This man's explanation was not accepted, however, and the people who had made the overture quickly communicated his response to other members of the church. Before very long the rumour circulated that the minister was not interested in young people and that caused a number to ask if he was a suitable kind of person to be a minister after all. These criticisms and queries reached the minister himself, they occurred at a time when other attacks were being made on aspects of his ministry. He reported to me that as a result he felt estranged from the congregation. He said: "I cannot be myself here, I don't belong here!" Soon after he resigned from the ministry.

Another minister who also resisted pressure to lead the youth group did so for different reasons. This man's approach highlights another source of alienation and threat to identity that could arise in parish work. In such instances, these problems arose for ministers because values, beliefs or practices they needed to implement to be true to their sense of identity, conflicted with crucial lay values or practices and thereby threatened the identity of lay people and sometimes the integration of the congregation or parish.

CONFLICTING VALUES AND IDENTITY

The minister I just referred to was convinced that the youth club along with church organisations generally was impeding the achievement of fundamental goals of his work as a minister. He believed the problem with most organisations in church life was this: they shifted the emphasis from the congregation as a whole to special interest groups and syphoned off energies that could have been devoted to breaking down barriers between male and female, young and old, prosperous and poor; energies and resources that could have been used to build up the congregation into a corporate body of caring people. This minister's stance drew a lot of criticism. After all, he was threatening the identities of many lay people by failing to support or by criticising activities that they had been closely involved in for many years. He too was estranged from his parishioners to some degree by this conflict. Yet he at least had the satisfaction of "affirming his principles in this matter". Often however, he was not successful in implementing programs with which he closely identified. He shared this problem with the majority of ministers in my sample. They also found themselves in parish situations where laymen resisted or were indifferent to ideas or plans that were of fundamental importance to their sense of identity. The nature of such ideas and plans did vary from minister to minister but many of them could be seen as expressing one or more of the following facets of identity. These were the convictions that: "I am an educator"; "I am a liturgist"; and "I am a pastor to pastors".

Almost all ministers in my sample believed that their calling and training equipped them to educate others. Here is how one of them expressed his belief: "When I went to X-town I was determined to educate people. I was sick of people rejecting the Christian faith on spurious grounds so I set out to prepare the way for replacing the morning worship with an all-age Sunday School and I used the pulpit to try and get people to think along the right lines". It was clear from my conversations with this man and with most other ministers, that their personal sense of well being as well as their identity as ministers depended to a significant degree on successfully engaging in educational activity. Usually however, their hopes and needs were not satisfied. For example, the all-age Sunday School lasted only one week because of opposition from powerful people.

Virtually all ministers attempted to get discussion groups of one kind or another going. Usually they were only attended by a few people and lasted only for a short period of time. The reaction of a minister of the 1980's to this type of lay response was very typical of what most ministers had to say on the matter. "I just cannot get them to attend a study group yet they really don't know what their Christianity is about and it seems they don't care." (All this was said with a considerable display of emotion.)

A minority of ministers, about eight in all, did attempt one or more forms of liturgical reform. Most of these attempts were criticised and in a number of instances they had to be abandoned. Almost always they generated a good deal of ill-feeling between the minister and at least some members of the congregation. In some instances they apparently caused members of long-standing to stop attending church. None of these outcomes helped ministers achieve the sense of identity they were pursuing. They estranged them from the congregation at least temporarily and reduced their sense of belonging.

Probably the ministers in my sample had the least success in the third area I singled out for comment: this was their attempt to encourage their lay people to be pastors on the premise that they (the ministers) were called and trained to fit them for such activity. So, for example, in the early 1980's the Council of Elders of one Uniting Church was generally neglecting its commission to share with the minister pastoral oversight of the parish and of its members. Only a handful of its members were, for example, visiting families that had been placed in their pastoral care. This type of response disappointed the ministers and also frustrated their attempts to wrest meaning for themselves from their jobs. This was also often frustrated by the experience and reaction of ministers' wives.

THE ESTRANGEMENT OF MINISTER'S WIVES AND THE MINISTER'S SENSE OF IDENTITY

Minister's wives were almost as vulnerable to criticism as their husbands. In the communities in which I have worked they were greeted on arrival with extensive and demanding expectations. These included presiding over or at least attending one or more women's organisations of the parish, assisting with fund-raising activities and running what was called an "open parsonage". The latter expectation meant they were to welcome and entertain whoever cared to call, whatever time of day or night. Like their husbands these women were often trapped by the breadth and demanding nature of lay people's expectations of them, particularly as they occurred in a context in which they were highly visible. The chances of them being found wanting were increased by the fact that a majority of them rebelled at least partially against these expectations. So ministers who could not turn to friends and colleagues for day to day psychological support because they were too geographically distant often found that their wives were unable to give them the support they badly needed as well. Actually seven of the ministers in my sample said that the serious problems their wives experienced in parish work helped them come to the decision to leave a particular parish or to leave the ministry altogether.

CONCLUDING COMMENTS

In this paper I have examined some of the reasons for the minister's work having such a large bearing on his sense of identity. At the same time I have tried to show that his work can frustrate his attempts to affirm or implement some of the more salient aspects of that identity. As a result his commitment to the ministry can be undermined, his need to belong can be thwarted and he can reach the point where he believes he can only hold onto his understanding of who he is by withdrawing from the situation or by giving up the vocation.

The major purpose of the paper has been to highlight the factors that can bring about such outcomes. However, in order to avoid overstating the case I must emphasise that things did not always work out as badly as they have appeared in the body of the paper for at least some of my ministers. For example, three said that their parish experiences had been, on the whole, quite worthwhile and another seven said they had found them tolerable and at least in some ways worthwhile. Predictably, those most likely to have perceived their parish experiences as worthwhile were those who had adopted a comforting and accepting rather than a challenging approach. They also had wives who happily embraced the traditional role of "the unpaid curate". These ministers were prudent enough to desist with a practice or a proposed change that was generating so much resistance as to put their ministry or the unity of congregational life in jeopardy. These three provided an excellent sample of how a sense of identity can be sustained because of the effect of what Mol calls symbol based elements. In this instance among the more pertinent of these were "... predictability of motivations and responses, common adherence (by ministers and lay people) to values and norms, common interpretations of experience ..." (1976:8). So, although strangers, the ministers generally avoided threatening the identities of lay people or the social identity and integration of the congregation (Mol, 1976: 32-33). Accordingly they were perceived as "one of us" and so their need for a sense of belonging was at least partially met. Seven others had a more tenuous relationship which oscillated between marginalisation and a fair degree of acceptance and integration. There was not the same affinity concerning values, norms

or year, but by his consistent life, 'and therefore there are very few people I can be sure of — though I feel it is no business of mine to judge men, but in faith to view them as Christians.'[18]

Such a longitudinally integrated character, though achieved by effort and decision, is also a product of luck or destiny. It 'happens' to the agent as he accomplishes it. Newman's impressive attempt to analyze the process of assenting to beliefs, in his *Grammar of Assent*, depicts this complexity in adopting the Christian ground project. Using a well-known series of distinctions, he identifies the 'real assents' which occur in the concrete experience of individuals. As distinguished from 'notional assents', they embody commitments to beliefs which, in many instances, we would call 'existential'. They may be commonplaces, reported in such propositions as that one is having a particular sensory experience, or that the world external to one's experience exists. They can also concern more transcendent things, such as the reality of oneself or God, but they always involve certitude. With the simple certainties, such as the existence of the self or the external world, this is obvious. He holds that the more complex are also certitudes, because they proceed from acts of the whole self, integrating intellectual, moral, aesthetic, psychological, and other responses, as well as conscious and unconscious presuppositions and tendencies.

All of this seems to represent the beliefs that ground morality as relative to individual characters and circumstances. In fact, Newman supports that interpretation of his theory when he quotes Pascal's argument that we should believe in Christianity because the accomplishments and precepts of Christians are so striking as to require a supernatural explanation. Newman remarks that the force of this argument depends on 'the assumption that the facts of Christianity are beyond human nature', so that, 'according as the powers of nature are placed at a high or low standard, that force will be greater or less; and that standard will vary according to the respective dispositions, opinions, and experiences, of those to whom the argument is addressed.'[19] In an earlier place in his exposition, Newman suggests that such individual characteristics could be compared to accidents:

> That this particular man out of the three millions congregated in the metropolis, was to have the experience of this catastrophe, and to be the select victim to appease that law of averages, no statistical tables could foretell, even though they could determine that it was in the fates that in that week or day some four persons in the length and breadth of London should be run over. And in like manner that this or that person should have the particular experiences necessary for real assent on any point, that the Deist should become a Theist, the Erastian a Catholic, ... are facts, each of which may be the result of a multitude of coincidences in one and the same individual, coincidences which we had no means of determining, and which, therefore, we may call accidents. For —

> There's a Divinity that shapes our ends,
> Rough hew them how we will.[20]

Thus he emphasizes two clusters of circumstances in the development of belief, namely, personal factors in the nature of the individual, and extra-personal accidents which could be called his destiny. Newman admits that we could doubt the truth of beliefs so acquired, and he mentions many reasons that might be invoked for doing so. He responds to such doubts, as is well known, with his argument that certitudes that are 'indefectible' can be obtained when the process of assent has gone on properly. Less explicit and less well-known, but equally effective, is his argument that the essential self of any individual is 'reserved', and therefore free from the vicissitudes of doubt. Let us first consider this latter, lesser-known appeal, and then return to the 'indefectibility of certitude.'

The reserved self, in Newman's thought, is the self separated from all the processes, associations, doctrines, and shared beliefs that we experience. It is the self as directly perceived, and for Newman it is the most real thing there is. As Vargish puts it,[21] 'Newman stresses the unreal nature of abstractions throughout his Anglican as well as his Catholic career. Reality, for Newman, is in nature always unique and individual'. However, this does not refer primarily to unique and individual external objects. Newman once wrote to his sister Jemima, 'What a veil and curtain this life is! Beautiful, but still a veil'.[22] In the *Apologia* he refers to an idealistic essay which he wrote as a boy, in 1816-17, to the effect that so-called reality is like a dream, and O'Faolain comments, 'For him the only real personality is the private personality, the anonymous secret, known inadequately even to ourselves.'[23] This belief recurs vividly in a sermon of 1833, entitled 'The Immortality of the Soul',[24] where he argues that each of us begins by supposing himself to be in union with the world, as just another part of it. But he continues, we gradually realize our separate existence, and that we have moral responsibilities. This develops into an awareness of the self as the most certain reality there is. Newman believes, as is well known, that full self-awareness is contiguous with knowledge of God. In addition, he attributes other important features to it.[25]

One of them is growth. Full self-awareness as simultaneously perception of God is not achieved suddenly. Just as doctrine is capable of development, so also is individual self-realization, as one 'advances to the fullness of his original destiny,' discovering 'the law of his being'.[26] However, there is never a final and complete discovery, because each self is a 'mystery',[27] in the ancient sense of a solemn process in which, as one goes further, there are ever-more-profound revelations.[28] In one extraordinary passage, Newman eloquently sketches the unity of microcosmic and macrocosmic events, in individual living things, in societies, and in 'this wonderful web of causes and effects'.[29] He concludes, 'all that is seen — the world, the Bible, the Church, the civil polity, and man himself — are types, and, in their degree and place, representatives and organs of an unseen world, truer and higher than themselves.'[30]

Yet we discover that Newman does not take doctrines about that unseen world too seriously. As he sees it, the true and serious realities are concrete, private, often inarticulate individual experiences. Thus, for example, his discussion of transubstantiation appears almost casual because, while not doubting the real presence, he does not believe that a particular verbal form is essential to explain it.[31] He has similar thoughts about the resurrection of the body. He believes in it, but freely speculates about the way in which it might happen.[32] O'Faolain says that Newman's discussion of creeds, in *The Arians*, reveals his belief that they are all (in effect) relatively inaccurate. They arise as regrettable necessities, when disputes within the Church must be settled.

> Inevitably, all his approaches to these early controversies are coloured by a sad regret for still earlier centuries when felt traditions took the place of spoken creeds, and the acceptance of things ineffable was as simple as the child's unenquiring trust.[33]

Thus, self-realization is complex, so that commentators regularly remark that Newman's thought has two foundations, the certainty of the unique, private self, and the certainty of God. Linking these two puts us in mind of conscience, in which self and God are related. Newman defines conscience in psychological terms as, 'a certain keen sensibility, pleasant or painful, ... attendant on certain of our actions, which in consequence we call right or wrong.'[34] Referring to externals, he speaks of "things which excite our approbation or blame, and which we in consequence call right or wrong."[35] Conscience discerns right and wrong in its judgemental character, and sanctions right actions in its magisterial character. It is reasonable, but it is also moral and spiritual. It is a response to something that strikes us as personal, which we encounter in our total experience. In "this special feeling" there are "the materials for the real apprehension of a Divine Sovereign or Judge."[36]

Newman expands upon this personal feature of conscience at some length in the *Grammar*. He describes conscience as 'always emotional', and says that it 'always involves the recognition of a living object towards which it is directed ... If, as is the case, we feel responsibility, are ashamed, are frightened, at transgressing the voice of conscience, this implies that there is One to whom we are responsible.'[37] Thus, he argues that conscience teaches us that God is, that He has certain characteristics, and that a certain form of life, spiritual as well as moral, is required of us.

Conscience, then, has a wider scope than has been supposed. It is the name of the most certain consciousness of reality, conveying direct awareness of the self and God in relationship. It therefore dictates our form of life and its aims in all details. In 1875, discussing the authority of the Queen and the Pope, Newman wrote (as if to present-day consequentialists and formalists) that, 'there is no rule in this world without exceptions, ... so I give absolute obedience to neither.'[38] He said quite explicitly that we would be mistaken if we supposed that rules and systems protect us from being "thrown upon what is called by divines, 'the Providence of God.'" Infallible authority can never shelter us from life's problems or from 'God's particular call.'[39]

But this again raises the question of certitude. How can a person be sure his conscience and the real assents that ground it are without error? Although the basic features of Newman's theory are well known, we can profit from a contemporary expression of it by M J Ferreira. He agrees that 'certitudes' fall within the class of assents. They are of many kinds, but all of them are assents which can stand up to reflection, which is the achievement of a decision by the intellect in combination with the conscience, the will, and other reactions of the whole person. That is why Newman characterizes such decisions in a special way, as products of the illative sense. By that term he refers to a process that combines the various functions just mentioned in an appropriate balance, which also has a reflexive character. It can include moral reflection on moral decisions, moral reflections on intellectual decisions, and various other such combinations. The illative sense therefore depicts man, as Newman would say, as ' ... not a reasoning animal, he is a seeing, feeling, contemplating, acting animal.'[40]

The spiritual certainty that such a process provides is not that of logical certainty. It is, rather, that kind explained by such thinkers as John Wisdom and Wittgenstein, who discuss the occurrence of beliefs that cannot be denied, within a given world-view and its linguistic expressions. Such beliefs provide ways of understanding experience systematically, grounding an effective way of life. In founding and organizing a world-view, they are presupposed throughout it, and they are beyond real questioning. Jamie Ferreira explicates this theory, as it occurs in various places in present-day philosophy. From Hacker, *Insight* and *Illusion*, he presents a repetition of Newman's (and others') ideas of how beliefs and certitudes arise. 'We create our forms of representation prompted by our biological and psychological character, prodded by Nature, restrained by society and urged by our drive to master the world.'[41] Ferreira emphasizes that, looking at certainty in this way, Newman and Wittgenstein are writing about a very widely-played language-game. It belongs to 'nothing less than the entire human community with the constitution given to it by God.'[42]

Now, this may seem rather poetic, but it does enhance our understanding of Newman's concept of 'certitude.' First, as Ferreira points out, Newman admits the fallibility and corrigibility of human beliefs.[43] Yet he also places limits on doubt.

> Both in his early and late writings Newman condemned the idea that we have a 'duty to doubt everything.' We need a reason to doubt; we only doubt *within* a system. Newman thus set forth quite clearly what C S Peirce, Wittgenstein, and others would later maintain — namely, universal doubt is unreasonable, since we need grounds for doubting ... Wittgenstein points this out in *On Certainty* — 'What I need to show is that a doubt is not necessary even when it is possible.' (*On Certainty* 392) Is not this what Newman meant by saying that doubt is often 'possible, but it must not be assumed,' since 'to be just able to doubt is no warrant for disbelieving.'[44]

Therefore, Newman's certainty about his ultimate beliefs is, in context, well founded. That is, given his moral luck (or destiny) that he was born and raised in a certain time and place, and that his decisions had the results that they did, he is correct in judging that his fundamental religious beliefs are 'indefectible.' He begins with certainty about himself, which leads to certainty about God, so that we may say that his destiny complements and elaborates his strong sense of identity. Yet, as a man aware of the skeptical currents of his time, he realizes that the belief to which he is destined can be questioned. Therefore, he points out that they are firmly embedded in a system of commonplace certitudes about self-identity, conscience, sensory experiences, and the external world. Admittedly, any one of those beliefs is theoretically open to doubt, but Newman sees them as interlocking building blocks in a practical way of life that embodies moral and spiritual integrity both at given moments and in the long run of life's development. Thus, they are really beyond question.

Newman's moral thought never occurs in separation from his spiritual and theological thought, and the drying-up of twentieth-century analytical ethics has helped us to understand why that is so. In contrast to rival secular moral theories in his own times, in contrast to the skeletal moral selves and moral aims of so much of this century's moral philosophy, Newman's thought contains a rich depiction of human moral life, set in a context of traditional narrative explanations of such puzzling moral experiences as weakness of will, moral responsibility in already-determined situations, good and bad moral luck, and hope of ultimate vindication. Even those who cannot accept such religious beliefs might well profit from studying their role in his moral theory, and the ways in which he justifies them.

END NOTES

1. G. Wallace and A. D. M. Walker (eds), *The Definition of Morality* (London: Methuen & Co., Ltd., 1970), p.156

2. Alasdair MacIntyre, *What morality is Not* in Wallace and Walker (eds.), *op. cit.*, p.30

3. *Ibid.*, p.38

4. Neil Cooper *Two Concepts of Morality*, in Wallace and Walker, *op. cit.*, p.90

5. Alasdair MacIntyre *After Virtue*, Second edition (Notre Dame, Indiana: University of Notre Dame Press, 1984)

6. Thomas Nagel *Moral Luck*, in *Moral Questions* (London: Cambridge University Press, 1974), pp.24-38

And quite often the content oscillates concretely between what fragments, divides and what makes whole, heals. For the Kwakiutl Indians of the south coast of British Columbia Baxbakualanuxsiwae ('Man Eater at the Mouth of the River') is the most formidable of great spirits. He is a cannibal and stands for destruction, bestiality and anti-social conduct. The myth of his taming is dramatized in the Kwakiutl winter dances the secret of which according to Locher (1932, 41) 'consists in the conception that life and light do not come into being without death and darkness, so that both these aspects not only may, but even must, be united.'

In Christianity too it would be difficult to attend a church service on any Sunday morning anywhere, in which not in some way or other basic themes of sin versus salvation, evil versus goodness, crucifixion versus resurrection, freedom versus constraint, chaos versus order, integrity versus fragmentation, the sacred versus the profane are dramatized by means of Bible stories or mundane illustrations. At first sight the dynamic quality of the dramatization seems to be denied when salvation is pronounced as being established once for all. Actually it is meant to say that underneath all decay and change there is the irrevocable changelessness of God. To put this more philosophically: in life the thesis (salvation, wholeness) contrasts with the anti-thesis (sin, fragmentation), but the outcome of the pull and counterpull between them is a new level of synthesis (God, Jesus, summing up in their Beings the salvation represented in the thesis).

These theological dramatizations correspond closely with the congruences and conflicts of the various units of social organization. The salvation/reconciliation elements correspond with basic forces of healing and wholemaking of individuals, families and communities. If the language is invariably couched in individual references, that does not mean that the integrity of family and society is not latently involved. Love is intimately tied to salvation in Christianity. Yet it is also a basic feeling linking individuals, families and communities and making each of them into a more cohesive unit. Sin is the opposite of salvation, but it also corresponds with the discords and frictions that weaken persons, groups and societies and the relations between them. Goodness and justice are part and parcel of God's Being. Yet they also correspond with human behaviour which facilitates the well-functioning of social organizations. Evil and injustice jar with what Christians believe to be God's purpose for human living. They also clash, as we all know, with the forces integrating our societies and the sub-systems within them. And so we can go on with each of the paired opposites in our myths, theologies and ideologies.

I have purposely used the word "correspond" when I linked the content of theology with what I previously called a field of jostling, contending, but also co-operating units of social organization. Social scientists with an atheistic bent (such as Durkheim, Freud and Marx) or with an inclination to make the sociological perspective sacred, tend to say that these religious forces and dramatizations are caused by, rather than correspond with, social needs. By contrast religious functionaries and believers also prefer the causal expression, but then start from the opposite angle: God causes individuals and social structures to become whole and rescues them from fragmentation. By using 'correspondence' I think that I am both avoiding atheistic and theistic biases and can point more accurately to mutual effect rather than one-way determination. Or to put it in other terms: inter-dependence reflects reality better than dependence or independence.

Apart from the hermeneutic component there are other elements of religion which contribute to the identity, identities, or jostling of systems which have survived the onslaught of time. By bringing in 'survival' we may, as a sort of bonus, also increase our insight into why religions have maintained themselves so well in all cultures.

When the late William Stanner (1972, 270) tried to sum up totemism he called it the principle of order transcending everything significant for Aboriginal man. Elsewhere (1966, 35) he calls it "the language of the ontological system". Religion then in the context of Australian Aborigines has something to do with ordering. Yet the 'identities' or units of social organization it ordered were incomparably simple (a tribe, a moiety, a clan, an individual, gender). Nor was the ordering very transcendental (the totem and the identity were one; neither nature in the abstract nor time nor history existed for traditional Aboriginal society). Religion and traditional Aboriginal society perished together. The former could not stretch its canopy sufficiently to cope with, or to absorb, the devastating change brought about by the coming of the whites in 1788.

By contrast, the religion of the whites colonising Australia possessed an ordering mechanism which was much more transcendental and therefore much less tied to the mundane. The sacred did not pervade everything. In its organizational form it was so powerless in fact that the first chaplain to the penal colony of New South Wales had to build his own church attended by about 3% of the population on Christmas day 1793, the year it was built. It was burnt down by the convicts five years later (Mol, 1985a). Personal and family identity where much more clearly separated within the social system as compared with Aboriginal society. And yet as in Aboriginal society, religion represented culture and moral order even when it was despised by convicts. It was therefore only natural that the first Catholic priests allowed into the colony in 1820 to keep the Irish convicts under control were paid from the Police Fund (O'Farrell, 1968, 16).

Transcendental ordering therefore is a second component of religion which comes to mind as we look at the context, even though there was quite a difference between the almost non-existent, embryonic transcendental quality of that ordering in Aboriginal society as compared with the full Christian panoply of abstract ideas such as atonement, revelation, eternity, providence, covenant, justification, sanctification, eschatology. In other words the more complex civilization became, the more the transcendental canopy stretched as if to contain sprightly progeny. Too long have scholars of religion stared at Otto's definition of the sacred as entirely other and Durkheim's and Eliade's separation of the sacred and the profane to see behind the gradual separating a sophisticated evolutionary process counterbalancing a complexifying field of jostling systems or a growing transcendentalism interacting with growing differentiation.

The social advantage of the separation is that now both spheres can retain the relevance for one another (as a blueprint is relevant for action and construction) and yet not contaminate the mundane with counterproductive rigidity or the sacred with maladaptive flexibility (transcendental order is by definition permanent and continuous).

In the West this separating of earth and sky had a variety of consequences. Transcendental ordering became two-faced. It relativized in two ways. Firstly it became a means for managing discord, disorder, disruption through relating them to, or placing them in, a context of order: personal identity could be restored if the traumatic event could be interpreted to be part of a larger blueprint (God's inscrutable design). In its Protestant guise it even began to legitimate certain forms of marginal individualism thereby advancing democracy, private enterprise and scientific objectivity (Mol, 1983, 27-31). This is the conservative face of relativization. The other side is the reforming one. Instead of reinforcing man's units of social organization through relating them to a source of legitimation in the beyond, it 'relativizes' them through diminishing their importance and 'holiness' in relation to this source in the beyond. In 1984 during his visit to Canada Pope John Paul II unambiguously endorsed the critique of Canadian society by his bishops who a year earlier had condemned the unalloyed chasing of the profit motive at the expense of better work opportunities for the unemployed. In other words the transcendental frame of reference contains standards of justice which may demand change rather than legitimation. This reforming face concerns itself with improving the justice, wholeness and viability of social identity. In a slightly oversimplified way the relation between the ordering component of religion and the various identities in modern society might be summed up by suggesting that the conservative evangelicals are primarily interested in saving, healing the individual, while the social activists are interested foremost in saving, healing society. For the latter it is necessary that the transcendental frame of reference provide both perspective and leverage for change.

In summary: the second component of what religion means in the context of both Australian Aboriginal and Christian religion shows that ordering kept pace with differentiation and complexification through increasing transcendentalization. It also suggests that surviving religions reflect the dialectic between identity and change in the environment by synopsizing order and anticipating disorder. More concretely, these surviving religions unify individuals, groups, societies through images of order, defining what each of them is about.

Yet consciousness of belief unifies less than strong loyalties to these beliefs and to the systems protected by them. That's why *emotional anchorage* or commitment is so often tied up with religion whenever it is practised or mentioned. In the Bhagavad Gita the warrior Arjuna defeats his uncle's army through clinging in utter devotion to Krishna, his charioteer and the incarnation of Brahman. Mutual loyalty between Yahweh and Israel was the essence of the covenant. Often when something went wrong morally or militarily the cause was squarely laid at the door of the nation's unfaithfulness. Yet God's loving, enduring commitment was assumed all along in spite of the nation's less than perfect response to His love. God became (or actually was) the personification of love, loyalty and commitment. And if God loved them, so the Israelites thought, how could they withhold affection from one another? God had commanded not just to love one's neighbour, but even an alien (Leviticus 19:34). National identity was cemented together through faith.

An altogether different context in which religion is used as commitment is the secular environment of the modern West. Commentators as well as the man in the street make fun of ardent feminists or ecologists for making their cause into a religion. Yet their own commitments to private enterprise, democracy or private goals of promotion, status, wealth, power is often just as strongly held. More importantly these commitments have often lead to the formation of common interest groups or lobbies separating themselves as effectively from the environment as tribes did who increased internal solidarity in order to be all the more capable of dominating that environment. Whether in ancient or modern times, feelings of loyalty or commitment have been crucial for the strength of the boundaries around the various systems now contending, now cooperating in the kind of jostling field I have used as our point of departure.

Yet in the same way as transcendental ordering can ossify and thereby become maladaptive, so emotional anchoring can anchor too much and obstruct adjustment to new situations. And similarly as transcendentalization and relativization can both comfort and open the way to change, so commitment has developed both attaching, unifying, welding characteristics and detaching, separating and stripping tendencies. Of course it would be difficult to still call the latter commitments when in actual fact they de-commit.

I would like to give a number of examples of religion both committing and de-committing. On the level of personal identity conversion in Christianity and satori in Zen Buddhism usually involve a clearing of the underbrush before the new foundation can be laid. It is also true for ideologies, such as communism. After reading Marx, Engels and Lenin, something clicked in Arthur Koestler's brain, he said (1951,32). The tortured past, full of doubts, conflicts and confusion had now become an area of darkness from which he had to constantly and consciously detach himself before his new faith could take hold. Christian conversion, Chinese brainwashing (Schein, 1961,119), Alcoholics Anonymous have in common that all vigorously and continuously dissolve old patterns in order to create new ones through an intervening phase of meaninglessness.

On the level of collective identity charismatic leaders have emerged all through history at times of stress and confusion. They emotionally strip the unsatisfactory past and weld their vision of the future in the minds and hearts of their people. In the second half of the 19th and the first quarter of the 20th centuries a variety of Maori leaders in New Zealand, such as Te Whiti (1832-1907) and Ratana (1873-1939) relativized tribal boundaries by forging a supratribal vision of the Pakeha enemy being driven into the sea or Maori identity being re-established. All the biblical themes of Exodus, Promised Land, and resurrection were grist for the mill. In the process they replaced defeatism with purpose, a defunct identity with a new one (Mol, 1982, 26-35).

Fourthly, religion is also very often used on contexts where it means ritual, or where it *enacts sameness*. In Transcendental Meditation the secret Sanskrit prayer formula or mantra has to be repeated for about twenty minutes in the morning and also in the evening. It retraces the grooves of order for the individual and reassures that the familiar has not succumbed to the unfamiliar. Family prayers do for a family what the five daily prayers do for a Muslim community and the national anthem for a nation. Ritual provides man with a sense of identity and belonging (Klapp,1969,125,37). In the Christian West hundreds of millions attend church each Sunday where again and again they hear which norms and values are judged to be good (altruism, caring, consideration, responsibility, etc.) and which are bad (selfishness, cruelty, self-assertion, unreliability, etc.) Common beliefs in God whose entire Being closely fits with what the group or society thinks of itself ideally are professed. Feelings of dedication to Jesus, the Lord of Life, are aroused on the correct assumption that in the bustle of existence ideas and sentiments tend to be consigned to oblivion unless the memory of them is refreshed.

Yet at the heart of ritual (as with transcendentalization or with commitment) there is also often a dialectic with variety. Variety on the periphery and in the forms of articulation contrasts with sameness at the core of values and beliefs. Ministers and priests may repeat the Apostles' Creed every Sunday, but they hate to be accused of preaching the same sermon.

More pervasive is the dialectic basic to rites of passage (birth, marriage, initiation, death). Here rites function to channel change within permitted boundaries. They form a very hardy, enduring form of ritual which has persisted from the most primitive to the most secular periods of history and in all cultures, irrespective of ideology. One can find them just as readily in the Christian West as in Communist East Europe. Wedding ceremonies are a good example of the phases of emotional detachment and attachment to a new, or re-aligned identity or unit of social organization. The bride is detached from the family in which she grew up and 'given away' by the father. The new family is now symbolically welded together with strings (in some Asian cultures) or with rings (in Christianity) and solemn oaths are sworn by the partners to be faithful and loving until death. The honeymoon underlines the separation from the household of which the partners were members and on return the husband carries the wife over the threshold to again accentuate the transition across the boundary between two families.

III RELATIONS BETWEEN RELIGION AND IDENTITY

We have already constructed a fair number of generalizations about the relationship. Here it remains to systematize, summarize, refine, amend and qualify these generalizations.

Elsewhere (Mol, 1976, 1) I have defined religion as 'the sacralization of identity'. A description of this kind may be short and pithy, and may do as a point of departure, but from the foregoing it is obvious that it needs refinement and elaboration. The advantage of the definition as it stands is two-fold: (1) it draws our attention to a process (sacralization) rather than fixity (religion) and therefore allows us to go beyond the indubitable separateness and otherness of the sacred to a better understanding of the contribution separation paradoxically makes to the integration of identities. (2) It links religion to survival in that the ubiquity of religion appears to have something to do with the way it increases the viability of systems and their relations in a field of cooperating, but also contending units of social organization.

Before qualifying the definition, I must for a moment summarize the ways various identities were and are indeed sacralized.

A transcendental frame of reference relates a welter of sometimes chaotic events and experiences to an underlying order which on the level of personal identity restores confidence and on other levels also swiftly repairs broken boundaries. Faith, loyalty and commitment strengthen emotional links between this point of reference and various units of social organization and thereby makes each of these units more cohesive. Ritual retraces the grooves of order so that integrative elements are not forgotten and remain uppermost in consciousness. Myths and theological themes dramatize the tension within and between the systems to which we belong, usually resolve them and thereby lessen their destructive impact. So far our definition holds.

It is already implied in the previous paragraph however, that in a system of countervailing identities sacralization of one may weaken another. In those countries to which Ukrainians have migrated in this century both the Ukrainian Catholic and the Ukrainian Orthodox churches have been the most formidable guardians of Ukrainian identity (Mol.1985, 71ff) and have often successfully battled those forces of the host country which advanced national identity at the expense of ethnic identity. By contrast the major denominations in those same countries carried out the kind of mission work amongst Ukrainians which implicitly strengthened the language and culture of the host country at the expense of the ethnic one. Examples of this kind can be multiplied many times over for other ethnic groups. These examples also show that structurally religious organizations can and do have their own identity and as such are in no way exempt from the boundary maintaining and boundary challenging forces impinging on them.

However, even on the functional level (the contribution mechanisms of sacralization make to the consolidation of units of social organization) there are many examples of sacralizations being accompanied by desacralization. I have already pointed to the inner dialectic within each of these components of our definition of religion. Transcendentalization can and does lead to sacralization/legitimation, but also to desacralization/censure. Commitment was often preceded by de-commitment, particularly in the cases of conversion and charisma. An important category of rites (rites of passage) always incorporates a phase of stripping one identity in order to weld a new one all the more effectively. Myth and theology act out basic disparities within a particular society, recognizing both boundary fusing and boundary fissioning elements.

There is more. I have advanced ideas with one hand (sacralization) some of which I then subsequently have taken back with the other (desacralization). This seems unpardonable, particularly when we have been taught that any scientific model must be logically consistent, aesthetically elegant and orderly hierarchic. And yet the data at our disposal somehow cannot be squeezed into such a model. As in the biological sciences, identity (heredity) and its tendency towards hierarchy and integration is countered (for the sake of survival) by change (mutation), or as Bertalanffy (1969,74) suggests, hierarchy and openendedness seem to both be necessary, if the model is to be comprehensive. This then brings us back to the dialectic model fitting best not only in the scientific study of religion, but also in the natural and social sciences (Mol, 1978, 22ff).

The correspondence between sacralization and units of social organization is also not neatly congruent. The transcendental frame of reference is usually cosmic enough (particularly in the universal religions) to be potentially as relevant for the international system as for national, social, communal, familial, personal ones. Yet the weakness of both the World Council of Churches and the United Nations shows that actual loyalties do correspond much more closely with lower level systems than with configurations of international brotherhood and such like. The Vatican is constantly engaged in moderating between its international ethos and the strength of competing national sentiments.

In summary: we can define religion initially and ideally as the sacralization of identity, but identities are always proximate and situated in a jostling field in which they have to be capable both of cooperation and contention in order to survive. Therefore we have to add to this definition (a) that sacralization of one identity may contribute to the weakening of another and (b) that the mechanisms of sacralization (transcendentalization, commitment, ritual, myth) have developed the wherewithal to desacralize in order to ensure both function and survival.

IV COMPARISON WITH OTHER WAYS TO STUDY RELIGION

(a) Phenomenology.

Phenomenologists ask themselves the questions: How does it appear? How can one observe religion as accurately and precisely as possible? While they observe, they think themselves into the situation of those who experience the various religious phenomena. In so far as phenomenology attempts to uncover the structure, essence and meaning of phenomena it has much in common with the dialectical method described above. However, phenomenologists are generally not interested in generalizations about the effect of religion, how it correlates with other phenomena or in latent analysis (the construction of these generalizations on the basis of what lies below appearances and beneath the surface of phenomena).

By contrast the above sketched dialectical method zeroes in on what lies beyond culture-bound surface categories and concentrates on 'identities', 'systems' and their opening and closing boundaries. It tries to answer the question: How does religion affect the strength or weakness of these boundaries? By doing so it claims that it can elucidate the functioning and survival of religious phenomena. However unique cultures are and however foolish it is to underestimate their differences, the dialectical or 'identity' method is particularly interested in underlying patterns they have in common. It is less afraid of being accused of cultural relativism, if only because it claims that by specifying identity levels it can analyze the relevance of religion for both intra- and inter-cultural systems.

The specification of identity levels also allows the dialectical method of studying religion to go beyond the generally subjective (or personal-identity oriented) treatment of meaningsystems. Weber (1964) and Berger and Luckmann (1967) correctly trace the emergence of systems of meaning in subjective terms. Yet objectification and unifying belief systems, group and social identities have in common with persons.

(b) Hermeneutics.

The search in hermeneutics seems to be for the key to unlock the interpretation of religion as it were from the *outside*. Yet what if this key is actually to be found *within* the religions we study? What if the sin/salvation dialectic in Christianity and its equivalents in other religions proves to be *more* rather than *less* sophisticated than the linear progressive thinking of Darwinists, the rationalist assumptions of the creationists and the cognitive positivism which has some of the sciences teetering on the brink of bankruptcy? I have taken the view that at the present state of scientific endeavour the integration/differentiation or identity/change dialectic is the best fitting and most comprehensive model for the interpretation of natural, social as well as religious data. On this assumption the ordering of religious phenomena cannot be arbitrary. The vantage point for ordering therefore must distinguish between superior and inferior hermeneutics.

From this angle the best interpretations result from a series of systematic questions. First: which units of social organization ('systems', 'identities' or more concretely persons, groups, societies) are implicitly or explicitly involved in the data (belief, commitment, ritual, myth)? Second: are these units congruent or are they in conflict, or both? Thirdly: do the religious phenomena reinforce, restore, reconcile each of these units and do they divide, disaffect others? A prayer of confession may reconcile a community or a family, but it may also repress the self-assertion necessary for the integrity of a particular individual. A rite may reinforce a sense of tribal identity, but thereby endanger super-tribal loyalties.

By implication, inferior interpretations ignore some units of social organization (a collectivity of some sort) and attach exclusive importance to others (individual perception, for instance). More frequently hermeneutics concentrates on religious ideas, beliefs rather than religious commitments, rites. In this way a partial account may be taken for the whole and so distort the total picture. Alternately surface intentions of individuals or groups may hide deeper motivations and structures and so lead to incomplete analysis if they alone are described.

(c) Structuralism

Levi-Strauss (1970,341) correctly felt that mythical thought portrayed the nature of reality and organized the diversity of empirical experience. To him (1969,29) the relation between myth and empirical fact was dialectical. It was not obvious to the naked eye. And yet it was the essence of the underlying structure of myth. Structuralists therefore look for binary opposites, or to put it in language I prefer, notions of integration and differentiation crystallized and synthesized in a suitable symbolic core.

There are two problems with structuralism as presented by Levi-Strauss. The first one it has in common with all other theories here reviewed: it may elucidate important aspects of religion, but it is not a comprehensive theory of religion and therefore runs the risk of taking the part too much for the whole. The fit of the myth in a particular culture may be just as important if not more so than its structure. Structuralism may have contributed substantially to our understanding of myth (and theology I may add), but it has little to say about ritual, faith and transcendentalization.

The other problem is the tendency of Levi-Strauss to reduce emotional drives to intellectual processes and therefore to underestimate commitment in relation to myth. A dialectical rather than a reductive relation between commitment and myth seems to reflect religious reality better.

(d) Psychoanalysis

The important contribution psychoanalysis (both in its Freudian and Jungian variant) made to the study of religion is that it delved below the appearance of religious phenomena by analysing their latent effect on the sanity (or insanity) of individuals. Sigmund Freud thought of religion as an emotional crutch which people interested in knowledge should avoid. Yet his own strong attachment to individual rationalism was not any less irrational and the fit of religious symbolism with reality as people experienced it was generally better than the fit of Freud's belief in rationalism. After all, reason proved to be a rather utopian interpreter and poor mender of man's predicament, whereas such irrational factors as love and loyalty, stressed by religion, had an indubitable effect on integrity.

Carl Jung understood this better. To him individuation (the whole-making of a person, personal integration) could be significantly assisted by religion. It provided the individual with a system of meaning outside him or herself in terms of which the patterns which the jungle of life had put into jeopardy, could be repaired. Psychoanalysis also detects much conflict between individual and culture (which Freud regarded as primarily a regressive institution). This emphasis on conflict between personal and other forms of identity and on latent factors involved in the opening and closing of boundaries around the self must be part of any theory of religion. Yet conflict and latency also exist between and in other units of social organization. Religion is as much, if not more, involved in these and psychoanalysis therefore lacks the comprehension which we have attempted to achieve in the dialectical approach.

(e) Functionalism.

Functionalism, like psychoanalysis was equally interested in what lay below the surface of appearances and Durkheim's importance for the study of religion lies in the link he saw between ritual and commitment (rather than belief) and social solidarity. This was progress, since almost all figures of the nineteenth century who thought about religion (such as Ludwig Feuerbach, Edward Tylor, Sir James Frazer) looked at it through the coloured glasses of individual rationalism. The problem was that in his enthusiasm Durkheim made the opposite mistake. He correctly pointed out that collective effervescence was not ancillary to the rational individual but had a life of its own. Yet he overlooked that even amongst the Australian Aborigines (the subjects of his *Elementary Forms of the Religious Life*) totems for individuals (associated with the conception site — the place where the mother had first felt the stirrings in the womb) were separate from, sometimes even in conflict with, tribal totems.

The problem with the functional approach therefore is that it too readily assumes that units of social organization harmoniously interact and that religion reinforces this harmony. It was for reason of conflict that Robert K. Merton introduced the concept of 'dysfunction' (whatever produces consequences of lesser adaptation for a given unit of social organization). An example: When in Central Australia Namatjira (the father of the famous aboriginal painter Albert Namatjira) eloped with a girl from the wrong kin-group, he was denied instruction in the sacred traditions of his own conception site (Strehlow,1970,122). In other words this knowledge was regarded as functional for Namatjira's confidence and integrity, but dysfunctional for clan solidarity (Mol. 1982a, 12).

(f) Conflict theory

Conflict theories stress the ubiquity of conflict, contradiction and change in society. They stand in contrast with functionalism, which emphasizes integration. From the point of view of our dialectical theorizing, the polar position of each underestimates the interaction between congruence and conflict, or the way both the factors moving towards identity and those moving towards change, are of vital necessity for survival. Conflict between units of social organization prevents sterile ossification, congruence prevents certain extinction following the wake of unimpeded change.

Conflict theoreticians are not particularly interested in religion. Negatively they point to religious organizations backing the powerful against the powerless. Positively they point to, for instance, the social gospel in Anglo-Saxon countries or liberation theology in South America as means to counterbalance the injustices perpetrated on the weak by the strong. In the dialectical approach religion is treated rather similarly. Here too social action is regarded as a means to heal broken societies. Yet more comprehensively religion is also regarded as the reinforcer of boundaries in primitive societies where the kinds of conflict the conflict theoreticians are interested in, are largely unknown.

More importantly, the relevance of religion is not confined to patching over economic friction (slums and poverty versus affluence), political conflicts (establishment power versus radical powerlessness), and racial strife (negro versus white). Its relevance also rests with its capacity to place frictions in a larger cosmic setting where threat and anxiety are relativized. In other words it too interprets reality — in the sects, for example, by means of the sin/salvation dialectic.

(g) Marxism

Marxism is closely allied to the conflict theory of society. It accuses religious organizations of supporting the ruling classes and there is indeed good evidence that this has been and is the case. Yet the Marxist assumptions were and are too narrow for the general state of affairs even in 19th Century England and Germany. Class was only one of a variety of units of social organization and religion was just as much concerned with the community, the family, the individual and their interactions, quite separate from the class-structure. Of course there is also considerable evidence that the same religious organizations which reinforced the status quo somewhat incongruously vigorously defended the workers against the injustices of a capitalist economy around the turn of the 19th Century.

More importantly, about the same time both in Britain and North-America Christian sects had often greater appeal for the 'exploited' than those political movements which promised paradise through the overthrow of capitalism and improvement in material conditions. The reason for the remarkable attraction of Methodism, the Salvation Army and the Baptists in Canada and the U.S.A. for the working class lay in their capacity to address themselves to the entire realm of human experiences (not just economic deprivation, but also family conflicts, alcoholism, death, birth, marriage, divorce, frustration, adultery, pain, ill health, plain human cussedness, evil, greed, fortune as well as misfortune, diffidence, etc.). All these could and did weaken personal identity in the same way as more globally culture contact, military conquest, trade, injustice, disaster damaged social identity.

(h) Deprivation theories

Like Marxism, deprivation theories of religion assume that in an undeprived state man would not need religion, because it is only a means towards the end of mastery. But looking at religion solely in terms of technological mastery or social differentiation ignores the function it has for the other side of the dialectic: the knitting together or integration of societies and individuals. Religion deals with the interpretation of any reality, not merely with ones which can be reduced to a form of deprivation. A win in the lottery can obviously not be reduced to a form of deprivation. And yet the event has to be fitted in a balanced set of interpretations if the lucky ticket holder is to survive the altered change in circumstances. The Jesus Freaks with their millennialism or the New Guinean cargo cults do not just compensate for the relative deprivations of this world, but, more fundamentally, interpret present disorder in the light of an anticipated event.

When religion reinforces identity, it thereby strengthens the side which complements rather than sugarcoats alienation. In other words the dialectical or identity approach to religion maintains that mastery (the profit motive, technical progress, efficiency, etc.) is not independent of the way facts and goals are interpreted. It maintains that there are no uninterpreted facts or goals and that the only alternative to interpretation is disorder or even chaos.

Both to Marxists and some of those who favour the deprivationist approach to religion, the transcendental point of reference is an unnecessary illusion which in the past led to exploitation and which in the present distorts reality. By contrast, in the dialectical or identity model of religion, this transcendental point of reference delineates and sums up an order in terms of which disorder and change can be better managed.

CONCLUSION

Deep down scientific papers of this kind are motivated by specific convictions, biasses, values or beliefs of the author. Making a clean breast of these basic motivations has the advantage for the audience that it can both understand why the address took the turn it did and facilitate the positive or negative judgment necessary for linking it with the variety of favoured approaches.

It is not accidental that the term 'comprehension' presented itself as often as it did. To understand religion systematically has been a much more demanding and puzzling intellectual exercise to me than any other topic in the social sciences. How could the large variety of religious data at my disposal be ordered and accounted for, given the most up-to-date theories of individual and social behaviour? Why had religion survived for so long and why were all those scholars of past generations predicting its inevitable demise so hopelessly wrong? It is this concern with comprehension which has made me judge the nineteenth century scholars of religion as overestimating both personal identity and rationalism at the expense of the social system and commitment. The first scholar not to do so (Emile Durkheim) made the opposite mistake (overestimating the predominance of the social system). He also underestimated the conflict between the various forms of identity. By contrast Sigmund Freud was quite aware of conflict and non-rational commitment, but underestimated the saliency of the social system and his own non-rational commitment to rationalism. Karl Marx correctly saw the sacralizing, legitimating characteristic of religion, but failed to see both its application to the numerous forms of identity not reducible to class and the internal, de-legitimating elements at the very heart of the surviving forms of religion. Max Weber made very astute observations about the effect of meaningsystems on social structures, but had little to say about commitment to transcendental beliefs. The phenomenologists have made important advances in the study of religion through stressing objectivity and understanding from within, but have tended to avoid generalizations based on latent analysis and for that reason have not looked as much as they could have, beyond the culture-boundness of their categories. The deprivation theories of religion were not any less partial in that they generally failed to see it operating in situations which could not be reduced to deprivation.

Criticism is easier than construction. With comprehension as the goal, how could we produce a fitting accounting scheme? Obviously the model of a jostling field of congruent and cooperating systems lacks in elegance what it gains in dynamism. Yet the dialectic between the variables making for identity and consolidation and the variables making for change and disjunction is obviously elementary in both the social and natural sciences. Arnold Toynbee's (1946,65) view of history as well as the intrinsic components of the major religions of the world (sin and salvation in Judaism, Christianity and Islam, ch'ien and k'un, yang and yin in Chinese religion, prakriti and purusa, adharma and dharma in Hinduism) fit as a hand in a glove with the dialectic emerging as the template of the sciences.

What is more, this comprehensive dialectical way of thinking about religion and identity has the advantage of operationalizing and concretizing what is essentially a rather vague grand theory. Identity can be translated into actual units of social organization being subject to boundary eroding and boundary reinforcing forces. Religion can be translated into the diachronic component of transcendentalization and the three synchronic components of commitment, ritual and myth. Most of this paper has attempted to sketch the effect that these mechanisms of sacralization have on the various forms of identity. In the process of doing so, we found it necessary to modify the simple idea that religion is the sacralization of identity. After all not only do units of social organization clash (thereby creating the dilemma that sacralization or strengthening of one implicitly leads to weakening another) but also the mechanisms of sacralization have their own in-built de-sacralizing potential to survive the onslaught of change and to absorb the latter back into order.

Paradoxical though it may sound, the prime motivation of comprehension has its own limitations. One cannot be single-mindedly scientific in the comprehensive sense and simultaneously avoid being a cultural relativist and a reductionist, two accusations which can be rightfully addressed to this dialectical interpretation of religious phenomena. And I may add, two accusations which render the approach unacceptable to many scholars of religion. All I can say to colleagues for whom these approaches determine scholarship is that an over-emphasis on the uniqueness of a culture tends to preclude the study of that culture from an exterior vantage point. On reductionism: any exterior vantage point (apart from the religious one intrinsic to the particular tradition under investigation) usually reduces religious phenomena to a framework of order at odds with the religious one. Objectivity and reductionism belong together. All scholars of religion and most theologians (Karl Barth, for instance, is an exception because he stood squarely within the Christian tradition) reduce religion by the mere fact that they treat it as an independent (affecting) or dependent (affected) variable, whatever the case. If anything this dialectical methodology is least reductionistic of all approaches in that the oscillation between salvation and change, yin and yang, prakriti and purusa on the one hand and the paired opposition of identity (wholeness, integration) and difference (fragmentation, dissolution) on the other belong to the same family of ontological assumptions.

The implication of all this of course is that however valid within the academic setting, the scientific study of religion cannot materially contribute to the well-being of religion, unless theologians and embattled Christians cry out for an apology of their existence. If the latter is needed, there are specific areas in which religious exposition is more sophisticated than scientific analysis. For instance the former is much more articulate about inescapable emotional commitment to basic ontological departures than the latter. Analytic procedures (so close to the scientific enterprise) are partisan explainers of reality. Synthetic procedures, much closer to the heart of what any religion is about, may also be partisan. Yet they are more likely to contribute to whole making than the former. After all salvation is seldom the expressed purpose of the academic communities in which I have worked and still work, in spite of the fact that the motto of my own university (McMaster in Canada) is: Ta Panta

Sunesteken En Christoi (In Christ everything hangs together). Nothing is further from the truth on our and any other campus.

All this leads to the inescapable conclusion well expressed by Ninian Smart (1979,7) that being a saint is more important than studying religion. Or to say the same with the theme of this congress: studying identity does not necessarily lead to having one, learning about salvation does not make one saved, religious scholarship does not produce religious people, in the same way as knowing all about love does not help one much to be in love.

REFERENCES

Berger, Peter L. and Luckmann, Thomas, *The Social Construction of Reality*, London, Allen Lane Penguin Press, 1967.

Bertalanffy, Ludwig von, "Chance or Law" in (Editors) Koestler, Arthur and Smythies, J.R. *Beyond Reductionism*, London: Hutchinson, 1969 pp. 56-84.

Bronowski, J. *The Identity of Man*, Garden City, N.Y.: Natural History Press, 1965.

Durkheim, Emile, *Elementary Forms of Religious Life*, Glencoe: Free Press, 1954.

Eliade, Mircea, *Australian Religions*, Ithaca, New York: Cornell University Press, 1973.

Erikson, Erik H. *Childhood and Society*, New York, Norton, 1963.

Erikson, Erik H. *Insight and Responsibility*, New York: Norton, 1964.

Erikson, Erik H. *Identity — Youth and Crisis*, New York: Norton, 1968.

Feuerbach, Ludwig, *The Essence of Christianity*, New York: Harper, 1957.

Frazer, James George, *Totemism and Exogamy* (4 Volumes) London: Macmillan, 1910.

Freud, Sigmund, *The Future of an Illusion*, Garden City, N.Y.: Doubleday, 1964.

Heidegger, Martin, *Identity and Difference*, New York: Harper, 1969.

Huxley, Aldous, "Culture and Individual" in Solomon, David (ed.) *LSD, The Consciousness Expanding Drug*, New York: Putnam, 1964, pp. 29-39.

James, William, *Principles of Psychology* (2 Vols.) New York: Holt, 1890.

Jaspers, Karl, *General Psychopathology*, Chicago: University of Chicago Press, 1963.

Jung, Carl Gustav, *Psychology and Religion: East and West* (The Collected Works of C.G. Jung, Vol. II), New York: Pantheon Books, 1958.

Kant, Immanuel, *Critique of Pure Reason*, New York: St. Martin's Press, 1965.

Kierkegaard, Soren, *Concluding Unscientific Postscript*, Princeton: Princeton University Press, 1941.

Klapp, Orrin E. *Collective Search for Identity*, New York: Holt, Rinehart and Winston, 1969.

Koestler, Arthur, *The God that failed*, London: Hamish Hamilton, 1951.

Laing, R.D. *The Politics of the Family and other essays*, New York: Random, 1971.

Leibniz, Gottfried Wilhelm, *Neue Abhandlungen über den Menschlichen Verstand* Vol. I and II. Frankfurt am Main: Insel Verlag, 1961.

Levi-Strauss, Claude, "The Story of Asdiwal" in Edmund Leach (ed.), *The Structural Study of Myth and Totemism*, London: Tavistock, 1969, p.1-47.

Levi-Strauss, Claude. *The Raw and the Cooked*, London: Jonathan Cape, 1970. (first publ. 1964)

Locher, G.W. *The Serpent in Kwakiutl Religion*, Leyden: Brill, 1932.

Locke, John, *Works* (10 Volumes), London: Johnson (ed.), 1801. (*The Essay concerning Human Understanding* published in 1690).

Marx, Karl, *On Religion*, (arranged and edited by Saul K. Padover), New York: McGraw-Hill, 1974.

Malinowski, Bronislaw, *Magic, Science and Religion and Other Essays*, Garden City, New York: Doubleday, 1954.

Merton, Robert G. *Social Theory and Social Structure*, Glencoe, Ill.: Free Press, 1957.

Mol, Johannis (Hans) J. *Identity and the Sacred*, Oxford: Blackwell, 1976 or New York: Free Press, 1977.

Mol, Johannis (Hans) J. *Wholeness and Breakdown (A Model for the Interpretation of Nature and Society)*, Madras: The Dr. S. Radhakrishnan Institute for Advanced Study in Philosophy, University of Madras, 1978.

Mol, Johannis (Hans) J. *The Fixed and the Fickle* (Religion and Identity in New Zealand), Waterloo, Ont.: Wilfrid Laurier University Press, 1982.

Mol, Johannis (Hans) J. *The Firm and the Formless*, (Religion and Identity in Aboriginal Australia), Waterloo, Ontario: Wilfrid Laurier University Press, 1982a.

Mol, Johannis (Hans) J. *Meaning and Place* (An Introduction to the Social Scientific Study of Religion), New York: Pilgrim Press, 1983.

Mol, Johannis (Hans) J. *The Faith of Australians*, Sydney, N.S.W.: Allen and Unwin, 1985a.

O'Farrell, Patrick, *The Catholic Church in Australia*, Melbourne: Nelson, 1968.

Otto, Rudolf, *The Idea of the Holy*, London: Oxford University Press, 1950.

Peter, Karl, "The Dialectic of Family and Community in the Social History of the Hutterites" in (Editor) Larson, Lyle E. *The Canadian Family in Comparative Perspective*, Scarborough, Ontario: Prentice-Hall, 1976, pp. 337-350.

Rickert, Heinrich, *Das Eine, die Einheit und die Eins*, Tubingen: Mohr, 1924.

Schein, Edgar H. *Coercive Persuasion*, New York: Norton, 1961.

Smart, Ninian, *The Science of Religion and the Sociology of Knowledge*, Princeton: Princeton University Press, 1979.

Smith, Wilfred Cantwell, *Faith and Belief*, Princeton, New Jersey: Princeton University Press, 1979.

Stanner, William E.H. *On Aboriginal Religion* (Oceania Monograph No. 11), Sydney: University of Sydney, 1966.

Stanner, William E.H. "The Dreaming" in (eds) Lessa, William A. and Vogt, Evon Z. *Reader in Comparative Religion*, New York: Harper, 1972. pp. 269-277.

Strauss, Anselm L. *Mirrors and Masks, the Search for Identity*, Glencoe, I11.: Free Press, 1959.

Strehlow, T.G.H. "Geography and the Totemic Landscape in Central Australia" in (ed) Berndt, Ronald M., *Australian Aboriginal Anthropology*, Nedlands, W.A.: University of Western Australia Press, 1970, pp. 92-140.

Toynbee, Arnold J. *A Study of History* (Abridgements of Volumes I-VI) New York: Oxford University Press, 1946.

Tylor, Edward B. *Primitive Culture*, London: Murray, 1871.

Weber, Max, *The Sociology of Religion*, Boston: Beacon Press, 1964.

Whaling, Frank, *Contemporary Approaches to the Study of Religion*, Vol. II, *Social Scientific Approaches*, Berlin Mouton, 1985

A RESPONSE TO PROFESSOR MOL'S KEYNOTE ADDRESS

Ninian Smart

*University of California, Santa Barbara, U.S.A.
and University of Lancaster, U.K.*

I am honoured to have been invited to respond to Professor Mol's address, and to be a cocelebrant of Australia's remarkable progress in the field of religious studies during the last decade. It is an especial pleasure to be here again in Sydney, especially as I am on my mother's side a descendant of Lachlan Macquarie.

Professor Mol has pointed to a multitude of ways in which his definition of religion as the sacralization of identity can set in train new reflections and stimulate new researches. In his opening remarks he cautions against cutting religion off from other elements in society, in our trying too easily to abstract religious from non-religious phenomena. Indeed I believe that in many ways it would be healthier if we talked more of the history and analysis of *worldviews* (including their practical and social expression) as a genus of which religions as traditionally defined are the major species, together with secular ideologies. In addition we may also want to stretch sacralization as a concept. It is the solemn loading of identities. So I take it that though for administrative and professional purposes we may characterize ourselves as students of *religion*, our interests are much wider, stretching horizontally to worldviews dubbed as secular, and vertically to the social and cultural context and embodiment of worldviews. And in directing our thoughts, Professor Mol's definition has great heuristic merit.

Also, it may be useful for us sometimes to make use of a Tillichianism in relation to group identity. We can ask of a person or of a collection of people what is her or their *group of ultimate concern*. For whom would they die, sacrifice a large portion of their goods and so on? Usually, today, it is the nation. Often religious or secular ideologies, whether Shi'ism or Maoism, have played a crucial role in restoring, refreshing or reordering national identity and dignity. So in all this I agree with Hans Mol's consistent emphasis, over the last two decades or more, upon the concept of identity in social and religious research.

In responding to him I would like to take up particularly the latter part of his paper where he compares his approach to other ways of studying religion: he lists phenomenology, hermeneutics, structuralism, psychoanalysis, functionalism, conflict theory, Marxism and deprivation theories. I do not have time to deal with all these, but let me concentrate, albeit briefly, on phenomenology, functionalism and Marxism. I do so because historians of religion have been much influenced by the first and social scientists by the second and third. I might say that Dr Mol does not think of his list as exhaustive, and some of the approaches labelled are more in the nature of theories or models within a general field or method, rather than such a method. But phenomenology is a sort of method (or more than one) and it has influenced us: so I shall begin there.

I myself have in one or two recent papers attempted to evolve what I call a 'position theory' in relation to religious and other traditions and subtraditions, in which

I take up the challenge of producing a 'moving phenomenology' (such a dynamic phenomenology was advocated a number of years back by Michael Pye). It is an interesting study to see how traditions, groups, subtraditions and cultures react when faced forcefully by others and by alien cultural themes, including both ideological (including symbolic) and economic or material ones. Consider the variety of Islamic responses to Western material and ideational incursions. In trying to work out such a theory (e.g. in my A Theory of Religious and Ideological Change: Illustrated from Modern South Asian and Other Religious Nationalisms, Arizona State University, Department of Religious Studies, 1984) I have been encouraged by Professor Mol's general approach to problems of identity. It is one way by which phenomenology, i.e. typology or morphology, can be dynamized. There is no reason why we should not collect kinds of changes in worldview as well as the static 'essences' more traditional phenomenology has tended to deal in. In doing such dynamic as well as static typology we are in effect compiling the vocabulary of religious meaning-systems. Here I endorse Professor Mol's question, at the end of his section on phenomenology, about the importance but insufficiency of subjective meanings. I think here phenomenology has quite a different sense from typology: in this second sense it amounts to the call for imaginative and informed empathy in walking in other people's moccasins (to echo a Native American proverb). That is the point of epochē and bracketing.

Next: his worries about functionalism are well taken. Indeed it may be that all theories of large-scale societies which are founded on observations of small-scale ones are problematic, in that it has typically been impossible for large and especially modern societies to exist as tightly integrated groups. It is true that for virtually all modern societies there is the concept of the nation, and we have divided the whole hard surface of the globe, save Antarctica, into sovereign nation-States. But normally each of these societies is highly porous to external influences, and we are finding that even relatively homogeneous societies are incorporating variegations of religion as well as other cultural manifestations into their fabric. Pluralism is, then, the norm. Such variegation helps to promote worry about group identity, as Professor Mol has well noted.

Third: regarding Marxist approaches to religion, Dr Mol rightly points to ways in which traditionally defined religions, including groups such as Methodism and the Salvation Army, had a widely conceived view of human experiences which gave them relevance to human beings caught in the trials of social change and dislocation during 19th century industrialization. This is in effect more of a critique of Marxism as an ideology rivalling religions than as a theoretical approach to the analysis of social problems, alienation and so forth. Indeed one of the crises of contemporary official Marxism lies in the unexpected vigour of religion in a socialist State. Religion persists both because of threats to national identity and because of concerns about personal identity and meaning.

I am not sure, however, that I agree with one of Dr Mol's conclusions, namely that any single-minded attempt at comprehending religion must be culturally relativist and reductionist. I believe, though I shall not argue the point here, that the social scientist and scholar of religion should be methodologically agnostic (assuming, that is, neither the truth nor the falsity of the faiths studied). We do not need to be either methodologically atheistic or theistic (or nirvanistic). I do not think we are correctly described as reductionistic if — as Dr Mol implies — we treat religion sometimes as the independent and not the dependent variable. Indeed it seems to me obvious that religious experiences, doctrines, myths, rituals and so on are often active and partly independent in human affairs. If it were not so no religion would be worth affirming and no worldview would be worth espousing. But it is true that dealing with these matters scientifically and with an appropriate warm dispassion does raise some interesting and disturbing philosophical questions, among them this: whether the experience and encounter with God or Emptiness or Brahman is quite enough, for what more would be added by adding her or his existence?

In conclusion, let me add a point which has only in part been made explicitly by Professor Mol. What is the connection between social and personal identity? It is indicated I think by the fact that the question "Who am I?" is so frequently answered by nominating the most ultimate group which we affirm (e.g. "I am a human being"). But of course some analyses, especially from within religions affirming a transcendent Focus, treat any group including the group of one constituted by myself, as provisional and of secondary importance compared to that Focus.

We should be grateful to Professor Mol for his correct concern with problems of identity in religion and society: for under the rubric of identity most of the important questions can be subsumed.

FEMALE IDENTITY AND THE HISTORY OF RELIGIONS

Ursula King

University of Leeds, England

This paper is placed towards the beginning of our discussions on the role of methodology and theory in the study of religion, a fast growing field of scholarly concern as is evident from numerous publications. The paper is mainly of an exploratory nature; it asks a number of questions rather than provides answers. But these questions may help to contribute an important orientation for the discussions of the many theoretical issues which will be raised over the next few days.

Much has been written on religious studies as an academic field with heterogeneous approaches which require a unified theory or at least a more explicitly formulated theoretical orientation (Honko 1979; Schmid 1979; Vernoff 1983; Wiebe 1983). In 1983 the American Academy of Religion established an ongoing 'Consultation on Theory and Methods for the Study of Religion' towards which a session of this Congress will contribute. In exploring the various questions concerning the field of religious studies and the nature of the academically disciplined means for studying religion, Charles Elliott Vernoff has spoken of 'the foundational issues of academic identity' and the deeper issue of 'fundamental intellectual clarity and integrity for individuals and collegial cohesion for groups of scholars in disparately staffed departments' (1983:110), whilst Ross Reat has pointed out that scholars in religious studies have been somewhat lax in developing 'a clear formulation of methodological identity' (1983: 465).

The area of methodology and theory is as crucial for the identity of our field as for us as individuals involved in a particular scholarly enterprise. To explain my own concern with methodology and situate this paper against a wider background, I need to mention that I published a survey on the 'Historical and Phenomenological Approaches to the Study of Religion. Some major developments and issues under debate since 1950'. It analysed the international discussions on methodology between 1950 and 1980 but appeared only recently in print in *Contemporary Approaches to the Study of Religion* edited by Frank Whaling (Berlin/New York/Amsterdam 1984). At a late stage of editing I added a final footnote to this survey which reads: 'The above discussion, and the language in which it is expressed, accurately reflect the major issues debated up till the late 1970s. It does not incorporate the more recent feminist critique of the study of religion. This would require a reassessment of the issues in another article' (King 1984a: 153).

It is not possible to undertake such a reassessment in this paper. But I would like to share some critical comments which have occurred to me more recently through my own change of awareness and a more thorough acquaintance with the work of feminist writers in religious studies and with critical feminist literature in other fields of the humanities.

The title of my paper 'Female Identity and the History of Religions' arose not only out of wider reflections on theoretical and practical issues pertaining to religious studies. It was also a direct response to the Congress theme of 'Religion and Identity' which invited an analysis of the 'sense of personal and corporate identity' which religion has provided for individuals and communities throughout history (Congress Brochure). 'History of religions' is here understood in the widest sense as embracing numerous methods and approaches applied in the study of religions.

The sections of the Congress pose a problem of personal identity for women scholars in religion as no major section has been allocated to the discussion of women and religion or the feminist critique of religious studies. A growing number of college courses and publications have appeared in this area over the last decade. The image and role of women, the place of women's religious experience, of their exclusion from or participation in ritual, of female imagery and symbolism in sacred scriptures and theological writings, is not only of great importance in the Judaeo-Christian tradition, but also in Hinduism, Buddhism, Islam, African, Near Eastern, Far Eastern and other religions. This subject is a growth area in religions studies, and it is well known that the American Academy of Religion has had a section on 'Women and Religion' since 1972. The last IAHR Congress in Winnipeg (1980) also included a special section on this subject, although it was somewhat oddly entitled 'Femininity and Religion'. It thus came as a surprise, if not to say a shock, when the current IAHR Congress did not include a section on women and religion. At a Congress devoted to 'Religion and Identity' one must not only investigate the importance of religion in general or of particular religions for personal, social, cultural and political identity, or enquire into foundational issues of academic identity; one must also ask when reading the titles of sections and papers, how far the categories of the past and the history of our field restrict our perception of breakthroughs and paradigm shifts occurring in the present. Women and religion are again nowhere on the agenda in Sydney and this in 1985, during the year which marks the end of the UN decade for women, and has recently seen the international women's conference in Nairobi. This situation highlights the invisibility and general marginality of women in the history of religions as a field of studies, so far largely defined by male scholars of religion. For contemporary female scholars, especially those who apply a feminist perspective to their work on different religious traditions, this marginality raises important questions about their own identity as well as that of their discipline.

The methodological debate is not only about the question *what* is the study of religion, what are its methods and theory, but it must also be concerned with the question of *how* and *by whom* the study of religion is undertaken and *who* can identify with it. Which perspectives, methods and approaches have until now been left out? So far, the study of religion has hardly been gender-specific, and insufficient attention has been given to sexual differentiation in the practice and theory of religion. There is no recognition of this differentiation and of women as a category in their own right in the study of religion in recent surveys on the field and its methods (Crosby 1981; Honko 1979; Waardenburg 1973, 1978; Whaling 1984a, 1984b).

In the methodological debate it is important to analyze the values, presuppositions and basic orientations which have consciously or unconsciously shaped the prevalent methods and theories in the study of religion. Contemporary feminist thought acts as a critical category for examining the unacknowledged ideological assumptions which inform all disciplines of knowledge as historically constructed. From a feminist-critical perspective one must investigate how far the major conceptual tools and interpretative theories used for the classification and interpretation of religious data have been developed in the gender-exclusive and therefore one-sided manner. This requires what has been called a hermeneutics of suspicion vis-a-vis existing models, theory and practice in the study of religion and vis-a-vis its own history.

To clarify this argument, I shall briefly explain what I mean by feminism and its importance as a perspective in religious studies (I). I shall then illustrate by some examples from past and present how female scholarly identity must call into question certain theoretical and practical perspectives in the history of religions (II). Finally, in my conclusion, I shall consider the question of how the change in contemporary consciousness may be an important influence in shaping new directions in our field of studies (III).

I

The new feminism which has emerged since the 1960s is not only an important social and political movement, but it also functions as a critical perspective which passes judgement on society and its institutions. Although very diverse in its manifestations and expressions, feminism has produced a wide-ranging body of theory and praxis which has affected many areas of contemporary culture. It has been said that 'consciousness raising is the essential first step in feminist theory' but also that 'feminist strategy and feminist scholarship at this moment in their development are hampered by the absence of a solid theoretical perspective' (Keohane, Rosaldo & Gelpi, vii, 99). Whilst there is no unified theory of feminism, there are a number of different theoretical perspectives available, often linked to specific political orientations. There is also a number of important elements which are common to the different forms of feminism. An absolutely basic one is the experience of consciousness raising already mentioned which gives expression to women's active determination to shape their own selves and the world around them, including history and culture. Finding a sense of self is not only a personal experience but it happens at the social level to women as a group today. This newly discovered and newly expressed sense of self at the personal and social level indicates a new identity among contemporary women, an identity which also affects women scholars and has produced a new feminist scholarship in different areas of the humanities, including religious studies.

Feminist thought has a negative and positive aspect. Negatively, it uncovers the dualistic and gender-exclusive assumptions of traditional knowledge and social practice whilst its positive task consists in developing more integral, holistic ways of thinking and living by linking together personal, social, political and spiritual dimensions of human life and envisaging alternative forms of society and culture.

The feminist critical perspective might be summarized as essentially a critique of patriarchy, androcentrism and sexism, terms which are often used interchangeably in feminist literature, although each has a different history and different connotations. Patriarchy, the rule of the fathers, is a theory about both the history and nature of society. Initially related to social, economic, religious and political power structures, it is now seen to be embedded in attitudes, values, language and thought as well as internalized in the character structures of both sexes. Androcentrism, a term first coined by the American sociologist Lester F Ward in 1903, indicates a perspective in which the male is primary and the female secondary. The term is widely used today to indicate any position or view where the male is taken as the norm, representing the generic view of all that is human without explicitly taking into account the experience and perspective of women.

As Rita Gross has written in her discussion of androcentrism in the methodology of the history of religions: 'The unconscious androcentric presuppositions undergirding almost all work done to date in the history of religions cause serious deficiencies, especially at the primary level of data-perception and gathering, and this deficiency in turn generates serious deficiencies at the level of model-building and theorizing whenever any hint of sexuality or sexual imagery is present in the data being analyzed' (1977, 7).

Sexism has been defined as an exclusive ordering of life by way of gender. Gender is understood as a socially and culturally constructed identity and role whereas biological sex is given. Sexist language, attitudes or behaviour can be exclusive of either sex but the occurrence of sexism is recognised as currently applying mainly to the situation of women. In works on religious studies, as in books on religious education, one might point more to a 'sexism by omission' (Trevett 1983) than to explicitly anti-feminist attitudes. 'Sexism by omission' is also an appropriate characterization for criticizing the structure of the Sydney Congress sections, but, in recognition of this omission, it is perhaps a small compensation that the two papers this morning have been grouped under the overall theme of 'Sexism, Identity and the Study of Religion'.

The feminist perspective addresses new questions to the different religious traditions and thereby discovers new data which were overlooked, lost or suppressed in the past. At the most basic level, one can ask how far women's experience has been taken into account at all in the articulations and theological reflections of the world's religions. What do the sacred scriptures, the theological and spiritual writings teach about women? Or how far do the different religions draw on feminine images and symbols in speaking about the fullness of reality and transcendence, about the nature and experience of the spirit? To what extent do women take part in ritual and religious practices, choose to follow the religious life or hold positions of authority in particular religions? Most important is women's own religious experience. Why has it been so rarely expressed in official theological literature whereas it has contributed so much to mystical and spiritual writings? With regard to the study of the past it has been said that the 'single greatest barrier to scholarship on the topic of women's lives and experiences, apart from androcentric consciousness, is that it is much more difficult to find the data in historical than in contemporary situations because fieldwork is more likely than texts to contain the potential information' (Gross 1983, 588 f).

It is particularly important to study women's religious experience in the present, and this for several reasons. What we know about the religious experiences of women in the past often concerns exceptional women who diverged from traditional female roles and thereby attracted the attention of their contemporaries. Yet we need to know much more about the everyday religious experiences of ordinary women (Holden 1983). Another area where little work has been done is the participation and place of women in new religious movements today. Yet another area of more than theoretical interest is the contribution of feminism to the transformation of contemporary religious consciousness (King 1983, 1986) and to the reinterpretation of traditional religious practices (1984b) which under the influence of a new feminist self-understanding have now become accessible to women whilst they were formerly forbidden to them. At the level of religious practice, the greatest challenge arises from the question of how far traditional religious beliefs and practices can still speak to women with a changed consciousness today and remain credible. Feminists have sometimes described the liberating group experience of consciousness raising and the newly found identity of sisterhood as a conversion experience of an almost religious nature. From the perspective of studying religion in contemporary society the emergence of a distinct spirituality and new religious cults among women is another important phenomenon worth investigating.

II

The task of feminism in religious studies according to Rosemary Radford Ruether is defined by the historical nature of female exclusion and male ideological bias in the tradition. 'The first task of feminist critique takes the form of documenting the fact of this male ideological bias itself and tracing its sociological roots'. 'The second agenda of feminist studies in religion aims at the discovery of an alternative history and tradition that supports the inclusion and personhood of women' (1981, 391). This provides not merely an additional, interesting agenda for religious studies with a separate focus on women, a mere addendum to our existing knowledge of religion whereby the past gap about the image, role and experience of women in religion is now being filled, but at its most radical it has the potential to induce a paradigm shift in the study of religion by creating a new orientation for all previous perspectives and theories, a radical change in consciousness affecting the gathering, description and comprehension of all data. This necessary paradigm shift was strongly expressed in Rita Gross' paper (1983) 'Women's Studies in Religion: The State of the Art, 1980' presented at the Winnipeg Congress. But so far, little institutional and organizational recognition has been given to the transformative power of the feminist perspective in religious studies. International surveys of the study of religion as a whole, such as Waardenburg's *Classical Approaches to the Study of Religion* (1973) or Whaling's *Contemporary Approaches to the Study of Religion* (1984), or major publications on methodology and hermeneutics, include little explicit reference to women as either subjects or objects of study in the history of religions field. It is not only the absence of women as either authors or objects of study, but even more the fact that their perspective and experience have not entered into the theoretical considerations pursued in recent methodological works which must be considered a contributory cause for the continuing crisis of identity among female scholars of religion. I shall list some past and present examples to illustrate the inherent androcentrism of the history of religions as a field of studies.

Looking at the historiography of our field from a contemporary feminist perspective, one discovers that the early women pioneers in the comparative study of religion are generally overlooked by historians. Women such as Hannah Adams (1755-1831), in L H Jordan's account of *Comparative Religion* (1905), still listed among the pioneers who helped to make the nineteenth century advance of the discipline possible, or Lydia Mary Child with her survey of oriental religions, or Carolyn H Dall, one of the first American writers on Shinto, or Annie E Cheney, working on Mahayana Buddhism, are virtually unknown today (Jackson 1981).

Similarly, history books frequently refer to the World Parliament of Religions, Chicago 1893, but there is never any mention of the contribution of 21 official women lecturers, including one Indian woman, whose addresses are part of the published proceedings (Burrows 1893). At the height of the first wave of feminism there were many women participants at Chicago, parallel women's congresses and meetings were held, women were part of the organizing committee and women reported on the Parliament in the press. There were not only women speakers such as Annie Besant or Mary Baker Eddy, the founder of Christian Science, but seven ordained women from different churches as well as some women scholars gave major lectures. Eliza R Sutherland from Ann Arbor lectured on 'The Importance of a Serious Study of all Religions' and Alice C Fletcher from Harvard spoke on 'The Religion of the North American Indians'. As Mrs Henrotin, the woman vice-president of the Congress, said in her address: 'That the experiment of an equal presentation of men and women in a Parliament of Religions has not been a failure, I think can be proved by the part taken by the women who have had the honour to be called to participate in this great gathering' (Burrows, 63). But posterity has not given these women the credit and acknowledgement they deserve. This is true of women scholars in the history of religions generally. If one thinks of the contribution of Mrs Rhys Davids to the study of Buddhism, of Mrs Sinclair Stevenson to the study of Hinduism and Jainism, or of Jane Harrison to the study of Greek Religion — to name but a few

— one must ask why it is that in such an important reference work as Waardenburg's *Classical Approaches to the Study of Religion* and other works on the history of the discipline not a single woman scholar is listed. It is not that women scholars did not exist — they existed in much smaller numbers for reasons we cannot go into here — but through lack of recognition in the annals of the discipline even the few are assigned to oblivion. The only entry on 'woman' in Waardenburg's index, for example, is to 'woman, religious capacities' referring to an extract from Bachofen's *Myth, Religion and Mother Right.*

Can one not say about women scholars in the history of religions what an art historian has written about the lack of recognition of women artists in official art histories:

> The most signal omission of feminist art history to date is our failure to analyse *why* modern art history ignores the existence of women artists, why it has become silent about them, why it has consistently dismissed as insignificant those it did not acknowledge. To confront these questions enables us to identify the unacknowledged ideology which informs the practice of this discipline and the values which decide its classification and interpretation of all art. (Parker and Pollock 1981, 49).

The contribution of women scholars is largely ignored in the official accounts of the history of the discipline because of the androcentric presuppositions with which data are selected as historically significant. This androcentric perspective becomes even more apparent where historians of religion write about women as objects of study in an externalised and objectifying manner without taking women's own subjectivity and personhood into account. A good example of this kind of writing is Heiler's substantial compendium *Die Frau in den Religionen der Menschheit* (1977), a veritable 'Gang durch die Geschichte der Stellung der Frau in den Religionen' (188), in positions assigned to her by others without even a hint of questioning this perspective and its underlying assumptions.

Such objectifying description has been called 'the most devastating component of the androcentric outlook'. When women *per se* are mentioned, as they sometimes must be in accounts of religion

> androcentric thinking deals with them only as an object exterior to mankind, needing to be explained and fitted in somewhere, having the same epistemological and ontological status as trees, unicorns, deities, and other objects that must be discussed to make experience intelligible. Therefore, in most accounts of religion, males are presented as religious subjects, as namers of reality, while females are presented only in relation to the males being studied, only as objects being named by the males being studied ... (Gross 1983, 583 f.)

It is not a question of simply adding a paragraph or chapter on women to history of religions books where there was none before. The investigation of the religious experience and lives of women, of cultural and religious attitudes towards women and of female imagery and symbolism, as currently undertaken by many women scholars, represents not only a further addition to the growth of knowledge in a cumulative sense, but it explicitly calls into question previous perspectives and methodologies.

At an analytic level this applies especially to a critique of the language and categories of thought used in the description and interpretation of religious data. Language is the key indicator of the androcentric thinking of male historians of religion and remains a source of profound alienation for women. Even today scholars write without a critical self-reflective attitude towards their use of exclusive language when dealing with the 'religious history of *man*' or describing religious studies as dealing 'with *man* in *his* religious dimension' or referring to 'the history and nature of *man's* religiousness' or *'man's* transcendence' (Whaling 1984b, 5, 25, 26). The subject matter of the study of religion is described as 'basically *man* rather than nature'; the field of religion includes 'the worldviews of *men* and a transcendent referent' (Whaling 1984a, 386, 389). A new interpretative theory is described as having the advantage of containing 'no explanation of why *man* is religious' (Crosby 1981, 291; all emphases are mine). These few examples could be multiplied at length. The generic use of 'man' in English, as in some other languages, often masks the unexamined assumption that the human male is simply taken as the generically human but often *excludes* women as a specific category.

At one level, language is the most obvious area to criticize, and some may consider it the most superficial, but given our contemporary level of differentiated consciousness about the place of gender in society, history and culture, it is simply no longer acceptable to write in a naive and unreflective manner. Feminists have worked a great deal on the analysis of language, and contemporary writers in religious studies ought to take note of the following comment:

> While language is the means by which we speak ourselves and communicate to others, on a deeper level it also controls what can be said or even thought, and by whom. It is therefore in the field of language that women's struggle must also take place: in the way women try to speak themselves and are spoken of, in the ways women represent themselves and are represented by culture. (Parker and Pollock, 114f.)

So many studies remain trapped in gender-exclusive language. This is particularly regrettable when the subject under discussion is 'the mystic', always referred to as 'he' by Horne (1983) even though women have made outstanding contributions to the history of mysticism and some of them are used as examples in the same book. Yet in his introduction the author says: 'One of the interesting characteristics of the mystic, which makes *him* especially relevant for a philosophic study of this subject, is that in spite of *his* usually being religious *he* is not always moral. I shall therefore explain *him* in both *his* modes ...' (X; my emphases).

Other authors are more perceptive and use more inclusive language by referring to 'person' rather than 'man' or speak of the student of religion as 'he or she' (Cahill 1985) or even 's/he' (Wiebe 1984), which becomes quite unpronounceable. In any case, changing vocabulary is relatively simple, but it may not necessarily imply a complete change of thinking. Several women authors have stressed that the major conceptual tools used in the study of religion require critical analysis and that we need to develop a truly comprehensive anthropology of *homo religiosus*. On closer analysis, previous scholarly works on religious anthropology often turn out to be mainly concerned not with *homo* but with *vir religiosus* with no space at all for the voices and experiences of women. One author naively refers to 'the predominantly male practitioners of religion' (Brenneman *et. al.,* 1982, 133) when in fact he means the official religious specialists, authorities and functionaries. Who are the people practising religion? If one understands practitioners as participants rather than specialists, it is well known that in many religions women adhere to religious beliefs and practices to a higher degree than men and represent a larger percentage of participants in religion. This fact has not been considered as a datum of significance in itself until very recently.

Another important aspect open to the criticism of exclusiveness is the whole area of the analysis of conceptualisations of the Divine, of the idea of the holy and the focus of the transcendent in the study of religions. Are the interpretative categories which have been developed so far sufficiently wide-ranging and comprehensive to take full account of the perspective of women? Similarly, the whole field of the study of religious experience on which much has been published in recent years, seems to have been rarely examined from a perspective giving adequate attention to sexual differentiation.

<h2 style="text-align:center">III</h2>

One could go on citing examples of the androcentric patterns of thought prevalent in the theory and praxis of the history of religions and thus highlight further the selectivity operative in the construction of our discipline as knowledge. One must always ask how far a particular perspective is inherent in the data being studied, or how far it is part of the outlook of the scholar studying the data. It is my contention that the current methodological debate still reflects a predominantly androcentric bias or sexism by exclusion and omission which is detrimental to the identity of the history of religions in the widest sense as a field of studies, and which adversely affects the personal identity of women scholars within it.

The introduction of the feminist critical perspective has methodological and practical implications (for the organization of the IAHR for example). At the practical level it is perhaps true to say that the change in consciousness arising out of feminism has affected the field of religious studies so far less than other disciplines. This is not only evident from the existing literature but also from the thematic orientations of the present IAHR Congress. Another example may be quoted from the German branch of the IAHR, the Deutsche Vereinigung für Religionsgeschichte. One member suggested as next year's conference theme 'Religion der Frauen, feministische Theorien der Gegenwart in der Religionswissenschaft' (DVRG 1985, 14), a theme which did not find general acceptance. As the feminist orientation and consciousness is, comparatively speaking, so little developed in our field, it is no wonder that in next year's programme on 'Feminism and the Humanities', developed by the Humanities Research Centre of the Australian National University, religious studies, as far as one can see at present, has not found a place in the three interdisciplinary conferences which have been planned (entitled 'Feminist Criticism and Cultural Production'; 'Feminism and the Humanities: Enrichment, Expansion or Challenge?'; 'Feminist Enquiry as a Transdisciplinary Enterprise', HRC 1985, 7f). Is this not a sufficient reason for questioning the identity of our field and its place within the world of scholarship and knowledge? Is it not imperative to examine whether our regulative ideals have become fossilized and are static remains from the past rather than dynamic and alive to the issues of the present?

At present, the crisis of religious studies and the crisis of method (Wiebe 1984) are often debated. If new directions in theory and methodology can contribute to a transformation of our existing discipline, the breaking of boundaries and the searching for new ground must also include a concern for the feminist critical perspective. I would like to make two concluding observations why this is important.

First, beyond all specific criticisms regarding the exclusiveness and dualism of language and thought, of androcentrism and sexism, the feminist perspective at its most comprehensive undertakes what has been termed a critique of the masculinity of our culture. It radically calls into question certain traditions of an exclusively objective, analytical and rational analysis which cannot reveal the full experience of being female, male, or simply human. This critical orientation meets other criticisms made elsewhere, in the debates about hermeneutics for example, or in the debates about paradigm shifts in science. So far the study of religion has been dominated by a heavily intellectualist and even scientistic approach with an emphasis on the cerebral production of ideas, concepts, doctrines, models and theories. The role of imagination and feeling, of symbol, story and image, are only slowly being recognized but have not been methodologically fully integrated into a general theory of the study of religion. The ongoing debates about the role of empathy, of the category of meaning, about the place of insiders and outsiders (Ross Reat 1983) are an indication of this.

Secondly, the emergence of the feminist perspective represents a new stage in the history of consciousness which will have profound effects on contemporary and future religious thought and practice. It acts as a catalyst and agent of transformation in human self-understanding. Throughout most of human history sexual differentiation was taken for granted without being critically reflected upon whilst now we have reached a stage of critical reflection which is often divisive through highlighting differences and introducing separatism. However, what is being sought is an integral meaning of human sexual differentiation for both female and male identity. One can correlate this search for a wider, more integral and holistic framework with current changes in religious consciousness and a critique of the dualistic thinking of the historical religions, with the renewed interest in the unitary forms of archaic religious thought and the search for a more integral system of symbols which can be witnessed in many areas of contemporary culture.

These ideas are all open to criticism and discussion. They have been presented in the belief that when discussing issues of religion and identity and developing further theories in our field of studies, we must not only be attentive to the religions of the past but be equally aware of the dynamic of religious life and thought in the present. If past knowledge shapes present knowledge, then the development of new knowledge for the future — whether in the gathering of data or their theoretical elucidation — must of necessity imply a critique of the knowledge accumulated in both past and present.

At present the feminist perspective is not yet part of the common horizon of our field. I have argued that the development of a truly inclusive framework for the study of religion, or more differentiated conceptual tools as well as of different perspectives of analysis and synthesis requires that full space is given to the voices and perspectives of women. If 'the accurate description and analysis of worldviews' is a basic task of the study of religion (Vernoff 111), then the worldviews of women must become an integral part of the dominant theorizing in religious studies. It is only when a critical shifting of the foundations of our discipline has occurred that its identity as a field of studies can be more clearly focussed and that, in turn, the identity of its practitioners, both female and male, can be more fully developed and recognized.

WORKS CONSULTED

Barrows, John Henry (ed) 1893 *The World's Parliament of Religions.* An Illustrated and Popular Story of the World's First Parliament of Religions held in Chicago in Connection with the Columbian Exposition of 1893. 2 vols, Chicago: The Parliament Publishing Company.

Brenneman, W. L., Yarian, S. O. & Olson, A. M. 1982 *The Seeing Eye. Hermeneutical Phenomenology in the Study of Religion.* University Park & London: The Pennsylvania State University Press.

Cahill, Joseph P. 1985 'Interpreting Religions', *Religious Studies and Theology* 5/1, pp 39-43.

Christ, Carol P. & Plaskow, Judith (eds) 1979 *Womanspirit Rising. A Feminist Reader in Religion.* New York: Harper & Row.

Crosby, Donald A. 1981 *Interpretive Theories of Religion.* The Hague/Paris/New York: Mouton.

DRVG 1985 *17 Mitteilungsblatt der Deutschen Vereinigung für Religionsgeschichte Tübingen.*

Gross, Rita 1974 'Methodological Remarks on the Study of Women in Religion: Review, Criticism and Redefinition' in J Plaskow & J A Romero (eds) *Women and Religion.* American Academy of Religion, distributed by Scholars Press, Missoula, Montana, pp 153-165.

1977 'Androcentrism and Androgyny in the Methodology of History of Religions' in R.M. Gross (ed), *Beyond Androcentrism. New Essays on Women and Religion.* American Academy of Religion, distributed by Scholars Press, Missoula, Montana, pp 7-19.

1983 'Women's Studies in Religion: The State of the Art 1980' in P Slater & D Wiebe (eds), *Traditions in Contact and Change. Selected Proceedings of the XIVth Congress of the International Association for the History of Religions.* Waterloo, Ontario: Wilfried Laurier University Press, pp 579-591.

Heiler, Friedrich 1977 *Die Frau in den Religionen der Menschheit.* Berlin/New York: Walter de Gruyter.

Holden, Pat (ed) 1983 *Women's Religious Experience.* Cross-Cultural Perspectives. London & Canberra: Croom Helm. Totowa, New Jersey: Barnes & Noble Books.

Honko, L. (ed) 1979 *Science of Religion.* Studies in Methodology. Proceedings of the Study Conference of the IAHR, held in Turku, Finland, 27-31 August 1973. The Hague: Mouton.

Horne, James R. 1983 *The Moral Mystic.* Waterloo, Ontario, Wilfried Laurier University Press.

HRC 1985 *Bulletin* no 40, June 1985. Humanities Research Centre, The Australian National University, Canberra.

Jackson, Carl T. 1981 *The Oriental Religions and American Thought.* Westport, Connecticut/London: Greenwood Press.

Keohane, Nannerl O., Rosaldo, Michelle A. & Gelpi, Barbara C. (eds) 1982 *Feminist Theory: A Critique of Ideology.* Brighton: Harvester Press.

King, Ursula 1983 'Der Beitrag der feministischen Bewegung zur Veränderung des religiösen Bewusstseins' in K Walf (ed), *Stille Fluchten. Zur Veränderung des religiösen Bewusstseins.* München: Kosel, pp 38-61.

1984a 'Historical and Phenomenological Approaches to the Study of Religion: Some major developments and issues under debate since 1950' in F Whaling (ed) *Contemporary Approaches to the Study of Religion* Vol I: The Humanities. Berlin/New York/Amsterdam; Mouton, pp 29-163.

1984b 'The Effects of Social Change on Religious Self-Understanding: Women Ascetics in Modern Hinduism' in K Ballhatchet and D Taylor (eds), *Changing South Asia: Religion and Society.* Hong Kong; Asian Research Service, pp 69-83.

1986 'Goddesses, Witches, Androgyny and Beyond? Feminism and the Transformation of Religious Consciousness', in U King (ed) *Women in World Religions Past and Present.* New York: Paragon House (in press).

Parker, Rozsika & Pollock, Griselda 1981 *Old Mistresses. Women, Art and Ideology.* London & Henley: Routledge & Kegan Paul.

Pye, Michael & McKenzie, Peter (eds) 1980 *History of Religions. Proceedings of the Thirteenth International Congress of the International Association for the History of Religions* (Lancaster 15-22 August 1975). Leicester, England: Leicester Studies in Religion II.

Reat, Noble Ross 1983 'Insiders and Outsiders in the Study of Religious Traditions', *Journal of the American Academy of Religion* L1/3, pp 459-476.

Ruether, Rosemary Radford 1981 'The Feminist Critique in Religious Studies', *Soundings* 64, pp 388-402.

Schmid, Georg 1979 *Principles of Integral Science of Religion.* The Hague/Paris/New York: Mouton.

Slater, Peter & Wiebe, Donald (eds) 1983 *Traditions in Contact and Change. Selected Proceedings of the XIVth Congress of the International Association for the History of Religions.* Waterloo, Ontario: Wilfrid Laurier University Press.

Trevett, Christine 1983 '"The lady vanishes": sexism by omission in religious education', *British Journal of Religious Education,* Spring number, pp 81-83.

Vernoff, Charles Elliott 1983 'Naming the Game: A Question of the Field', *The Council on the Study of Religion Bulletin* 14/4, pp 109-114.

Waardenburg, Jacques 1973 *Classical Approaches to the Study of Religion.* Vol I. Introduction and Anthology. The Hague/Paris/New York: Mouton.

1983 *Reflections on the Study of Religion.* The Hague/Paris/New York: Mouton.

Whaling, Frank (ed) 1984a *Contemporary Approaches to the Study of Religion.* Vol I: The Humanities. Berlin/New York/Amsterdam: Mouton.

1984b *The World's Religious Traditions.* Current Perspectives in Religious Studies. Edinburgh: T & T Clark.

Wiebe, Donald 1983 'Theory in the Study of Religion', *Religion* 13, pp 283-309.

1984 'The failure of nerve in the academic study of religion', *Studies in Religion/Sciences Religieuses* 13/4, pp 401-422.

Related works by the author of this paper:

"Historical and phenomenological approaches to the study of religion. Some major developments and issues under debate since 1950" in F. Whaling, ed., *Contemporary Approaches to the Study of Religion,* Vol. 1. Berlin/New York/Amsterdam: Mouton, 1984. pp. 29-163.

Voices of Protest — Voices of Promise: Exploring Spirituality for a New Age. The Hibbert Lecture. London: The Hibbert Trust, 1984.

THE REAL ZOROASTRIAN DILEMMA[1]

Alan Williams

University of Manchester[2]

If the sheer antiquity of a religion can impart a sense of identity to a community in spite of the many disruptive conditions of modern urban life, then Zoroastrians — in India, Iran and around the world — may take pride in that they can claim to belong to a tradition founded upon a revelation older than that of any other living faith, stretching back to Zoroaster in the 2nd millennium B.C. Iran, which is still seen as the 'homeland' of the tradition, has long been at the junction of imperial, cultural and mercantile exchanges. In the religious domain also one would expect syncretization and the hybrid to be the norm, continuous tradition to be impossible. The traumas of repeated invasions and conquests which Greeks, Arabs, Mongols and, latterly, Europeans imposed on the Iranian people would surely have destroyed any continuous tradition from ancient Iran, just as they decimated texts, temples and populations, one might have thought. However, there is ample evidence to show that Zoroastrian doctrines, rituals, observances, ethics and eschatology are genuinely ancient and derive from the prophet Zoroaster himself and his world.[2]

A historical continuity can thus be traced extending back over three thousand years; yet this fact may remain merely theoretical if the great majority of modern Zoroastrians no longer experience that continuity and if they do not wish to maintain it. The Zoroastrian identity, in India particularly, is still very distinctive, for the Parsis are, as Paul Axelrod found, an exclusive community who have a strong self-image, holding, as they do, a position outside the caste system: "On the one hand, they see themselves as somehow nobler than other Indians; on the other, they recognize that their minority status requires a good deal of tolerance, respect, and even diplomacy"(162).

Although Zoroastrians are now one of the world's smallest religious communities, with only ca. 130,000 members in all, their interpretations of the religion vary enormously. Since the last century, many Zoroastrians have sought to find an "original" Zoroastrianism which they can translate into modern terms to answer contemporary needs — an endeavour in which they have often felt free to purge the religion, so to speak, of what they see as useless archaism and medieval accretion. Western scholarly interest in translating all available texts has had the effect of publicising traditional teachings which have their place in the theological context but which appear to create difficulties for the reformist, who would have a rational, practical religion for now and the future.

One such difficulty is the dualism of Zoroastrian theology. This is not a controversial matter of the magnitude of the major issue on which the worldwide Zoroastrian community is now divided, namely, conversion (whether or not to allow non-Zoroastrians formally to enter the faith and community). For two principal reasons, however, this latter issue has not been taken as the subject of this paper, although superficially it might seem to be more relevant to the Congress theme of "Religion and Identity". First, the conversion issue is very complex and is not compatible with a brief paper, lacking as we do a full historical/sociological study of the issue. Second, the question of dualism is possibly more representative of the uncertainty manifested in the traditionalist-reformist split in the community: it discloses the factors which have caused the contemporary anxiety and may be seen as a litmus test of acceptance or rejection of the traditional teachings of Zoroastrianism and the boundaries of Zoroastrian identity.

The most ancient source for the religion is the prophet Zoroaster's own words recorded in the *Gāthās*, composed in the Gāthic Avestan language, dated late second millennium B.C. Although other, later texts are theologically more explicit, because they were written to be doctrinally definitive, it is to the sublime, yet often cryptic, verses of the *Gāthās* that the religious practitioner and enquiring scholar turn to establish the first principles of Zoroastrianism. As prophetic revelation, the *Gāthās* do not disappoint, for they are at once resounding, numinous utterances, and also veiled, symbolic, even obscure. Zoroaster's teaching is perfectly clear in depicting his vision of God, Ahura Mazdā, and his message is couched in dialogue with, and praise and exhortation of, the one, good God. Zoroastrianism has long been regarded by "outsiders" as "dualistic",[3] and so enquirers have tried to establish finally from the *Gāthās* alone whether Zoroaster taught that there are two first principles in the universe or just one. Opinion among modern Zoroastrians is divided, with the ranks of reformists and traditionalists in confusion, and today the majority are, to a greater or lesser extent, embarrassed by the description "dualist" and shun it.[4]

It is necessary to venture into the history of Iranian religious ideas to understand what has happened to the doctrine in the modern period. We may identify three reasons for the rejection of traditional doctrine in sections of the modern community: (1) the increase of education among the laity, and their business success in urban Bombay which gave them (a) an independence from the traditional community identity and (b) access to religious doctrine now in the form of printed texts, which access formerly had been restricted to priests (they had been guardians of an oral tradition which was regarded as superior to written texts); (2) 19th century Christian missionary activity which forced Parsis into a defensive position so that they were constrained to explain and justify their faith in the terms used by the agressor, i.e., a "biblical" style of exegesis in which it is expected that doctrines can be established as metaphysical propositions derived from the sacred text. The sacred text is viewed as the "word of God", therefore self-existent and free from the contextuality of history and the religious tradition of devotion, observance and learning which has enshrined and transmitted the "sacred word"; and (3) the existence of a precedent for the homogenization of Zoroastrian dualism into a vague monotheism in the Zurvanite heresy. This had originated in Achaemenian times (early 4th century B.C.) as a result of influence from Near Eastern religions which tended towards monism and fatalism.[5] Most significantly the development of this heresy "can be seen as being ... linked to an Iranian response to the intellectually exciting scientific advances made by Babylonian astronomers in the fifth century B.C." (Boyce 1982:241).

In relation to (1)(a) above it may be suggested that the structure of Zoroastrian society had changed very radically in the 19th century and religious changes may be seen as merely symptomatic of those structural changes. It is worthwhile pausing to reflect on Max Weber's brief comments on the nature of Zoroastrian religion which he saw as exceptional in devolving on the ideal of the peasant:

> Only rarely does the peasantry serve as the carrier of any other sort of religion than their original magic. Yet the prophecy of Zoroaster apparently appealed to the (relative) rationalism of peasants who, having learned to work in an orderly fashion and to raise cattle, were struggling against the orgiastic religion of the false prophets, which entailed the torture of animals ... In the religion of the Parsees, only the cultivated soil was regarded as pure from the magical point of view, and therefore only agriculture was absolutely pleasing

to God. Consequently, even after the pattern of the religion established by the original prophecy had undergone considerable transformations as a result of its adaptations to the needs of everyday life, it retained a distinctive agrarian pattern, and consequently a characteristically anti-urban tendency in its doctrines of social ethics. (1978:470)

Though such an ideal may be true for a bygone age and may be the root of the distinctive work ethic of Zoroastrianism which has been compared with Weber's Protestant variety,[6] Weber does not acknowledge the effects urbanization and westernization have had upon the Zoroastrian community in the last century. He does, however, explain that, generally, in contrast to the religious propensities of peasantry and nobility, there is, with the rise of a petty bourgoisie and artisan class, a definite tendency towards congregational religion, and an increase in the diversity of religious attitudes. The new social identity gives rise to a new religious perspective: "In the Occident particularly, the congregational type of religion has been intimately connected with the urban middle classes of both the upper and lower levels. This was a natural consequence of the relative recession in the importance of blood groupings, particularly of the clan, within the occidental city. The urban dweller finds a substitute for blood groupings in both occupational organizations, which in the Occident as everywhere had a cultic significance, although no longer associated with taboos, and in freely created religious associations" (1978:482). Such a shift from agrarian based traditionalist identity to a congregational religious propensity and diversification in the urban environment is clearly an oversimplification of the complex reality, and it merely remains frustrating to us that Weber gave no fuller consideration to Parsi society. In Axelrod's essay on Parsi self-image and the rivalry between priestly and lay identities, the author concludes: "If the Parsis 'internal' charter for their distinctiveness as a community is provided by their religion, it is marked 'externally' primarily by social and economic considerations" (164). These latter are as complex as those of any modern community.

In the remainder of this paper the two other reasons given above will be examined in relation to the history and nature of the traditional identity. The combined effect of Christian missionary influence and Western scholarly emphasis on text and *urtext* in the 19th century brought about an attempt to fathom the *Gāthās* as metaphysics, without reference to the general religious context of Zoroaster's revelation, his *Weltan-schauung*, and the long tradition which is descended from him. As long ago as 1913, J.H. Moulton pointed out: "There is nothing to prove that Zarathushtra wasted on metaphysics time that he needed for practical teaching" (133). Only direct quotation of a key passage in the *Gāthās* (*Yasna* 30.3-6), will serve to present the foundations of thought which are the subject of the rest of this discussion. Here, in archaic, poetic language, which is evocative rather than speculative in purpose, the prophet warns man of the all-important choice and responsibility:

3. Yes, there are two fundamental spirits, twins which are renowned to be in conflict. In thought and in word, in action, they are two: the good and the bad. And between these two, the beneficent have correctly chosen, not the maleficent.

4. Furthermore, when these two spirits first came together, they created life and death, and how, at the end, the worse existence shall be for the deceitful but the best thinking for the truthful person.

5. Of these two spirits, the deceitful one chose to bring to realization the worst things. (But) the very virtuous spirit, who is clothed in the hardest stones, chose the truth; and (so shall those) who shall satisfy the Wise Lord continuously with true actions.

6. The gods did not at all choose correctly between these two, since the deceptive one approached them as they were deliberating. Since they chose the worst thought, they then rushed into fury with which they have afflicted the world and mankind (translated S. Insler:33).[7]

These are the two spirits, the very virtuous spirit and the deceitful spirit, who are personifications of Ahurā Mazda (Pahlavi Ohrmazd), "the Lord of Wisdom", and Angra Mainyu (Pahlavi Ahreman) "the Hostile Spirit". In the fully developed tradition of exegesis and translation (zand) of Avestan and Pahlavi scriptures the structure of religious dualism is drawn out in doctrine, ethics, ritual and mythology in quite unambiguous terms. This dualistic structure has its origins, in general designs and in many details, in the Avesta and even the Gāthās. In brief, the picture of the world as given in the Pahlavi books is as follows: there is one good God, Ohrmazd, who is creator of all the good creation, comprising the blessed immortals (amahraspands) and other beings worthy of worship (yazads), spirits of the blessed (frawahrs) and the seven physical creations (sky, earth, water, plants, beneficent animals, mankind, fire). This created world has been invaded by a hostile, evil spirit, Ahreman, whose will is to destroy everything. He has no physical existence of his own but, with his demonic miscreations, he insinuates himself, parasitically, into the good world, bringing suffering, wrongdoing, injustice and death. Ohrmazd has been always aware of his presence from eternity, and knows that the ultimate banishment of Ahreman can only be effected if he is engaged in battle in this world, in limited time. Man has chosen to help Ohrmazd in this struggle. Zoroaster showed man how to carry out his mission through truth, goodness, worship and praise of Ohrmazd.

Original to the prophet's message is the doctrine of heaven and hell, emphasising man's responsibility for his own personal, as well as societal and cosmic, well-being. Already in the Gāthās we see a profound eschatological vision — one which was to be adopted by the Western faiths, particularly Christianity and Islam. Zoroaster's teaching hinges on the act of choosing, exemplified in the Gāthic passage above, and indeed, although his hymns address and invoke God, his appeal is to man to act in accordance with the law of divine truth and cosmic order (Av. aša, Ved. rta), to smite the forces of untruth (Av. drug-). Zoroaster's passionate concern is with the realization of his cosmic, social and personal responsibility to uphold aša. S. Insler has summed up the distinctiveness of the message as "the extraordinary contribution of Zarathustra in the profound realization that man can both serve and honor God more meaningfully in the enactment of the lordly principles of truth and good thinking among his fellow men than in the awesome reverence founded upon fear and dread" (22). This does not mean that religious commitment and devotion are lacking but that in Zoroastrianism these things are motivated by mankind's recognition of the beauty of God's order and truth.

Here we come to an important point that will deliver this paper from merely theological curiosities. The Zoroastrian tradition has been a flowering and development of an original prophetic message in which, by the ascendancy of a priestly class (appropriately, since Zoroaster was himself a priest), the primary modes of expression and perpetuation of religious identity have been theological and liturgical. The originally ethical, dynamic and non-speculative teachings of the prophet were codified and propagated in both priestly forms (doctrine, ritual, purity laws) and popular forms (devotional practice, mythology, legend). To some the assertion that the tradition has been faithful to the prophet's message seems to be a distortion of truth (since the Pahlavi books abound in genres of writing which are lacking in the Gāthās, e.g. philosophy, scholasticism, science, mythology etc.). In fact it is no different from any other religion where tradition has developed and expanded the original prophetic message.

Yet, in a profound respect, this tradition is faithful to Zoroaster's fundamental vision that the world is held in a state of opposition and conflict: life is a struggle because existence is opposed by non-existence, order by chaos, creation by destruction. Only when the perspective of opposition or, as we shall call it, *dialectic*, is established in mind, can the principle of order be distinguished from the chaos which has invaded that order. This dialectical structure is seen to be present throughout the universe, and originates from the ultimate opposition of irreconcilable principles. As the *Gāthās* put it "Yes, I shall speak of the two fundamental spirits of existence, of which the virtuous one would have thus spoken to the evil one: 'Neither our thoughts nor teachings nor intentions, neither our preferences nor words, neither our actions nor conceptions nor our souls are in accord'".[8] Here Zoroaster emphasises that the opposition of good and evil (and thus the act of choosing) is one which obtains at the highest level of reality (i.e. divine). The dialectical structure of this world is a result of the evil spirit having succeeded in corrupting the perfect creation of God. Man, however, is still capable of actively participating in the divine struggle against evil, the maintenance of life and restoration of perfection to the physical world. So far from being caught in the sense of determinism or existential despair inculcated by the dialectics of some modern philosophy, Zoroastrianism is fully optimistic as it aspires to an eventual rehabilitation of the universe through the triumph of wisdom, order and goodness over chaos, destruction and injustice.

In modern times a large number of Zoroastrians believe that the "dualism", as they understand it from what they know of the tradition, is a blatant misrepresentation of the Avestan texts and is a result of malevolent Greeks', Romans', Arabs', and, especially, scholastic Middle Persian priestly theologians' tampering with Scripture. Modern alternative reinterpretations of Zoroastrianism are patently modelled upon Christian, Vedāntic and other theological, even occultist, understandings.[9] It will be suggested here that the need which has been felt for such alternative representations of the religion is symptomatic of a crisis in the religious identity, in fact, another dilemma for the Zoroastrians.

First, to examine the dialectical structure of the traditional identity of Zoroastrianism we turn to an anonymous text from early 10th century A.D. Iran. Now called *The Pahlavi Rivāyat Accompanying the Dādestān ī Dēnīg*,[10] the text is largely a compilation, by a priest, of earlier traditional material, for the purposes of reassuring and guiding a community who were then under direct physical and psychological threat from the majority religion, Islam. The text has been regarded as an anthology, and thus as having no central unity, being a miscellany of sixty-five chapters of very unequal length and varied material. However, although it does not reveal the thought of *one* Zoroastrian mind, it may, in its highly traditional content and structure, indeed disclose certain distinctive features of *the* Zoroastrian mind, i.e. of the traditional identity. *The Pahlavi Rivāyat* is a title dubbed on by comparison with later Zoroastrian texts, in New Persian, called *rivāyats* 'communiqués', which were written by Iranian priests to their Indian co-religionists from the 15th century onwards.[11] These later *rivāyats* range over a wide area of life, for the practical ritual observances in respect of maintaining orthodoxy and ritual purity extended very widely. It is a mistake to regard the earlier *Pahlavi Rivāyat* as similar to those texts, however, as the compiler, working in 10th century Muslim Iran was addressing a community who, unlike the later, exiled, Parsi Zoroastrians living in religious freedom in India, were besieged in their own land by the dominant religion. In the earlier text the large number of problems, some perennial, some particular to the time, are characterised as stemming from the fact of worldly existence (Pahl. *gūmezišn*, lit. "mixture") in the state of *gētīg*, i.e. "the world" conceived as the locus of forces of opposition of Ahreman against the creations of Ohrmazd. The dialectical structure is perceived in all aspects of life, personal, public and spiritual. It may be seen that a common element in this anthology is the fundamental apprehension of the world as a *dialectical process*, and the basic aspiration that religion provides for all circumstances the *resolution* and synthesis. The actualities of life, individual and collective, are regarded as intrinsically good, yet they are besieged by danger of one form or another. The text deals with a large number of these actualities, and each chapter has one or more of the dualities as its theme. In most cases the writer attempts to resolve the problem either explicitly in doctrinal or ritual prescriptions from the orthodox tradition, or more allusively, in legendary narrative, cosmological symbolism or religious mythology. The idea of resolution of a dialectic through human enterprise and, in the widest sense, "cultivation" is in accordance with the grand eschatological vision of *wizārišn* "resolution" of the present state of mixture (*gumēzišn*) of opposites in strife (*petyāragōmandīh*). Some examples of these oppositions will suffice to demonstrate the importance of the dialectical approach to the world:

— a house is an abode and refuge, but when evil enters (e.g. death) it becomes a trap: the problem is resolved by ritual observance and purity (ch. 2).

— Trade (and profit) is a wholesome activity, but its opposite, greed (and meanness), poses a problem: this is resolved by the giving of righteous charity, i.e. to a priest (ch. 42.2).

— Sexual relations in marriage are wholesome, but the demonically originating menstrual processes of woman are heavily polluting: the problem is resolved by a purity code and by the procreation of children — a productive and doubly meritorious act, because it stops menstruation (ch.43).

— Food is essential and life-giving, but can be ritually polluted so that it is a poison: resolved by strict regulations (ch. 2).

— The Good Religion (Zoroastrianism) is opposed by Evil Religion, and contamination and attrition from contact with the latter are difficult to avoid: *xwēdōdah* "next of kin marriage" minimises such contact (ch.8) as does abstaining from trade with outsiders (ch.30).

— Beneficent animals are considered holy, but men eat their meat: righteousness resolves the problem, for the wicked suffer punishment for the sins of the animal they eat, as well as their own (ch.14).

The resolutions which are provided in nearly all cases are not merely descriptions of practices and rites, nor, importantly, are they theological, pertaining to the nature of God, his grace and action in the world. They are rather normative religious ideals and dramatizations of doctrine, for the purpose of the text is to persuade the reader to apply the normative resolutions to the problems posed. In this text the dominant resolutions (in order of their frequency of occurrence) are righteousness, practical observance, retribution and reward, wisdom, eschatological optimism. In all of these it is clear that emphasis is placed upon human endeavour to win the harmony that is promised in the eschatological vision.

The Zoroastrian, priest and laymen, is exhorted to smite evil by ordering the world through ritual action and virtuous behaviour, and by establishing the boundaries of self and community so that all alien elements (e.g. irreligion, hostile forces and wickedness) are excluded. This ethic is derived from the fundamental assumption that man and creation are intrinsically good, because they derive solely from the good Creator. Thus the dialectical structure (what is seen as theological dualism) is essential in order to

a) define the goals of the religion,

b) organise the religious endeavour in a hierarchy of values, and

c) objectify the nature and source of imperfection and disorder which abound in this world.

For example, abhorrence of contact with Muslims is an anxiety which pervades much of this text; it is dramatized not only in terms of the opposition, Good Religion/ Evil Religion, but in many others also e.g. marriage/homosexuality, good divinities/ demons, Ohrmazd/Ahreman, beneficent animals/noxious creatures, fire/the extinguishing, pollution of fire, etc. Islamic oppression only compounded the difficulties of a world already under attack from evil. The resolutions of the problems fall roughly into two types 1) of righteousness (purity) and 2) of eschatological hope. Both put the evils of the day into a greater perspective and thus urge that triumph over mundane, ordinary problems is symbolic of, and will result in, "victory", i.e. in the revitalization of tradition, the consolidation of the boundaries of Zoroastrian identity and eventually the attainment of *Frašegird*, the final rehabilitation of the world and resurrection of the dead. Righteousness is the most effective means of resolving conflict, whether it is enacted liturgically or in practical moral and spiritual virtue; for righteousness, and other resolutions, serve to *seal off the community* from outside influence and thus to minimize the effects of oppression and scarcity. Eschatological hope is also fundamental as a socially cohesive ideal, and is expressed both explicitly in soteriology and apocalyptic, but also frequently as a general attitude.[12]

In 10th century Iran, Zoroastrianism was suffering two problems which are still with the Parsi community: conversion to other religions (then to Islam, now to materialism, agnosticism, and other faiths), and, second, attrition and impoverishment of the priesthood. From a brief look at an old, traditional text we see the dialectical structure of Zoroastrian religious apprehension is as appropriate for the modern problems as it was in the past. It derives not from the specific social-historical situation of Sassanian or early Islamic Iran but rather from an original Zoroastrian religious attitude towards the state of worldly existence and the nature and integrity of human endeavour.[13]

Presented in its full theological form Zoroastrianism contrasts dramatically with other religions. Such a comparison of religions originated not in the university but from the Christian missionary presence among the Bombay Parsis from the early 19th century. The most articulate voice to preach was the Church of Scotland missionary John Wilson, who had unfortunately discerned from his reading of classical and oriental texts not the orthodox version of Zoroastrianism, but rather the Zurvanite heresy. This latter doctrine perverted the dialectically structured religious optimism of Zoroastrianism into a fatalistic ditheism of Ohrmazd the good god and Ahreman the evil god,[14] both born of a high god Zurvan, "time". Wilson was, presumably, unaware that his attacks on Zoroastrianism in fact applied to a heresy which had been extirpated from text and tradition by the 9th century A.D. However, Wilson failed utterly to realise the hope to convert all the Parsis (expressed in the introduction to his notorious polemical work),[15] for the Parsis were not willing to foresake their community. They were, however, severely shaken by Wilson's onslaught, and the confusion he caused only served to destabilize further the rapidly changing state of Parsi society.[16] For some of the laity the traditional religion had indeed become irrelevant and for lay reformists, such as Dosabhoy Framjee, a Christian style of monotheism, though lacking altogether in rituals, was preferable, for they required a modernized religion compatible with European tastes and notions of science and progress.

The basis for a thoroughgoing rethinking of Zorastrianism was provided not by such reformists but by another European, the German philologist Martin Haug.

Haug had worked on the difficult Avestan scriptures and in the 1860's took up a position as a university teacher in Poona, and his theories on the religion were, and are still, widely known in India. He rejected all but the *Gāthās* as the authentic teaching of Zoroaster, and provided the reformists "with exactly what they had been seeking, namely, scholarly justification for rejecting everything in the faith which did not accord with nineteenth century enlightenment" (Boyce, 1979:203). He seems also to have been attempting to reconcile the Zoroastrian scriptures with Christian monotheism, yet in so doing he was actually drawing towards the fatalistic monism of the Zurvanite heresy by positing the two spirits as co-equals under a higher omnipotent divinity, thus making evil both a necessary part in a divine plan, and also as originating from the one source.[17] In this twisted form of the religion the dialectical structure of orthodox Zoroastrianism is destroyed, leaving a vague monism interrupted by a crude ditheism. Some modern Christian writers[18] still mistake this for Zoroastrianism.

Such a drift towards an undistinguished monotheism has been reinforced by the influx of ideas from Indian religions. With the 19th century revival of Hinduism and the publication of the classical scriptures such as the *Upanishads* and *Bhagavad Gita*, Parsi savants were attracted by Vedantic philosophy and attempted to interpret their own scriptures accordingly.[19] For Parsis, recourse to the ocean of Indian spirituality and religious philosophy, and to the syncretic approach of Indian teachers may have been taken in response to their increasing exposure to the religiously pluralistic environment of the Indian city, after the walls of identity of their own religious establishment had been ransacked. Theosophists, Vedāntins, Sūfīs and other groups could easily absorb the Zoroastrians, for was not Zoroaster another *avatar* of the all-embracing totality of God? Is not Zoroastrianism part of the *sanātana dharma*, "eternal truth", of Hindu teaching? Cannot the supposed dualism simply be a medieval misunderstanding of ancient sublime truth? Such questions strike a very discordant note for most Parsis, just as Parsis do not, generally, identify with Indian culture and values, preferring to look Westwards. Indeed, Zoroastrianism has more in common with traditional Judaism and Christianity than with Hinduism or Buddhism.

In concluding we would reflect upon the role of historians of religions as they seek to assemble the patterns of tradition and development, mindful that a modern community has a vital need to reinterpret the past for the future. As has been said before, the variety of reinterpretations of Zoroastrianism is enormous as the traditional identity has fragmented. In this case, however, academics and theologians have not been mere bystanders, for as Boyce puts it "the blame for the confusion lies largely with the West, and the ruthless self-confidence of nineteenth century scholars and missionaries" (1979:225). The identity crisis in the community in the late 20th century is perhaps worsening, as Zoroastrians have now been geographically fragmented across the world to the centres of business and commerce.

In California or London, Sydney or Singapore, their work ethic, sense of history and racial identity are still sufficient to keep the Zoroastrians in search of what they have only recently lost. It is here tentatively suggested that the suppression of the dualistic structure and other elements of the religion, which are seen as archaic and obsolete, is symptomatic of a form of self-suppression. Both in British and independent India, in post-revolutionary Iran, and now abroad in Western countries, Zoroastrians are constrained to accept more and more the identity of the host culture and to suppress their own identity. When, in the past, the Zoroastrians were strongly self-possessed and self-contained (for different reasons in Iran and India) they maintained their identity not *in spite* of the external world being alien but *because* it was alien — for such was, as we have seen from a traditional source, their dialectical structure of thought: life is struggle, religion is resolution.

Hans Mol's four mechanisms of the sacralization process were working at full power it would seem, only a century and a half ago in the Zoroastrian community. The mechanism of objectification he describes (Mol: 202 ff.) was fully operative in the projection of a dualism of transcendental forces (not to mention the objectification of space as two worlds — physical and spiritual — and of time as a vivid, linear eschatological plan). The mechanisms of commitment (216 ff.) and ritual (233 ff.) were efficient and exact, especially in the elaborate dramas of sacrifice and liturgy and in the rigorous purity code. Lastly, the mechanism of myth (246 ff.), whose power is perhaps least capable of objective analysis, was abundant in texts, oral traditions and throughout all elements of the religious life. The deterioration of such mechanisms would seem to be attributable to two main causes:

1) the scientific-rational worldview, which both relativizes objectification, and debunks (or psychologizes) myth, theology and religious symbolism

2) the laicization of the religion and lowering of the status of the priesthood which has brought the decline of both commitment and ritual.

It is likely that 2) is a direct effect of 1). As Mol warns, however, sacralization processes do not grind to a halt, for though they may be interrupted and prevented from maturing "they appear to be as viable as ever"(7).

The social problems and community strife over controversial issues such as intermarriage, conversion and rituals are not to be solved merely by getting the doctrinal theology right. Nevertheless, perhaps the theology is symbolic of attitudes, priorities and above all solidarity (or the lack of it) in the community. Zoroastrians face what is after all the original dilemma announced by their prophet: to choose between a decision for existence, identity and truth or a decision for oblivion — yet there is no agreement on which decision leads where.

NOTES

1. I am grateful for the opportunity to present this paper to the I.A.H.R. Congress; the subject requires more introduction than space allowed, and I therefore apologize for obscurities which remain.

2. This has been most fully demonstrated by Mary Boyce, who has published two volumes (1975, 1982) to date of her *History of Zoroastrianism.* The first volume is particularly useful for the comparative religionist, as it includes a detailed account of Zoroastrian religious thought. This history has already superseded previous standard works on the subject (e.g. Zaehner, 1961: Duchesne-Guillemin, 1962). Valuable for the general reader is her one-volume history, 1979. See 1977 for bibliography of articles by Boyce.

3. Plutarch gives a summary of the dualistic teachings of Zoroaster the Magus in what is perhaps the most important of all fragments on Zoroastrianism extant from Greek antiquity, *De Iside et Osiride* 45-47, 369D-370D; this, and many other sources from the ancient world on Zoroastrianism, is given in Bidez & Cumont, II.

4. The study of Zoroastrianism was for a long time impeded by theological assumptions of western scholars. The following is an example: "... this idea of the coexistence of the two eternal principles, distinct from each other, is more repugnant to the human mind than polytheism itself. Sooner or later the mind will push further its theories in order to repose in an original unity of principles" (Casartelli 3-5). Max Weber too suggests an explanation for the demise of dualism which, surprisingly, is frankly theological: "Zoroastrianism was the prophetic religiousness which realized this conception (dualism) most consistently ... It involved renouncing the omnipotence of a god whose power was indeed limited by the existence of a great antagonist. The contemporary followers (the Parsees) have actually given up this belief because they could not endure this limitation of divine power" (1948:358).

5. On Zurvanism see Boyce, 1982:231-242; Zaehner, 1955 is monumental but eccentric and unreliable.

6. See especially Kennedy.

7. For a discussion of this passage and on Zoroaster's thought generally, see Boyce, 1975:192-4; chs.8 and 9.

8. Yasna 45.2; transl. Insler:75.

9. For a discussion of reinterpretations of dualism see Williams, 1985.

10. This is the subject of an unpublished PhD. dissertation, Williams, 1984.

11. Text Unvala; transl. Dhabhar.

12. E.g. a work ethic in which accumulation is seen as preferable to consumption; see Kennedy: 15f.

13. Cf. the social psychologist John J. Ray's findings on Parsi behaviour and economic enterprise, and his conclusion that "Zoroastrianism ... is very strongly concerned with the struggle between the forces of light and darkness. That an acceptance of the need for struggle could lead to economic enterprise is therefore easy to see" (178).

14. Ahreman is never considered a god in traditional orthodoxy.

15. "The Parsi community is daily rising in intelligence and enterprise, and ... we cannot but look forward for its ultimate, and probably speedy, approach to God through Him who is the Way, the Truth, and the Life" (18).

16. On events in this period affecting the community in India and Iran see Boyce, 1979: ch.13.

17. Haug:302-4.

18. E.g., Küng: 428; Hick:25.

19. A notable example is Taraporewala, whose work reflects Indian influence even in the title, reminiscent as it is of Kṛṣṇa's own "Divine Song".

LIST OF WORKS CONSULTED

Axelrod, Paul
1980 "Myth and Identity in the Indian Zoroastrian Community", *Journal of Mithraic Studies*, III,150-65.

Bidez, Josef and Cumont, Franz
1938 *Les Mages Héllenisés*, I and II, Paris: Societé d'Editions "Les Belles Lettres".

Boyce, Mary
1975 *A History of Zoroastrianism*, vol. I, "The Early Period" Leiden/Köln: E.G. Brill.
1977 *A Persian Stronghold of Zoroastrianism*, Oxford: Clarendon Press.
1979 *Zoroastrians: Their Religious Beliefs and Practices*, London: Routledge & Kegan Paul.
1982 *A History of Zoroastrianism*, vol. II, "Under the Achaemenians".

Casartelli, L.C.
1889 *The Philosophy of the Mazdayasnyan Religion Under the Sasanids*, Bombay.

Dhabhar, Bamanji, N.
1932 *The Persian Rivayats of Hormazyar Framarz*, English Transl. Bombay.

Duchesne-Guillemin, J.
1962 *La Religion de l'Iran ancien*, Paris: Presses Universitaires. Transl. in English by K.M. Jamasp Asa, *Religion of Ancient Iran* Bombay, 1973.

Framjee, Dosabhoy
1858 *The Parsees*, Bombay.

Haug, Martin
1878 *The Parsis, Essays on their sacred language, writings and religion*, London, repr. 1978, Delhi: Cosmo.

Hick, John
1977 *Evil and the God of Love*, London: Macmillan.

Insler, S.
1975 *The Gāthās of Zarathustra*, Leiden: Acta Iranica 8.

Kennedy, Robert E.
1962-3 'The Protestant Ethic and the Parsis', *The American Journal of Sociology*, vol. 68, 11-20.

Küng, Hans
1978 *On Being a Christian*, London: Collins (Fount).

Mol, Hans
1976 *Identity and the Sacred*, Oxford: Basil Blackwell.

Moulton, J.H.
1913 *Early Zoroastrianism*, The Hibbert Lectures 1912, London: Williams and Norgate.

Ray, John J.
1983 'Ambition and Dominance among the Parsees of India', *The Journal of Social Psychology*, 119, 173-179.

Taraporewala, Irach J.S.
1951 *The Divine Songs of Zarathushtra*, Bombay: Taraporevala.

Unvala, Maneckji R.
1922 *Darab Horomazyar's Rivayat*, text, 2 vols. Bombay.

Weber, Max
1948 *From Max Weber: Essays in Sociology*, Transl. Gerth, H.H., Wright Mills, C., London: Routledge & Kegan Paul.
1978 *Economy and Society*, ed. and transl. Roth. G., Wittich, C., Berkeley and Los Angeles: Univ. of California Press.

Williams, Alan
1984 *The Pahlavi Rivāyat Accompanying the Dādestān ī Dēnīg*, Ph.D. thesis, University of London, publication forthcoming.
1985 'The Concept of Evil in Zoroastrianism', *Journal of the K.R. Cama Oriental Institute*, Bombay.

Wilson, John
1843 *The Parsi Religion as contained in the Zand-Avasta and propounded and defended by the Zoroastrians of India and Persia, unfolded, refuted, and contrasted with Christianity*, Bombay: American Mission Press.

Zaehner, R.C.
1955 *Zurvan, A Zoroastrian Dilemma*, Oxford: OUP
1961 *The Dawn and Twilight of Zoroastrianism*, London: Weidenfeld and Nicholson.

Related works by the author of this paper.

See under Williams, Alan (above)

THE KHALSA NAMIT:
The Sikh Identity Defined*

W.H. McLeod

University of Otago, New Zealand

Rahit: The Sikh Rahit is the code of discipline which all who enter the Khalsa order must vow to observe ...
Rahit-nāmā: A rahit-nama is a manual which records any version of the Rahit ...
The Penguin Dictionary of Religions, pp. 265-66

Sikhs have been much in the news during the past year. Although reports have been dominated by acts of violence, questions of custom, belief, history and aspirations have inevitably been raised. One such issue has been the problem of distinguishing Sikhs from Hindus, an elementary question which many seem able to answer without hesitation. The mobs which assaulted Sikhs and their property in the days following the assassination of Mrs Gandhi evidently had little difficulty with this particular problem, and even the inexperienced foreigner commonly believes that a Sikh can be easily identified. There is a strong likelihood, however, that the points of recognition will be strictly limited. A brief question or two usually reveals that for the foreigner at least it is only the male Sikh who can be recognised, and then only if he presents to outward view the more obvious features of the Khalsa discipline. Most aspects of the discipline remain unrecognised and the poor foreigner will commonly find it quite impossible to distinguish Sikh women from Hindu.

The apparently simple question of a visible Sikh identity quickly becomes an obscure and complex issue when we move beyond the well-known turban and beard. The turban and beard nevertheless serve as an appropriate introduction to the larger issue, for as we have just noted they are prominent features of the Khalsa discipline. We are led directly to the essential nature of Sikh identity and to the substance of this paper. We are led, in a word, to the Rahit.

It is perhaps surprising that the word 'Rahit' should be so little known and so seldom used. A single word which expresses normative Sikh belief and behaviour certainly deserves to be well known and a primary purpose of this paper is to encourage its usage. It shares in the neglect which is typically bestowed on those other key terms 'Gurmat' and 'Panth'. How much closer we should be to understanding the Sikhs and their distinctive beliefs if we possessed even a rudimentary grasp of Gurmat, Panth and Rahit. All three terms are intimately related, each to the other two, and although I shall be concentrating on Rahit I should note in passing that 'Gurmat' may be briefly defined as the corpus of Sikh doctrine and Panth as the Sikh community. I should also mention that the terminology used in this paper is further explained and illustrated in *Textual Sources for the Study of Sikhism* (Manchester University Press, 1984).[1] Chapter 4 of this collection is largely devoted to the Rahit.

What then is the Rahit? The Rahit is the code of discipline which all members of the Khalsa must vow to observe. Sikh tradition binds Khalsa and Rahit inextricably together. According to well-founded tradition the Khalsa order was inaugurated by Guru Gobind Singh on Baisakhi Day 1699. Following the dramatic choosing of the first five members the Guru is said to have initiated them with a form of baptism and then to have promulgated the Rahit or code of discipline which all Sikhs of the Khalsa must thereafter follow.[2] Sikh tradition also affirms that the Guru restated the Rahit in an amplified form immediately prior to his death in 1708. At his death the Rahit was sealed. The Lord of the Khalsa had delivered, once and for all, the pattern of belief and behaviour which his loyal followers must thereafter observe.

The reality of the situation is, needless to say, rather more complicated than the tradition allows. It is slightly complicated by developments which precede the founding of the Khalsa in 1699; and it is vastly complicated by those which follow that crucial event. Pre-1699 sources indicate that a rudimentary Rahit was evolving prior to the founding of the Khalsa. Contemporary sources fail to deliver an authenticated 1699 version. Post-1699 sources demonstrate that much of the Rahit crystallized during the eighteenth century and that the discipline as a whole has ever since continued to mutate. In response to changing circumstances it has predictably introduced items which earlier versions lack, amended some which have come to be unacceptable in their original forms, and discarded others which could no longer be sustained. This should not suggest, however, a process of change so radical that the Rahit of today bears little resemblance to its early eighteenth-century precursor. Plainly this is not the case. The fact that the Rahit testifies to an ongoing evolution quite rightly implies continuity, a continuity which can easily be traced throughout the entire history of the Khalsa.[3]

Pre-1699 sources do little to complicate the issue because there is little in them which one identifies as typical Rahit material. Attention has frequently been drawn to an apparent difference in the spirit and general approach which evidently distinguishes the practices of the tenth Guru from the teachings of the first (the so-called 'transformation of Sikhism'). This particular controversy is essentially irrelevant in that the Rahit is recognisably a product of the later period. The early period, best expressed in the Adi Granth collection, is largely concerned with the interior discipline of meditation on the divine Name. This particular emphasis has ever since remained a conspicuous feature of Sikh belief, and as such it finds a place in the Rahit. Ever since the first versions of the Rahit were formally enunciated Khalsa Sikhs have neen enjoined to rise at an early hour and meditate on the divine Name. The injunction has, however, become one amongst many. Although it retains a fundamental importance the Rahit which was to emerge during the eighteenth century includes much more than this Adi Granth inheritance. A few other items evidently derive from the early practice of the Panth. Most belong to the period of the later Gurus and to the turbulent decades which followed the death of Guru Gobind Singh in 1708.

It was during the fifty years following the death of the tenth Guru that the earliest extant version of the Rahit was committed to writing. This brings us to the rahit-namas, the recorded versions of the formalised Rahit.[4] It has been widely assumed that Guru Gobind Singh himself must surely have instructed scribes to prepare copies of the Rahit which he had promulgated at the inauguration of the Khalsa. Earlier Gurus had already begun the practice of despatching *hukam-nāmās* or 'letters of command' and the tenth Guru had continued the practice. Although a *hukam-nama* might well include instructions of a kind which could have been incorporated in a rahit-nama these 'letters of command' never supplied the comprehensive list which constitutes the latter form. No extant rahit-nama can be safely traced to the lifetime of the Guru himself. All belong to the years following his death.

Sikh tradition acknowledges that the earliest rahit-namas may have been recorded after the tenth Guru's death, but it does not countenance a significant gap. Several rahit-namas claim to derive directly from the words of the Guru himself and if, in fact, the recording took place after he had died, the injunctions which they contain express his actual words and authentic intention. Such is the claim lodged by most of the writers responsible for the earliest versions. One purports to be the work of the Guru's most trusted servant, a faithful retainer who had cared for the Guru during his childhood and who had subsequently remained by his side as a close confidant. Another declares itself to be the record of a conversation held with the Guru shortly before his death in South India. Three different rahit-namas are attributed to Nand Lal Goya, a celebrated poet of the Guru's entourage.

The earliest of these claimants apparently dates from the middle of the eighteenth century (between 1740 and 1765). This is the *Chaupā Singh Rahit-nāmā*, attributed to the tenth Guru's tutor and aide Chaupa Singh Chhibbar.[5] In its extant form it presents considerable difficulties from an orthodox Khalsa point of view, difficulties which seem plainly to explain the general neglect which it has suffered. These include the composite nature of the text (it includes narrative anecdotes and apocalyptic prophecy as well as rahit-nama material); its insistence upon traditional deference towards Brahmans (Chaupa Singh was himself a Brahman); and its embarrassing involvement in the Devi cult. The neglect is thus understandable, but it is nevertheless unfortunate in that no existing rahit-nama carries us nearer to the time of Guru Gobind Singh than this work attributed to Chaupa Singh Chhibbar. It must be added that its value, though considerable, should not raise too many expectations. It emerges almost half a century after the Guru's death and there is insufficient evidence to sustain the claim that its rahit-nama portions are the work of the Chaupa Singh who served as an intimate member of the tenth Guru's retinue. What this means is that the *Chaupā Singh Rahit-nāmā* testifies to a later perception of the role of the Khalsa and the duty of the individual Sikh. It must also be remembered that it represents the views of a group which had once been influential within the Khalsa but which had since become disaffected.

In spite of these shortcomings the *Chaupā Singh Rahit-nāmā* can at least be dated and located within its appropriate context. Most of the other claimants to an early eighteenth-century provenance are more difficult to fix in terms of time or context. It is obviously safe to assume that like the *Chaupā Singh Rahit-nāmā* they do not derive from the period of Guru Gobind Singh and in the case of the Nand Lal versions their attribution is obviously contrived. If claims to authenticity were to be established it was essential that the relevant text should assert a context involving direct dictation by Guru Gobind Singh. Amongst his retainers none would have better qualifications as an amanuensis than Nand Lal Goya and he thus became a natural candidate for the role of rahit-nama author. The actual texts do nothing to sustain these claims, plainly indicating that they belong to a later period. That is the easy part. The difficult bit is to locate them within the decades (or centuries) following the Guru's death, and to identify the groups or individuals who produced them.

One of these later rahit-namas which does permit cautious conclusions is the work variously known as the *Prem Sumārg* or the *Param Sumārag*. This particular manual obviously belongs to the middle years of the nineteenth century, a conclusion which follows from its author's obvious knowledge of the rule of Maharaja Ranjit Singh and from his evident nostalgia for that period. The only outstanding question with regard to dating concerns the precise time of its composition, whether shortly before the British annexation of the Punjab or shortly after that event.[6] The *Sau Sākhīān* or 'Hundred Episodes' also belongs to the same period, though in its extant form it probably emerged a decade or two later.[7] Like the *Chaupā Singh Rahit-nāmā* the *Sau Sākhīān* combines Rahit injunctions with apocalyptic prophecy. As such it was to provide comfort and inspiration to the Kukas in their opposition to the alien British.[8]

Much more difficult to place and evaluate are four brief rahit-namas written in verse form. Two of these rahit-namas are attributed to Nand Lal; one to a disciple variously called Prahilad Rai or Prahilad Singh; and one to Desa Singh, also said to be a contemporary follower of Guru Gobind Singh.[9] This cluster constitutes the principal problem associated with the rahit-namas. Their contents are far too important to be ignored and if we are to trace the growth of the Khalsa satisfactorily it seems imperative that these verse rahit-namas should be firmly fixed in terms of time and context. It is, however, impossible to draw adequate conclusions at this stage. We can certainly detach all four from their purported origins and thereby bring them forward in time. Their language is not that of the period which they claim to represent and the kind of verse which we find in them could scarcely be the work of the highly skilled Nand Lal Goya. But how far forward should they be brought? That precisely is the problem and no sufficient answer has yet been supplied.

The same problem also attaches to one of the two remaining earlier rahit-namas. These two are both brief collections of injunctions expressed in prose. One of them (another of the Nand Lal rahit-namas) is invariably found in association with the *Chaupā Singh Rahit-nāmā* and like its dominant colleague can probably be placed in the middle years of the eighteenth century. The second is attributed to Daya Singh, one of the first five Sikhs to be initiated by Guru Gobind Singh at the inauguration of the Khalsa in 1699. As with the four verse rahit-namas this prose product can safely be detached from its putative author. A nineteenth-century provenance is indicated by the nature of its language, but at this stage any such verdict must be a cautious one.

Whatever their dates and origins these were the formal rahit-namas which existed when representatives of the Singh Sabha reform movement turned their attention to the Rahit late in the nineteenth century.[10] Given their interest in restoring the purity of Sikh doctrine and practice it was inevitable that the Singh Sabha reformers should have directed a portion of their zeal to the Rahit and its formal enunciation. Their task was not easy. The legacy of the two preceding centuries was a sparse one and much of its content was plainly unacceptable to the educated men who led the movement. The Khalsa allegiance of the various rahit-namas may have been obvious, but so too were their many contradictions and the injunctions which no enlightened product of late nineteenth-century education could possibly accept.

One response was to prepare commentaries on the Rahit or on particular features of it, and several of the works published during the Singh Sabha period belong to this category. A prominent example of this genre was Avatar Singh's *Khālsā Dharam-śāstr Sanskār Bhāg*, first issued from Lahore in 1894.[11] A few years later that most influential of all Singh Sabha intellectuals, Kahn Singh of Nabha, published a different kind of response, one which clearly signalled the true nature of the problem.

Kahn Singh's *Gurmat Sudhākar*, first issued in 1901, was a compendium of works relating to the person and time of Guru Gobind Singh. Such a collection was bound to include material relating to the Rahit, but how could the rahit-nama wheat be sifted from the chaff and the weeds? Kahn Singh solved the problem by publishing what appeared to be abridged versions of the principal rahit-namas. In reality, however, his selections were expurgated versions rather than abridgements. Portions which were unacceptable were deleted (as well as those which were insignificant) and only those items which matched the reformist philosophy of the Singh Sabha movement were retained. Anything which conflicted with that philosophy must *ipso facto* conflict with the original intention of Guru Gobind Singh. As such it must surely represent interpolation by an enemy, a deviant, or (at best) an ignorant Sikh. Purging these excrescences should produce a version of the Rahit much closer to the original version than that of any extant rahit-nama. Although this reasoning was not spelt out it seems clearly implicit in the procedure adopted by Kahn Singh.

Other attempts have subsequently been made to utilise the early rahit-namas. It is, however, a method doomed to fail if the objective is to be a comprehensive statement of the Rahit appropriate to contemporary circumstances. This awareness prompted a lengthy quest for the definitive rahit-nama, one which would draw into a single agreed manual the various injunctions which together constitute the sum total of approved Khalsa practice. Extant rahit-namas could contribute to this process, but alone they must be inadequate. Other sources had to be used for the details which they delivered; and a consensus had to be achieved with regard to inclusion, omission, and the actual form of words. The task was an exceedingly difficult one and the final result bears all the marks of committee procedure. It was nevertheless achieved after several decades of negotiation, a feat of no mean scale.

The attempt made during the Singh Sabha heyday was actually a failure. This was the manual of Sikh rituals published as *Gurmat Prakāś Bhāg Sanskār* in 1915, a work which incorporated Rahit injunctions in proposed orders for various rites and ceremonies. Its failure was implicitly acknowledged in 1931 when the Shiromani Gurdwara Parbhandhak Committee (which by then had become the dominant voice in Sikh affairs) appointed a sub-committee to prepare a new rahit-nama. Although a draft was ready within a year the process of discussion was protracted and it was not until 1950 that an agreed version was finally published as *Sikh Rahit Maryādā*.

The brief introductory portion of *Sikh Rahit Maryādā* appropriately offers a definition of a Sikh.

> A Sikh is any person who believes in God (*Akāl Purakh*); in the ten Gurus (Guru Nanak to Guru Gobind Singh); in Sri Guru Granth Sahib, other writings of the ten Gurus, and their teachings; in the Khalsa initiation ceremony instituted by the tenth Guru; and who does not believe in any other system of religious doctrine[13].

The remainder of the manual is divided into two sections, a lengthy 'Personal code' and a much shorter 'Panthic code'. The former includes instructions concerning modes of personal devotion; gurdwara worship and administration; approved methods of reading the sacred scripture; practices which are either enjoined or proscribed; and orders to be followed in the conduct of birth and naming-ceremonies, marriage and funerals. The second section consists largely of the order to be observed in conducting the Khalsa initiation ceremony (*amrit sanskār*). Several basic injunctions are incorporated within this rite as portions of the homily delivered to all who receive initiation. The manual concludes with a brief segment on penalties to be imposed for violations of the Rahit.

Sikh Rahit Maryādā has stood the test of thirty-five years remarkably well. Having acknowledged this considerable achievement one must add some predictable qualifications. For some the problem has been the evident fact that whereas the manual defines *normative* Sikh behaviour, *operative* practice is very different. The answer to this particular objection is, of course, that such manuals are by definition normative statements and that as such they serve to stabilise religious practice in the quicksand world of ignorance and self-interest. A second criticism is that although *Sikh Rahit Maryādā* grapples with the problem of the so-called Sahaj-dhari (or non-Khalsa) Sikh, it finally fails to provide a satisfactory place for the latter. To this the answer must be that *Sikh Rahit Maryādā* is, after all, a statement of khalsa practice. It does not pretend to cover the needs of the uninitiated who yet regard themselves as Sikhs.

A final comment is that although *Sikh Rahit Maryādā* was meant to be definitive, later editions have introduced surreptitious amendments. It is this comment which brings us to that most basic of all questions associated with the Rahit. Is the Rahit immutable, established once for all by the tenth Guru and subject to no acceptable change thereafter? Or is it to be regarded as firm yet flexible, adapting its forms as the world and its manifold pressures force change on the society of the faithful? The historian and the sociologist may find this an easy question to answer. For the believer it may not be quite so simple.

FOOTNOTES

1. *Textual Sources for the Study of Sikhism* will hereafter be cited as *TSSS*. See also W. H. McLeod, *The Evolution of the Sikh Community* (Oxford, 1976), pp. 51-52. Relevant entries in *The Penguin Dictionary of Religions* may also be helpful.

2. *TSSS*, p. 34-37.

3. *TSSS*, pp. 9-10 and chap. 4.

4. W. H. McLeod, 'The problem of the Panjabi *rahit-nāmās*' in S. N. Mukherjee, *India: History and Thought. Essays in honour of A. L. Basham* (Calcutta 1982), pp. 103-26.

5. *TSSS*, pp. 74-75.

6. S. S. Hans, '*Prem Sumarg* — a modern forgery'. *Proceedings of the Punjab History Conference 1982* (Patiala, 1982), pp. 180-88.

7. An early translation of the *Sau Sākhīān* was published by Attar Singh of Bhadaur as *Sakhee Book, or the Description of Gooroo Gobind Singh's Religion and Doctrines* (Benares, 1873).

8. W. H. McLeod, 'The Kukas: a millenarian sect of the Punjab' in G. A. Wood & P. S. O'Connor (ed.), *W. P. Morrell: a Tribute* (Dunedin, 1973), pp. 85-103, 272-76.

9. *TSSS*, pp. 75-79.

10. *TSSS*, pp. 14-17. W. H. McLeod, 'The problem of the Panjabi *rahit-nāmās*', p. 119.

11. Titles are listed in N. Gerald Barrier, *The Sikhs and their Literature* (Delhi, 1970).

12. One such work was Sant Sampuran Singh's *Rahit-prakāś*, first published in 1923. See also Piara Singh Padam, *Rahit-nāme* (Patiala 1974).

13. *TSSS*, p. 79. *TSSS*, pp. 79-86, supplies a substantial part of the text of *Sikh Rahit Maryādā* in English translation.

Related works by the author of this paper:

Early Sikh Tradition: A study of the janam-sākhīs. Oxford: the Clarendon Press, 1980.

Textual Sources for the Study of Sikhism. Manchester: Manchester University Press, 1984.

*Most of this paper has been incorporated verbatim in the introduction to the author's forthcoming *The Chaupā Siṅgh Rahit-nāmā: the rahit-nāmā attributed to Chaupā Siṅgh Chhibbar and the associated prose rahit-nāmā attributed to Nand Lal.* Gurmukhi text and English translation with introduction and notes. University of Otago Press, Dunedin, 1986.

VAISHNAVISM, BRAHMANISM AND HINDU IDENTITY IN MEDIEVAL BENGAL

M. H. Klaiman

La Trobe University

According to available evidence, the worship of Krishna as a form of popular Hinduism originated in north-central India at least several centuries prior to the Christian era.[1] Since then the Krishna cult has funished the basis of numerous sects and movements within popular Hinduism, and has been one of the most powerful forces in religious and cultural history on the Indian subcontinent. In the sixteenth century, in Bengal, there arose a highly organized and lately much studied sect of Krishnaite Hinduism, the Guadiya Vaishnava sect. This movement and its sociohistorical basis will be the focus of the present paper.

Gaudiya Vaishnavas credit the foundation of their sect and its early leadership to the charismatic and saintly Caitanya, born Visvambhara Misra in 1486. After his death in 1533, the movement attributed to his vision and teachings took on the philosophical and theological apparatus of a distinct religion. Moreover, the Caitanyite or Gaudiya Vaishnava movement was phenomenally successful in eastern India, though it has by no means been confined to that area. The modern Hare Krishna or ISKCON organisation is essentially an offshoot of Gaudiya Vaishnavism, and it is with the emergence of this offshoot or subsect that Krishnaism can be said to have evolved today into a world religion.[2]

But despite its impressive advance during the more recent era, in its early history the Gaudiya Vaishnava movement operated amid unusual and turbulent material and political circumstances, as I will outline in some detail in this paper. Nonetheless, scholars of Indian religious history have by and large given little importance to the temporal conditions of medieval Bengal in their reconstruction of the early intellectual and social milieu of the Vaishnava movement there; instead, the impetus and inspiration for the movement is attributed by most present scholars to the charisma, activities and vision of a single religious leader. It is in this context that the religious historian AK Majumdar refers to Caitanya as "the founder of the last great Vaisnava sect".[3] Edward Dimock credits "the intense and unprecedented revival of the Vaisnava faith in Bengal" of the 16th century to "the leadership and inspiration of Caitanya."[4] Another scholar, S.C. Mukherji, characterizes the time preceding Caitanya as an era of "lamentable decadence of religious life and ideals in Bengal."[5] Dimock[6] cites early Gaudiya sources deploring the intemperance and gross standards of personal conduct, such as the practice of sacrificial rites and of bloodthirsty goddess worship, prevalent among the Bengali masses of Caitanya's period — masses that, the same Gaudiya sources assure us, were woefully ignorant of the divinity and grace of Krishna.

Despite the tenor of these views it is undeniable that Krishna did receive some form of popular worship in eastern India prior to the time of Caitanya. If nothing else, there is Jayadeva's 12th century poem *Gitagovinda* to provide evidence that Vaishnava lore had found a place in the consciousness of easterners prior to the rise of the Gaudiya movement. What is more, there is a massive song collection in archaic middle Bengali, Baru Candidasa's *Srikrsnakirtana*, that attests to Krishna's having been a popular hero of early eastern legend and romance. Even the literature of the Gaudiya movement furnishes evidence that possibly Caitanya himself, and certainly his disciples and contemporaries, were aware of this text.[7] I have discussed this in the introduction to my translation of SKK, which has been just published by Scholars Press. As I mention there, distinguished scholarly opinion has dated SKK to the late 14th century, making it the earliest surviving Krishna devotional literature in eastern India, and the only such work that predates Caitanya.[8]

Some writers, however, dispute SKK's antiquity and authenticity. A.K. Majumdar, for instance, comments that in view of the work's "gross nature" it must be concluded that "Most probably Caitanya had not read the SKK".[9] Also, Sukumar Sen has claimed that SKK cannot be an authentic pre-Caitanya text because:

> ... the main note of the poem running through the whole of it is frankly erotic, so much so that it is really hard to believe that these songs had obtained approval from Caitanya.[10]

On the other hand, several scholars, including S.K. Chatterji, have held that SKK is the earliest, most important and one of the best of the Middle Bengali texts.[11] Still, the evidence furnished by SKK as to the antiquity and popularity of Krishna devotionalism in eastern India tends to be discounted, and even cautious religious historians, tracing the development of Bengal Vaishnavism, place overweening emphasis upon Caitanya's life and leadership. Typical is the view of the scholar S.K. De, who states:

> Although the term Bengal Vaishnavism is not co-extensive with the religious system associated with the name of Caitanya and his adherents ... Caitanyaism ... is Vaisnavism *par excellence* in Bengal. .... It is difficult to say in what particular form Vaishnavism existed in Bengal before Caitanya.[12]

I would suggest that the difficulty S.K. De alludes to must be compounded to the extent that scholars are reluctant to examine material and ethical conditions for a Vaishnava movement in Bengal prior to Caitanya. Particularly worthy of scrutiny are certain factors of geography and social history, factors that — it can be argued — were causally related to the advent and progress of the Gaudiya movement. What is more, I shall claim that Caitanya could not have fomented the human and material conditions which gave rise to Bengal Vaishnavism as a socioreligious force, inasmuch as these conditions had been in the making for centuries before his time. Ironically, however, they are attested to by incidents in Caitanya's own life, as I'll demonstrate with examples.

The structure of the argument is basically two-fold: first, that the rise of some Hindu reform movement along the lines of Gaudiya Vaishnavism was inevitable, given the conditions in eastern India at Caitanya's time; secondly, that this revival had as its vehicle the already popular folk cult of the divinity Krishna, whose pre-existence is supported by an archaic vernacular tradition of lore and legend as exemplified by Srikrsnakirtana. We will now proceed with these claims in order, beginning with an argument that relates the activities of the early Gaudiyas to the social and material conditions of early medieval Bengal.

One vital factor which has had a particular impact upon the pattern of human settlements in Bengal occurred between the 12th and 16th centuries AD. This was a major shift in the course of the Ganges River.[13] Prior to the shift, agriculture and civilization tended to be concentrated in a narrow strip of territory running north and south in western Bengal. This was the Ganges' original course, presently the course of the Bhagirathi-Hooghley. About the twelfth century, after silting up its original channel, the Ganges embarked on a gradual "Eastward March"[14] which brought the eastern territories and their tribal inhabitants into first time contact with outside civilization.[15] The shift was also responsible for opening up Bengal's underexploited eastern tracts to material development at the hands of entrepreneurs from the west.[16]

Coincident to the Ganges' movement toward and eventual convergence with the Padma River system in what is now Bangladesh came the onset of Islamic rule in Bengal. This process began with the conquest of the Hindu seat of power at Nadiya, in western Bengal, in 1204. The Ganges' gradual eastward shift worked hand in glove with Islamic designs for the economic and cultural assimilation of eastern Bengal. The culmination of these intertwined processes may be seen in the establishment of the seat of Moghal rule in the east, at Dacca, in 1610.[17]

During the period of these developments the locus of Hinduism in Bengal, socially and culturally speaking, did not shift substantially from its old base along the Ganges' original course. However, the Hindu community was profoundly affected by the new political and geographical realities, in several ways. The Muslim conquest deprived the Brahmanical authority structure of the political devices for upholding its own legitimacy. Also, the domination of the outsiders called the ritual purity of all caste Hindus who lived under their rule into question. And, finally, if not most importantly, the hegemony of Islam made the Hindus' adherence to their own religious practices conditional upon the pleasure of an alien authority. One event of Caitanya's lifetime attests to this:[18] early in the days of Caitanya's movement the local representative of the Islamic powers, the kazi or Muslim magistrate, issued a prohibitive order against the religious practices of the Gaudiyas. Caitanya responded by leading a procession of followers *en masse* to the magisterial residence, where negotiations insured the privilege of the Vaishnavas to worship as they saw fit. This incident, documented in Caitanya's biographies, attests to the pressures that confronted the Brahmanical community of Bengal under Islamic rule.

Another manifestation of the changing political and sociogeographical situation of the era was the increased importance of the eastern districts in the social and economic life of the country. The Hindu mainstream, concentrated in the western districts, was obliged to look on as the political and demographic epicenter of Bengal gradually shifted eastward. Moreover, in connection with this shift, the tribals occupying the eastern territories came into a position to be assimilated into the greater Bengali society. These tribals had previously, according to Richard Eton, "had but the lightest contact with the Hindu religious or caste structure"; and they, to the exclusion of the Hindus in the west, were the principal targets of Islamic conversion.[19]

Faced with an increasing body of indigenous converts to a previously alien religious and cultural system, Hindu society in Bengal had come to be trivialized numerically as well as neutralized politically by the end of the fifteenth century. In response to this, standards of ritual purity and obedience to traditional Brahmanical authority were sought to be reinforced within the community, and with a vengeance. As S.K. Mukherji describes the situation at and just before Caitanya's time: "The tyranny of the foreign ruler was ... accompanied by the greater oppression of dominant Brahmanism with its conservative outlook and despotic spirit." Moreover, "Minute rules and restrictions of an unchanging and stringent code of religious and social duties were prescribed ..."[20] Although the intent was to hold the Hindu society of Bengal intact, the tightening of ritual restrictions and caste rules largely seems to have accelerated the disintegration of the community by alienating some of its most creative and enterprising members.

For an illustration of this point we need look no further than the case of the brothers Rupa and Sanatana. These were contemporaries, and eventual followers, of Caitanya. Moreover, they were men of scholarly acumen and refined Brahman upbringing.

Notwithstanding, the two brothers had consorted with Muslims by taking employment in the court of the ruler Husein Shah; and, consequently, were regarded as fallen Hindus — ineligible for the caste privileges to which they had been born. Yet they won rehabilitation and distinction in the highest echelons of the Gaudiya Vaishnava movement, becoming important theologians and philosophers of the sect after Caitanya's death.

Medieval Bengal had many Rupas and Santanas. After the Muslim conquest, practical necessity obligated many educated Hindus to seek employment outside their community. The Muslim court, for its part, had a demand for servants of high calibre; i.e., Hindu entrepreneurs and administrators who, with their efficiency and skills, could be utilized to further the economic and political objectives of Islam. As an increasing number of caste Hindus acceded to this need, Hindu religious authorities increasingly responded by reclassifying these persons on a par with untouchables.

Clearly, the tossing out from Hindu society of its most elite and industrious members was a practice the community could not affort to pursue indefinitely. In addition, the impending assimilation of the tribal masses in the east was at issue. It must have been plain by the close of the fifteenth century that the tribals would obtain some place in the life of the country, with or without the cooperation of the Brahmanical Hindus.

In sum, a convergence of trends was gaining momentum, one that could end in only one of two ways: with the extinction of Brahmanical Hinduism itself, or with a massive restructuring of Brahmanical religious doctrine and social ethic.

It would be impractical and unnecessary here to elaborate on the well known revolution which Gaudiya Vaishnavism brought about in Hindu religious doctrine and practice.[21] However, the changes which the movement inspired in social ethic merit discussion. I will argue that Gaudiya Vaishnavism was neither unbrahmanical nor anti-brahmanical, even though, as a social institution, its willingness to accommodate its followers at the expense of traditional orthodoxy is well documented.

It is known, for one thing, that from its inception Caitanya's movement accepted the dispossessed and outcasted. What is more, the movement has tended to provide adherents with a definite place within a reconstituted social order. Gaudiya Vaishnava doctrine is emphatic that neither personal background nor social circumstances are bars to spiritual attainment. Historically, the movement has broken with traditional orthodoxy by permitting persons of extremely varied backgrounds to embrace the faith, including fallen Hindus, untouchables, and even occasional recanting Muslims. Still, this does not mean that all members are admitted into the Vaishnava community on precisely the same basis. The social makeup of the Gaudiya movement over the centuries has a definite and revealing outline.[22]

Geographically, Vaishnavism has acquired the bulk of its adherents in an area where Islam was also highly successful: the lower Gangetic delta of eastern Bengal.[23] this would suggest that, after Caitanya, Bengal Vaishnavism broke with the Hindu tradition centered on the old course of the Ganges, and that the community adapted its expansion as the demographic, cultural and economic epicenter of Bengal shifted to the east.[24]

Sociologically, too, Bengal Vaishnavism has tended to follow the general pattern of Islam, though with some particular differences.[25] Like Islam, Vaishnavism has acquired its numerical base in Bengal among agriculturalists, artisans and service castes. It has been traditionally under-represented, however, at the two extremes of the caste continuum. In contrast to Islam, Vaishnavism has hardly any representation among the lowest ranking menial and laboring castes. Also relatively few in number are Vaishnavas from the highest Hindu castes.

Notwithstanding, the Brahman element unquestionably comprises the apex of the Gaudiya community. Caitanya himself was a Brahman, a Brahman who is said to have adhered to the rules of his own caste, and who did little to sway others from obedience to theirs.[26] Likewise, among the six lieutenants he deputed to the northern India town of Vrndavana to provide the religion with a liturgical and theological basis, five, including Rupa and Sanatana, had been born into the Brahman caste. The same held of many leading figures of the Caitanyite movement who remained in Bengal.[27]

Gaudiya Vaishnavas to this day exhibit a strong affinity for Brahmanical social standards and also enjoy a certain degree of identification with Brahman social ranking in the public consciousness.[28] This even applies to the movement's recent spinoff, the Hare Krishna organization. Its more adept participants receive initiation as Brahmans, and it is only from their ranks that cooks are recruited for the feeding of the membership.[29]

It follows, then, that however hostile Caitanya and his companions may have been to the orthodox component of Hindu society — and Caitanya's biographies make clear that there was considerable tension between his followers and Bengali Hindu orthodoxy in the movement's earliest days — nevertheless the Caitanyite movement is not and has never been an anti-Brahmanical movement. It has functioned, instead, to bring about a revision in Brahmanical standards, both in religious doctrine and in social ethic.

What I wish to suggest is that this revision came about when, faced with the catastrophic prospect of the total extinction of the Brahmanical Hindu community, the progressives of the Bengali Hindu elite took advantage of a pre-existing, popular cult of the deity Krishna as the hero of legend, folklore and romance, and used this cult to promote a restabilization of community identity and re-establishment of Brahmanical ethical values and authority. The text Srikrsnakirtana which was referred to earlier does suggest the antiquity of a folk dimension to Vaishnava faith in Bengal. Also, the text shows clearly the popular nature of the pre-Caitanya Krishna cult there. However, there is a problem with using SKK as evidence that the early Caitanyite movement drew on some such pre-existing Bengali Krishna cult.

The problem is not that Vaishnava scholarship largely rejects a pre-Caitanya dating of the text; the evidence for the early dating is strong, and the arguments against it can be shown to be weak and unscientific.[30] The problem is not SKK's dating, which is definite even if controversial. The problem is that this text is one which Vaishnava scholarship, not to mention the present Vaishnava community, rejects. That the text undeniably predates Caitanya and reflects popular tastes, lore and tradition in itself does not establish that Caitanya and his contemporaries drew on that tradition. On the other hand, if Caitanya and the other early Gaudiyas did not draw upon some earlier popular eastern Indian tradition, then to determine whence and by what reasoning the cult of Krishna was incorporated into their philosophy and theology is problematic.

Srikrsnakirtana is evidently the only surviving pre-Caitanya Vaishnava text in the Bengali vernacular. In the view of some it is also the most grossly erotic text in the Bengali vernacular. To be sure, eroticism *per se* is nothing unusual in Indian devotional literature, least of all in Vaishnava poetry; witness *Gitagovinda*. But the eroticism in *Srikrsnakirtana* goes beyond mere description of characters' physical charms, or suggestion of their psychological scenarios as is the mainstay of Jayadeva's poem.

Srikrsnakirtana contains detailed accounts of the sexual intercourse of Radha and Krishna. The dialogue, moreover, includes lurid teasing, suggestive banter and swapping of the coarsest of insults. One character of the text, the go-between Barayi, is an obvious caricature of the *sakhi* character of *Gitagovinda*; Barayi is portrayed as an aged woman of grotesque demeanor, familiar with magic spells and formulas and, what is more, a seasoned procuress.

In one section of SKK, Krishna compels Radha to submit to him sexually after detaining her in the guise of a revenue official (*Danakhanda*, Episode of the Tax). Another section (*Naukakhanda*, Episode of the Boat) has Krishna forcing himself on Radha under the implicit threat that he will otherwise allow her to drown in the Yamuna River. Krishna replicates his body (in *Vrndavanakhanda*, Episode of the Vrndavana Gardens), not to dance with the dairymaidens as per the traditional description of *raslila*; but in order to take the cowmaids into separate arbors and have his way with every one of them, to the unlimited outrage of Radha.[31]

These contents, and more, have likewise provoked the outrage of a significant segment of the Bengali community. This is why *Srikrsnakirtana's* potential for the investigation and reconstruction of the milieu of pre-Caitanya Bengal Vaishnavism has been suppressed, suppressed under the weight of scholarly conviction that the text can have nothing to do with the Caitanyite movement, that it is so inimical to the standards of piety and taste propounded by Caitanya that its very authenticity must be questioned. Above all, this text is contradictory to the Gaudiya movement's image of itself. It is an image carefully cultivated in the movement's liturgical writings and in biographies of Caitanya, and it is this image of Gaudiya Vaishnavism which is usually accepted uncritically by scholars of the movement both Western and Eastern. Yet there is evidence from within the movement itself that, among the original adherents, standards of literary taste, at least, were less fastidious.

According to S.K. De,[32] a number of Caitanya's contemporaries and followers composed literary pieces on the Radha-Krishna theme for entertainment. For instance, the degraded Brahman brothers Rupa and Sanatana, together with their nephew Jiva, contributed to this body of writing, as did several other early Gaudiya Vaishnavas. It may accordingly be assumed that these works were written for the approbation of others in the movement and were not considered inconsistent with Vaishnava piety. However, De has provided summaries of many of these pieces, making clear their comic and erotic content. They include themes also found in *Srikrsnakirtana*, such as Krishna demanding amorous favours in lieu of revenues from the dairymaids; Radha stealing Krishna's flute; Krishna replicating himself to make love to Radha's friends; etc.

One work of this class, available in a recent critical edition, is a play called *Danakelikaumudi* or "Moonlight on the Sports of Tax-Collecting" by Rupa Goswami[33] — the Rupa mentioned earlier. His play "Moonlight" portrays Krishna's activities as a bogus revenue agent; and thus it is essentially another treatment of the tax episode that occupies quite a prominent place in the SKK. As in the SKK version, Rupa's version likewise has Krishna accosting Radha with the help of an older cowherd woman as the dairymaidens travel together to market. After this opening, Rupa's play is largely taken up with the protracted dispute that occurs between the two sides, carried on with much erotic double entendre and suggestive bantering. At one point, for instance, Krishna tells Radha that he is anxious to perform a "great service" for her — *uruseva*, a pun on "attendance on the thighs". In turn, the older woman character suggests that Radha raise her garment a bit and satisfy Krishna with a glimpse of her breasts. At this, all the young women turn on the older lady in irritation and denounce her as a *dubuddhie*, a dirty minded woman. At length the play comes to an end as Krishna is placated with the promise of a tryst with Radha that evening.

The point of this is that present scholarship tends to downplay the existence of a class of erotic and comic interpretations of the Radha-Krishna legend by the early Gaudiya Vaishnavas. Nevertheless such a body of writing exists, and the significance of this literature for reconstructing the intellectual origins of the movement is, of course, considerable. It demonstrates, for one thing, that eroticism and irreverence in the recounting of Krishna's adventures are no gounds *per se* for excluding a work from the Bengal Vaishnava tradition. From Rupa's contribution in particular, it is apparent that Caitanya's own associates appreciated such material, and more: they composed it. This fact provides strong evidence, in turn, that Gaudiya Vaishnavas drew on an earlier, popular Krishnaite tradition of eastern India as a vehicle for the propagation of their ethical, social and religious doctrines. This Krishnaite folk tradition of religious belief naturally underwent great revision at the hands of the Gaudiyas. Its original popular character is nevertheless proven by the literature which Rupa and the other early Gaudiyas composed for entertainment — literature which, in thematic and stylistic structure, has obvious affinity with a pre-existing Bengali tradition of popular Krishnaite lore as represented by Baru Candidasa's *Srikrsnakirtana*.

This paper is intended to provoke a rethinking of certain matters that have long passed unchallenged in scholarly approaches to medieval Bengal Vaishnavism. If it has been successful, it should have at the very least suggested the need for a reappraisal of Caitanya's role in religious developments in eastern India. The principal role he has played historically has been that of a religious symbol. Furthermore, his leadership, charisma and personal piety indisputably have been reflected in the success of the Gaudiya movement. It is too much, however, to credit him with the inspiration for the Krishnaite socioreligious revolution in Bengal. As discussed in this paper, the inspiration for such a movement did not and could not lay in the personality of a single man. Rather, it can be attributed to converging factors of social, physical and economic history. The pressures exerted by these factors upon the Bengali Brahmanical community were enormous; religious and social reform were mandatory for the very survival of Hinduism. A pre-existing, popular cult of Krishna, supernatural hero of lore and romance, became the vehicle of socioreligious reform in Bengal. The resulting movement proved successful in expanding the community's social base without sacrificing Brahmanical authority and values. In the final analysis, a movement along these lines was inevitable in medieval eastern India, whether or not Caitanya had trod the soil.

FOOTNOTES

1. Jan Gonda, *Visnuism and Sivaism: A Comparison* (London: Athlone Press, 1970), chs. 2-3; Suvira Jaiswal, *The Origin and Development of Vaisnavism* (Delhi: Munshiram Manoharlal, 1967), ch. 2 "Sources"; Sir R.G. Bhandarkar, *Vaisnavism, Saivism and Minor Religious Systems* (Benares: Indological Book House, 1966); Hemachandra Raychaudhuri, *Materials for the Study of the Early History of the Vaishnava Sect* (Calcutta: University of Calcutta, 1920).

2. The Hare Krishna (ISKCON) organization was founded in New York in the mid nineteen-sixties by an adherent of Caitanyite Vaishnavism. This individual, commonly known under the name of A.C. Bhaktivedanta Swami, was originally named Abhay Charan De and was born in Calcutta on September 1, 1896. Some Indian scholars have been quick to recognize ISKCON as the continuation of and heir to the Gaudiya Vaishnava movement. For instance, O.B.L. Kapoor's *The Philosophy and Religion of Sri Caitanya* (Delhi: Munshiram Manaharlal, 1977) is subtitled *The Philosophical Background of the Hare Krishna Movement*. In the Preface,

Kapoor credits Bhaktivedanta Swami with going over a prepublication draft of the text. Since the latter in fact deals entirely with the medieval Gaudiya sect, it is clear that the author regards the ISKCON leader as the contemporary spokesperson for the Gaudiya tradition.

3. A.K. Majumdar, *Caitanya: His Life and Doctrine* (Bombay: Bharatiya Vidya Bhavan, 1969), p.25.

4. Edward C. Dimock, Jr., *The Place of the Hidden Moon* (Chicago: University of Chicago Press, 1966), p.25.

5. S.C. Mukherji, *A Study of Vaisnavism in Ancient and Medieval Bengal* (Calcutta: Punthi Pustak, 1966), pp.161-162.

6. Dimock, *Place*, p.112.

7. The biography *Caitanya-caritamrta* of Krsnadasa Kaviraja, completed approximately in 1615, states that Caitanya listened with approbation to the songs of Candidasa on several occasions. *Vaisnava-tosani*, a commentary on *Bhagavatapurana* by Caitanya's associate and disciple Sanatana, mentions Candidasa in connection with the names of two of the actual episodes of *Srikrsnakirtana*. For further discussion and critical evaluation of such evidence see Klaiman, *Singing the Glory of Lord Krishna: Baru Candidasa's Srikrsnakirtana* (Chico, CA: Scholars Press, for the American Academy of Religion, 1984), Introduction.

8. See *inter alia* Suniti Kumar Chatterji, *Origin and Development of the Bengali Language* (London: Allen and Unwin, 1970), vol. 1. The introduction to Klaiman, *Singing the Glory*, contains some discussion of problems of the text's dating. For an extended treatment of the topic see Asitkumar Bandyopadhyay, *Bania sahityera itibrtta*, 3d ed. (Calcutta: Modern Book Agency, 1970-), vol. 1 (in Bengali).

9. Majumdar, *Caitanya*, pp.78-79.

10. Sukumar Sen, *Chandidas* (Delhi: Sahitya Akademi, 1971), p.13.

11. Since its discovery in 1910 followed by its publication (various editions since 1916, principally by the Bangiya Sahitya Parisat of Calcutta), *Srikrsnakirtana* has received almost simultaneously the richest scholarly praise as well as the most damning criticism. Whereas S.K. Chatterji in *Origin and Development*, p.129, compared it to the works of Layamon, Orm and Chaucer in English, Sukumar Sen in *Chandidas*, p.52, attributes to *Srikrsnakirtana* a quality of "coarseness", saying that its tone is "jarred at times by obscenity". On the other hand, Bandyopadhyay asserts in *Itibrtta*, 1:348, that *Srikrsnakirtana* "is a work of unprecedented choiceness, not only for the middle ages, but for the whole of Bengali literature" (my translation of the original Bengali: *srikrsnakirtanakabya sudhu madhyayuge nahe, samagra banla sahityera ekakhani abhinaba upadeya grantha.*

12. S.K. De, *Early History of the Vaisnava Faith and Movement in Bengal* (Calcutta: K.L. Mukhopadhyay, 1961), pp.1,8.

13. See N.D. Bhattacharya, "Changing Courses of the Padma and Human Settlements," *National Geographic J. of India* 24.1-2 (March-June, 1978), pp.63-65.

14. *Ibid.*

15. Richard M. Eaton, "Approaches to the Study of Conversion to Islam in India," in *Islam and the History of Religions*, ed. Richard C. Martin (Berkeley: University of California Press, 1983).

16. According to the Gaudiya movement's standard biographies even Caitanya, as a young Brahman teacher not yet converted to Vaishnavism, made a financially successful teaching tour of eastern India. For details see Majumdar, *Caitanya*.

17. For a concise treatment of Islam's cultural and material repercussions in Bengal see Richard M. Eaton, "Islam in Bengal," in *Bengal: The Islamic Heritage*, ed. George Michell (London: Art and Archaeology Research Papers, 1983).

18. This episode is reported in biographies of the saint and in several secondary sources, including Kapoor, *Philosophy and Religion*, p.24, and Majumdar, *Caitanya*, pp.108ff.

19. Eaton, "Approaches," prepublication copy, p.7.

20. Mukherji, *Study of Vaisnavism*, p.162.

21. See inter alia De, *Early History*, chs. 4-6; Majumdar, *Caitanya*: Dimock, *Place*, chs. 4-5.

22. For one of the most detailed existing treatments of the demographics and internal organization of the Caitanyite movement see Joseph Thomas O'Connell, "Social Implications of the Gaudiya Vaisnava Movement" (Ph.D. diss., Harvard University, 1970).

23. Nicholas, "Vaisnavism and Islam," pp.39-40.

24. Significantly, the largest single Vaishnava community in Bengal comprises a depressed agricultural caste situated in the eastern region, the Namasudras (Candalas). For an account of the socioreligious and political history of this community see Sekhar Bandyopadhyay, "Caste and Politics in Eastern Bengal: The Namasudras and the Anti-Partition Agitation, 1905-1911" (Occasional paper, Centre for Southeast Asian Studies, University of Calcutta, 1981).

25. Nicholas, "Vaisnavism and Islam," p.40.

26. De, *Early History*, pp.108-109; Dimock, *Place*, p.79.

27. They included Nityananda, Advaita Acarya, Srivasa Pandita and his grandnephew Vrndavana-dasa, Gadadhara Pandita, and Srinivasa; see De, *Early History*, pp.72, 30-31, 79, 48 and 60.

28. Surajit Sinha, "Vaisnava Influence on a Tribal Culture," in *Krishna: Myths, Rites and Attitudes*, ed. Milton Singer (Chicago: University of Chicago Press, 1971), pp.64-89.

29. Faye Levine, *The Strange World of the Hare Krishnas* (Greenwich, CT: Fawcett, 1974).

30. See Klaiman, *Singing the Glory*, pp.1-22 ("Introduction").

31. Complete synopses of *Srikrsnakirtana* are carried in Sen, *Chandidas*; in Klaiman, *Singing the Glory*, pp.15-16; and in M.H. Klaiman, "Vanamali as Forest Gardener: The *Srikrsnakirtana*", in *Proceedings of the 1981 Bengal Studies Conference*, ed. Ray Langsten (East Lansing: Michigan State University, South Asia Series Occasional Paper 34,1983), pp.9-11.

32. De, *Early History*, ch.7 ("The Literary Works").

33. Rupa Goswami, *Dana-keli-kaumudi* ("Moonlight on the Game of Tax Collecting") ed., trans., and with commentary by S.N. Shastri (Indore: Bharati Research Institute, 1976).

Related works by the author of this paper

1. *Singing the Glory of Lord Krishna: Baru Candīdāsa's Srikrsnakīrtana*. Chico, CA: Scholars Press (American Academy of Religion Classics in Religious Studies No. 5),1984.

2. "Religious Revolution and Religious Tradition: the case of Vaishnavism in Bengal." *South Asia* 6,2: 28-38 (1983).

3. "Masculine Sacrality." Forthcoming in *The Encyclopedia of Religion* (Macmillan).

THE ISMAILI MUSLIM IDENTITY AND CHANGING CONTEXTS

Professor Azim Nanji

Oklahoma State University, U.S.A.

INTRODUCTION

The Shia Ismaili Muslims constitute one of the branches of Islam and represent a minority within the Muslim *Ummah*. They are found at present in some 25 different countries of the world, primarily in western Asia (including India, Pakistan, Iran, Afghanistan and Syria), Central Asia including the Soviet Union, China in the Northern Himalayan areas of the Indo-Pakistan Subcontinent, Eastern Africa and now increasingly in the western world, primarily in Great Britain, Canada and the United States.[1]

The purpose of my paper is to explore within the changing contexts of the last 150 years, the interaction between identity and change in the Ismaili community, with a focus on those members of the community whose roots were in the Subcontinent, who subsequently migrated to East Africa and then in the last quarter of a century, have begun to make their home in the West. For comparative purposes I also wish to give as an example the situation of Central Asian Ismailis in the Northern areas of Pakistan. My method will be to treat the various transitions that mark modern Ismaili history and to relate these to the way in which the Ismaili identity has been defined and itself defines the type of institutional, religious and ritual change that has enabled Ismailis to maintain their religious identity in changing contexts.[2]

My starting point is the definition of the initial boundaries that circumscribe the Ismaili community during its first significant phase of change in the middle of the 19th Century and the subsequent redefinition and extension of these boundaries.

ISMAILIS OF THE INDO-PAKISTAN SUBCONTINENT

In the mid-nineteenth century groups of the Indian Ismaili community were to be found in Sind, Gujarat, Punjab and other centres in northern and western British-ruled India. The migration of the *Imam* of the time, Hasan Ali Shah (Aga Khan I) from Iran to India, and the eventual establishment of his headquarters in Bombay in 1848, created the initial context for changes in the community's future organization and development.

The Aga Khan and his successors, Aga Khan II (d. 1885) and the well-known international figure Aga Khan III (d. 1957), adopted in subsequent years a program of reorganization and modernization of the community's structure which sought to establish continuity with past tradition even while creating connections with institutions and patterns of economic life under the British.

Since the present Imam, Shah Karim, Aga Khan IV, assumed the position of Iman in 1957, there have been many fundamental political and economic changes that have affected Ismailis all over the world. Under his leadership, the programs initiated in previous years have been consolidated and additional steps taken to meet new community as well as national requirements, primarily in the Third World.

Overall, the strategy adopted by the Imams for effecting change in the community was to introduce modern administrative and educational institutions into the community and to relate these changes to an interpretation of the role of Ismaili Islam as a transforming agent. The key to this process was the mobilization and reorientation of traditional values. If, as it is generally maintained among Ismailis, their transition to modernity has been a successful synthesis of religious continuity and adaptive capability, then it is to their traditional insititutions and values that one must look for clues as to how they perceive this to have been achieved.

In addition to the affirmation of its religious values, the Ismailis have also been concerned in the present global situation of Muslims, to build bridges with other Muslims and non-Muslim communities. As articulated by their present Imam, his main objectives have been to:

> ... help the Community adjust to increasingly rapid forces of modernization and what I would call threats of extreme secularisation, the imbalances which one notes in certain parts of the world caused by the unequivocal search for material wealth, which passes the limits of reason. I think that was a problem; not of one time but a continuing problem. A delicate balance had to be found between living in the Twentieth Century, with all that means in terms of technological knowledge, of aspirations for material well-being and, at the same time, the actual turning into practice of the spirit of the Muslim brotherhood, the practice of one's faith and the concern for the betterment of the people. That was one issue which I sought to deal with. The second issue was the adjustment of the Community to new economic and political situations and that, of course, must also remain a continuing problem. There is no doubt that the situation in Africa between 1957 and 1983 has changed very radically, the situation in the Indo-Pakistan sub-continent has changed, the situation in the Middle East has changed very rapidly, new communities have established themselves in the Western World and adjustments to these new political and economic realities have been of major concern to me. A third area has been to build upon the institutional structure which my grandfather had created so that the members of the Community and others would use these institutions which were not only responding to the existing problems but were sufficiently well managed to anticipate future requirements and to grow in such a way that they became strong pillars of support for the Community in fields of education, health, housing and economic development. Another element which has been of concern to me, has been to try to build bridges amongst the various 'Tareeqas' in Islam. I have felt that Islam must not be exposd to increasing polarisation and division — after all the consequence would only breed weakness. I have encouraged my Community and, through my own actions, tried to build unity. ...[3]

The implementation of these goals and the enlargement of boundaries, also incorporated adjustments in the practice of the faith that had developed and became ingrained in the community over the period of its history and development in India. Some of these had been retained with the tradition as part of the process of conversion from Hinduism to Islam in previous centuries. Examples of these were Indian or Hindu customs of inheritance, marriage, etc. These were discouraged and a stronger affirmation of Ismaili Shiite tradition came to be integrated in the personal and family law. Certain ritual practices were retained and modified and even acted as agents of change in the movement towards greater self-identification with modern Ismaili Islam.

This process of change was extended and given wider application in the social context, as well. As an example, the Imam also encouraged women to participate actively in the public performance of prayers. When studying the community in a comparative context, one finds the role of women in ritual practice more pronounced among Ismailis of Indo-Pakistani origin than perhaps among other Muslim groups; the wider role envisaged for women by the Imams was facilitated and prepared for in part by their growing role in the religious life of the community. Certain rituals thus played a crucial role as agents of social change and were linked to the overall policy of the community in encouraging education among girls and indeed in creating a stronger role for them in the modernized institutions of the community. When viewed diachronically, Indian Ismaili rituals may be very useful tools for analyzing in more detailed fashion how patterns of belief and community organization are interdependent, and may provide significant clues to how a religious community adapts its symbols and concepts in new or changed situations.

As is well known, the Ismailis, like other Shia in general, have evolved through Muslim history their own framework for implementing the *Shariah*. The above process indicates a reestablishment of the fundamental practices with reference to that historical framework and a realignment of practices that were congruent with past practice as well as the normative Ismaili traditions among its communities in other parts of the world such as Syria, Iran, Central Asia and East Africa. These communities were also going through similar periods of transition, albeit at a differing pace and within varying historical circumstances.

An example of one such community, is that of Ismailis of Central Asian origin who today live in what are known as the Northern Areas of Pakistan.

ISMAILIS OF THE NORTHERN AREAS OF PAKISTAN

These Central Asian Ismailis are located in probably what is among the most spectacular geographical settings in the world, where three great mountain ranges of Central Asia—the Himalayas, the Karakorums, and the Hindu Kush converge. Several major peaks such as the K-2, the Nanga Parbat, and the Rakaposhi, all rise majestically within this setting. The River Indus flows through the region carving out valleys that make human settlement possible.

It is in this setting in Central Asia and more particularly in Gilgit, Hunza, and Chitral, now part of the Northern Area of Pakistan, that one finds the presence of Nizari Ismailis of Central Asian origin. It must be noted that Pakistan and India are also home to the ancestors of those Ismailis already referred to in North America.

A BIRD'S-EYE VIEW OF HISTORY

The early history of this region has yet to be written. There has been no systematic collection of the oral tradition that constitutes by far the most significant source. What has been recorded by political agents, travellers and now local historians is sketchy and vague, and refers mostly to legends that range from tracing the origin of people of the area to remnants of Alexander's soldiers or to Indo-Scythian tribes who came up the Indus Valley and settled there. The languages spoken in the area and reflecting the oral culture of pre-modern times, Burushaski in Hunza, Khowar in Chitral, and Shina in Gilgit are considered Dardic or Kafiric languages bearing little resemblance to either Indian, Iranian, or Turkish language patterns. Current studies on these languages by French-Canadian scholars, and archeological and ethnographic studies initiated by professor Karl Jettmar of Heidelberg University, will, one hopes, throw some light on their origins and relationship to other Central Asian languages and cultures.

One thing is certain: The physical barriers and remoteness of the region helped sustain the autonomy both of language and culture. Buddhist artifacts, as in Afghanistan, are found in the area, indicating the presence of some form of Buddhism, but this may have been the result of contact in China, that constituted for a long time the major point of contact with this area. There were three trading routes that allowed for trade between Central and South Asia through this region. Raiding of caravans was therefore an important aspect of the economic life of the region.

In the nineteenth century, this area became a part of the struggle for Central Asia that pitted Britain against Russia. Hunza's strategic importance, lying as it did on the direct line of Russian advance to the Subcontinent, caused the British to divert the caravan route away from the Hunza Pass, causing the people to change their tactics and raid the alternative route. It is said that as a result the British decided to move against the area and in 1891 captured it and integrated it into the Indian Empire, putting it under the control of Kashmir. In 1935 a separate Gilgit Agency was set up to oversee the area; and in 1947 the partition of British India led to a dispute over the whole Kashmir region. After the ceasefire in 1948, the area came under Pakistani control and was managed until the 1970s as a special territory, with a degree of local autonomy granted to the ruler known as *Mir* and then finally designated and integrated as part of the Northern Areas of Pakistan.

It is not known when conversion to Islam took place. Tradition has it that a *pir* introduced Islam in the area during the medieval period and that he converted its people to Shiism. It has also been suggested that the adoption of Ismailism in some areas may be no more than five generations old. Prior to that they are believed to have been Ithna Ashari. Until the oral tradition and other historical materials have been fully analyzed and evaluated, we remain in the dark about the introduction of Islam and Ismailism to this area.

CHANGING CONTEXTS

The last decade or so has witnessed major changes for the people of the region. By way of contrast with other Ismaili communities, I want to examine three significant contextual changes that have affected the Ismailis here.

The first context is broadly political and involves the integration of the Northern Areas into the political framework of what remained of Pakistan after the emergence of Bangla Desh in 1971. As part of this integration, the area was also drawn into the larger context of the development process affecting Pakistan. The autonomous control in local matters exercised by the Mir in Hunza or the Political Agents in Gilgit or the Special Administration of these "disputed" territories was now replaced by centralized government institutions.

A second major change was effected by the building of the Karakorum Highway, a 600-mile metalled dual highway that winds its way through the mountains and links the capital of Islamabad to the Northern Areas, up to the Kunjerab Pass bordering on China. The KKH, as it is known, was officially opened in 1978.

This has had tremendous economic implications for the area; Gilgit has become a major trading center and the primarily subsistence agricultural life of the Northern Areas is being complemented by other commercial activity, including the mining of precious minerals.

The third, and for our purposes most significant change, is in the widening of their sense of religious identity. The integration of the Nizari Ismailis of the area into the national, i.e., Pakistani, and global development policies of the present Imam has led to major institutional and administrative change. The focus of change has been community initiative, engendered by guidance from the Imam and channeled through new and appropriate institutions that blend private, national, and international resources, and intended to benefit not only Ismailis, but to a great extent all those who live in the area.

In the case of the Northern Areas, this has meant the creation of Councils and other administrative structures similar to those among other Ismailis. This process had been initiated by the previous Imam, Sultan Muhammad Shah; but in time the institutions have involved much larger segments of the community, so that at present there are local Ismaili councils in each of the four main regions of the Northern Areas — Hunza, Gilgit, Chitzar, and Chitral, and institutions that look after the health, economic, housing, and educational needs of the community.

As with other Ismailis, religious life was built around the *jamat khanas*, of which there are now twenty-six in the Northern Areas. Contact with other Ismailis has also brought about a great deal of uniformity in practice, though the specifically Central Asian character of the Ismaili heritage has been maintained. Persian Ismaili literature and literature in the local languages remain the main source; and the Arabic script with additional Urdu characters is now employed to record material in the local languages. All these changes reflect the growing consciousness of an Ismaili identity within the larger context of a Pakistani Muslim nation and bring in its wake all the ambiguities that accompany the larger transition going on in the Muslim world and the transition the Ismailis of the Northern Areas have to make as a minority within this larger *Ummah*.

CONCLUDING REMARKS

The above developments raise general questions about how change comes about in traditionally religious communities like the Ismailis, where the religious heritage has obviously constituted one of the sources of vitality in modern times. It also raises broad questions about how religions like Islam may adapt to existing conditions and the tension and ambiguity inherent in both processes of change and adaptation and their relationship to an Islamic sense of identity.

In a recent essay, Mary Douglas argues that "events have taken Religious Studies by surprise".[4] As an example, she cites the fact that scholars were unable to foretell the so-called resurgence of Islam. Their inability to perceive the vitality and revival of traditional religious forms is traced to the absence of a critical methodology and undue focus on secularization as the major tool for comprehending responses in societies where modernization is taking place. In the case of modern and contemporary Islam, it can be argued that some of the methodological shortcomings identified by Mary Douglas have recently led scholars to overemphasize one particular aspect, namely, the conjunction of faith and political power. It is noteworthy that several recent scholarly books have incorporated this notion as a central concern, so much so that the word "power" occurs in the titles of the works themselves.[5]

In societies that have come to believe that the power of religion has been neutralized by secularization and modernity and shifted to other domains, such a trend in religious consciousness appears only to be menacing and threatening. And an overemphasis on it causes one to miss or ignore much of the transformative potential within the religious consciousness. Misleadingly simplistic perspectives obscure the complexity of the search for self-identification within the Islamic tradition and the efforts of particular Muslims to confront the issues of the modern age. The situation demands, as Robert Bellah indicates,[6] more than the simplistic paradigm of a movement from "traditional" to "modern". It requires a focus on how religious tradition acts as a "moderating" or "equilibrating" force that does not withdraw from the crisis of modernity through utopian or authoritative modes but rather responds to it and shapes the direction in which society is to move.

In this paper, I have tried to show how one Muslim group has sought to address itself to the problems of modernity and to develop solutions and strategies for maintaining continuity and equilibrium by anchoring its sense of identity in its vision of Islam. In common with many other fellow-Muslims, the Ismailis believe that the disengagement of the issues of modern life from an Islamic perspective would create a dichotomy and an artificial division in their approach to the world, and that such a posture would in any case be antagonistic to the spirit and experience of Islam. The crux of the experience as reflected specifically in the approach adopted by the Nizari Ismailis, revolves around the ideal of creating a society to serve both material and spiritual needs. As Jacques Berque has pointed out, the acceptance of modernity and the challenges it poses necessitates one of two attitudes: first, adapting while preserving certain safety mechanisms; and second, and more complex, integrating what he calls the "movement of the world" into one's own system.[7] Among Muslims, these processes can by no means be homogeneous since they are diverse peoples with different backgrounds and contexts. Yet at the heart of all their responses appears to be a shared concern for establishing a balance among all the elements of the system: the practice of faith, the threat of secularization, the aspiration for material development and growth, and the building of bridges between Muslims and others in an increasingly shrinking and interdependent world. By focusing on how two segments of the Ismaili community, living under totally different material conditions, have addressed these various issues, I hope the paper has illustrated both the unity and the diversity of Muslim responses to modernization, and thrown some light on the dilemma highlighted at the Congress in Hans Mol's opening address regarding the balance religions try to achieve as they seek to maintain order and transcendence in the face of increasing complexity and the threat of disorder.

NOTES

1. For the Ismailis in general, see W. Madelung, "Ismailiyya", Encyclopedia of Islam, New Edition (Leiden: E.J. Brill, 1954-), Vol. IV, 198-206 and S.H. Nasr (ed.) Ismaili Contributions to Islamic Culture (Teheran: 1977).
2. The material for the paper is drawn in part from two other studies, see Azim Nanji, "A Religious Minority in Transition: The Case of Two Ismaili Communities", in Papers in Comparative Studies: Religion in the Modern World, Vol. 3 (1984) 169-182, and "Moral Principles in Tension: The Case of the Nizari Ismaili Muslims" in Shariat and Alternative Codes of Behaviour in Southern Asian Islam (Berkeley: University of California Press, forthcoming).
3. From an interview with H.H. The Aga Khan in Pakistan and Gulf Economist (March 12-18, 1983), p. 11.
4. Mary Douglas, "The Effect of Modernization on Religious Change," Daedalus, 3/4 (Winter, 1982), 1.
5. Examples include A.S. Cudsi and Ali Dessouki (eds.) Islam and Power (Baltimore and London: The Johns Hopkins University Press, 1981); E. Mortimore, Faith and Power (New York: Vintage Books, 1982); and Daniel Pipes, In the Path of God: Islam and Political Power (New York: Basic Books, 1983).
6. Robert Bellah, "Religion and Secularization in Societies" in Papers in Comparative Studies, see n. 2.
7. Jacque Berque, "Islam and Innovation," in Islam, Philosophy and Science (Paris: The UNESCO Press, 1981) 73.

DESCRIPTIONS OF THE IMMORTALS AND THE TAOIST IDENTITY

Bartholomew P. M. Tsui

Chinese University of Hong Kong

INTRODUCTION

Like the lives of saints in Christianity, the biographies of Taoist immortals (*hsien*) provide exemplars for the Taoist life. They are models for imitation and identification. In so doing, these stories reveal the true significance of the teaching of a religion in a manner often missing in philosophical discussions, for, in a biography, abstract thoughts are translated into possible practical actions.[1] Specific to our interest, stories of the immortals reveal the nature and state of the Taoist goal, the extraordinary powers they enjoy, the religious practices they follow and the conduct they prefer. To anticipate our conclusion, the Taoist exemplar reveals in every respect the classic functions of a religion. The immortal provides an identity which defeats the fundamental limitations encountered in human life: death, sickness, old age, powerlessness and social evil. On becoming an immortal, human life is ultimately transformed.

Such a conclusion differs significantly from current interpretations of the Taoist goal. Current interpretations of Taoism show particular interest in those aspects of the Tao which equate it with the order of nature. The latter is understood to mean that all things change by themselves according to certain regular patterns. To follow the Tao means to acquiesce in the unfolding of the process of life and death. To participate in the natural rhythm is all there is to human destiny. Assuredly there are concepts in *Lao Tzu, Chuang Tzu, Huai-nan Tzu* and others which lead to the naturalistic interpretation. Lao Tzu says, "The Way conforms with Nature (*Tao fa Tzu-ian*)." (ch. 25) Chuang Tzu's attitude towards death, shown in a few stories, is that one should resign oneself to the natural process.[2] Yet the concept of Tao presents another aspect which is difficult to reconcile with the order of nature. Tao is the trancendent reality behind the world of phenomena. The one who possesses the Tao rises above the limitations imposed by nature. Chuang Tzu's emphasis on unlimited freedom, mysticism and the extraordinary powers acquired by the Perfect Man seems to indicate that there is no simple answer to his position with respect to death or nature. To delve deeper into this question is beyond the scope and intention of this paper. Here I only want to draw attention to the inadequacy of drawing a conclusion with respect to the Taoist view of religion on the basis of the simple equation of Taoism with naturalism.

Being convinced of the equation of Taoism with naturalism, some scholars interested in the Taoist belief in the immortality pill seek to explain that immortality can be completely natural. To support their case they sometimes exerted a free hand in their interpretations. For example, they say that Taoist paradises are simply secluded scenic places within this world. They consistently avoid extensive discussions of inner alchemy (*nei-tan*) and the experiences of these Taoists because it is hard to see how these are natural processes.

The upshot of these interpretations is that the Taoist is seen as seeking nothing but to be natural. The logical conclusion from this position is that the Taoist does not seek any ultimate transformation. In other words, the Taoist has no religious consciousness. And since naturalism is also thought to be widely accepted by persons who call themselves Confucians and Buddhists of the Ch'an school, it is sometimes said to be the Chinese world-view. The conclusion is, if the equation of Taoism with naturalism be correct, the Chinese have no religious consciousness and they have no need of religion. My analysis of the biographies of the immortals shows that this opinion could not be farther from the truth. In fact, the biographies can be fully understood only in terms of a religious quest. The main bulk of this essay is to enter into dialogue with one of the current chief interpreters of *hsienhood* and to show how material from the biographies can serve as correctives to his interpretation.

NEEDHAM'S INTERPRETATION

The most celebrated interpreter of the *hsien* phenomenon in recent years is Joseph Needham. In volume 5 part 2 of his momumental work *Science and Civilization in China*, which deals with alchemy and chemistry, he sets out to answer the question as to why belief in the drug of immortality and its active pursuit occurred in China and China alone.[3] It is assumed that the effect of the elixer is the indefinite prolongation of this life and its rejuvenation. Needham thinks that there are two pre-conditions for the rise of the belief in the drug of immortality: (i) there must be a great love of life on earth;[4] and (ii) there must be an absence of belief in another world the entrance to which is ethically determined.[5] If ethics becomes the determining factor for entrance into another world, there would be no point in seeking the elixer. If the only world that exists is this world, then it makes sense to look for some sort of medicine which may prolong this life indefinitely. If ethics makes no difference to the span of life, then the only means of prolonging life is material.

Needham thinks these two conditions existed in ancient China and they permitted the belief in the drug of immortality to rise. Needham's characterization of *hsienhood* entails two corollaries. First, an indefinite prolongation of life is not contrary to nature.[6] Since the pursuants of elixer are Taoists and Taoists are said to be followers of nature, it is imperative, assuming a consistency to exist within the Taoist view, that the above be true. Second, all phenomena associated with *hsien* must show naturalistic characteristics. For example, Taoist paradises are not inaccessible other-worlds but are only some actual far-away mountains or islands of this world. The Yellow Spring (*huang ch'üan*) is not abysmal hell but merely some sort of a cave a few yards below ground. The existence of Earthly-immortals (*ti-hsien*) who refuse the Taoist paradise indicates the ethos for the natural.

Needham went to great lengths in search of supports for these corollaries. In order to clarify what he meant by the absence of other-worldly belief in Chinese culture, he made a comparison of the beliefs about the after-life in all religions. For this purpose, he constructed a diagram on page 78. A discussion of this diagram will be made below. What Needham intended to do is very clear. He has determined that the world-view of the Taoist is the order of nature. A superior will, spirits, demons and ghosts do not exist. The only reality is the world of nature. Man arranges the best he can from whatever forces he can summon from nature. Thus, he makes the Taoist a believer in modern materialism. The pursuit of immortality is only a little skill one acquires along the way of discovery of nature, almost a pastime on the same level as the harnessing of natural forces by the invention of machines. As Needham sees it, the Taoist is so perfectly happy with life in this world that he does not feel the need for a radical change. The Taoist is devoid of a religious sense. I would suggest, however, that Needham's characterization of the Taoist immortal does not tell the whole story and that the phenomenon of the *hsien* will be better understood in terms of a religious quest.

REPLY TO NEEDHAM

The unsatisfactoriness of Needham's interpretation of the immortals springs from the fact that he seeks a strict consistency in Taoist thought and action that may not have been there in the first place. To Needham, Taoism means the belief that the universe operates according to its own inbuilt laws alone. That is the only reality. A Taoist is one who seeks to allow nature to play out its own development to the full. That is the meaning of *wu-wei*. Needham, therefore, sets himself the task of proving that all other Taoist thought and activities must be consistent with the above definition. This task is wholly unnecessary! First of all, we do not have a defined essence called Taoism. Considering that diverse and even contradictory doctrines are grouped under Taoism, we are not sure if the word is anything more than a bibliographical label.[7] We are not sure if the Taoists who express belief in the order of nature are also those who experimented with immortality drugs. Second, even if they were the same people, it is still not necessary to assume that they felt urged to connect belief in the order of nature with the experiment in immortality drugs, anymore than liturgical Taoists feel the necessity of reconciling the theory of *yin-yang* and five phases with the belief in gods. Taoists themselves never claimed that in seeking the immortality pill, they were following *wu-wei*. On the contrary, there were Taoists who scorned those who attempted to lengthen their lives by various means. Chuang Tzu chided those who practice "bear-hangings and bird-stretchings, hoping to lengthen their lives".[8] Following nature would be to accept death with an even mind, if Chuang Tzu's several stories on death are admitted as significant.[9]

On the meaning of "following nature" it should be pointed out that Needham understands the term differently from the ancient Chinese. The consequence of Needham's view that the only reality is that of Nature is that man may do whatever he wants to do and yet still be within nature, for the only course of action that may have any effect must be bound by the laws of nature. "We cannot command Nature except by obeying her."[10] Man cannot not be bound by the laws of nature. He is powerless in acting against nature. In effect, Needham allows the Taoist all sorts of experiments and inventions of techniques and declares that none of these activities are against *wu-wei*. That may be Needham's thinking, but it is certainly not Taoist thinking. Needham's understanding would have made the Taoist injunction *wu-wei* redundant, for if man is completely powerless if he acts against nature, what is the point of telling him not to act against nature. He could never harm nature or anybody anyway. For the ancient Chinese, *tzu-jan* means the regular outcome of events. The deliberate interference of the normal pattern like the use of the immortality drug and other techniques is unnatural. That is why the immortality pill is called an unnatural thing (*pu jan chih wu*).[11] Naturalism would mean, according to Chuang Tzu, acquiescence in the natural life-span.[12]

This-worldly/other-worldly

It would be so much easier to equate Taoism with naturalism if one could show that Taoists have no conception of another world, and that paradises and hells are actual places on earth. Needham designed a diagram which represented the major types of beliefs with respect to the after-life.[13] The major division in this diagram is between the belief in the other-world and the belief that the immortals and the dead are bound within this world. The "other-worldly" type of belief stemmed from Indo-Iranian sources which spread to Hinduism, Buddhism, Christianity and Islam.

The "this-worldly" type included the Israelite belief in Sheol, the Greek in Hades and Chinese beliefs. It is not clear how Needham distinguishes the "other-worldly" from the "this-worldly". It seems that for him, it is the presence of a judgment and the separation of the good from the evil that makes these abodes other-worldly, for these places are unthinkable within this world.[14] In a note in which he disagrees with Yu Ying-shih's distinction between the "this-worldly" and the "other-worldly", it can be deduced that Needham was thinking of actual physical worlds.[15]

Though appearing simple and attractive, Needham's diagram opens a can of worms when his concepts are examined closely. He thinks that entrance to the other-world is ethically determined. Any beginning theology student can tell him that Heaven is a gratuitous gift, that is, man is saved by God's grace. In the Indian scene, no matter how much good work one may do one may never attain *moksha*. Only true knowledge (*jñāna*) can free man from this world (*samsāra*). These are minor errors compared to the major difficulty of his diagram.

The major difficulty with Needham's scheme is his distinction between the this-worldly and the other-worldly. When Needham talks about the other world, he means an actual, physical other world. Now, we moderns, well-used to the rounded earth and the solar system, have no difficulty at all in conceiving of another world. But for the ancient people to whom the earth is flat, it is impossible to conceive of another world which is not continuous with this one. Either it is Amitabha's paradise, which is extremely far away to the west, but still on earth, or it is Heaven above the dome of the sky, but still our sky. *Huai-nan-tzu* says, "Being circular the heavens have no edge and that is why they cannot be observed; being square the earth has no limit and that is why none can spy out her gates."[16] Hell is below ground. The point is, it is impossible to distinguish between the Christian or the Indian Heaven and the sky abode of the Taoist immortals with respect to their this-worldly or other-worldly character. Dante toured Hell through a cave that led below ground. Ought one then designate the Christian Hell as this-worldly? Needham was not unaware of the difficulty of the concept of actual physical other-worlds. That is why he retreated to a different criterion for distinguishing the other-world from this one: the presence of a judgment or ethical determination. But why should the presence of an ethical determination be a criterion for distinguishing the other-world from this world? The Christian Heaven is not ethically determined inasmuch as Christ saves by his grace. The entrance to the Taoist paradise is ethically determined in the sense that, according to an almost unanimous Taoist view, only the moral person can advance in the Taoist path.

Taoist paradises

The most damaging evidence against the usefulness of Needham's this-worldly other-worldly scheme is in the descriptions of the Taoist paradises themselves. How happy would Needham be if it were true to say that "the deathless being remained among the scenic beauties of earth or ascended as a perfect immortal to the ranks of the Administration on high — in either case within the natural world suffused by the Tao of all things."[17] But Taoist paradises are never as natural as Needham wished them to be. Let us examine a few examples. In the first chapter of Chuang Tzu, there is a description of a Holy Man living on faraway Ku-she mountain.[18] This Holy Man is invariably taken to mean a Taoist immortal. Not only is he an etherealized being capable of climbing the clouds and riding a flying dragon, but he is also capable, by concentrating his spirits, to protect creatures from sickness and plague and make the harvest plentiful. In short, he has miraculous powers. He escapes from the limitations confronted by mortal men. Would that not go against Needham's concept of the Taoist after-life, where both good and evil men indifferently find their abode? Just what on earth is a "flying dragon" in the natural world? I have already pointed out that it is impossible for the ancient people to conceive of an other-world in Needham's sense. When the story mentions a faraway Ku-she mountain, it is tantamount to saying "in another world." This Taoist paradise is so fantastic that Chien Wu, the man who related the story, thinks it "wild and wide of the mark, never coming near human affairs."[19] After telling the story, Chien Wu said, "I thought this was insane and refused to believe it."[20] This paradise is so great a contrast from ordinary human life that it represents an ultimate liberation from the limitations of life on earth. The story makes religious sense.

The book *Lieh Tzu* has the same story, but it contains a longer description of the idealized condition of the holy mountain.

> There, the *yin* and the *yang* forces are always in harmony; the sun and the moon are always bright; the four seasons rotate in smooth succession; the wind and the rain are always well-balanced. Living things get their timely sustenance and harvests of grains are always bountiful. The earth will not cause death or injury; the inhabitants will not harbour malice; myriad things will not bring disease and ghosts will have no baleful influence.[21]

A natural place on earth may have scenic beauty but it may never be conceived to be in such an ideal condition. Furthermore, the cause of those conditions is the presence of the Holy Man in the mountain and not vice versa.

The Taoists themselves were well aware that such paradises were mythological and not actual places on earth. In a description of another paradise, the Kingdom of Hua-hsü, Lieh Tzu has this to say:

> The kingdom of Hua-hsü was situated I know not how many tens of thousands of miles distant from the Ch'i State. It was beyond the reach of ship or vehicle or any mortal foot. Only the soul could travel so far.[22]

This paradise is incalculably faraway from the Middle Kingdom. This is the ancient people's way of saying that it is in another world. It is unreachable by all modes of transportation. It can only be visited by the spirit. Will this story not lay to rest Needham's theory that the Taoist paradise is this-worldly? The idealized condition of the Kingdom of Hua-hsü is similar to that of the Ku-she:

> This kingdom was without head or ruler; it simply went on of itself. Its people were without desires or cravings; they simply followed their natural instincts. They felt neither joy in life nor abhorrence of death; thus they came to no untimely ends. They felt neither attachment to self nor indifference to others; thus they were exempt from love and hatred alike. They knew neither aversion from one course nor inclination to another; hence profit and loss existed not among them. All were equally untouched by the emotions of love and sympathy, of jealousy and fear. Water had no power to drown them, nor fire to burn; cuts and blows caused them neither injury nor pain, scratching or tickling could not make them itch. They bestrode the air as though treading on solid earth; they were cradled in space as though resting in a bed. Clouds and mist obstructed not their vision, thunder-peals could not stun their ears, physical beauty disturbed not their hearts, mountains and valleys hindered not their steps. They moved about like gods.[23]

The isles of the blessed are also unattainable places.
Again Lieh Tzu says:

> To the east of the P'o sea — I do not know how many hundreds of millions of miles away — there is the Grand Chasm. It is actually a bottomless ravine

... In it there are five mountains. They are namely Tai-yü, Yüan-ch'iao, Fang-hu, Ying-chou and P'eng-lai.[24]

These islands are more than hundreds of millions of miles away to the east. This is a way of saying that they do not belong to this world. *Shih-chi* also says:

The three holy mountains, P'eng-lai, Fang-chang and Ying-chou are said to be in the P'o sea, not far from human habitation. If one were to go there, his boat would invariably be led away by a wind. It is reported by those who have gone there that on these mountains various immortal beings and the drug of immortality are found. All objects and living creatures are white in colour. The palaces are made of gold and silver. When viewed from a distance, the mountains look like clouds. When one arrives at the location, the three mountains appear from under water. When one goes near them, a wind immediately blows him away. In effect, no one is able to reach these mountains.[25]

"No one is able to reach these mountains." This is a way of saying that these islands are mythological. They are not actual places on which one can set foot.

Contrary to Needham's beloved idea that the Chinese love life on earth, the immortal can become weary of the world and depart from it. Chuang Tzu recorded such a case:

When the world has the Way, the sage joins in the chorus with all other things. When the world is without the Way, he nurses his Virtue and retires in leisure. And after a thousand years, should he weary of the world, he will leave it and ascend to the immortals, riding on those white clouds all the way up to the village of God. The three worries (old age, sickness and death) never touch him, his body is forever free of peril.[26]

If the immortal leaves the world, does he not go into another world? Is the village of God not another world?

Lastly, I want to recall the story of Hu Kung.[27] Hu Kung was an immortal who carried an empty gourd with him. Every night, when he retired, he jumped into his gourd. Later, his secret was discovered. When asked why he jumped into the gourd, Hu Kung invited the questioner to jump after him. Lo! What opened up within the gourd was a paradise complete with doors, paths, buildings, servants and so on. Does this paradise not belong to another world?

None of these descriptions of Taoist paradises fit with Needham's idea that they are "within the natural world suffused by the Tao of all things." They are all idealized places where the causes of human unhappiness are expurgated. Living there is a contrast to life on earth where there is old age, sickness and death. Paradises are frequently marked with geographical directions, but that does not mean they can actually be found. That is why they are said to be millions of miles away. Their phony directions must have been deliberate. On the one hand, geographical directions must be provided to indicate their reality. On the other hand, they must not be thought to be normally accessible. That is to say: Paradises are real but they are beyond this world.

Indeed, Needham's distinction between this-worldly and other-worldly paradises serves no useful purpose in religious interpretation. In terms of religious meaning, it is not important whether paradise is in another solar system or in some rather distant corner on earth. The relative inaccessibility of paradises in the latter case render them to have the same values as other-worlds. What is religiously significant about paradises is their unusual, idealized conditions which cannot be described as natural. In providing a scenario where life's defects are made whole, Taoist paradises serve to define the Taoist identity. In other words, stories about after-life should be treated as mythological in the sense that myths in other religions serve to define man's situation in the Universe.

The hsien's Transcendent Life

Needham's thesis on why alchemy flourished in Taoism depends on three assumptions: First, nature must be regarded as the only reality. There must be a belief that only this world exists. Taoist paradises are merely scenic locations somewhere on earth. Second, it is possible, by harnessing the forces of nature, to extend human life indefinitely. Third, Chinese love life in this world. One of the consequences of these assumptions is that *hsienhood* is nothing more than an indefinite prolongation of this life on this earth. I have already discussed extensively part of the first assumption in connection with Needham's distinction between the this-worldly and the other-worldly. Here I shall take up the other assumptions and shall try to show that contrary to his view the *hsien* leads a transcendent life, an existence on a higher plane.

Needham writes, "In accord with the basically this-worldly ethos of the Chinese, life on earth was found good and greatly treasured, so that from the Shang period onwards emphasis on longevity grew and grew, length of life in some quiet hermitage or surrounded by one's descendants being the greatest blessing the Heaven could confer."[28] "The ancient Chinese were a very this-worldly people, full of the love of life and a zest for its joys and pleasures."[29] As a general description, it is true to say that the Chinese love life, but it would be a mistake to single it out as a characteristic which marks the Chinese off from other members of the human race. So did the Aryans love life, the Hebrews, the Greeks. Can we find any people who does not treasure longevity? Why is it in all nations royal subjects cannot find a better salutation than to wish long life to their kings?

Needham lays great store on the "this-worldly ethos of the Chinese." Paradoxically, while Confucians may be said to have a this-worldly ethos, it is uncertain whether this designation fits well with Taoists. Those things which constitute this-worldly happiness — a lot of wealth, numerous children and grandchildren, hearty appetite, reputation among peers — are exactly what Taoists despise. Taoists reject having a good name and official positions. They reject rich food, fine dress and any sign of opulence which goes with worldly happiness. They prefer seclusion and quiet in mountains and caves. Disenchantment with the world was what drove Ch'ü Yüan to follow the steps of Ch'ih Sung Tzu, who had washed off the world's dust.

Yü Ying-shih expressed doubt whether rulers, well used to the pleasures of the palace, could whole-heartedly pursue the way of the immortals even though they desire everlasting life.[30] Taoists do these things precisely because they are not satisfied with what the world can offer. That is why paradises are invariably depicted as far superior to this world. To be sure, in the stories about Taoists, longevity is frequently mentioned as a sign of their accomplishment, but desire for longevity may not be used to indicate a love of this world. It indicates a desire for life as opposed to death. If, perchance, someone should use the story of Mr White-Stone, who preferred to stay in this world rather than to go up to heaven, to prove that the Taoist loved this world, it could be pointed out that it was precisely the unusual preference for this world which has made this story so famous.[31] It is the exception which makes the rule. The story originally may have an axe to grind. The reason why Mr White-Stone did not want to go to heaven was that he did not want to take a place among the celestial bureaucracy. The story may have been intended to serve as a criticism of the earthly bureaucracy. All discussions of the immortals rank *t'ien-hsien* (heavenly immortal) superior to *ti-hsien* (earthly immortal).

In Needham's naturalistic interpretation, becoming a *hsien* simply means an indefinite prolongation of this life through the power of immortality drug. If this were true, there should be a smooth transition from being a mortal to being an immortal. The biographies of the immortals, on the other hand, present a different picture. There is a clear disjunction between ordinary human life and life of an immortal. An immortal proper must invariably be taken up to heaven. Those Taoists who were left behind, like the *ti-hsien*, were not properly immortals. T'ai P'ing Ching says, "For this reason, when a man has not yet obtained the Tao he remains but a man. When he has obtained the Tao he will be transformed into an immortal. Being an immortal, he will be wafted up to the heavens, and will undergo transformations according to Heaven."[33] It is proper for a *hsien* to ascend to heaven. In the story of P'eng Tsu in *Shen-hsien ch'uan*, a distinction between *hsien* and *ch'ang sheng* (longevity) or *Te Tao Che* (possessor of the Way) is made several times:

> "Please explain to me the way to lengthen my life." P'eng Tsu replied, "If you wish to raise your body up to heaven ... you should employ the golden pill ... That is why one is wafted up to heaven in broad daylight. That is Tao in its highest order. For the next in order, one should love to cultivate one's spirit and ingest herbal medicine. One may then attain longevity (*ch'ang-sheng*) but he cannot order the ghosts and spirits to serve him, or to fly in the air."[34]

There is a story about a Taoist called Mr Blue Essence (*Ch'ing ching hsien sheng*). He had lived a thousand years and yet his appearance was that of a boy. He could walk five hundred miles a day. He could abstain from food for a whole year and yet he could also eat nine meals in a day. On being asked what kind of *hsien* Mr Blue Essence was, Tsu replied, "He is merely one who has obtained Tao, he is not yet a *hsien*."[35] Again, P'eng Tsu said, "If a man learns a little about Tao, he can live up to two hundred and forty years. If he knows a bit more, he may live up to four hundred and eighty. If he knows all about Tao, he can be exempted from death. But he is not yet a *hsien*."[36] The point about P'eng Tsu's speeches is clear. Being a *hsien* entails much more than Needham's indefinite prolongation of life on earth. Even the story of Mr White-Stone makes this distinction: "Mr White-Stone ... was already 2000 years old in the time of P'eng Tsu. He refused to practice the way of the ascending immortal (*scheng t'ien chih tao*) but only pursue the undying (*ch'ü yü pu ssu*)."[37]

Again, the story of I-chün wang-lao makes the distinction between the *hsien* proper who flies up to heaven and one who lives on indefinitely. Wang-lao and his entire household, including house, dogs and children, were wafted up to heaven while his servants were left behind a tree in the next village. The latter also attained eternal life (*ch'ang-sheng*).[38] Being able to fly into heaven is the dividing line between the *hsien* proper and those who are only on the way to becoming *hsiens*. Such an understanding is suggested by the *Hsü hsien ch'uan* which divides the biographies into two parts, the "Wafted-up-to-heaven" (*fei-sheng*) and the "Retire-to-transform" (*yin-hua*).[39] The preface of this book also says, "The one who follows the way of 'retire-to-transform' is one who, (dwelling) in a cave, retains his skin, changes his bones, preserves his breath and strengthens his body in the manner of a cicada, then, having completed becoming a true immortal, he is wafted up to heaven."[40] In other words, "retire-to-transform" is only a stage in the process of becoming a full-fledged hsien who can fly at will.

This ability to fly into a mythological world is carefully recorded in the biographies. In the *Lieh-hsien-ch'uan*, the characters used to indicate this ability are *sheng* (wafted up), *sheng-t'ien* (wafted up to heaven), *shang* (going up), *tu* (transcend), *chü* (depart).

For example, it is said of Neng-feng-tzu that he went up (*shang*) with smoke; of Ma-shih-huang that he departed (*chü*) on the back of a dragon; of Huang-ti that he was wafted up to heaven (*sheng-t'ien*); of P'eng Tsu that he rose up (*sheng*) to become a *hsien* and departed (*chü*); of Ch'ih-chiang tzu-yu that he said, "It is possible to walk in the clouds and human life can be made transcendent (*tu*)". The character *chü* is used in at least ten biographies in the *Lieh-hsien-ch'uan*. The terms *sheng, shang, tu, chü* represent a disjunction of the life of a *hsien* from those of mortals who live in this world. Even though it is hard for Taoists to conceive of other-worlds physically, their paradises are other-worldly in terms of religious meaning.

Enough has been said to demonstrate that Needham's naturalistic interpretation of the Taoist immortal is erroneous. Immortality is not simply an indefinite prolongation of this life in some scenic spot on earth. Becoming a *hsien* entails a disjunction from this life and an advancement to an otherwise inaccessible state where conditions of life are idealized and where all human limitations are transcended. The phenomenon of immortality is not a corollary of the philosophy of the order of nature. It arises from a religious concern that is common to humanity. It is for this reason that ultimate transformation is offered to the accomplished immortal.

NOTES

(1) The point that biographies are exemplars and that they reveal the truth of the religion is recognized by the collector of biographies himself. One example is the Yüan Dynasty collector Chao Tao-i, who said, "I shall discuss the Way and its Power with fair-mindedness; I shall reveal the exemplary lives of the immortals so as to make manifest the authentic teaching and to exalt the Great Transformation." *Li-shih chen hsien ti tao t'ung-ch'ien.* TT139 or Harvard-Yenching Index no. (HY) 150, *hsü*, 8a.

(2) Burton Watson, tr., *The Complete Work of Chuang Tzu* (N.Y.: Columbia University Press, 1968), ch.6, p.85, story about Master Lai; ch.18, pp.191-2, death of Chuang Tzu's wife.

(3) Joseph Needham, *Science and Civilization in China* (Cambridge: Cambridge University Press, 1974), p.71.

(4) *Ibid.,* p.82.

(5) *Ibid.*

(6) *Ibid.,* p.83.

(7) Arthur F. Wright, in "A Historian's Reflections on the Taoist Tradition", *History of Religions*, Vol.9 nos.2 and 3, (1969-70), 248-255, valiantly suggested, very tentatively, common attitudes among the various strands called Taoist. However, he has not examined whether the three common attitudes he put forward are compatible among themselves or not.

(8) *Chuang Tzu*, ch.15; cf. Watson, *op. cit.,* p.167.

(9) See note 2 above.

(10) Bacon's saying quoted by Needham, *op. cit.,* p.84.

(11) *Han-fei-tzu*, ch.32, as quoted in Needham, *op. cit.,* p.95.

(12) See note 2 above.

(13) Needham, *op. cit.,* p.78, table 93.

(14) *Ibid.,* p.80.

(15) *Ibid.,* p.95, note c. See also last sentence on p.77.

(16) *Huai-nan-tzu*, ch.15, p.253. Translation by Michael Loewe, *Chinese Ideas of Life and Death* (London: George Allen & Unwin Ltd., 1982), p.52.

(17) Needham, *op. cit.,* p.82.

(18) Watson, *op. cit.,* p.33.

(19) *Ibid.*

(20) *Ibid.*

(21) Translated from *Lieh-tzu chi shih*, p.45.

(22) Lionel Giles, *Taoist Teachings* (London: John Murray, 1947), p.35. Slight adjustment made to translation.

(23) *Ibid.*, pp.35-36.

(24) Translated from *Lieh tzu chi shih*, pp.151-152.

(25) *Shih Chi*, chüan 28, pp.1369-1370.

(26) Mainly Watson's translation, *op. cit.*, p.130, with modifications.

(27) *Shen-hsien ch'uan*, cited in *Tai-p'ing kuang chi*, chüan 12.

(28) Needham, *op. cit.*, p.82.

(29) *Ibid.*, pp.93-94.

(30) Ying-shih Yü, "Life and Immortality in the Mind of Han China," *Harvard Journal of Asiatic Studies*, vol.25 (1964-65), pp.94, 102.

(31) Needham, *op. cit.*, p.107.

(32) For example, *Tai Shang Ling-Pao Wu Fu Ching, Pao P'u Tzu*, cited by Needham, op. cit., p.106.

(33) *Tai P'ing Ching*, p.282.

(34) *Shen-hsien -ch'uan*, cited in *Tai p'ing kuang chi*, chüan 2, p.9.

(35) *Ibid.*

(36) *Ibid.*, p.10.

(37) *Li-shih chen hsien ti tao t'ung-ch'ien* (TT139), chüan 4, 1.

(38) *Hsü hsien ch'uan* (TT138), I chün wang lao, first chüan, pp.3-4.

(39) *Ibid.*, first chüan, p.1; second chüan, p.1.

(40) *Ibid.*, hsü, p.1.

Related works by the author of this paper:

"Tan Tse Tao: A Contemporary Chinese Faith-healing Sect in Hong Kong". Forthcoming in the *Journal of the Royal Asiatic Society*, Hong Kong Branch.

GLOSSARY

ch'ang-sheng	Huang-ti	sheng-t'ien
Chao Tao-i	I chün wang lao	Shih Chi
Ch'ih-chiang tzu-yü	li	T'ai P'ing Ching
Ch'ing ching hsien sheng	Li shih chen hsien ti tao t'ung ch'ien	T'ai p'ing Kuang chi
chü	Lieh hsien ch'uan	T'ai Shang Ling-pao Wu-fu Ching
ch'ü yü pu ssu	Lieh Tzu	Tai-yü
chüan	Lieh tzu chi shih	Tao fa tzu-jan
Fang-hu	Ma-shih huang	ti hsien
fei-sheng	nei tan	t'ien hsien
Han fei tzu	Neng-feng-tzu	tu
hsien	Pao P'u Tzu	tu-shih
hsü	P'eng'lai	tzu-jan
Hsü hsien ch'uan	P'eng Tsu	wu-wei
Hsü Ti-shan	pu jan chih wu	yin-hua
Hu Kung	shang	Ying-chou
Hua-hsü	Shen-hsien ch'uan	Yüan-ch'iao
Huai-nan-tzu	sheng	
huang ch'üan	sheng hsien chih tao	

NEO-CONFUCIANISM:

Theism, Atheism or Neither?

Paul Rule

La Trobe University
Bundoora, Victoria, Australia

There has been a quite extraordinary about-face in the study of Confucianism in the last generation. When I first began to study Confucianism, and was constantly struck by what I took to be overtly 'religious' elements in the theory and practice of the Confucian school, I felt myself a member of a defensive minority. I had on my side the earliest Western sinologists, the Jesuit missionaries of the 16th to the 18th centuries; a few missionary sinologists of the 19th century — including the great James Legge; and hardly any twentieth century authorities. Herlee Creel, of course, in the 1930's had denied that Confucius was an agnostic, but had backed off to some extent in his late work. James Ware with his uncompromising translation of *t'ien* as 'Sky' rather than Heaven, and his assertion that Confucius was an out-and-out rationalist represented the consensus position of Chinese as well as Western authorities, although the motives of the former were often more complex than those of the latter.

Today the position has been reversed, at least so far as early Confucianism is concerned. Our major Western authorities — including Tu Wei-ming, Donald Munro, Herbert Fingarette — all now take for granted that Confucius accepted and used as the underpinning of his moral and social teaching the Chou belief in a personal God, *t'ien* or Heaven; that personal spiritual development rather than political success was his aim; and that Confucianism should be seen as one of the great world religions, not in some strained or applied sense, but of right. Curiously, even in the People's Republic of China the view that Confucianism is a religion has recently been vigorously promoted, although, I suspect, for reasons that are not strictly or exclusively academic.

The religious dimension of Neo-Confucianism, however, remains more problematic. The early Jesuit position on Neo-Confucianism, adopted largely for polemic purposes, was to regard it as at best a kind of spiritual monism, at worst pure materialism and atheism. Religious practices, such as meditation, were attributed to Buddhist influence and its high moral tone to the persisting influence of an earlier Chinese natural religion. There are occasional flashes of insightful dissent from this party-line on the part of, especially, the more skilled sinologists amongst the missionaries. Some — Niccolo Longobardo and Claude Visdelou being the best known — wished to destroy what they saw as an artificial distinction between early Confucian theism and Neo-Confucian atheism. The classics and the four books, said Longobardo, are always read in the light of the Sung commentaries; whatever they might once have meant, they now are understood only in the light of Neo-Confucian materialism. Visdelou, on the other hand, at the height of the controversy over Chinese Rites i.e. the permissibility of Chinese converts to Christianity continuing to practice some at least of the domestic and public rituals prescribed by Confucianism, argued that Confucian practices were thoroughly enmeshed in Chinese superstition and idolatory. At least these Jesuit dissenters were more consistent than the arch-enemy of the Jesuits, Charles Maigrot, the Vicar-Apostolic of Fukien, who argued that seventeenth-century Confucians were simultaneously atheists and idolaters. The majority view, however, which was shared by most 19th and early 20th century commentators was that Neo-Confucianism was materialistic, acknowledged no personal God, and was a system of practical if theoretically inconsistent atheism.

The revaluation of Confucianism that has proceeded apace in the last decade or so has been extended from earlier to later Confucianism. Again, it is the religiousness of Confucian practice that has attracted most attention. The Columbia University seminar on Neo-Confucian thought and the several conferences whose proceedings have been edited by W.T. de Bary, have placed great emphasis on Neo-Confucian 'cultivation' and 'enlightenment'; on meditation practices such as 'quiet sitting'; on the dimension of transcendence in the moral, social and even political activities of Confucian scholar-officials. Studies of individual leading Confucians by Tu Wei-ming, Julia Ching, Rodney Taylor, Irene Bloom, and, of course, Liu Ts'un-yan, have shown them to be far from the austere deistic rationalists of the French *philosophes'* view of Chinese intellectuals. They emerge as passionate, committed and, yes, — religious leaders.

Comparatively neglected, however, has been the question of the status of Neo-Confucian metaphysics. We still await a philosophical and theological reassessment of the main concepts of Neo-Confucianism. Leibniz's pioneering attempt in his *Discourse on the Natural Theology of the Chinese* has recently been revived in the form of an annotated English translation, but it suffers from second-hand (often third-hand *via* missionary commentators) knowledge of the Chinese sources. Julia Ching devotes a stimulating but tantalisingly brief chapter to 'The Problem of God' in her *Confucianism and Christianity.* Wing-tsit Chan's many essays on Neo-Confucianism in *Philosophy East and West* and elsewhere, while focusing on clarifying the metaphysical concepts, are not concerned with comparative or theological evaluation. Such a task has not been attempted since the early 1920's when John Percy Bruce's *Chu Hsi and His Masters* and his annotated translation of some chapters of Chu Hsi's collected works, under the title of *The Philosophy of Human Nature,* appeared.

This paper has no ambitions to fill the gap so lightly disclosed. It is rather concerned with establishing the state of the question, the *problematik.* I wish to suggest that it is a matter of concern not only to China specialists, but also to the general phenomenology of religion and to contemporary theology. Here we have a major system of thought and practice, flourishing over a thousand years from the eleventh century to the present day, engaging men's deepest convictions, yet apparently unassimilable under our common analytic categories. As Bruce pointed out sixty years ago, there is something eminently unsatisfactory about our understanding of a system to which such apparently contradictory labels can be given as monotheism, pantheism, monism, spiritual dualism, materialism, theism and atheism. The fault may lie as much in our categories as in the subject of investigation.

NEO-CONFUCIANISM

For non-specialists amongst my audience, and with apologies to the experts, I must begin with a brief sketch of the origins of the system under discussion. And, in the first place, I must point out that 'Neo-Confucianism' itself is a misnomer. The Chinese have only used the term, *hsin-ju-hsueh,* 'New or Neo-Confucianism' quite recently, and then as a label for the 20th century revival of Confucianism as a philosophy of life. The Chinese themselves refer to the new metaphysical system that began in the Sung, based on the much older Confucian tradition but incorporating new perspectives, a new language and a much wider ambit, by names such as *li-hsueh*, 'the study of li (or Principle)'; *tao-hsueh*, 'the study of *tao*, the Way'; and, in its Ming development, *hsin-hsueh*, 'the study of Mind'.

To generalize grossly, the dominance of Confucianism during the first Imperial Dynasty, the Han (2nd century BC — 2nd century AD), was challenged, during the period of division and disorder after its collapse, by a revived Taoism and an imported Buddhism. It was only in the late T'ang/early Sung (9th and 10th centuries) that Confucianism began to recapture the ground lost, and, above all, to challenge its rivals on their own ground, metaphysics and spirituality. It would be myopic to see this as their explicit motivation. The old Confucian concerns with good government, historical precedent and correct human relationship are still dominant. But there is a recognition that new questions were abroad, the answers to which could not be read off the pages of the Confucian canon, and which had to be answered if Confucianism's claims to exclusive control of the state system and the educational establishment were to be justified.

The problem, then, was how to draw on Taoist cosmology, and Buddhist spirituality and metaphysics while appearing to base the new synthesis on the classic texts. It was Chou Tun-i (1017-1073) who found the way through by a piece of creative commentary on one of the more obscure passages in the most enigmatic of the classics, the *I Ching* or 'Book of Changes'. The passage occurs in the Third Appendix to the *I*, possibly of no earlier than Han date, and, as James Legge argued, probably of Taoist origin (Introduction to *The I Ching, Sacred Books of the East*, p.12). Legge translates it as follows:

> Therefore in (the system of) the Yi there is the Grand Terminus (*t'ai-chi*, Great or Supreme Ultimate), which produced the two elementary Forms. Those two Forms produced the Four emblematic Symbols, which again produced the eight Trigrams. The eight trigrams served to determine the good and evil (issues of events), and from this determination was produced the (successful prosecution of the) great business (of life).
>
> I Ching, p.373

What we have here is a typical piece of Han cosmology, a model of the production of the physical and moral universes. All that had to be added was Taoist/Buddhist metaphysics, and this was done through a new concept, the 'Non-Ultimate' or *wu-chi*, with its echos of Taoist 'nothingness' *(wu)* and Buddhist emptiness *(hsu)*.

So, Chou Tun-i begins his 'Explanation of the Diagram of the Great Ultimate' (*T'ai-chi-t'u shuo*):
The non-ultimate, but also the Great Ultimate!
wu-chi erh t'ai-chi

— perhaps the most commented on passage in Chinese literature. I haven't time here to go into the problems. *Chi* itself is ambiguous, meaning primarily a pivot (as of a door or gate), then the ridge of a roof, the zenith of the sky, the geographic poles, and finally the ultimate or limit. *T'ai-chi*, then, appears to be the ultimate source of all, the end of the chain of derived being. But *wu-chi*? Does it mean 'without limit' hence limitless or infinite in time and space? Or, simply, not limited, its limits indeterminate? Or absolute nothingness? and how is it related to *t'ai-chi*? The linking *erh* can mean simply 'and', 'also', 'moreover' but it may be taken in a qualifying sense as 'but', 'yet'; or as indicating temporal sequence, 'and then', and hence, here, differentiating rather than identifying *t'ai-chi* and *wu-chi*.

The 'Explanation' goes on to depict, as in the accompanying diagram, the generation by the Great Ultimate of *yang* and *yin*, which in turn generate the five agents —water, fire, wood, metal and earth — which are assimilated to *ch'i*, 'material-force' or 'matter-energy' of the universe. Hence *t'ai-chi* which is without limit, *wu-chi*, infinite, yet produces all the finite beings, and especially man.

> It is man alone who receives (the material forces) in their highest excellence, and therefore he is the most intelligent. His physical form appears, and his spirit develops consciousness. The five moral principles of his nature (humanity or *jen*, righteousness, propriety, wisdom, and faithfulness) are aroused by, and react to, the external world and engage in activity; good and evil are distinguished; and human affairs take place.
>
> (W.T. Chan, *A Source Book in Chinese Philosophy*, 463)

And so we are back with the Confucian concern for morality and social activity, but anchored in a new overarching framework.

Chou Tun-i's contemporary Chang Tsai (1021-1077) contributed to the conceptual armoury of Neo-Confucianism a developed concept of *ch'i*, 'material-force'. We have seen Chou's use of *ch'i* to describe the activities of the five agents. Much earlier the Han cosmologist Tung Chung-shu had written of *ch'i* as a 'limpid, colourless substance surrounding man as water surrounds a fish' (De Bary, *Sources*, 466) and like the ether of early modern physics, invoked to provide a physical connection and hence causal link between material objects. Like ether, too, etymologically it implies 'vapour'. Chang Tsai saw *ch'i* as in constant interaction with *li* or 'principle', which ordered this formless or disordered material-force into the myriad beings. He then identified *ch'i* with the *wu* and *hsu* of the Taoists and Buddhists, and argued that it was not in opposition to existence and existents, but their source (i.e. Chou Tun-i's *wu chi*).

The high-point of Chang Tsai's thinking was a vision of unity — cosmological, ethical and metaphysical — expressed in the famous 'Western Inscription' on the west wall of his study:

> Heaven is my father and Earth is my mother, and even such a small creature as I find an intimate place in their midst.
> Therefore that which fills the universe I regard as my body and that which directs the universe I consider as my nature.
> All people are my brothers and sisters, and all things are my companions.

There follows a detailed exposition of Confucian virtue, and moral examples from early Chinese history. And it concludes:

> Wealth, honour, blessing, and benefits are meant for the enrichment of my life, while poverty, humble station, and sorrow are meant to help me to fulfilment.
> In life I follow and serve (Heaven and Earth).
> In death I will be at peace.   (W. T. Chan, *Source Book*, 498)

I will not comment in detail on the 'Western Inscription' since its religious tone and the note of transcendence that it strikes are self-evident. 'Heaven' and 'Earth', however, deserve some notice. The coupling of Heaven with Earth, suggests that Heaven, *t'ien*, is not the early Chou God-concept, but more cosmological. Yet, neither are they impersonal or material. It is not a 'proto-scientific' concept. The universe is personal, responsive and ultimately moral.

The decisive steps in the systematising of these inchoate concepts were taken by Chang Tsai's nephews, the Ch'eng brothers, Ch'eng I (1033-1107) and Ch'eng

Hao (1032-1085). Ch'eng I, especially, took up the hints of his uncle about *li* or Principle, and made it the key-stone of the new *li-hsueh*. It was always hard to see how, in Chang Tsai's thought, the material world could be the vehicle for ethical and spiritual values, and how *ch'i* could be the common or linking principle between man and the ultimate. But *li*, principle or law, the ordering force, logically if not actually prior to and independent of *ch'i*, could play such a role. It could serve, too, as a metaphysical foundation for the old argument of Mencius for the innate goodness of human nature. The man who understood *li* would adopt an attitude of 'seriousness' (*ching*) towards the world and other men, expressed in the extension of knowledge to the utmost (another borrowing from early Confucianism) and *jen* or benevolence.

Ch'eng Hao, in anticipation especially of the School of Mind (*hsin-hsueh*) of the Ming, took the theory of *li* a decisive (and to many a dangerous) step further, by identifying *li* with both the individual human mind and 'the mind of the universe':

> The constant principle of Heaven and earth is that their mind is in all things, yet of themselves they have no mind; and the constant principle of the sage is that his feelings are in accord with all creation, yet of himself he has no feelings.
>
> (De Bary, *Sources*, 1, 506)

This is too inchoate to be regarded as a full blown pantheism of the Spinozan variety, or even a spiritual monism. However, this universal mind or Principle is clearly contrasted with matter, is spiritual. I suspect that, were it not for the shadow cast by Buddhist monism — and invoked by the more dominant *li-hsueh* interpretation in condemnation of *hsin-hsueh* — such passages would be read, like Chang Tsai's 'Western Inscription' as no more than a vigorous affirmation of the unity of all things.

It was Chu Hsi (1130-1200) who created the final synthesis of these ideas into what became Neo-Confucian orthodoxy. In many respects Chu was both less creative and less penetrating than his predecessors. But he was more systematic (one might even say 'scholastic'), prolific in his writings, and a politician of great ability and perception in a time of perpetual political crisis, the declining years of the Southern Sung.

Chu Hsi took from Ch'eng I (hence the common label of the Ch'eng-Chu School) the idea of building the new systematic exposition of Confucian metaphysics around the concept of *li*. If there is to be any reductionism it is in the direction of *li*. *Tai-chi* is ultimately *li*; *Tien* is, in manifestation at least, *li*; *hsin*, 'mind', is in the final analysis *li*; and Tao is the moral facet of *li*. This raises some very difficult and fundamental problems. Is *li* a category, a label, or is it a metaphysical reality? If the latter, it is certainly not an entity i.e., it cannot exist independently of *ch'i*, yet it has a certain priority, logical, causal, and perhaps, in Chu Hsi's mind, temporal. The best known passage on this comes from the *Li/Ch'i* section of Chu Hsi's *Complete Works* (Ch. 49 of the K'ang-hsi edition, *Chu Tzu Ch'uan-shu*):

> In the universe there has never been any material force (*ch'i*) without principle (*li*) nor principle without material-force.
>
> Question: Which exists first, principle or material-force?
>
> Answer: Principle has never been separated from material-force. However, principle is above the realm of corporeality whereas the material-force is within the realm of corporeality. Hence when spoken of as being above or within the realm of corporeality, is there not a difference of priority and posteriority? Principle has no corporeal form, but material-force is coarse and contains impurities.
>
> Fundamentally principle and material-force cannot be spoken of as prior or posterior. But if we must trace their origin, we are obliged to say that principle

is prior. However principle is not a separate entity. It exists right in material-force. Without material-force, principle would have nothing to adhere to. Material-force consists of the five agents of metal, wood, water, fire, and earth, while principle contains humanity, righteousness, propriety, and wisdom.

(De Bary, *Sources*, I, 481)

Where does *Tai-chi* fit into this scheme?

The Great Ultimate is merely the principle of Heaven and earth and the myriad things. With respect to Heaven and earth, there is the Great Ultimate in them. With respect to the myriad things, there is the Great Ultimate in each and every one of them. Before Heaven and earth existed, there was assuredly this principle ... The Great Ultimate is not spatially conditioned; it has neither corporeal form nor body. There is no spot where it may be placed ... However, activity is after all the activity of the Great Ultimate and tranquillity is also its tranquillity, although activity and tranquillity themselves are not the Great Ultimate.

[De Bary, *Sources*, I, 484]

How does all this link up with the concept of Heaven (*t'ien*) in early Confucianism? True to his general guiding light, Chu Hsi argues that *t'ien* is Principle, is *li*. Frequently in his commentaries he glosses *t'ien: t'ien chi li ye*, (*t'ien* here means *li*). He appears, however, uncomfortable with the concepts. It cannot be dismissed since it is so centrally canonical. Yet one feels he would prefer to restrict the use of *t'ien* to the physical sky.

Nowadays, it is maintained that Heaven does not refer to the blue sky. In my view [this interpretation] cannot be left out of account.
[But, he goes on]
Principle is the substance of Heaven, while destiny [t'ien] is the function of principle.
[Chan, *Source Book*, 612 from *Chu Tzu Ch'uan shu* 42]
[and a little further on]
If I investigate principle to the utmost and fully develop my moral nature, then what I have received is wholly Heaven's moral character, and what Heaven has endowed me with is wholly Heaven's principle.
[Chan, *Source Book*, 613 from *Chu Tzu Ch'uan-shu* 42]

Yet, despite this discomfort with the personalistic *t'ien*, he does not hesitate to attribute personality to *t'ien*:

The production of a man by Heaven is like the command of the throne to a magistrate.
[*Chu Tzu Ch'uan-shu*, 43 in Bruce, *Philosophy of Human Nature*, 117]

And when specifically questioned as to whether the Decree of Heaven (*t'ien-ming*) is not personal, but rather due to the interplay of the physical forces of the universe, he strongly upholds the traditional view:

The phenomena may be such as would lead one to think that there is not really One imparting the Decree; but that there is a personal being above us by whose command these things come to pass, seems to be taught by the "Odes" and "Records" — in such passages, for example, as speak of the wrath of the Supreme Ruler. But still, this Ruler is none other than Law [*Li*, 'Principle'].

In the whole universe there is nothing higher than [Principle] and hence the term Ruler.

[*Chu-Tzu Ch'uan-shu*, 43 in Bruce, *Philosophy*, 147]

Again, two other key terms, Nature (*hsing*) and *Tao* (Moral Order) are reduced to being expressions of *li*. *Tao* is *li* in its ethical form: '*Tao* is the ethical principle which every phenomenon has' [Bruce, *Philosophy*, 274-5 from *Chu Tzu Ch'uan-shu*, 467] while 'Nature is the concrete expression of the Moral Law (*Tao*) [Bruce, *Philosophy* 275 from *Chu Tzu Ch'uan-shu* 46], a phrase Chu Hsi borrows from Shao Yung, and to round the circle, he quotes with approval Ch'eng I: 'Nature is Principle, and what we call Principle is really nature. [Quoted Bruce, *Philosophy*, 16].

Finally, we might look at Chu Hsi's treatment of Ch'eng Hao's theme of the 'mind of Heaven and Earth'. In a section of Ch. 46 of his *Complete Works*, he rejects the Buddhist conception of Mind as remote from human relationships and distinct from the world:

Here we have the Mind of Heaven and Earth, the Source of the universe. There are not two sources in the universe ... Every form, produced and reproduced, has each the nature of Heaven. This is the reason for the inseparableness of the creature from its source. Receiving its spiritual essence we become man, and within the confines of the four cardinal principles it resides, inscrutable, formless, still, and, it would seem, unnameable. Tzu Ssu, having regard to the absence of any leaning to one side or the other, called it The Mean. Mencius, having regard to its perfect purity called it Good. The Master [Confucius] having regard to its life-producing substance called it Love [*jen*]. The terms differ but the thing named is the same, and is not separable from everyday life. This is why you said that its meaning is manifest without our seeking it.

[Bruce, *Philosophy* 282, from *Chu-Tzu Ch'uan-shu* 46]

The 'Mind of Heaven and Earth', then, is not to be sought by abstraction from experience, but is immersed in our daily life. The spiritual life is a dimension of our everyday existence, the substance of our ethical struggle for authenticity. And, in this at least, he was thoroughly Confucian. Religion, for Chu Hsi, as for Confucius, was not a matter of worship of spirits but of service to men, as the following commentary suggests:

When Fan Ch'ih asked about wisdom, Confucius said: "To devote onself earnestly to the duties due to men, and to respect the heavenly and earthly spirits but keep them at a distance, may be called wisdom." Let us understand those things that should be understood. Those that cannot be understood let us set aside. By the time we have thoroughly understood ordinary daily matters, the principle governing the heavenly and earthly spirits will naturally be seen. This is the way to wisdom. When Confucius said: "If we are not yet able to serve man, how can we serve the earthly spirits?" he expressed the same idea.

[De Bary, *Sources*, I, 487, from *Chu Tzu Ch'uan-shu* 51]

To round off this sketch of the evolution of Neo-Confucianism I should have something to say of the School of Mind, *hsin-hsueh*, and its development by Chu Hsi's contemporary Lu Hsiang-shan and especially by the Ming dynasty thinker, Wang Yang-ming (1472-1529). However, since I am convinced, and the recent works on Wang by Julia Ching and Tu Wei-ming confirm my reading of him, that Wang differs from Chu Hsi in emphasis rather than substance, and that his key notion of discovering *li* within the mind, rather than in the external world ('the investigation of things') is implicit in Chu's synthesis, there seems no need to discuss his views in detail.

The attempts to label Wang Yang-ming a 'Buddhizer', as a proponent of Buddhist idealism and monism, or of Buddhist meditation practices, or of Ch'an Buddhist social irresponsibility are now seen as largely derived from the strains of the late Ming political crisis and a selective reading of Chu Hsi himself by Ch'ing apologists. The substance of *hsin-hsueh* was already there in the *li-hsueh*.

A THEOLOGICAL ASSESSMENT

This is the point in the paper at which I firmly step right out of my depth. I am not a theologian nor a philosopher of religion, but an historian. In the last capacity I have an acquaintance with many theological systems, and their terminology, but I may be, in the eyes of the professionals, guilty of crass irresponsibility in throwing them around. I beg to be corrected.

The Jesuit missionaries in whose writings I have been immersed for so many years, when faced with the task of a theological evaluation of the *li-hsueh* instinctively attempted a comparative conceptual analysis. They had a fixed criterion for orthodoxy: the scholastic, Greek (especially Aristotelean) categories or 'attributes' of the Christian God which they sought for in the categories and concepts of Chinese thought. In the Classics they struck oil: the personalised *t'ien* and *shang-ti* appeared to be conceived of, however vaguely, as creator, sustainer, pure spirit, transcendent etc. In Neo-Confucianism, on the other hand, the classic attributes proved elusive. Was their referent, the substantive Being to whom they were attributed, *t'ien* or *t'ai-chi* or *li*? And was it a 'whom' at all? Was not this all-pervasive *li* a pantheistic concept, a fatal confusion of creator and created, the *Deus sive Natura* of Spinoza? On the whole, the Jesuits eschewed systematic discussion of Neo-Confucianism, preferring to concentrate on the safer classical Confucianism and a blanket condemnation of the modern *atheopolitici*. The only exception, Alexandre de la Charme's *Hsing-li chen-ch'uan* (1753) takes up the *hsing-li* philosophy only to parody it. *Tai-chi*, for example, is seen as a sort of Neoplatonic Demiurge, subordinate to the real creator, and fundamentally material (*ch'i*).

The only thoroughgoing modern attempt along these lines is that of John Percy Bruce whose London University D.Litt. thesis, published as *Chu Hsi and His Masters* in 1923, constantly applies the categories of Christian theology (he was himself on the faculty of the Shantung Christian University) to Neo-Confucian concepts. He finds in the *t'ai-chi/wu chi* equation an attribution of infinity to the creative principle. *Tien*, he argues, using the passages I have already referred to, is clearly personal, equated with *t'ai-chi* and *li*. *Li* itself is spiritual, independent of and prior to matter. But does this make Neo-Confucianism a theism? Rightly, I believe, he hesitates over labels:

> We shall perhaps arrive at a truer understanding if we content ourselves with not labelling it at all, though careful comparison may serve the useful purpose of teaching us something of what it is by showing us what it is not.
>
> [Bruce, *Chu Hsi and His Masters*, 120]

And, of what it is not, he is, again rightly in my view, certain:

> The charges, therefore, which have been brought against Chu Hsi of materialism and antitheism would alike appear to be without sufficient foundation. In the statement that Heaven is [Law: Principle], on which these charges have been largely based, he does not deny personality, but asserts the spirituality and ethical perfection of the Divine Being; and ... his assertion of personality in the Supreme Ruler is unequivocal and complete.
>
> [Bruce, *Chu Hsi and His Masters*, 300]

Logically, then, Neo-Confucianism would seem to be a kind of Theism. But what kind? Not Deism, as Voltaire and others thought, since this 'God' is very much involved in the activities of the universe. Not Pantheism, since there is a logical and metaphysical distinction drawn between the spiritual 'Principle' and 'Matter'. Not quite Monism, since there is a certain dualism; the ultimate reduction of matter to spirit is avoided.

If we must apply Western categories — and I would question the necessity — perhaps Panentheism is the best label. Hans Küng in *Does God Exist?* applies the label to the early Hegel, before what he calls his 'mind-monism' was developed.

> Hegel does not deify the empirical world, he does not make everything God, as if the finite were simply absorbed in the infinite. But we may certainly speak of a pan-en-theism in the widest sense, of a vital unity of life, of love, of all-embracing Spirit — these three notions are typical of Hegel's Frankfurt period. God as Opposite seems to be conquered by Deity as all-encompassing. Consequently, in describing the relationship between God and man, personal categories are now avoided as much as possible.
>
> [*Does God Exist?*, 136]

Certainly, there are many echoes of Chu Hsi in this description, just as the Hegelian emphasis on 'mind' and 'spirit' has resonances of *hsin* and *li*. So, too, the conflation of the ethical with the ontological; the avoidance of the language of personality. Why, then, hesitate to call Neo-Confucianism a kind of Hegelian Panentheism?

My reasons for caution lie in the very enterprise of drawing conceptual analogies, especially those based on Western categories. It is this that has bedevilled the study of Buddhism and Taoism as much as Confucianism. Leaving aside the fundamental question of the influence of the structures of the Chinese language or what can and cannot be said in Chinese, I would raise the general problem of the functional as opposed to the structural implications of key philosophical or theological categories. Does *li* function within the system as 'Spirit' does in early Hegelianism? I am not proposing to answer my own question definitively, but simply to suggest that functional analogy both gives warrant for the drawing of comparisons — enables one, for example, to speak of 'salvation' in Buddhism — and demands a different kind of analysis, one focussing on behaviour, practices, not systems; on faith, not theology.

And 'faith' there seems to be in Neo-Confucianism. W.T. de Bary in the Preface to his *Neo-Confucian Orthodoxy and the Learning of Mind-and-Heart* draws attention to the faith dimension of Chu Hsi style orthodoxy. The school, he says, called itself *tao-hsueh* out of 'a sense of religious certitude ... [a] powerful sense of mission in the world' (p.xvi). Men endured persecution and died for the convictions imbued by Neo-Confucian teachers. The Late Ming Tung-lin school almost courted martyrdom at the hands of the eunuchs and court officials. Rodney Taylor in his study of Kao P'an-lung, the Tung-lin leader, stresses his conversion, his enlightenment experience, his embracing of sagehood as an ideal [*The Cultivation of Sagehood as a Religious Goal in Neo-Confucianism*]. Sagehood was attained primarily by studying the classics, but was only possible after a basic reorientation achieved by meditation. This pillar of Ch'eng-Chu orthodoxy, bitter opponent of Wang Yang-ming's Buddhist 'perversions' advocated and practiced meditation, quietly sitting (*ching tso*) in order to realise one's fundamental nature (*pen-t'i*).

Faith, then, but faith in what? Presumably not in a person, certainly not in a historical figure. Confucius himself was a sage, a teacher and a model, but not the object of faith. Ultimately Confucian faith was in a way of life and action, the Confucian *tao*. And the Neo-Confucian word for it was *ching*, 'seriousness' or 'reverence'. This was what was acquired by quiet sitting, envisioned in political decision-making, embodied in the life of the true Confucian. So, the Confucian ideal was not faith in an object of worship, but 'seriousness' about living:

> The object of reverence [says de Bary] was not understood in the theistic or devotional sense as an object of worship, but as a definite form of action to which the attitude of seriousness and respect attaches. *Ching* in this sense meant collecting the mind and directing it toward one thing. Often this "one thing" represented the unity of all things in principle.
>
> [*Neo-Confucian Orthodoxy*, 14]

Philosophical discourse, in this mode, was neither pure rationalism nor pursued for its own sake. *Ching*, 'seriousness', endowed it with purpose and charged it with commitment. Tu Wei-ming, characteristically Chinese in his reluctance to call this 'religion' or 'theology' but recognising the faith elements, proposes a new term 'religiophilosophy':

> Since this form of philosophizing involves a kind of religious commitment, to distinguish it from the philosophical study of religion we shall call it "religiophilosophy", a tentative definition of which is: the inquiry into human insights by disciplined reflection for the primary purpose of spiritual self-transformation. Religiophilosophy thus defined charactizes the nature and function of philosophizing in all the major historical traditions of the East. In addition, it truthfully represents theological thinking in Judaism, Christianity, and Islam.
>
> [Tu Wei-Ming, *Humanity and Self-Cultivation*, 84]

I doubt that we need a new word. I would argue, in fact, that this 'religious commitment' characterizes not just theological thinking but also philosophy in the European tradition, the pursuit of truth with seriousness, the 'love of wisdom'. It is when it falls away from seriousness into word-games or manipulation (the red flag for which is 'philosophy of . . .') that it abandons its own vocation.

What is the prime characteristic of this kind of philosophical reflection? Inwardness. A sensitivity to one's spiritual states; a consciousness of spiritual realities experienced within one's reflective self-consciousness; of the unity of knowledge and action. In theistic terms it is an experience of immanence rather than transcendence. But it is precisely this Eastern tradition — of Eastern Christianity, as well as Buddhism, Taoism, Neo-Confucianism, Hatha Yoga and so on — that challenges the validity of the Western Transcendence/immanence dichotomy. God, as God, must be the 'Coincidence of opposites', the point where such conceptual differentiation ceases to have meaning. Rather than the wholly other, to use Rudolf Otto's very Western formula, God is the 'not other', the *non aliud* of Nicholas of Cusa, the 'centre of the centre, end of the end, name of the name, being of being and non-being of non-being' [Nicholasof Cusa, *Directio speculantis seu non aliud*, quoted in Kung, *Does God Exist?*, 601] — or in Neo-Confucian terms, *wu chi erh t'ai chi.*

Related works by the author of this paper
1. *K'ung-tzu or Confucius? The Jesuit Interpretation of Confucianism.* Allen and Unwin, 1985.
2. *Mao Zedong.* University of Queensland Press, 1984.

RELIGION AND IDENTITY:
New Religious Movements in Québec

Roland Chagnon

Université du Québec à Montreal, Canada

Over the past fifteen years, Western societies have been experiencing an unprecedented influx of religious movements. Some draw their inspiration from Christian tradition but most of these movements are of Eastern origin and lean heavily on Hindu-Buddhist thought. In Québec, the number of new religious movements is estimated to be around 250 (Bergeron 1982: 14). A survey conducted by the Centre de sondage de l'Université de Montréal showed that 5.4% of Québec's population are presently participating or have already participated in one or another of these Eastern-inspired religious movements and that 19.9% of this same population had read books or articles on Eastern spirituality. The poll made no reference to the involvement of persons in evangelist or fundamentalist movements which have reached a certain level of importance in Québec today. The poll likewise did not attempt to measure the impact of Christianity-inspired sectarian literature. These data, on the other hand, give us a good idea of the influence Eastern-inspired religious movements have on Québec. Although we are not talking in terms of a mass social phenomenon, the influence these new religions have in Québec has, nonetheless, awakened the interest of religion sociologists. Because these movements appeared in Québec within the context of a sweeping drive towards secularization, we will begin by rapidly recalling the religious and social history of Québec and will then show how these new religious movements are an attempt to answer this recent secularization and the profound identity crisis that has resulted.

1. FROM A NATION-CHURCH TO A NATION-STATE

1.1 Religious and social history of Québec

Created in 1867 at the time of the Canadian confederation, Québec province remains distinct from the other provinces. Its inhabitants are mainly descendants of French colonists who settled in Canada during the French Regime (1608-1760). The British Conquest of 1760 was decisive for the future evolution of the "Canadians", a term which was first used to designate french "paysans" and which later came to describe, in its anglicized form (Canadians), English Canadians who had settled in Canada after the Conquest. In order to be distinguished from English Canadians, the French were progressively called French Canadians. They differ from English Canadians not only in language, but also in culture, history and especially religion. French Canadians form a nation distinct from English Canadians. Indeed, their group corresponds to the definition of a nation given by Pascale Mancini: "a natural society of men, united by territory, origin, custom, language conforming to the community of life and the social conscience" (Quoted in Shafer 1972: 14).

Whereas English Canadians were for the most part Protestant, French Canadians had always been almost uniquely Catholic. French Canadian historians have always stressed the tremendous role played by the Catholic Church in the formation and protection of the national identity of French Canadians (Brunet 1958, 1969, 1971; Quellet 1962; Séguin 1970; Voisine 1971). Jean Hamelin wrote "Catholicism is the constitutive characteristic of French Canadian nationality. The collective will-to-live existing in the conscience of the people is embodied in a "Nous religieux" (Hamelin 1984: 48). After the Conquest when the elite had returned to France the Catholic Church took charge and assumed the management of the French Canadian destiny in all areas: religious, political, economic, social and cultural. The failure of the Patriots revolt in 1837-38, merely increased the power of the Church over the French Canadian society. From 1840 to 1960, the Catholic Church was to remain the ruling institution of French Canadian life. According to Nive Voisine, the apex of the Church's power over the French Canadian society was reached in the period from 1896 to 1940, a period which he likens to the triumphal Church (Voisine 1971: 55).

During the century in which the Church reigned, it held a complete monopoly on social institutions. It controlled education on all levels. Monks and nuns oversaw a network of hospitals, homes and orphanages. The Church also held influence on the economy. For decades it favoured the expansion of agriculture and colonization. At the beginning of the 20th century, when the labour movement appeared in Québec alongside the shaping of a movement towards industrialization, the Church sought to confront the situation by creating in 1921 a Catholic union: the Confédération des Travailleurs Catholiques du Canada (C.T.C.C.). Every effort of the Church was consecrated to fighting against what it considered to be the two greatest dangers facing French Canadians: the threats of Protestantism and anglicism.

While industry was in the hands of English Protestants, the Church sought to protect French Canadians by isolating them on their lands. Agriculture became the national vocation. In 1923, Cardinal Bégin stated: "We are essentially a people of agricultural calling" (Bégin quoted in Hulliger 1958: 16). Within this context, colonization of new lands became a national as well as religious crusade in Québec. This reverence for agriculture as a way of life was so strong during the second half of the 19th century and the beginning of the 20th century that, along with messianic and anti-state attitudes, it became a dominant characteristic of the French Canadian national ideology (Brunet 1958).

Distrust of State was nourished by the same fears as devotion to agriculture. They were both counter-reactions to the English Canadians use of State as an instrument of domination. According to the views of the Church, the State should be held at a distance. French Canadians should especially not consent to placing their values and most esteemed institutions into the hands of the State: their networks of schools and hospitals, their legislative system, language and culture ... French Canadians were encouraged to entrust all these things to the hands of the Church or to the weak provincial government which was subservient to it.

The ecclesiastical elite had finally legitimized the political and economic inferiority of French Canadians by immersing them in a supernatural and messianic vision of their unique destiny in North America. L.A. Pâquet expressed the essence of this messianic vision when he wrote:

Now, my brother, — why should I hesitate to say it? — we have the privilege of being entrusted with this social priesthood granted only to select peoples. I cannot doubt that this religious and civilizing mission is the true vocation and the special vocation of the French race in America. Yes, let us not forget, we are not only a civilized race, we are pioneers of a civilization; we are not only a religious people, we are messengers of the spirit of religion; we are not only dutiful sons of the Church, we are, or we should be, numbered among its zealots, its defenders, and its apostles. Our mission is less to handle capital than to stimulate ideas: less to light the furnaces of factories than to maintain and spread the glowing fires of religion and thought, and to help them cast their light into the distance. (Pâquet quoted in Cook 1969: 154)

This passage from a sermon given in 1902 on the vocation of the French race in America is an accurate reflection of the mood of this period when French Canadians were still holding on to the characteristics of a traditional society. During the years of the Quiet Revolution (1960-1966), this society was to undergo a series of profound mutations.

1.2 Secularization during the period of the Quiet Revolution (1960-1966)

Québec's entry into the modern era was neither abrupt nor impromptu. Since World War II, major changes had taken place in its socioeconomic infrastructure. Urbanization and industrialization were both forces which had shaken the foundations of a traditional French Canadian society. Urbanization increased from 58% in 1931 to 78% in 1971 (Posgate and McRoberts 1976: 48).

Posgate and McRoberts interpreted the Quiet Revolution as an adjustment, long expected, in ideologies and mentalities in the world of socio-economic infrastructures. It would only make sense that French Canadians, having lived for 20 or so years in a modern, industrialized society, should decide to implicate this reality where ideas were concerned. They ceased to continue living between two worlds and opted enthusiastically for a modern perspective on life.

The State played a determining role in Québec's attainment of modernity. In its haste to catch up and modernize, Québec gave the State control over the educational system and the network of social welfare fields. The Church suddenly found itself robbed of former functions. The secularization of social institutions created deep repercussions in the orders of the Church. Recruitment started to drop. From 164 ordinations to the priesthood in 1958, the number had dropped to 33 in 1976 (Voisine 1971: 84). The total number of priests went from 5,382 in 1961 to 4,687 in 1976 (Rouleau quoted in Johnson 1979). The number of men and women in religious communities was reduced from 55,295 in 1969 to 34,041 in 1976. Finally, the number of Sunday churchgoers fell drastically: 87% in 1956, 83% in 1965, 59% in 1974, 37% in 1978 and 38% in 1984 (Crysdale and Wheatcroft 1976: 6; Johnson 1979; Proulx 1984).

For Quebeckers, the Quiet Revolution marked a real paradigm shift in terms of symbolic integration in their society (Kuhn 1970). It represented a transformation from integration symbolico-religious to integration symbolico-politicus of the collective. The nation-state succeeded the nation-Church. To promote its reforms and to give coherency and momentum to its undertakings, the State resorted to nationalistic ideology which, as religious ideology had done in the past, was successful in uniting the entire collective into one body through recourse to common symbols. The old national identity, formerly inspired by religion and linked to a pessimistic nationalism of survival, was progressively downgraded and replaced by a new identity inspired by secularism and linked to a modern, liberal nationalism centered on promoting the nation of Québec in North America (Dion 1957, 1962, 1964). The term Québécois (Quebecker) replaced the term French Canadian. Nationalism was the central mobilizing idea for Quebeckers throughout the Quiet Revolution (1960-1966) and the years following until the beginning of the 1980's. During this period, nationalism indeed became, as Carlton J.H. Hayes suggests concerning contemporary nationalism in general, a dominant religion among Quebeckers. Hayes writes: "Modern and contemporary nationalism appeals to man's "religious sense". It offers a substitute for, or supplement to, historic supernatural religion. Persons indifferent or hostile to the latter are apt to find a compensatory satisfaction and devotion in this worldly nationalism, that is, in what is essentially a religion of modern secularism" (Hayes 1960: 176).

1.3 The quiet disillusionment of the 1980's

The defeat of the referendum in 1980, the unilateral repatriation of the Canadian Constitution in 1981, and the economic crisis in 1981-1982 caused irreparable damage to the Parti Québécois, the nationalist government in office since 1976. Since the beginning of the 1980's nationalist ideology could no longer move the masses. A certain moroseness settled over Québec.

It is within this context of secularization, which rendered any dream of a Catholic French Canadian Québec impossible and which dulled the nationalist ideological spirit, that we should examine the appearance and development of another phenomenon — new religious movements. The inability of Church and State today to offer Quebeckers inspiring collective projects would explain the infatuation some have for the promises made by new religious movements. The dwindling feeling of belonging to a dynamic and promising community life, and the ever increasing feeling of anomy which is pervading Québec are the two main factors inciting many to a feverish search for a general meaning in life and for a personal reason to live. The theory of religion-identity relationships expounded by Hans Mol sheds some precious light on understanding this phenomenon of new religious movements in Québec.

2. THE THEORY OF RELIGION-IDENTITY RELATIONSHIPS

In their works dealing with the sociology of knowledge, Peter Berger and Thomas Luckmann accurately described the relationships between religion and the social construction of reality. To survive, societies must invent an ORDER, in other words, ways of thinking and acting which are acceptable to others and are a source of social consensus such as to assure communication between members of a society. Because this order is arbitrary and precarious, societies feel the need to solidify it by founding it on a sacred and transcendent universe. Berger writes: "Religion has been one of the most effective bulwarks against anomy throughout human history" (Berger 1969: 87).

Societies have always constructed their reality to be in opposition to the manner in which societies surrounding them conceived theirs. What was a source of disorder for one could be a source of order and harmony for another. Anthropologists like Mary Douglas and Louis Dumont showed well how, through rules of pure and impure, societies sought to protect their own rules of operation from the threat of interference from the outside.

Historically, the great religions have always had an important role to play in the social construction of reality of various peoples and various cultures, a reality which at the same time defined their particular identity. The ties which are established between reality, order and identity justify the definition that Hans Mol gives of religion: "Religion is the sacralization of identity" (Mol 1976: IX). Mol also recognizes that the sacralization of a collective identity is much easier within the context of traditional societies than within modern and differentiated societies. He writes: "The waning capacity of universal religions to sacralize a social identity can be related to the decreasing extent to which highly differentiated societies are capable of being integrated ... Sectarian groups in these highly differentiated societies seem to derive at least some of their success from being buffers between the heterogeneity of the social whole and the threat of personal alienation" (Mol 1976: 10).

The distinction Mol makes between social identity, group identity and personal identity (Mol 1976: 149) proved fruitful in the research I made on new religious movements in Québec (Chagnon 1985a, 1985b, 1985c). It was the inspiration of my typology on new religious movements in Québec. According to whether members of these movements had or had not experienced radical ruptures of identity in their spiritual development, I noticed their tendency to integrate, be it into sects having rigid community structures, or into the mystics where the structures were more open and flexible. Members of sects had been generally subjected to a process of conversion which lead them to find security in the identity of the group and, in becoming so absorbed, to lose their personal identity. Members of the mystics, on the contrary, would be better characterized as "alternants" (Travisano 1971), more concerned with asserting their own personal identity and individuality through the practice of certain rituals.

Travisano presents conversion as a radical passage from an old to a new identity. The converted adopts an entirely new perspective on existence. This perspective pervades his life from thereon and divides it into two essential periods: life before conversion and life after conversion. The converted presents himself in an entirely new manner to others. Finally, the converted is also someone who has changed groups of belonging. The alternant, on the other hand, does not undergo such radical change. His new identity does not seem cut off from his old one. On the contrary, it seems to him to be a prolongation of his former identity which he still keeps. The alternant seems to tend to territorialize his new identity; it does not pervade his whole existence as it does for the converted.

Finally, my typology was able to establish links between, on the one hand, spiritual progression of conversion, participation in a sect and refusal of modern values and, on another hand, spiritual progression of alternation, involvement in mystic conception and acceptance of modern values. The "marginal church" type was created for groups who, though subjecting their members to a process of conversion, do not stand in opposition to modern values.

In light of this typology, the majority of these new Eastern inspired religious movements in Québec should be interpreted as mystic. We are talking here of groups in which rituals aid the individual to live and develop in spite of the anomy prevalent in modern society. Sects tend to group together persons who are marginal and alienated from modern conditions of living and who seek religious compensation for their alienation in the sect. Mystics, on the other hand, tend to gather together persons who, though pushers of the cogwheel of modern living, do not find satisfaction in the roles they play or the opportunity to come to a full realization of themselves.

This remark brings us to another important distinction proposed by Mol between the role-playing self and the niche-constructing self (Mol 1978: 2). It is a question of two different theories of identity. The first which relates the identity of a person to the collection of roles he plays in his community, is expressed by Strauss, Mead, Berger and Luckmann, Soddy and Klapp. According to them, "Identity is a product of interaction with others in social groups" (Strauss cited in Mol 1976: 58), "identity emerges from the dialectic between individual and society" (Berger and Luckmann cited in Mol 1976: 58), "identity is an anchorage of the self to the social matrix" (Soddy cited in Mol 1976: 58). The second theory envisages the identity of a person as something difficult to confine and which conceals itself behind the roles it holds. Several theoreticians claim this theory, notably Wheelis, Eissler, Kramer, Jung, Goethe and Mol. They seem to share a like definition of identity, considering it to be "the most essential nucleus of man which becomes visible only after all his roles have been laid aside" (De Levita cited by Mol 1976: 60). Wheelis defines it as "a coherent sense of self" (Wheelis cited by Mol 1976: 60). As for Mol, he defines it as "a stable niche where man is found in the midst of a chaotic world" (Mol 1976: 8).

In elaborating on the development of new religious movements in Québec, the theory of identity I have worked out makes abundant use of Mol's distinctions between collective identity, group identity, and personal identity on one hand and between the identity of roles and identity-niche on the other. Indeed, the old collective identities proposed in turn by Church and State have had such a weak effect on Quebeckers that their search for group identity (sect type) and personal identity (mystic) is quite plausible. It is also true that because they are dissatisfied, to one degree or another, with their identity of roles (layman identity) Quebeckers today are looking for their identity-niche (sacred identity). Mystics will alternate between the two whereas the sects will tend to become totally absorbed in the latter. Though sects encourage refusal of the world and the loss of self by fusion in a sacred US or in a group identity, the mystics, to the contrary, socialize their members in values of modernity by proposing sacralization of personal identity.

3. NEW RELIGIOUS MOVEMENTS AND SACRALIZATION OF SELF

3.1 The return to individualism

For several years now, numerous authors have noted a wave of individualism sweeping over Western societies (Lasch 1980; Dumont 1983; Lipovetsky 1983, Gallo 1984; Bellah 1985; Laurent 1985). Contemporary individualism promotes such values as autonomy, right to one's own specificity and differences, the primacy of the individual over the collective and the right to pleasure. Several definitions have been given to individualism. According to Georges Palante "To be an individualist is to delight in the feeling, not of one's superiority, but of one's differentness, one's uniqueness" (Palante quoted in Laurent 1985: 40). For Théodore Zeldin, individualism was "the idea in which the individual is an autonomous being, having the right to act according to his own judgment and to submit all authoritarian norms and values to an independent and censorious examination" (Zeldin quoted in Laurent 1985: 40). Finally, Friedrich Hayek gave the following definition: "Individualism consists of recognizing the individual as judge in the last resort of his own ends and to believe that, to the extent it is possible, his own opinions must govern his acts" (Hayek quoted in Laurent 1985: 49).

All these definitions of individualism give primacy to the individual over the collective through all walks of life. In his praise of contemporary individualism, Alain Laurent shows that it represents a reaction against diverse collectivisms, communityisms and groupisms which had known a lot of favour in France, especially in the years from 1968 to 1981. Following the thought of Roland Jaccard, he adds "The man of modernity lives in a world of each man for himself, each in his own home, private, personal and intimate dimensions prevailing over those of community, social and collective" (Jaccard quoted in Laurent 1985: 47). Today's withdrawal into one's self was also noted by Gilles Lipovetsky who writes: "Everywhere it is the search of one's own identity and no longer of universality that motivates individual actions . . . Radiant days following the revolution and progress are no longer believed in . . . hedonist and personalized individualism has become legitimate and is no longer opposed" (Lipovetsky 1983:11).

3.2 Sacralization of self

New religious movements should be understood within the context of culture's new fashion which is contemporary individualism; be it sects and their refusal of individualism or mystics and their adaptation to it. A myriad of individualist traits appear in mystic religions. We could mention a few; their insistance on personal experience as a criterion for evaluating religious statements, their mechanistic ethic centered around the law of karma and reincarnation, their essentially individualist rituals and finally, their emphasis on a sacred inner self which exists in every person and which they name, according to the group as: self, essential being, soul, thetan, etc. Paul Heelas has combined the individualist traits of these various new religions and designated them as "religions of self" (Heelas quoted in Barker 1982: 69). This same opinion was expressed by Roy Wallis in the following terms:

> The beliefs of these movements are essentially individualistic. The source of suffering, of disability, of unhappiness, lies within oneself rather than in the social structure. The spiritual dimension in particular is a matter of individual experience and individual subjective reality rather than social reality or even social concern. Moreover, God is not perceived as a personal deity imposing a set of ethical prescriptions upon human society. If God is referred to, it is primarily as a diffuse, amorphous and immanent force in the universe, but present most particularly within oneself. For many of these groups and movements, the self is the only God there is, or at least the only one that matters. (Wallis 1979: 196)

Thomas Robbins and Dick Anthony also show how sacralization of self, promulgated by these Eastern-inspired new religions, could serve to justify a new individualist and permissive ethic made possible by the evolution of American capitalism from "enterpreneurship" to "managerism" (Robbins and Anthony 1981: 9).

From the above considerations it is very clear that these new movements are all preoccupied with the individual. But the individual they are concerned with is not the outer being, visible to all. It is rather the essential being present in every man, sheltering in the depths of himself and which the new religions call by various names: self, soul, thetan, and so on. The new religions are interested in the secret and hidden identity. They attempt to convince man that his true identity (identity-niche) is not to be identified with his empirical personality, but that it actually transcends his identity of roles. By convincing their members that their sacred and real identity overflows their illusionary and profane identity, the roles everyone confronts as necessary to survival are rendered trite or commonplace. In so doing they socialize their members to the values and demands of modern living. Contemporary mystics bring together people who may experience difficulties in living in an individualist climate, but who can succeed in doing so because they are assured that they are not essentially affected by the uneasiness of their times. In examining their rituals we are even further convinced.

3.3 Rituals of the sacralization of self

The new Eastern-inspired religious movements are essentially centred on the practice of exercises and rituals. Doctrines hold little weight in these movements. The principal rituals are initiation, witnessing (satsang) and especially meditation.

Witnessing (satsang) creates the heart of the spiritual reality. Through it, one is assured that a universe of peace, happiness and serenity can be achieved "here and now" in the heart of a troubled, turbulent world. Whether it is called Knowledge, Energy, Soul or God, one conviction remains: that perfect happiness is possible in this world. Initiation awakens the disciple to the world of peace and serenity for the first time. Meditation provides the means for the individual to attain states of consciousness that allow him to make contact with the energy deep inside him which is the guarantee of his happiness.

Arnold Van Gennep and Victor Turner stressed the religious crisis which accompanies the celebration of rituals. This crisis is generally brought about by a passage from one territory to another, from one state of living to another, or even, from life to death. To guarantee this transition which provokes anxiety, rituals are created which are essentially "rites of passage".

In her study entitled "The Complex Forms of the Religious Life. A Durkheimian View of New Religious Movements", Frances Westley makes a fundamental contribution to the study of the significance of ritual in new religions. She claims that the rites of traditional societies can be said to attempt to pass the individual from one state of being to another with the idea of avoiding statuslessness, but the same is not true of modern, differentiated societies. Inspired by the works of Irwing Goffman and Mary Douglas, she states that for the latter societies the purpose of the rites is not to pass the individual from one status or one stage of life to another, but rather to help him adopt the attitudes which circumstances at any given moment might require of him. Modern men are governed by rules of etiquette. In the evolving circumstances of their lives, they must always be ready to pass from one role to another and to adopt appropriate attitudes to those roles. If not, they can "lose face". This brings Frances Westley to maintain that modern man is not so much afraid of "statuslessness' as he is afraid of "facelessness", or of presenting the wrong face. She writes:

> In a stable society, one's identity is relatively changless. The role one plays, the image one has, the people one knows, remain fairly constant. Identity is not being continually tested and the rules for its maintenance are fairly well understood by all participants in a given situation. In these societies, ... rites of passage are partly created to deal with the danger those in transition present to others and to themselves.
>
> "Face", however, with its ephemeral implications, is much better suited for our society. Increasingly, it may be argued, criteria for public and private face-work are becoming obscure. Each new contact we make requires anew the establishment of "face". (Westley 1983: 104)

The concept of "face" sheds some light on the rituals of modern religious movements. Practiced daily, meditation permits the individual to release himself from all the faces and roles he has successively played throughout the day. It favours a re-centration of the self, a contact with the self which is really above and beyond the daily *mascarade* everyone puts on. By encouraging individuals to not identify with any one of the faces they must wear, the ritual of meditation makes members of the new religious movements better capable of playing their roles in society and of accepting the incessant shifts it requires of everyone.

Meditation is a therapeutic ritual in that it restores the true being by ridding it of its impurities. Meditation is a way of moving beyond false identities, which one is constantly tempted to adopt, towards the true identity hidden within. It is thus a passage from impurity to purity, from illusory identity to true identity, from anguish to serenity ... By the distance one is invited to maintain between self and the various roles each must play in society, meditation helps its members to survive in modern society while making them well adapted to modern conditions. The new religious movements, at least those of the mystic type, are closely attuned to modernity.

CONCLUSION

This rapid scan of the religious and social history of Québec shows that after having long been in search of a collective identity, first in a religious sense, then in a secular one, Quebeckers are now seeking group identity (in sects) or personal identity (in mystics). This evolution can be explained in part by the secularization which was provoked by the Quiet Revolution (1960-1966) and partly by the more recent disappointments in nationalist ideology. Many Quebeckers today are distrustful of collective and community projects. We are presently witnessing a general movement of withdrawal into the self and a kind of triumph of individualism.

This new cultural mode has penetrated Churches which must reckon with followers who are making religious experiments in the areas of beliefs, practices, values and styles of living. It has made a big impression on those who are looking for no other salvation than what is offered by a consumer society governed by mirages. In other respects, individualism has adversaries in a few isolated groups and minorities such as religious sects or politically radical groups of the same inspiration. Finally, contemporary individualism has found a precious ally in mystics of Eastern thought who encourage their members to adopt this predominant value of our era. Through their rituals, especially meditation, mystics assist their members in the difficult quest for individuality. By sacralizing the self, mystics encourage their members to not take the daily games they play too seriously.

REFERENCES

Bellah, Robert N., Richard Madsen et al ... 1985 *Habits of the Heart*. Individualism and Commitment in American Life. Berkeley: University of California Press.

Berger, Peter 1969 *The Sacred Canopy*. Elements of a sociological Theory of Religion. New York: Doubleday & Company Inc.

Berger, Peter and Thomas Luckmann 1966 *The Social Construction of Reality*. A Treatise in the Sociology of Knowledge. The Penguin Press.

Bergeron, Richard 1982 *Le cortège des fous de Dieu*. Un chrétien scrute les nouvelles religions. Montreal: Editions Paulines & Apostolat des Éditions.

Brunet, Michel 1958 La présence anglaise et les Canadiens, Montréal: Beauchemin.
1969 L'Eglise Catholique du Bas-Canada et le partage du pouvoir à l'heure d'une nouvelle donnée 1837-1854, in *Canadian Historical Papers*, 37-51.
1971 *Canadians et Canadiens:* études sur l'histoire et la pensée des deux Canadas. Montréal: Editions Fides.

Chagnon, Roland 1985a *La Scientologie: une nouvelle religion de la puissance*. Montréal: Hurtubise HMH.
1985b *Trois nouvelles religions de la lumière et du son: La Science de la spiritualite, Eckankar et La Mission de la Lumière Divine*, Montréal: Editions Paulines & Médiaspaul.
1985c Les nouvelles religions dans la dynamique socio-culturelle re-cente au Québec, dans Religion/Culture. *Comparative Canadian Studies*, eds William Westfall and Louis Rousseau, Association for Canadian Studies.

Cook, Ramsay 1969 *French-Canadian Nationalism*. An Anthology. Toronto: Macmillan of Canada.

Crysdale, Stewart and Les Wheatcroft 1976 *Religion in Canadian Society*. Toronto: Macmillan of Canada.

Dion, Léon 1957 Le nationalisme pessimiste: sa source, sa signification, sa validité, in *Cité Libre* 18, 1957, 3-19.
1962 Vers un nationalisme positif, in Montréal: *Le Devoir*, 8 décembre 1962.
1964 Genèse et caractère du nationalisme de croissance. In *Les nouveaux Québécois*, Québec: P.U.L., 1964.

Douglas, Mary 1967 *Purity and Danger*. London: Routledge & Kegan Paul Ltd.

Dumont, Louis 1966 *Homo hierarchicus*. Le système des castes et ses implications. Paris: Gallimard.
1983 *Essais sur l'individualisme*. Une perspective anthropologique sur l'idéologie moderne. Paris: Seuil.

Gallo, Max 1984 *La troisième alliance*. Pour un nouvel individualisme. Paris: Fayard.

Goffman, Erving 1973 *La mise en scène de la vie quotidienne*, 2 vols. Paris: Les Editions de Minuit.

Hamelin, Jean and Nicole Gagnon 1984 *Histoire du catholicisme québécois*. Le XXè siècle. Tome 1. 1898-1940. Montréal: Boréal Express.

Hayes, Carlton J. H. 1960 *Nationalism: A Religion*. New York: The MacMillan Company.

Heelas, Paul 1982 Californian Self-Religions and Socializing the subjective, in *New Religious Movements*. A Perspective for Understanding Society, ed. Eileen Barker, New York and Toronto: The Edwin Mellen Press.

Hulliger, Jean 1958 *L'enseignement social des évêques canadiens de 1891 à 1950*. Montréal: Fides.

Johnson, W. 1979 Church-going still going strong. *Globe & Mail*, 14 and 15 August 1979.

Kuhn, Thomas S. 1970 *The Structure of Scientific Revolutions*. Chicago: University of Chicago Press.

Lasch, Christopher 1980 *Le complexe de Narcisse*. La nouvelle sensibilité américaine. Paris: Robert Laffont.

Laurent, Alain 1985 *De l'individualisme*. Enquête sur le retour de l'individu. Paris: Presses Universitaires de France.

Lipovetsky, Gilles 1983 *L'ère du vide*. Essais sur l'individualisme contemporain. Paris: Gallimard.

Mol, Hans 1976 *Identity and the Sacred*. A sketch for a new social-scientific theory of religion. Oxford: Basic Blackwell.

1978 *Identity and Religion*. International, Cross-Cultural Approaches. Sage Studies in International Sociological Association, 16.

Ouellet, Fernand 1962 Les fondements historiques de l'option séparatiste dans le Québec, *Canadian Historical Review*, Vol. 43, No. 3, pp. 27-42.

Posgate, Dale and Kenneth McRoberts 1976 *Québec: Social Change and Political Crisis*. Toronto: McClelland and Stewart Limited.

Proulx, Jean-Pierre 1984 La pratique dominicale hebdomadaire s'est stabilisée à 38%. Montreal: *Le Devoir*, 8 septembre 1984.

Robbins, Thomas et Dick Anthony 1981 Culture Crisis and Contemporary Religion, in *In Gods We Trust*. New Patterns of Religious Pluralism in America, eds Thomas Robbins and Dick Anthony, New Brunswick and London: Transaction Books.

Séguin, Maurice 1970 *La nation canadienne et l'agriculture, 1760-1850*. Trois-Rivières: Boréal Express.

Shafer, Boyd C. 1972 *Faces of Nationalism*. New Realities and Old Myths. New York: Harcourt Brace Jovanovich Inc.

Travisano, Richard V. 1971 Alternation and Conversion as Qualitatively Different Transformations. In *Social Psychology through Symbolic Interaction*, eds. Gregory P. Stone and Harvey A. Farberman, Waltham: Xerox College Publishing.

Turner, Victor 1977 *The Ritual Process*. Structure and Anti-Structure. Cornell University Press.

Van Gennep, Arnold 1909 *Les rites de passage*. Paris: Librairie Critique Emile Nourry.

Voisine, Nive 1971 *Histoire de l'Eglise catholique au Québec* (1608-1970). Montréal: Editions Fides.

Wallis, Roy 1979 The Elementary Forms of the New Religious Life, in *The Annual Review of the Social Sciences of Religion*, 191-211.

Westley, Frances 1983 *The Complex Forms of the Religious Life*. A Durkheimian View of New Religious Movements. Chico, California: Scholars Press.

Related works by the author of this paper:

La Scientologie: une nouvelle Religion de la puissance. Montréal: Hurtubise HMH, 1985.

Trois nouvelles religions de la lumière et du son. Montréal: Editions Paulines, 1985.

"Les nouvelles religions dans la dynamique socio-culturelle recente au Québec" in *Canadian Issues, Religion/Culture, Comparative Canadian Studies*, eds., W. Westfall and L. Rousseau. The Association for Canadian Studies, 1985.

RELIGIOUS ENCOUNTERS OF THE THIRD KIND:

Spiritual Technology in Modern Nigeria

Rosalind I. J. Hackett

Georgetown University, U.S.A.

Information is abundant on the arrival of Islam and Christianity in Nigeria, as well as on the later influx of Christian denominations (mainly from the United States). Far less is known about a third wave of religious imports, which we shall refer to as the "spiritual sciences", whose main focus is on the development of spiritual power and knowledge and whose origins are as diverse as India, Indonesia, Korea, Britain and California. Forerunners of this very varied collection of movements have been present in Nigeria since the 1930s, although the majority have arrived since the end of the Civil War in 1970.

Our main interest in this paper is not just in specific institutional forms, but also in the wider and more diffuse religious phenomenon which we are describing as "spiritual technology". This refers to those beliefs, practices and attitudes which seek to manipulate the divine or the spiritual and achieve specific, this-worldly ends. Magic is not considered to be an appropriate term to refer to this widespread phenomenon; certainly some degree of magic is involved, if we take this to mean the manipulation of impersonal forces using prescribed ritual techniques (usually administered by an intermediary specialist) to attain desired results. But the concept of spiritual technology is broader than this: it permeates the beliefs and practices of individuals and religious institutions; it is manifested through prayers, rituals, religious literature and sacred objects.[1]

This religious instrumentalism and concern for techniques and results derives from both indigenous and exogenous sources. We may identify the this-worldly pragmatism of the traditional world-view as well as the esoteric and mystical claims of Western and Eastern metaphysical and occult groups offering direct access to the sacred and knowledge of the infinite. It is an attitude which pervades both institutional and organized forms of religion as well as the more popular and informal types of religious expression. There is an attendant emphasis on the cognitive and experiential dimensions as opposed to the ethical, the mythical and the social.

Our awareness of the growing importance of spiritual technology emerged from eight years of field work on all aspects of religious life and activity in Nigeria. It was highlighted during a recent survey of religious institutions in the town of Calabar, south-eastern Nigeria (1983) when an unexpected number of spiritual science movements were identified (14 or approximately 12% of all distinct religious bodies in the town).[2] This paper therefore stems from a desire to single out the phenomenon for further investigation.

The first part of the paper will focus on particular movements, while the second and third parts will be concerned with those indigenous religious institutions which have incorporated spiritual science teachings, either totally or partially into their belief systems. We shall then examine the various aspects of spiritual technology which are available to the consumer, before discussing, in conclusion, the implications of these new forms of spirituality for religious behaviour and identity in Nigeria as a whole.

I SPIRITUAL SCIENCE MOVEMENTS

There is no easy definition of a spiritual science movement since this is an extremely heterogeneous category with virtually no doctrinal, historical or cultural unity. These movements nonetheless share certain definable characteristics, namely, a quest for higher states of consciousness, increased spiritual power and knowledge and a direct religious (sometimes ecstatic) experience, as well as the use of procedures, techniques and practices which draw on hidden or concealed forces in order to manipulate the empirical course of existence. In a Western context movements of this nature would be referred to as "cults". For obvious reasons, this would be confusing in the African context. The term "spiritual science movement" is preferred since the search for spiritual knowledge and power through the use of scientific, or at least pseudo-scientific means, characterizes most of these groups.[3] It is also a term used by Nigerians themselves.

These movements are highly eclectic, drawing on a variety of sources: metaphysical, spiritualist, psychic, occult and mystical. There are important differences between the above: for instance, the metaphysician believes that he/she can have knowledge of the world and the cosmos through human reason (though not as a result of logical knowledge). The mystic, on the other hand, believes that direct knowledge of God, of spiritual truth, or of ultimate reality, is attainable through immediate intuition, insight or illumination, in other words in a way which differs from ordinary sense perception and which is not dependent on the medium of human reason. The psychic is considered to be subject to non-physical forces, while the occultist is concerned to discover the concealed, the unknown, the esoteric, that which lies beyond the realm of human understanding, but which is not necessarily supernatural — astrology or parapsychology for example.

We have not used the above terms as classificatory labels because of the loose organizational structures and tendency to eclecticism of many of the groups in Nigeria today. The data is therefore divided up in terms of origins, i.e. whether a movement is Western- or Eastern-related, since this is to some extent indicative of particular orientations.

Given the relative lack of information on the spiritual sciences on a national scale, we have centred our discussion on the town of Calabar in south-eastern Nigeria, where data was collected regarding the origins and development of movements operative in that region. Wherever possible, reference will be made to the activities of these movements in Nigeria as a whole. Calabar, however, serves as a good illustration, having benefited from the expansion of Lagos-based groups as well as being the headquarters for at least three movements. Some details of the world-views and cosmologies of the movements have been included, particularly of the lesser known groups, since this may help us to understand their potential appeal in the Nigerian context.

The Rosicrucians (AMORC) are today the most well known spiritual science movement in Calabar, even in Nigeria, largely owing to their extensive publicity campaign and the fact they have been active in the country since 1925. An impressive, Egyptian-style temple, which is the administrative headquarters for the whole of Nigeria, stands in the centre of Calabar and Rosicrucian literature, such as the "Mystic Life of Jesus", is readily available in the town's bookstores. The appeal of AMORC lies not just in its historical continuity with an ancient Egyptian occult order (several Nigerian historians trace their ancestral roots to Egypt), but also that it claims not to be a religion but a "mythical philosophy" and a "worldwide cultural fraternity" which can help people discover their secret powers of inner vision and cosmic consciousness and attain greater personal success.[4]

One of the reasons that could be adduced for the success of the AMORC in Calabar and in Nigeria as a whole, is its similarity to the Masonic model. While operating as a secret society, with initiation into different grades and esoteric knowledge, AMORC as an organization is not restricted to particular ethnic groups, as in the case of traditional secret societies. The AMORC world-view has international, even cosmic dimensions, and a content which is seen as "scientific" and "modern". (It claims not to be a religion.) This has obvious attractions for migrant professional men who have become disillusioned with conventional church worship and yet still want to be part of a support network, which may equally satisfy their religious needs. By the same token, it is the secret society image which has engendered hostility towards the AMORC. The esoteric rites are popularly linked with "magic" and "witch-craft", particularly those that surround the burial of their members.

The Aetherius Society was publicized, on the occasion of its introduction to Calabar in 1982, as an "international spiritual brotherhood". It is perhaps more accurately described as a "flying saucer" cult with an explicit religious structure which incorporates the teachings of occultism and yoga.[1] Founded by a British medium in 1955, the society claims to be able to communicate with extra-terrestial beings for advanced spiritual and material powers through spiritual discipline and "scientific prayer". Groups have reportedly been established in Calabar and Port Harcourt to date.

Swedenborgian literature has been circulating in Nigeria for over fifty years, and branches of the **Church of the New Jerusalem**, founded on the teachings of the Swedish mystic, Emmanuel Swedenborg (1668-1772), have existed for almost as long in the eastern and western regions. A group of refugees initiated a small group in the Calabar area during the Civil War (1967-70). Works by Swedenborg where he describes the supernatural spheres and their activities, such as "Heaven and Hell", "The Last Judgement", as well as doctrinal studies such as "The True Christian Religion" are the most popular, as from his concrete visions he sought to give answers to the sort of questions ordinary Christians would ask, such as, What is heaven like? What really goes on in hell? How do spirits live?[5] His work was, however, tinged with spiritualism and Kabbalism.[6] In later years he claimed that he had received revelations directly from God about the hidden spiritual meanings in the Bible.[7]

The Institute of Religious Science, which has a very small following in Calabar, stands in the New Thought tradition.[8] Its metaphysical teachings on healing, as purveyed through the publication *The Science of Mind*, are the most popular in the Nigerian context. There are currently seven branches or study groups throughout the country. **The Superet Light Mission** is primarily concerned with psychic phenomena; it was founded in Los Angeles by Dr Josephine Trust (Mother Trust), an aura scientist who claimed to have the mission of bringing into the world Jesus' light teaching. Superet literature found its way to eastern Nigeria in the 1950s, but has only generated two or three groups; the members are barely educated, but claim to be attracted by this "scientific religion".

The Eastern-related groups are a far more recent phenomenon. **Eckankar** or the Secret Science of Soul Travel, based on the teachings of the ECK master, Paul Twitchell, teaches the direct path to God or the path of total awareness.[9] An extensive campaign launched the movement in earnest in the early 1980s and there are now 64 branches throughout Nigeria. Eckankar makes frequent use of the broadcasting media to communicate its teachings and the Area Mahdi, Benjamin Anyaeji, is a popular speaker with accounts of his reincarnations, his "higher" powers and ability to stop rain. **Hare Krishna** devotees (of the **International Society for Krishna Consciousness**) have been visiting major Nigerian cities since the 1970s, distributing literature from the "Hare Krishna Bookmobiles". Nigerians are initially drawn to the movement because of the feasts and the festivals, as well as the emphasis on devotionalism, but few become committed devotees because of the monastic rules of conduct, notably regarding marital relationships and offspring. The appeal of the highly structured family life of the Krishnaite group can only be to those individuals who are alienated from the mainstream of African life.

The **Unification Church** has been operating in Nigeria since the 1970s but has not been as successful as in Zaire for example. They managed to take over two small independent churches in eastern Nigeria to effect government registration and they have a small staff of foreign missionaries at the headquarters in Lagos. But as in the case of the former movement, Nigerians are averse to the kind of total commitment required to be a member of the Unified Family and, in addition, are unused to Japanese missionaries (which was one of the reasons that the Calabar branch was closed in 1981). The church has been able to exert some influence in the academic world through the participation of African scholars in its global congresses, and has recently been involved in negotiations with a spiritual church in Calabar over a joint fishing project.

The **Subud Brotherhood** is a movement with Indonesian origins which is seeking to gain a foothold on Nigerian soil. The founder, Bapak, taught that through a series of spiritual exercises, known as "latihan", one can gain access to God's power by complete surrender of the self and the senses. People of all faiths are invited to participate in the direct religious experience of Subud. The National Spiritual Centre is based in Calabar but claims only a few regular members and occasional enquirers. **The Grail Movement** has been active on university campuses since the 1970s in Nigeria; people are invited to public lectures on spiritual knowledge and "any issue concerning human existence in Creation". The teachings of the founder, Abd-ru-shin, are found in his major work: In the Light of Truth.[10]

We have included the worldwide religion of Iranian origin — **Baha'ism** — even though its emphasis is on social, ethical and practical realities, rather than on mystical questions. The movement entered Nigeria from the Cameroons in 1956 via a Ugandan missionary and has since spread to both rural and urban areas of Nigeria.[11] Membership is limited to those with sufficient education to appreciate the egalitarian and global ideals of the organization.

Japanese new religions are not excluded from the spectrum of movements that may be found today in Nigeria. **Tensho-Kotai-Jingu-Kyo** toured Nigeria in 1979 advertizing itself as "the universal spiritual religion for World Peace and Redemption of evil spirits". It is not known whether this movement with its Buddhist/Shinto elements was able to gain a following. **Soka Gakkai** has branches in Lagos and Zaria.

II INDIGENOUS SPIRITUAL SCIENCE MOVEMENTS

The indigenous spiritual science movement is still a relatively rare breed, but is likely to grow in time as more people seek to indigenize and institutionalize the spiritual science teachings and ideas of overseas groups.

The Spiritual Fellowship (SF), founded by Mr A. Peter Akpan in 1980, emerged as a response to the book he wrote in 1977 entitled: The Path of Holiness. The main theme of the book is "spiritual development", which the author understands as a graduated path of knowledge by which the student attains higher levels of consciousness and spirituality: "Spiritual development leads to higher knowledge and, in all realms, knowledge is power."[12] The author's teachings regarding the acquisition of spiritual power stem from a variety of religious, mystical and occult sources.[13]

At their weekly meetings on a Sunday evening, Mr Akpan delivers a lecture on a theme such as reincarnation, love, service, money, the human mind or the reappearance of Christ. There are no prayers or hymns; Mr Akpan considers "churchly religion" to be inferior to the more mystical and metaphysical variety. And yet his renunciation of "esoteric individualism" and call for service as the fruit of study and meditation, reflect his Methodist upbringing as well as his African sense of community. He carefully vets incoming participants and demands a high level of literacy (in English), which has tended to restrict membership, particularly in terms of women. The group currently meets in a private house (although they have recently acquired a plot of land) and includes people from a variety of religious backgrounds: Muslim, Presbyterian, Apostolic Church and Brotherhood members.

The Esom Fraternity Company (Nigeria) is another example of an indigenous spiritual science movement, which is based on the mainland part of the Cross River State; it is known in Calabar because of its relationship with the Brotherhood of the Cross and Star, the largest independent or spiritual church in the region. The director, Professor Assassu Inyang-Ibom F.E.O., L.E.C., B.Sc., claims to have been converted to the Brotherhood after having encountered Obu on his astral travels and through mystical and occult research.[14]

Despite Professor Inyang-Ibom's declaration that he is the "Harbinger of the Brotherhood of the Cross and Star", he seems to maintain a certain degree of autonomy. In 1980 he announced that he was in the process of establishing an inter-denominational institution in Ukanafun Local Government Area, for the training of "priests" and "nuns" in the "healing arts and sciences".[15] Plans have also been released for the building of a "cosmic hospital" at Ibiak-Keffe in Oruk local government area. The project is a joint venture of the Society of Metaphysicians in Britain, the Grace Bible Church of Florida and the Esom Order. Drugs and personnel are to be supplied by Indian associates. The cosmic hospital will treat sicknesses which "defy medical cures" by means of "mystical impulses".

Strictly speaking **TUB** or **The Universal Body** exists more as a blueprint than in reality, but it is a good example of a nascent spiritual science movement. The founder, Cyril Owan, who comes from Ikom in the north of the Cross River States, owns and runs a bar and restaurant in Calabar. In his late thirties or early forties, he is of a very easy disposition and receives a steady stream of visitors who come to him for friendly and spiritual advice, particularly seeking his "mystical predictions". He was born and bred a Catholic, but left the church seven years ago because he considered it to be a "selfish church which hides secrets", likening it to a "mystical organisation" since salvation is only available, in his opinion, to the reverent fathers and sisters.[16]

Then followed a period of searching: he experimented with a local spiritual church but felt that his spiritual intellect was insufficiently stimulated and moved on. He discovered the "Psychology School of Thought" in 1977 and started to receive their letters and metaphysical tests, mainly concerning predictions. He attended a four-month course conducted by a European in Lagos.

For many years, Cyril Owan had kept up his membership of AMORC, following their training programmes and advancing to the rank of "Frater" in the Rosicrucian hierarchy. In the last few years he has become dissatisfied with their "slow, solid training" and has decided that he does not want their type of knowledge, that is, how to attain the link between human knowledge and the Universal Mind and how to tap the source of life. He nonetheless retains some Rosicrucian paraphernalia — an altar, candelabra, incense, bust of Nefertiti, etc., and has their "Supply Bureau" catalogue at hand should further ordering be required.

Now he feels the need to be more spiritually independent, although he admitted to having planned his own religious organization since 1974. He intends to call it THE UNIVERSAL BODY or "TUB" for short and construct a building on a small plot of land that he acquired in 1981. He has no helpers as yet but plans to isolate himself for three months in spiritual preparation for the "explosion" of his "church". He wants it to be a place where people from all social levels can "come and reason" and "know what they are worshipping".

The above comments relate to the importance that he attaches to knowledge, particularly of an esoteric kind. At times he calls this knowledge "Christ-consciousness", a state of being "Christlike" and having greater illumination and hence greater impregnability to dangers and evil forces. He also has a predilection for symbolism, having designed and made his own altar banner, with elaborate symbols reflecting the spiritual life and protection (weapons) that TUB will offer its members. Much of this symbolism is based on biblical sources, but it is in the area of his mystical predictions and calculations that the influence of his associations with spiritual science movements is more apparent.

There also appears to be a growing trend amongst traditional healers and "native doctors" to supplement their knowledge of herbalism and divination with spiritual science teachings, astrology, astral projection, tarot card readings etc.[17]

III INFLUENCE OF THE SPIRITUAL SCIENCES ON OTHER RELIGIOUS INSTITUTIONS

In this section we examine the ways in which some religious institutions have incorporated and adapted spiritual science teachings into their own beliefs and practises.

The Brotherhood of the Cross and Star, which has established itself as one of the largest spiritual or independent churches in eastern Nigeria, is drawing increasingly on the support of occultists and metaphysicians. This is done primarily to enhance the image and status of the Sole Spiritual Head and founder, Leader Olumba Olumba Obu. For instance the front page of one of the Brotherhood newspapers — the Herald of the New Kingdom (May 18-24, 1984) — reveals how three of the "world's great occultists" have acknowledged Obu to be the source of Ultimate Power. Professor Assassu Inyang-Ibom describes how he travelled to various planes and into the astral world to test the power of Obu — "Every result was that the leader of the Brotherhood of the Cross and Star was a Super-Human Being". Dr J.S. Bazie (alias Dr Aggarwal), an occult and mystical specialist based in Delhi, wrote in 1972 (in reference to Obu) to say: "I am convinced that God has his representative here on earth who comes into the world as God in disguise". Dr Bazie's letter, as well as a later declaration that he had been visited by Obu in spirit in India, have been much publicised by the Brotherhood as testimonies to the power of their leader. Dr Bazie and a small entourage from India visited Calabar in the late 1970s.

The Brotherhood also publishes numerous testimonies by its members (both in Nigeria and overseas) regarding their visions and auditions of Obu and their miraculous cures performed by him. He is generally believed to be omnipresent and omniscient. Obu claims that the power of Brotherhood is above that of any church or secret society or cult. Nonetheless, a Brotherhood delegation visited the Rosicrucian (AMORC) headquarters to San Jose, California in 1981 and there have been negotiations with the Unification Church concerning a joint fishing industry on the Cross River.

The **Crystal Cathedral Church** began in 1964 as a small healing home in Lagos. The founder, Leader Brother A.E. Inyang, who is from Oku-Iboku in the Cross River State, is a fairly well educated man, with a Presbyterian background. He has read a number of spiritual science works and this is partly reflected in some of his teachings on spiritual power and communication which are set down in a booklet on the history of the church. For instance there is reference to the leader's "premier psychic initiation" in a dream and to the later development of his "clairvoyance, clairaudience and strong inspiration of the body".[18] Inyang is described as a "great mystic"; in a Revival address he stated the following: "I invoke the Light of the Ancient Power to encircle you all and may the vibration of the creation demonstrate its power today."[19]

There are examples of other independent church leaders being influenced in similar ways by their readings of occult and mystical texts. Bishop Dr V.A. Oluwo, the founder of the **Cross of Christ World Ministry** in Ibadan, confesses to being an avid reader of comparative religious texts, as well as theosophical, magical and mystical materials. While he sees this in terms of his own personal edification and not as a determinant of church ideology and activities, it nonetheless influences his teachings on spiritual power and discipline. **The Cherubim and Seraphim Church** (an Aladura or spiritual church) regularly places the following advertisement regarding its London branch in the news magazine, **West Africa**:

PRAYER AND SCIENCE
Prayer books, candle burning Psalms,
and Seraphic Sciences.
For your difficulties, knowledge, success
and easy life Contact:
Mother Prophetess Janet Awojobi

CHERUBIM AND SERAPHIM
7 Ranelagh Road, Tottenham

The introduction of the concept of "science" has occurred over the last few years.

We may also include here the influence of the spiritual sciences on the media. For example, a popular evening television programme in Calabar is "Contemplation", billed as "our spiritual and metaphysical programme for mature minds". It features local leaders or representatives of spiritual science movements or any prominent "thinker" who is able to express himself on "philosophical" (i.e. non-church) issues. The local Sunday newspaper in Calabar, the *Sunday Chronicle*, carries a lively column entitled the "Philosophy of Life". The writer, Mr B.I. Otu-Udofa, a lecturer in General Studies at the University of Calabar, is described by his readers as a "Christian mystic". He admits to having had early training in lodges and philosophical schools before recognizing the "power of Jesus". In his articles he addresses himself to moral and religious issues of the day, with a language heavily infused with concepts such as "karma", "power" and "reincarnation". The beginning of each calendar year is also an important time for Nigeria's parapsychologists whose front-page predictions proclaim Nigeria's fate for the coming twelve months. The increasing influence of these metaphysicians and parapsychologists is the object of a satirical play — "Requiem for a Futurologist" — by the Nigerian playwright, Wole Soyinka.[20]

IV THE INDIVIDUAL AND SPIRITUAL TECHNOLOGY

Two concepts which are particularly appropriate for understanding the mass of beliefs and practices which characterize the religion of the individual in Nigeria today are power and protection. The two go hand in hand; the acquisition of spiritual power entails protection against evil forces and enables the individual to progress in life, unimpeded by "spiritual obstacles". Both concepts must be understood in the context of beliefs concerning the activity and intervention of the supernatural in human affairs. It is generally held that in addition to the actions of deities and spirits, human beings may actively influence, if not manipulate, supernatural forces to achieve desired ends, whether good or evil. This they may do directly (if they have spiritual knowledge or power) or through intermediaries such as diviners, "native doctors" and prophets.

Many of the beliefs and practices which would come under the rubric of spiritual technology at the individual level exist as "additives" to the type of spiritual power and knowledge people normally hope to acquire from their regular major affiliations (unless of course they belong to a spiritual science organization). These supplementary sources are more eclectic in nature and range from objects sold as direct sources of power and protection, such as charms, concoctions, and magical rings, to more indirect sources such as books on faith-healing, yoga, hypnotism, powerful prayers, the "Astrology of Accidents", etc.[21]

We must also include the use people make of sacred objects which they extract from their "regular" contexts and employ in their personal worlds. For instance, holy oil, water and incense become agents of personal protection. The objects take on a manipulative and magical power in addition to their symbolic value. The Christian cross or images of Christ may be used in this way. Those who have had association with the spiritual churches tend to use their white soutanes as garments of protection — sleeping, working or travelling in them at times of "spiritual need". It is also possible to see people sitting in their offices on "sanctified handkerchiefs" or sprinkling holy water around their place of work in the early morning. For members of the Brotherhood of the Cross and Star the letters of their leader's name — O.O.O. — are believed to have a sacred, protective quality and are seen painted on houses, car doors, lapel badges, etc. Rosicrucian paraphernalia have become popular for creating domestic altars and their Egyptian symbols are believed to be a source of special power.

The above symbols and artefacts are obtained from both local and international sources. An organization such as Okopedi Enterprises (Mystic Division) in Calabar, which advertizes itself as "Merchants, Mystic Adepts and Master Occultists", is able to obtain a wide variety of items and literature — herbal products, Indian amulets and talismans, "lucky jewelry", "love-potions", lodge accessories and books on Kabbalism, astrology, Egyptian religion, yoga and "secret" biblical texts.[22] As in so many other areas of Nigerian life, overseas products seem to hold a greater attraction.

The appeal of this supplementary religiosity is its versatility. The power of manipulation and control can be obtained through a variety of sources: through personal consultations with specialists — the majority are locally based, although some may be peripatetic (for example, two "great divine masters, mystical consultants and professors in Metaphysics" — one a Nigerian, one a Sierra Leonean, both claiming a variety of Indian qualifications in astrology, spiritualism, homeopathy, psychotherapy and metaphysics — toured around Nigeria in 1981 for an "international healing crusade");[23] through objects and books which may be ordered by mail;[24] through prayer sheets, "orations" and chain letters received from organizations such as St Anthony of Padua Mission in America and the "Sociedad de Jesus, Maria y Jose' in Caracas, Venezuela; through a chance meeting in the street with an itinerant Hausa diviner, who will offer his blessing to anyone with the promise that their money will be doubled if his palm is crossed with silver;[25] and through personal practices such as fasting, prayer and libations.

An increasing number of techniques reflect Christianizing influences. Christian symbols and methods are frequently incorporated, partly because they are readily available and partly because many would consider the power of Christian (or Islamic as the case may be) symbols to be greater than traditional or occult ones. For example, the exorcism of evil spirits and "medicines" from homes and places of work, formerly undertaken by traditional specialists, is becoming more and more the responsibility of the spiritual churches. Many would claim that the spiritual churches in general have helped reduce the power of witches through their use of prayer. It is popularly believed that witches fear the name of Jesus, particularly when it is shouted. Fasting has also become popular as a technique as a result of the influence of the spiritual churches.

In contrast, destructive power (notably witchcraft) appears to draw more readily on traditional means. Many believe that witchcraft is a mystical force acquired from diviners or sorcerers. Many of the traditional channels of redress against witchcraft — accusations, poison ordeals, oath-taking, confessions — have been eradicated. And yet the conditions which generate witchcraft beliefs still exist — economic and political tensions, family and ethnic disputes, and personal failure. Most people would affirm that education and Christianity have not succeeded in eradicating the witchcraft phenomenon. The insecurities of a modern, urban existence have served to sustain, if not aggravate, witchcraft beliefs and fears.

V SPIRITUAL TECHNOLOGY: THE SHAPE OF THINGS TO COME?

In conclusion we need to examine the type of religiosity represented by the spiritual science movements and the religious needs fulfilled by the various aspects of spiritual technology. We are not concerned with assessing the contribution, negative or otherwise, of the former to Nigerian society or religion.[26]

First and foremost, spiritual technology offers the possibility of a direct contact with the sacred, allowing the development of a "religious self-sufficiency". Increased access to the sacred, while this may entail for some a more intensely emotional experience and a deeper and more satisfying spirituality, essentially encourages an instrumentalist and manipulationist type of religion, with the development of techniques and methods which lead to "higher", "deeper" or "inner" levels of existence and consciousness. This spiritual power and knowledge is believed to have direct empirical and beneficial consequences in the life of an individual.

Ways in which the spiritual science movements differ from the mainline and exogenous Christian groups include their denial of the personal attributes of the divine, which is balanced by the central role played by charismatic "guru" figures in several of the movements. There is a tendency to reject historical traditions and conventional ecclesiastical structures and hierarchies. Individualism predominates over group structures; the Rosicrucians (AMORC) advertize "Your Home is Your Temple" with photographs of affluent-looking white males pouring over metaphysical texts in the comfort of their own armchair. Once the devotee has acquired the teachings and techniques, he/she is responsible for his/her own spiritual destiny; soteriological responsibility has shifted away from the divine or divine/human mediator to the individual. This has obvious consequences for group structure and identity, but does not automatically entail a thoroughgoing anti-institutionalism. Some forms of social expression occur but they are not binding or absolute.[27]

This type of religiosity has obvious attractions for those who are disillusioned and dissatisfied with more institutional and conventional forms.[28] Many of the spiritual science groups in fact renounce the status of "religion". Being involved with these groups may therefore constitute a source of supplementary religiosity in addition to church affiliation, for example. It is common to find people experimenting and dabbling with the various groups and techniques — what could be described as "amateur occultism".[29] Some groups are aware of their complementary status and have developed appropriate structures (mid-week meetings, mail order) to cater for this type of affiliational mobility.

Within the Western context, the spiritual sciences have been labelled as "counter-cultural" and as part of an "alternative reality tradition".[30] These terms are inappropriate in the Nigerian situation. As far as the churches are concerned, the spiritual sciences represent a deviant form of religiosity and constitute "modern and sophisticated forms of witchcraft and superstition". The spiritual churches of indigenous origin have displayed mixed reactions; some, such as the Brotherhood of the Cross and Star, have openly incorporated occult teachings, others condemn such religious organizations under the rubric of "demonic" or "worldly societies". The greatest continuity and affinity would appear to be with the traditional world-view, with the emphasis on the integration of the spiritual and material worlds, the esoteric and initiatory aspects, as well as in terms of such concepts as "power". Many amateur occultists therefore see their attempts to attain higher levels of consciousness as a revitalization process and as consonant with the world-affirming and pragmatic orientation of traditional religious beliefs and practices.

While no statistics are currently available, it is still possible to observe the types of recruits which are drawn to the spiritual science movements. They are usually middle-aged men, well-educated professionals, civil servants, bankers, technologists or businessmen. There are very few women, except in those movements which emphasize creativity, such as Eckankar, or emotional and ecstatic experience. There is virtually no evidence to suggest that these religious groups in Nigeria have a greater appeal for alienated or marginal individuals, or those seeking a sophisticated form of escapism. Rather they are drawing into their ranks people who have become dissatisfied with conventional religious world-views and who are instead searching for new sources of meaning and spiritual power. They are enticed by the challenge of an "advanced path" and "superior knowledge", as well as by the time-honoured values of discipline, love and service. Elements of the traditional ethos here merge comfortably with the message of modernity. The nature of the clientele must also be linked with the fairly high standard of literacy which is required for immersion into the spiritual sciences, as well as the economic means to have access to these sources.[31]

It is perhaps too early to predict an "occult explosion", but we have nonetheless been able to demonstrate the interest being shown in these new movements and their techniques, as well as the influence they are having on religious attitudes and behaviour in general. As we emphasized earlier, there are significant implications for the concept of identity — the importance of the individual in the process of spiritual self-realization and development of spiritual power is encouraging the circumventing of conventional religious structures and authorities, and de-emphasizing the need for a sacred community as determinant, provider and legitimation for one's religious actions. We should not ignore either the way in which the (imported) spiritual sciences are being modified by the Nigerian context: there seems little interest shown by Nigerian devotees in the concepts of "new community" and total commitment as promoted by some of the movements. There is therefore a tendency to promote a greater instrumentalism — the techniques and knowledge are seen as a means to an end, usually healing and an increase in personal power, rather than as an end in themselves, such as the "transformation of desire" or the "ultimate transformation of self".[32] In other words, amongst spiritual science devotees and amateur occultists in Nigeria, an intensified, more "spiritual" religious experience is considered as a means to an end, rather than as religion for religion's sake. We would argue that this "applied spirituality" is a characteristic feature of Nigerian religion, in all its dynamism and vitality, and does not represent a regression from lofty, other-worldly spiritual ideals. The appeal of the spiritual sciences therefore, lies not just in their pragmatic spirituality, but also in their unique blend of tradition and modernity and religion and "science" on an international, even cosmic level. The combination of these features, together with their adaptability, their neutral, non-denominational stance and absence of fanaticism, suggest that this type of religious orientation will continue to develop within the Nigerian context.

END NOTES

1. Cf. L. Schneider and S.M. Dornbusch, "Inspirational Religious Literature: From Latent to Manifest Functions of Religion" in *Religion, Culture and Society*, ed. L. Schneider (New York: John Wiley and Sons, 1964), pp.157-158.

2. See R.I.J. Hackett, *From Ndem Cults to Rosicrucians: a Study of Religious Change, Pluralism and Interaction in the Town of Calabar, South-Eastern Nigeria*, Ph.D. dissertation, University of Aberdeen, 1985/86.

3. It is not possible here to enter into a philosophical discussion concerning the rationality or scientific status of these movements, but since they tend to be concerned with super-sensible and non-experiential knowledge, we shall continue to use the terms "pseudo-scientific" and "pseudo-rational". Neither of these terms is however indicative of an empiricist aversion to, or criticism of, such knowledge.

4. See J. Gordon Melton, *The Encyclopedia of American Religions*, vol. 2 (Wilmington, NC: McGrath, 1978), p.178.

5. See R.S. Ellwood, jr. *Religious and Spiritual Groups in Modern America* (Englewood Cliffs, NJ: Prentice-Hall, 1973), p.65.

6. Melton, vol. 2, p.88.

7. A.M. Shulman, *The Religious Heritage of America* (San Diego: A.S. Barnes, 1981), p.462.

8. Ellwood, pp.3-4.

9. Shulman, p.379.

10. The movement was begun during the First World War by Oscar Ernst Bernhard while a prisoner-of-war on the Isle of Man. He later moved to Austria where the headquarters are still based. He claimed to be an incarnation of the Holy Ghost and to bring the truth about the legends of the Holy Grail. There are possibly 1000 members in Nigeria, about 7% of the worldwide total. (Information received from C.J. Lammers, Lienden, the Netherlands.)

11. The movement claims to have 10,000 members in 150 local groups in Nigeria with many more in Cameroun and Zaire.

12. A. Peter Akpan, *The Path of Holiness*, ((Calabar: the author, 1977)), p.131.

13. Mr. Akpan claims to have read over 100 "mystical and spiritual books" from organizations such as AMORC, Rosicrucian Fellowship, Lopsong Rampa, White Eagle, the Arcane School and Theosophy. He has been a member of White Eagle, the Arcane School and the Rosicrucian Fellowship. Interview, Calabar, April 20, 1983.

14. See Prof. A. Inyang-Ibom, *Beyond Prejudice*, vol. 1 (Calabar: The Brotherhood of the Cross and Star, reprint (of 1971? ed.)).

15. Courses at the school include Bible knowledge, Allied Alchemy and Hermetic Mathematics.

16. See H.W. Turner, "The Hidden Power of the Whites: the Secret Religion Withheld from the Primal peoples" in *Religious Innovation in Africa: Collected Essays on New Religious Movements* (Boston: G.K. Hall, 1979), pp.271-88.

17. See for example, "We Are Born Seven Times" (*Sunday Times*, May 25, 1980) — an interview with Dr. John Nkameyin Ibok, a Lagos-based "parapsychologist, metaphysicist, research psychic and an accomplished traditional healer". This tendency to acculturation and eclecticism is also confirmed by investigation into healing homes in the town of Calabar; very few confine themselves to traditional healing techniques alone. For example one healing home signboard proclaims: "Homeopathic and Botanic Medical Clinic: Occultist, Astrologer, Physician".

18. See *Short History of the Crystal Cathedral Church* (Lagos: the Church, 1976), p.6f.

19. Ibid., p.13.

20. London: Rex Collings, 1985 (in press).

21. A visit to the Ubeh Bookshop in Calabar in March 1983 revealed a religion section stocked with books on Zen, meditation, "Self-Control, Will and Word-Power", astrology, as well as a full range of Rosicrucian and Lopsong Rampa books. Cf. Harold Turner's article on "Searching and Syncretism: A West African Documentation", *International Review of Missions*, 49 (1960):189-94; republished in *Religious Innovation in Africa*, pp.159-164.

22. See their *Okopedi Healing Home Catalogue*, 1978/79 edition, where over 100 items are listed; one of the major sources appears to be De Lawrence of Chicago.

23. *The Nigerian Chronicle*, February 5, 1981.

24. Popular texts are the *Sixth and Seventh Books of Moses*, (an occult book), the Aquarian Gospel of Jesus the Christ, as well as books on Egyptian magic, Kabbalism, spiritual healing, black magic, secret biblical texts, positive thinking, dianetics, yoga and meditation, astrology, astral science. Cf. Turner, "Searching and Syncretism" pp.159-164. It is common to see books on "occultism" advertized in local and national newspapers; for example, the *Sunday Times* (Lagos) carried a full-page advertisement on June 5, 1980 by the Hermetic Science Centres (Lagos, Benin City and Aba) for the 1000-plus books on occultism that one could order as a member of their book club. The books ranged from "Seven Keys to Power", "Alchemic Treatise", "Instant Mind-Power", "Esoteric Astrology", "Evolution through the Tarot" and "Islamic Science".

25. These wandering Muslim diviners became more numerous during the dry season, many of them having migrated down from northern Nigeria or Niger to avoid the drought.

26. Cf. Turner in "Pagan Features in West African Independent Churches", pp.165-172.

27. See Ellwood, p.20.

28. See M. Eliade, "The Occult and the Modern World" in his *Occultism, Witchcraft and Modern Fashions* (Chicago: The University of Chicago Press, 1976), p.63.

29. N.B. Occultism tends to predominate over mysticism and metaphysics.

30. Ellwood, p.42f.

31. The literature of the Grail Movement and AMORC is to be noted in this respect, although in general it could be argued that spiritual technology is very conducive to commercialization.

32. See J. Needleman, *The New Religions* (New York: E.P. Dutton, 1970), p.13; Ellwood, p.5f.

Related works by the author of this paper:

"Sacred Paradoxes: Women and Religious Plurality in Nigeria", in *Women, Religion and Social Change*, eds., Yvonne Y. Haddad and Ellison B. Findly. Albany: SUNY Press, 1985. pp. 247-271.
"The Spiritual Sciences in Africa", *Religion Today* 3, 1 (January), 1986.
Editor: *New Religious Movements in Nigeria: A Current Perspective*. New York and Lagos: Nok Publishers, forthcoming.

RELIGION AND IDENTITY, AND THE STUDY OF ETHNIC MINORITY RELIGIONS IN BRITAIN

Kim Knott

University of Leeds, England

If we consider religion, identity and ethnicity, and the vast quantity of research and writing that has been undertaken on each we may be surprised when we find, if we take the three together, a relative scarcity of published material. Of course, many empirical accounts on the subject of ethnicity entail a discussion of the religious life of a group, and religion and ethnicity are not infrequently mentioned in theoretical works on identity. Serious studies on religion which discuss its relation to ethnicity and identity, however, are few and far between.

In 1972 Arnold Dashefsky wrote an article which comprised all three terms: 'And the search goes on: the meaning of religio-ethnic identity and identification'. In this paper Dashefsky concentrated on explaining identity and identification amongst what he called 'religio-ethnic' groups. In this context he chose to define an ethnic group as 'a group of individuals "with a shared sense of peoplehood" (M. Gordon, p.24)'(239). A religio-ethnic group, he added in a footnote, was the same thing. He used the terms interchangeably throughout, suggesting that he saw religion as playing a significant role in the life of an ethnic group. Despite Dashefsky's admission that religion and ethnicity could be separated when circumstances demanded it, he did not discuss them separately in this paper. Religious belief and practice were not central to his discussion, and while we learnt a considerable amount about the nature of identity in such groups, we were given no account of the particular role of religion or the effects on religion of religio-ethnic identity. Dashefsky's main aim in mentioning religion was to respond negatively to the earlier conclusions of Glazer and Moynihan (1970) that religion had declined as an instrument in ethnic identity formation.

Other studies of ethnicity have given more attention to religion. In his book entitled *Interethnic Relations* Francis devoted a chapter to the relation between ethnicity and religion. In this he discussed the role of religion in ethnic identification, precisely that which Dashefsky had presumed, but had not discussed in detail. In his conclusion he wrote,

> It is the ethnic group which sanctions a particular church affiliation, and which supports a religious congregation and its institutions as an effective means for its own maintenance and the preservation of its cultural traditions. Thus, when religious affiliation and ethnicity are coextensive, both tend to support and sanction each other. In other cases, however, instead of increasing the unity and coherence of an existing group and of protecting it against the influences of the social environment so that assimilation is inhibited by religious taboos on intermarriage and apostasy, religious differences may weaken and divide ethnic groups, promote union with different ethnic groups, and facilitate transculturation, assimilation, and eventually absorption. (157)

This reflects his particular interest — the role played by religion in ethnic identification — but also shows his awareness of the effect ethnicity itself has on religious organization and affiliation.

These concerns were also taken up by Abramson in his 1979 article on migration, and religion and ethnic identity. He asks 'Is there any ethnic group or ethnic identity which does not have a distinctive religious component? ... Is there any religion or religious group which does not have a unique sense of peoplehood or ethnicity?'(8). Abramson answers 'No' to both, but he does not choose to follow Dashefsky in conflating the roles of religion and ethnicity in identity formation. He continues instead to treat the two as separate but related variables. From his discussion of the socio-cultural consequences of migration he says 'we may learn something more about the meaning of ethnicity and religion in individual lives'(29).

It is perhaps the work of Hans Mol which most consistently discusses the relationship between these concepts. In an article in 1979 he reviews some of his own contributions to this subject, stating that the earliest works suffered from an 'oversimplified treatment of religion' (32). This had certainly changed by the early seventies when, in a discussion on migrant socialization, religion was 'defined in terms of its function to reinforce specific views of reality' (1979:33). This idea was later used in *Identity and the Sacred* and in the introduction to *Identity and Religion: International Cross-Cultural Approaches*. In these the discussion had moved away from a particular interest in ethnicity, although the theory, of religion as the 'sacralizer' of identity and the 'harnasser' of social change (1979:34-5), continued to hold good for situations of ethnic pluralism. Lewins, for example, in his chapter on 'Religion and ethnic identity' in Mol's 1978 book, makes use of Mol's theoretical material on identity in his account of Italian and Ukrainian Catholics in Australia. Turning to the perennial question of the relation between religion and ethnicity he asks whether religion reinforces ethnic identity or is a separate focus of identity? Lewins, like Mol, sees it as reinforcing ethnic identity, although the nature of this process depends on the particular ethnic group and its situation. He points out though that this relationship is not the one described by Glazer and Moynihan in their essay volume (1975), that of religion as an instrument in the advancement of ethnic group interests. In both relationships, however, religion is seen as functioning in a certain way for ethnic identity. In the former it is seen as a reinforcement of ethnic identity; in the latter as a vehicle in the pursuit of ethnic power interests. We will return to this distinction later. Two other studies are worth mentioning before this, however.

The first is Will Herberg's *Protestant, Catholic, Jew*. It is probably true that little of Herberg's theory actually holds water in the cold light of historical development. However, this does not wholly devalue its contribution to the sociology of religion. Of course, today we are beyond, *Beyond the Melting Pot* (Glazer and Moynihan, 1970). The 'melting pot thesis' itself now lies forgotten. Herberg's book, however, written in the mid-fifties, provides an early account of the relations between religion, ethnicity and identity in the USA.

Coming up-to-date and crossing the Atlantic, we have a recent article by Muhammad Anwar entitled 'Religious identity in plural societies: the case of Britain'. Anwar has written a number of books and articles on South Asians in Britain, particularly on the Pakistani Muslims. In this article he concentrates on the religious identity of this particular group, and, more specifically, on the question of the attitudinal differences of the different generations. Here he takes seriously the pressures, caused by migration and the new location, which are being brought to bear on Muslim religious identity. He considers this identity and attempts to characterise its history and development by asking questions of the old and the young. While he does not deny the effect of religion on ethnicity — he sees Islam 'as a regulating agency for all aspects of life ...' (1980:111) — he concentrates instead on the effect of ethnicity on religion.

Anwar's work is refreshing because it is one of the few pieces of research which puts religion squarely at the centre of discussion. In the British tradition of ethnic and racial studies, religion has been still more peripheral to discussion than it has in the American equivalent. When it is mentioned one sometimes gets the feeling that religion is like stamp-collecting or playing squash, a minor hobby. This is more often the case in statistical, sociological and geographical studies of ethnicity than in anthropological or phenomenological writing or in studies conducted by researchers who are members of the religious and ethnic communities themselves.

During the course of this short review several different perspectives and orientations have surfaced which relate to the complex relations between identity, ethnicity and religion. First of all there are those perspectives which relate to the question of status of religion and ethnicity vis-a-vis identity. Are they both variables of identity, independent but related, and of equal importance and strength? Is religion a part of ethnicity, either in the sense that religion might be like stamp-collecting to an ethnic group with an important tradition of philately, or in the sense that it is an instrument in the pursuit of ethnic group interests? Are religion and ethnicity qualitatively different in relation to identity, perhaps as Mol suggests, with religion the sacralizer of identity, ethnic and otherwise? Then there is the question of directional influences. Does religion affect ethnicity, or vice versa? Or are the influences mutually felt? Which questions one chooses to ask, and even which answers one chooses to give, may well be the result of one's particular research interest. Sociologists, geographers, political theorists, anthropologists, religious studies scholars, statisticians etc., may well have quite different views. Three in particular seem to have arisen in the review of research on religion, ethnicity and identity presented above.

Firstly there is what has been called the Marxian view, in which religion is seen as a means of advancing the interests of the group, in this case the ethnic group. Many writers have adopted this perspective in some form or another (e.g. Cohen, Glazer and Moynihan (1975), Tambs-Lyche) in their discussions of ethnicity and its social and political context. The second is more Weberian in character, perceiving religion as a significant element in the social change which is experienced in the context of ethnicity (e.g. Mol: 1978, 1979; Lewins). In both these views religion and ethnicity are seen as different features of personal or group identity. In the first, religion, like other aspects of culture, is superstructural in character. It is selected as a vehicle for the pursuit of interests at the infrastructural level. In the second, ethnicity is given its particular quality by religion. Religion 'sacralizes' ethnic identity. Ethnic identity is the name given to the particular kind of identity experienced by migrants; religion is that which gives this identity its character.

The third perspective — I call it perspective and not theory because we are concerned here with ways of looking at data on religion and ethnicity rather than uncovering watertight explanations — is that which explores the influence of ethnicity upon the religion and religiousness of groups (e.g. Abramson, Anwar: 1980). Ethnic identity is not a static phenomenon. The migration experience and its immediate context clearly produce very different types of identity and identification from the experience of the established settler. Religion is not static either. Both its content and its effect on its adherents alter according to social circumstances. Migration is the very type of crisis event which could be expected to affect religion. Abramson's account suggests he sees both religion and ethnicity as candidates for such an impact: 'It is only in contact between cultures, as in the classic role of migration, that ethnicity and religion assume a dynamic and social reality of their own'(8). The consequences of this impact are underlined in a different way by Pye: 'Since religion is subject to the passage of time, religious leaders and believers are forced to respond to ever-lengthening perspectives. In particular the transmission of religion from one culture to another whether geographically or chronologically means that new cultural elements are introduced to the tradition and new demands are made upon it'(1979:17).

This general, religious perspective is the one I plan to concentrate on here. A great deal of work, both empirical and theoretical, has been done already in which ethnic identity is put at the fore, with religion to one side, either supporting, influencing, or being used in the pursuit of ethnic identity. Focusing on religion does not imply a denial of these other perspectives. For example, it is quite clear when one looks at South Asian ethnic groups in Britain that on occasions religion is used as an instrument in support of either caste interests or religio-ethnic interests (e.g. the Gujarati Lohana caste (Michaelson), and the Punjabi Sikhs (Helweg)). Neither can such a focus be maintained without reference to the related social changes encountered in the migration and post migration experience. This becomes clear if we look at the different levels of identity in relation to religious change in such situations.

If we take Mol's three levels, of personal, group and social identity (1978), we can appreciate how all three are of significance in relation to the experience of ethnicity. At the individual level, ethnicity forms an important part of personal identity, sometimes competing with other features such as age or gender as a focus for identification, and at other times contributing to an expression of such features. At the group level, ethnic identity is of great importance, although sectarian identities frequently cut across it (e.g. caste, kinship and religion in South Asian groups) causing divisions within the ethnic community. Then, at the third level, the ethnic group is subsumed within the overarching category of the society of which it forms a part. This type of identity is of less immediate importance but comes into force in particular circumstances (e.g. war).

Religion and religious choices are clearly influenced by the way in which the individual, the group and the society see themselves. At the individual level the degree of religious participation may well be determined by a desire to be identified as part of an ethnic enclave. The same is true for groups. The increase in Hindu temple practices in East Africa and Britain compared with the Indian subcontinent is evidence of the way the migration experience has affected religion at this group level. Then, at the third level we have the example of the education debate. While many Muslims, Hindus and Sikhs are keen to see separate schools for their children, many reject this idea on the grounds that as members of British society such sectarianism is divisive and against the interests of both children and the religious groups themselves. The formation of the identity of ethnic groups and their members is thus not without influence on their religion and religiousness.

Religion, of course, makes its own impact on identity. Life cycle rites, and the beliefs and practices which are related to them, have a tremendous impact on the nature of personal identity. Then, at the next level, traditions of religious authority and organization help to determine the shape and nature of the group's ethnic experience. Hinduism, for example, is a relatively 'unorganized' tradition without a geographical centre or a bureaucratic structure or regular temple practices (although its sectarian movements are not without these). As a result, it contributes to the production of less formal religio-ethnic identity than Sikhism, with its history of brotherhood and persecution, its Punjabi background and its tradition of collective ritual practice. Then at the level of social identity we can see the influence of religion in the case of ecumenism. The leaders of minority religions have been keen to participate in encounter and dialogue because they have recognised that their communities are part of something wider than the religio-ethnic group. This has had an important impact at the local level in terms of community relations and community education.

As other writers like Abramson and Anwar have suggested, both religion and ethnicity influence identity. It is not necessary to assume, however, that they are alike in their relation to identity. Ethnicity would seem to be a particular type of identity, experienced by people in particular circumstances. Religion is clearly something which can be part of this type of identity or indeed of other types. For migrant groups religion and ethnicity are not without mutual influence. Religion, however, in the meaning and function it has for individuals and groups, is of a different order to ethnicity. Mol calls it the 'sacralizer' of identity. I think this helps us to know how it works in general, and how it operates in specific relation to ethnic identity. It is important to remember, however, that in addition to performing a function — that of 'sacralizer' — religion has content. It is this content with which our work in the Department of Theology and Religious Studies at Leeds is concerned. Our interest is in the complex and changing relations between migrant religions, their adherents, and their social, political and geographical locations, and, in particular, in the effect these relations have on religions and religiousness. Quite simply, this represents a 'religious studies' approach to the question of religious and ethnic identity.

Most of the writers reviewed earlier have a commitment to studying religion as a serious factor in identity formation. As sociologists, however, most are interested primarily in religion as social function and as social structure. Our interest certainly includes this: sectarianism, and the role of the place of worship and its leadership structure are of vital importance in understanding the religions of ethnic minorities. The other dimensions of religion and religiousness are also studied: to use Pye's categorization, the conceptual, the behavioural, and the psychological or experiential (1979). Perhaps the most important dimension, however, referred to by Pye as the 'dynamics of religion' (after Van Der Leeuw (Pye, 1969:234; 1979:17)), is religious change. We are concerned to record and understand religious change as it occurs through migration and settlement experiences. No religion remains unchanged through such occurences. Beliefs, practices, social organizations and religious experiences adapt and develop as a result of the new geographical and social location. In a sense, then, this is a 'comparative religion' exercise: How does a religion and the religiousness of its people change in an alien milieu? How are they different from their parent traditions in the homeland?

These are some of the current concerns of the Community Religions Project at the University of Leeds. Begun in 1976 as an informal research group with an interest in local religions (both the established religions and the new ethnically-related religions), it has in recent years focused on the religions of those ethnic minorities most recently settled in Britain.[1] This includes the South Asian religions — Islam, Hinduism, Sikhism, Jainism, and related sectarian movements — and the Afro-Caribbean groups: the Black Churches, and black allegiance to established Christian denominations.

Since 1983 the Community Religions Project has been engaged in full-time research to undertake a national survey of the religions of these ethnic minorities.[2] This survey includes the collection of geographical, historical and statistical information (on the geographical location and numerical distribution, ethnic composition, history of immigration, religious affiliation, and beliefs and practices of the members of ethnic minority groups), the production of maps, and an analysis of the religious dynamics of ethnic minority groups within British society as well as of indigenous reactions to the presence of religious beliefs and practices originating from different cultures.

Within this broad aim of conducting a national survey, there are a number of practical objectives. These include the production of a handbook on the religions of ethnic minorities in Britain for the use of students, teachers, and those working in the fields of community relations, education and social work, and the production of a series of research papers and monographs on related topics. The other major task is the establishment of a computerised data base for the provision of materials, minority contacts, and parallel studies in this general field. Support continues to be given to research students studying in this area, and for an undergraduate course currently running in the Department of Theology and Religious Studies at Leeds on the 'Religions of Ethnic Minorities'.

On the one hand this is largely an empirical task, a task involving the collection of secondary source materials on the religions of these minorities and, where necessary, of primary fieldwork information. The scope for particular studies in this area is immense. To date, two postgraduate theses have been completed in conjunction with the Community Religions Project, one on Bengali Muslims in Bradford, the other on Hinduism in Leeds (Barton, Knott:1982). Others are underway: for example, one is shortly to be completed on the Hindu Satya Sai Baba movement in Britain, and this year another is to be undertaken on the reinterpretation of Islam by young Muslim women in Britain. In addition, project staff give information to other researchers, to community relations workers, church leaders and the media on the religious beliefs, practices and organizations of Britain's ethnic minorities.

However, this kind of research cannot be pursued without a consideration of the theoretical issues involved in the study of ethnic minority religions. Of course, it is impossible to say that either A or B is happening to the religions of these groups in Britain. Each group is very different, and so is its religion. Some groups have arrived in Britain direct from the homeland (e.g. Bengali Muslims); others have experienced a lengthy settlement in East Africa before arriving on Britain's shores (e.g. the majority of Gujarati Hindus). Some groups share a general allegiance to the host faith, albeit a complex and pluralistic one (e.g. Afro-Caribbean communities); most come from alien philosophical and religious traditions (e.g. the South Asian groups). In addition to such broad differences, there are the internal ones of caste, sect, kinship, and so on. Quite apart from such diversity, however, the Community Religions Project, and the minorities themselves, have not been established for long enough for general trends in religious change to be fully observed.

Less speculative theories have been of greater value, however. For example, it has been necessary to attempt to construct a framework for understanding what happens to a religious group and its tradition when it moves to a new geographical and social location. When such a change in circumstances occurs a number of factors contribute to producing new patterns of religious behaviour, organisation, experience and self-understanding. These can be classified as follows.

(a) Home traditions
Those who have come recently to Britain from the countries of the New Commonwealth have not come empty-handed. They have brought their own religious and cultural traditions. It is these, in interaction with the new environment which produce consequent religious changes — new interpretations, new forms of religion and religiousness, and a new self-consciousness concerning religious matters. The precise nature of the changes which occur will stem partly from (i) the nature of the religion itself (e.g. its unity or diversity, its universality or its ethnic particularity) and (ii) the nature of the other cultural factors such as language, customs, food and dress, etc.

(b) Host traditions
On arrival and throughout the consequent period of settlement migrants come into contact in various ways with the established traditions of the 'host community'. In the case of Britain this means a form of religious and cultural pluralism, impregnated with a deeply ingrained and commonly understood and shared 'English' cultural tradition. Like all societies, Britain also has an overarching political framework into which newcomers are fed. This includes its laws and legal traditions, its educational and welfare systems, its immigration and settlement procedures.

(c) Nature of migration process
Individuals and groups who have arrived in Britain in the last fifty years have not all followed the same routes or had the same intentions. Some have come from their original homelands; others from other migration situations. Some have been migrants; others refugees. Some have planned to return; others to stay. The characteristics of the migrant group, and its consequent religious development have been greatly affected by these conditions. (These questions have been considered by Anwar:1979, Barton, Knott:1982, Michaelson.)

(d) Nature of migrant group
As the migration processes differ so too do the groups themselves. As those who have worked on or with ethnic minorities will know, it is generally rather futile to talk, for example, of Hindus, Muslims and Sikhs, of South Asians, of Indians and Pakistanis, or even of Gujaratis, Bengalis and Punjabis. These terms, while helpful descriptive categories, do not give a true indication of how people associate or how groups form and assert themselves in the wider society. To understand more about the dynamics of the migrant communities it is necessary to give serious consideration to group size, geographical dispersion, division, and cohesion (especially in relation to place of origin, history of settlement, caste, and kinship).

(e) Nature of host response
The other major set of influences is that which comprises the host response. Admittedly, this is a rather nebulous category, including general social attitudes rather than cultural traditions. Racism, attitudes concerning assimilation and integration, and ecumenism are examples of such responses, which are many and various in type and scope.
Together, these factors contribute to the development of religions, and to the religiousness of those who adhere to them in migration and settlement situations. The complexity of these factors, and the way in which they interrelate, is evidence of the variety of types of consequent religious response. As we saw earlier, in the quotation from Francis, the different religious and cultural backgrounds of migrants can, on their own, produce startlingly different religious forms. We can see this if we compare the institutionalization of Hinduism and Sikhism in Britain. Both religious groups face the problem of caste divisiveness but nevertheless, because in Sikhism religion and ethnicity are what Francis calls 'coextensive', the Sikhs have been more effective in forming a local and national religious network. There is a close fit between being Sikh and being Punjabi, and this has had important consequences for religious development outside India. In Hinduism, where adherents come from a variety of geographical and cultural backgrounds, institutionalization has been more complex and less effective. Mixed ethnicity has produced unstable institutional structures (temple management bodies, religious leadership etc).
The religions of ethnic minorities take a variety of forms, therefore, according to factors relating to the religious, social and cultural traditions of the group, and the many characteristics of the new location. These forms are not stable, however.

They change over time. The processes of institutionalization and of the reinterpretation of traditional beliefs and practices are without end. This dynamism is itself important. Whether those who comprise a religion, according to place and time, choose to standardize their beliefs and practices, to reject their 'little' traditions at the expense of their 'great' traditions, to retraditionalize, to 'ethnicize', to spiritualize, to denominationalize, they are involved in the making of their religious tradition in its contemporary forms. Young people are a perfect example of this. What young British Asians and West Indians choose to do in the name of religion will contribute to the future face of British Islam, Hinduism, Sikhism, Black Christianity etc. Their experience of English culture and religion, of the religion of their parents, of new religious movements and sects both inside and outside their home traditions, of feminism, political involvement, education, language learning, and so on, will all contribute to the development of their person identity and the subsequent development of the identity of the groups to which they belong.

Like the other perspectives on ethnicity, religion and identity, the 'religious studies' approach has considerable empirical and theoretical potential. This is only just beginning to be realised, although, as I hope this short paper shows, in Britain as elsewhere this potential is in great need of unleashing. In the sense that the religions of ethnic minorities are dynamic we know they will always be there in some form or other to quench our research interest. However, in order to understand the nature of this dynamism, it is important that its stages — from migration onwards — are closely observed and examined. The results of ignoring such phenomena might well be that vital evolutionary developments go unnoticed and that the meaning and significance of the religious changes which occur become impossible to interpret and understand.

NOTES

1. See Knott (1984) for an account of the historical development of the Community Religions Project. Since its inception its affiliated members have pursued a variety of research tasks, many of which are written up in research papers, monographs, or theses. A list of such works can be found in the research paper cited above. Brief details of the aims and objectives of the current scheme of research can be found in the brochure 'Ethnic Minority Religions in Britain', produced by the Community Religions Project.

2. This scheme of research is funded by the University of Leeds for a three year period from October 1983 to September 1986. I am employed as the full-time research fellow on the project. In addition, there is part-time secretarial help and general departmental support. This year we have also been awarded grants from The Hibbert Trust and the British Academy to fund a part-time temporary research assistant to work specifically on the Black Churches and on Afro-Caribbean religiosity.

LIST OF WORKS CONSULTED

Abramson, Harold
1979 'Migrants and cultural diversity: on ethnicity and religion in society', Social Compass 26:1, 5-29.

Anwar, Muhammad
1979 The Myth of Return: Pakistanis in Britain. London: Heinemann.
1980 'Religious identity in plural societies: the case of Britain', the journal of the Institute of Muslim Minority Affairs 2:2/3:1, 110-121.

Barton, Stephen
1981 'The Bengali Muslims of Bradford: a study of their observance of Islam with special reference to the

function of the mosque and the work of the imam'. Unpublished M Phil thesis, Department of Theology and Religious Studies, University of Leeds. (Forthcoming, CRP monograph.)

Cohen, Abner
1969 *Custom and Politics in Urban Africa: A Study of Hausa Migrants in Yoruba Towns.* London: Routledge and Kegan Paul.

Dashefsky, Arnold
1972 'And the search goes on: religio-ethnic identity and identification', *Sociological Analysis* 33:4, 239-245.

Francis, E.K.
1976 *Interethnic Relations.* New York: Elsevier.

Glazer, N. and Moynihan, D.P.
1970 *Beyond the Melting Pot.* Cambridge, Mass.: Massachusetts Institute of Technology Press.
1975 *Ethnicity: Theory and Practice* (editors). Cambridge, Mass.: Harvard University Press.

Gordon M.
1964 *Assimilation in American Life.* New York: Oxford University Press.

Helweg, A.W.
1979 *Sikhs in England.* Delhi: Oxford University Press.

Herberg, Will
1955 *Protestant Catholic Jew.* New York: Doubleday.

Knott, Kim
1982 'Hinduism in Leeds: a study of religious practice in the Indian Hindu community and in Hindu-related groups'. Unpublished PhD thesis, Department of Theology and Religious Studies, University of Leeds. (Forthcoming, CRP monograph.)
1984 ' "Community religions" at the University of Leeds', *Community Religions Project Research Paper (NS) 1.*

Lewins, Frank
1978 'Religion and ethnic identity' in *Identity and Religion: International Cross-Cultural Approaches*, edited by Hans Mol. Beverley Hills: Sage.

Michaelson, Maureen
Forthcoming
'Religious and devotional diversity in a Gujarati caste' in *Hindus in Britain*, edited by Richard Burghardt. London: Tavistock. *different title . Reviewed for SHAP 1987.*

Mol, Hans
1977 *Identity and the Sacred.* New York: Free Press.
1978 *Identity and Religion: International Cross-Cultural Approaches* (editor). Beverley Hills: Sage.
1979 'Theory and data on the religious behaviour of migrants', *Social Compass* 26:1, 31-39.

Pye, E.M.
1969 'The transplantation of religions', *Numen* 16, 234-239.
1979 'On comparing Buddhism and Christianity', *Studies* 5, University of Tsukuba, 1-20.

Tambs-Lyche, Harald
1980 *London Patidars.* London: Routledge and Kegan Paul.

Related works by the author of this paper
See Knott 1982 and 1984 above.

MILLET OR MINORITY — MUSLIMS IN BRITAIN

Dr. Penelope C. Johnstone

Oriental Institute, Oxford, England

This research report considers some aspects of the Muslim community in Britain, its constituent groups, their origins and affiliations, and their place and identity in relation to the wider community. The terms 'millet' and 'minority' indicate two possible tendencies, towards, respectively, being a separate entity with their own laws, or integrating with British society while retaining their own cultural traditions. The two may not be mutually exclusive, and eventually neither may be applicable.*

Muslims in Britain cannot at present be classified as a homogeneous group, due to their variations as regards national origins, language, background, present occupations and future aspirations.

BACKGROUND AND ORIGINS

Although Muslims have lived in Britain since the 19th century, these were small and fairly self-sufficient groups. It was chiefly after World War Two, and the subsequent Partition of India in 1947, that large numbers came to seek work, generally single men from India or Pakistan intending to return home after having saved sufficient money. Since the early 1960s, due largely to immigration restrictions, the emphasis has been on family reunion, which has meant the establishment of a more settled community, with its own social and religious infrastructure.[1]

The main body of Muslims here today hold British nationality and originate from the Indian sub-continent: India, Pakistan and Bangladesh. Like Hindus, Sikhs and others, these Muslims constitute an 'ethnic minority', the official term for non-indigenous national groups. There are also professional and business men, probably mostly Arabs; diplomatic staff, often with their households; political exiles; students and long-term visitors, from the Arab countries, Malaysia, East and West Africa, Indonesia, South-East Asia. There are converts of European origin, varying greatly in motivation and their degree of cultural adaptation, who may be attracted to one or other Sufi tariqa.

Estimates of Muslims at present resident in Britain vary widely, the most realistic being somewhere below one million.[2]

As with nationality, so with religious affiliation. Muslims include Sunni, Shi‘a, Isma‘ilis; from the Indian sub-continent, there is a division between Deobandis ('Wahhabis') and Brailvis, though in some cases this polarisation perhaps really represents tribal or geographical differences, as between Pathans and Punjabis. There are members of the controversial Ahmadiyya, well organised and particularly active in da‘wa.

WHAT IS MUSLIM IDENTITY?

Although the Muslim community is thus divided, it can also be seen to be searching for a common identity. Being Muslim may be a way also of preserving national and cultural identity. So, does religious or national loyalty come first? —

---

*For further details and documentation: J.S. Nielsen, 'Muslim Immigration and Settlement in Britain' Selly Oak *Research Paper* No.21, March 1984; P. Johnstone, 'Christians and Muslims in Britain', *Islamochristiana* 7, 1981, 167-199.

especially for a British citizen. Are some customs actually 'islamic' or 'cultural'? Is the idea of *umma* betrayed by integration with the host community? Is true Islamic life possible in the West, where Muslims are in a minority? What is the place of the shariᶜa? Not all these questions have an answer, but they highlight the issues.

THE BRITISH RESPONSE: OFFICIAL

The comparatively rapid growth of the Muslim population, as indeed of other 'ethnic minorities', was mainly in large urban centres with, initially, good opportunities for employment. The presence of large numbers of Muslims was perceived in the first place as an increased demand upon educational and health facilities and the social services. In the attempt to prevent discrimination, the Community Relations Commission (CRC) was established in 1968, then in 1977, under the Race Relations Act, was merged with the Race Relations Board, to become the Commission for Racial Equality (CRE) with informative, supervisory and advisory functions.[3]

EDUCATION

Education authorities have responded with a 'multi-cultural' syllabus; and, to overcome language problems, have provided special English teaching for new arrivals, extra tuition, training for their teachers, centralised or at-home language tuition for women, and where possible, mother-tongue teaching in schools.[4]

Religious Education (RE) has changed radically in recent years, in recognition of this new 'multi-religious' character of Britain's schools. The 1944 Education Act, envisaging a basically Christian background for most pupils, required RE in schools, and a daily act of worship ('Assembly'). Today, in some large conurbations, schools may contain up to 90% Muslim pupils. The existing RE system has been revised and many schools have, instead of the older syllabus, something on the lines of 'comparative religion'.[5] Sometimes this can bring about a response from local residents which shows confusion between religious and ethnic identity: any reduction of Christian content in the syllabus is seen as an attack upon British identity.

To the Muslims, a 'comparative' approach is unsatisfactory, since it puts other religions on an equal footing with Islam. Specifically Islamic instruction is provided by the local Muslim community, generally in the mosque in the evenings, though sometimes school premises are made available. Classes are divided into age groups, and teaching includes Urdu and instruction in the basics of Islam, Qur'an recitation and memorisation. The whole system is strongly traditional, and the contrast with the western style of schooling during the day can place a burden upon even the most bright and adaptable youngsters.[6]

ISLAMIC SCHOOLS

Traditionalist bodies, with a strong sense of their responsibility concerning the preservation of Islamic values, are inclined to think that such part-time instruction is not sufficient. Their call for separate Muslim schools is not always echoed by the parents, who may simply want their children to get on well and profit from the British educational system. Almost all agree, however, on wanting single-sex schools for their daughters.

The establishment of separate Islamic schools would meet with some problems. However, in 1974 a section of the Muslim community adapted a large disused building near Bury, in N-W England, for use as a madrasa. In 1975 'Darul Uloom al Arabiya al Islamiya' was formally opened. Students come not only from Britain but from abroad, and a strict daily time-table is followed, on the mediaeval madrasa pattern. Several more such schools have been established: in the north (Bradford, Dewsbury) and in London; none has as yet been given status as a 'voluntary' school within the public sector.[7]

ORGANISATIONS AND IDENTITY

The Muslims' own sense of identity may be indicated by their official organisations, whose chief priorities are the provision of facilities for ritual worship and education. Both are significant for the preservation and continuity of Islam.

In the early stages, a number of small, usually local, advisory groups were able to care for the needs of the community; but as numbers increased, larger, national organisations were established.

MOSQUES

The acquisition of a place for ritual prayer is one of the first concerns of a local Muslim community. This may involve adapting a house or other building, or later, constructing a purpose-built mosque, where funds permit. The number of mosques today is not known precisely, since a *masjid* varies from a converted terrace house or rebuilt warehouse to a large *jami*[c] mosque. A fair estimate would be between 450 and 500.

The first of the purpose-built mosques date from the 1890s, at Woking and Liverpool. Others, with considerable financial support from Muslims locally and abroad, have existed since the 1960s at Manchester and South Shields; since the 1970s at Preston (two, 1970 and 1974); London; Birmingham; Glasgow and Bristol (1981). The Central Mosque in Regent's Park, completed 10 years ago after negotiations dating back beyond the 1940s, sees itself as a centre for the whole Muslim population of the U.K., as well as a place of prayer for those in and around London. It contains a library, several large classrooms, and a residential unit, and to it is linked the Islamic Cultural Centre, which publishes the Islamic Quarterly. Two new mosques are planned for Birmingham, and a large one is being built in Whitechapel, East London.

The mosque can also have a symbolic value both as a reminder of a traditional way of life and as a 'resource of identity' in relating to British society. In planning and building its mosque, 'islamic' in style, the local Muslim community states its presence as part of the wider community, while at the same time preserving cultural and religious identity, with an easily recognisable base.[8]

The first organisation to which a Muslim may belong will be the Mosque Committee, with its educational and welfare concerns. At a meeting in London, 22-24 April 1983, a British Council of Mosques was established,[9] a new organisation to clarify the role of the mosque and to encourage Muslim education, while seeking friendly contacts with official bodies outside the muslim community.

Larger organisations include three which, with some overlap of personnel, reflect views of the Jama'at-i-Islami. These are the U.K. Islamic Mission (1962), with centres in more than a dozen large cities; the Islamic Foundation, Leicester (1966), which publishes books on Islam, and has produced a useful Muslim Guide for the help of teachers, social workers and others; the Muslim Education Trust (1964), which provides peripatetic teachers of Islam and publishes primers for schoolchildren. It was instrumental in forming a National Muslim Educational Council (1978).[10]

The Union of Muslim Organisations was formed in July 1970 with the aim of co-ordinating the activities of all Muslim groups in Britain; much concerned with education, it favours separate Muslim schools and has hopes for an Islamic university.[11]

At a more international level, the Islamic Council of Europe, established in May 1973 with headquarters in London, seeks to integrate the Muslims in Britain with those on the Continent. Its concerns are actually more world-wide, and its publications include the Universal Declaration on Human Rights in Islam.[12]

SPECIALISED GROUPS

Smaller groups are also represented. The Ismaᶜilis have a research Centre in London, with a well-stocked library, and conduct an MA programme in conjunction with London University and McGill. They publish a journal *Ilm*, and hold symposia and open meetings. A new centre was opened in London on 24 April 1985, built with assistance from the Aga Khan Trust.

A Shiᶜa Sufi organisation based in Texas publishes translations of classical texts and original works, and a journal *Nuradeen*. They are represented in the U.K. by the Muhammadi Trust and the Zahra Trust.

For students in Further and Higher Education, there are Islamic societies in most cities, which concentrate on preserving the Islamic allegiance of their members, for whom they provide welfare and other assistance. There is a central body, the Federation of Islamic Students Societies (FOSIS), to which individual societies can relate.

Rivalries do exist within and between some of the larger mainstream societies as well as smaller ones, and sometimes within local communities. All, however, are united in seeking a specifically Islamic upbringing for the younger generation, however precisely this may be envisaged.

LAW AND SHARIᶜA

The legal situation in the U.K. does not allow for 'recognition' of Islam as a religious community, as can happen, for instance, in Belgium, Germany and Austria. Religious requirements of Muslims will, in the main, be classified under education, public health, etc., and be negotiated with employers or local authorities rather than with central government. Points of law which often concern Muslims as religious questions, include Islamic education; Islam in English family law; planning permission for mosques; and the food law of the U.K. (obtaining halal meat). These questions were discussed at a symposium held in April 1980, under the auspices of the Islamic Cultural Centre and the Centre for the Study of Islam and Christian-Muslim Relations, Birmingham.[13]

A more specific and difficult question is the request that shariᶜa family law be applied to Muslims in Britain. For some years, this issue has been regularly aired and persuasive arguments advanced at, e.g., a conference in Birmingham convened by the Union of Muslim Organisations in 1975. Main areas of relevance would be marriage and divorce, where the question of custody of children after a marriage break-up causes particular problems.

Not all Muslims support the demand for introduction of shariᶜa law, and it may be assumed that some in fact prefer to live under the British legal system while resident in this country.

The formation of a 'millet' might well be a result of separate Islamic law, setting the community apart from their fellow-citizens; whereas 'minority' status is common to several groups, is less closely defined, and is more socio-psychological than legal or economic.

INDEPENDENT RESPONSES: CHURCH AND EDUCATIONAL

Non-government organisations also take an interest in Muslims, aware of the specifically religious nature of this ethnic minority. The Leeds University Community Religions Project, within the Department of Theology and Religious Studies, was set up in 1976, and in 1983 the work was broadened into a study of ethnic minority religions in Britain, its main aim being to undertake a national survey of the religions of ethnic minority groups recently settled in Britain.[14]

In 1976, largely in response to the World of Islam Festival, the British Council of Churches formed an Advisory Group on the Presence of Islam in Britain. This Group developed in 1977 into the Committee for Relations with People of other Faiths (CRPOF), with consultative groups to examine special issues. In 1981 the Committee published *Relations with People of Other Faiths: Guidelines on Dialogue in Britain*. Other individual churches are providing their members with information on Islam and other faiths. As a side-effect, the encounter with Islam has in some cases helped to strengthen Christian identity in a positive way, putting denominational differences into perspective.[15]

Also in 1976 was established the Centre for the Study of Islam and Christian-Muslim Relations, at the Selly Oak Colleges, Birmingham: a centre which was to be a joint venture of Christians and Muslims, seeking to explore the living traditions of the two faiths 'in total obedience to their respective faiths and in a spirit of openness to one another and of trust.'

Activities have expanded over the past nine years, and include M.A. and Ph.D. supervision for the University of Birmingham; teaching of Arabic; extension work and courses for specialised groups; an annual Summer School; two Survey projects, on the presence of Islam in Europe and in Africa; a programme dealing with resources in Christian-Muslim relations, linked to the two survey projects but focusing on theological issues. Information gathered is made available through the Centre's publications: *Newsletter, News of Muslims in Europe; Abstracts: European Muslims and Christian-Muslim Relations; Research Papers* on specialised subjects; the *Bulletin of Islam* and *Christian-Muslim Relations in Africa*.

The Centre's work is at a practical and academic level, and its concerns cover most of the issues which affect Muslim 'identity' in Britain and on mainland Europe. The Centre and its publications, backed up by visits, interviews and publications of other organisations, have been my own main source of information and assistance in preparing this Report. Although this is necessarily a view from outside of the Muslim community, every effort has been made to present a balanced, though brief, outline of the present situation of Muslims in Britain.

REFERENCES

1. M.M. Ally, 'The Growth and Organization of the Muslim Community in Britain', Selly Oak *Research Paper* No.1, March 1979; V. Saifullah Khan, 'Pakistani women in Britain', *New Community* 5 (1-2), 1976, 99-108.

2. Nielsen (1984), 2-3; *Census 1981; Country of Birth* (London: HMSO, 1983); K. Knott and R. Toon, 'Muslims, Sikhs and Hindus in the UK: Problems in the estimation of religious statistics', *Religious Research Papers*, no.6, Leeds University, 1981.

3. *Between Two Cultures: A Study of Relationships in the Asian Community in Britain*, CRC, 1976.

4. *Meeting their Needs: An Account of Language Tuition Schemes for Ethnic Minority Women*, CRC, 1977; A. Little and R. Willey, *Multi-Ethnic Education: the way forward*, Schools Council Pamphlet 18, London 1981; EEC: Council Directive 25 July 1977 (77/486/EEC).

5. The issues of multi-faith education have been approached by among others the Standing Committee for Interfaith Dialogue in Education (established 1973), and by the SHAP Working Party (so named after the original meeting place, in North West England), which publishes an annual *Calendar of Religious Festivals* and *Shap Mailing* for teachers.

6. S. Crishna, *Girls of Asian Origin in Britain*, YWCA 1975.

7. Primers available at the I.C.C. include: M.E. El-Geyoushi, *Primary Islamic Teachings for Children*, Parts I & II; M.A.E. Siddiqi, *Elementary Teachings of Islam*, M.E.T. On Darul Uloom, cf. D. Shepherd and S.W. Harrison, *Islam in Preston*, 2nd edn., 1979, 72; 'Muslims get their own school', *New Society*, 28 June 1979.

8. S. Barton, 'The Bengali Muslims of Bradford', Selly Oak *Research Paper*, No.13, March 1982.

9. *Times*, 25 April 1983; *News of Muslims in Europe*, 20, 27 March 1983.

10. M.Y. MacDermott and M.M. Ahsan, *The Muslim Guide*, Leicester: Islamic Foundation, 1980.

11. *Guidelines and Syllabus for Islamic Education*, UMO 1976; *National Muslim Education Council: Background Papers*, UMO 1978.

12. al-bayān al-ᶜālamī ᶜan ḥuqūq al-insān fi-l-islām, London 1981; an English version, *Universal Islamic Declaration of Human Rights*, London 1981. Literal translations in English and French, in *Islamochristiana* 1983.

13. 'Islam in English Law and Administration: A Symposium', Selly Oak *Research Paper*, No.9, March 1981.

14. Leeds University, Dept. of Theology and Religious Studies, Research papers.

15. The CRPOF has produced, apart from *Guidelines* (revised edn., 1983), *Can We Pray Together?* 1983, and by K. Cracknell, its secretary, *Why Dialogue? a first British Comment on the W.C.C. Guidelines*, BCC 1980; *Considering Dialogue (Theological Themes in Interfaith Relations 1970-1980)*, BCC 1981. More recently, a translation by K. Cracknell of the German *Christen und Muslime im Gespräch* has appeared' *Christians and Muslims talking together* (BCC 1984).
Other churches' publications include: *With People of Other Faiths in Britain: A Study Handbook for Christians*, Mission and Other Faiths Committee of the United Reformed Church, 1980; *Shall we greet only our own family?* Division of Social Responsibility, Methodist Church, n.d.

Related works by the author of this paper:

1. "Christians and Muslims in Britain", Islamochristiana 7, 1981, 165-199.

2. "Medicine in Islam", in *World Religions and Medicine*, Institute of Religion and Medicine, 1983.

Note: The recently-published "Swann Report" *(Education for All: Report of the Committee of Inquiry into the Education of Children from Ethnic Minority Groups*, HMSO 1985) draws attention to the value of RE. It can help to "broaden the horizons of *all* pupils ... to enhance their understanding of a variety of religious beliefs and practices, thus offering them an insight into the values and concerns of different communities". The Committee considered that religious *instruction* should be properly the responsibility of the community concerned, whereas religious *education*, giving a wider view and appreciation of other faith communities, would be part of the school curriculum. But they noted that the attitude of some Muslims was that the two were synonymous, seeing no need for a broader approach to religious education. (Such attitudes can probably be found elsewhere too).

The majority of the Swann Committee concluded that the provision of separate schools would not contribute to the welfare or development of the ethnic minority communities themselves. A group of six members, however, prepared a statement to the effect that ethnic minorities do have a right to establish voluntary aided schools.

THE ARTS OF *MA*:
Religio-Aesthetic Values and Cultural Identity in Japan

Richard B. Pilgrim

Syracuse University

INTRODUCTION

The central thesis of this paper is that *ma* ("interval", "between"), together with the various meanings that it carries, points to a central value system — even a "cultural paradigm" as a fundamental "way of seeing" — within the culture of Japan. This central value system is found expressed most consistently and explicitly in the traditional arts of Japan — performing, visual, or literary arts — and, in that context, is both deeply religious and aesthetic simultaneously. While this particular paradigm and its artistic expression can be found in other cultures (notably traditional China), it so permeates Japanese culture that it could be argued that it is one significant element within a generalized Japanese cultural identity.

The discussion which follows focuses primarily on the meaning and function of *ma* — or *ma*-like phenomena — in specific, exemplary arts. Where relevant and useful, the possible connections of this idea to the religions of Japan — particularly Buddhism and Shinto — will be mentioned. By focusing on a paradigm or underlying value, however, the paper will only be suggestive as to the characteristics of the aesthetic forms that make up these arts; in short, I will be more interested in an underlying philosophy (or theology) of art in Japan than in the specific kinds of artistic expression that arise from that.

This paper is one expression of a continuing research project on *ma*, a project in large part inspired by an exhibit on *ma* put together by major figures in contemporary Japanese architecture and design (e.g. Arata Isozaki) and held at the Cooper-Hewitt Museum of New York City in 1979. The exhibit, and the catalogue which represented it *(MA: Space-time in Japan)*, is primary but relatively unspoken evidence (at least in *this* paper) for the nature and importance of *ma* in Japan. Subsequent research has only borne this out, though the admittedly ambiguous, vague, and often implicit presence of *ma* has not made it either obvious or easy. It is my hope that this paper might help articulate that which remains so difficult and inarticulate even to the Japanese.

However, the inarticulate character of *ma* is precisely one of its central features. The term refers, at least within the context of the arts, more to a "poetic" sense of reality than a descriptive one. The descriptive mode of articulation will always tend to break down or "deconstruct" as one attempts to get closer to the underlying meaning of a poetic "world".

That the "world" of *ma* is more poetic than descriptive is perhaps suggested by the original Chinese character for *ma*: a combination of the character for gate or doorway and moon. It is as though the very word itself invites one to experience the moonlight as it filters through (or between) the cracks and gaps in the gate.

Speaking of the root meaning of *ma*, the contemporary *nō* actor Kunio Komparu says:

> This word (*ma*) can be translated into English as space, spacing, interval, gap, blank, room, pause, rest, time, timing or opening ... Of course both understandings of *ma*, as time and as space, are correct. The concept apparently first came from China ... and was used in reference only to space, but as it evolved in Japanese it came to signify time as well ... Because it included three meanings, time, space, and space-time, the word *ma* at first seems vague, but it is the multiplicity of meanings and at the same time the conciseness of the single word that makes *ma* a unique conceptual term, one without parallel in other languages.[1]

In general Japanese usage, however, the word *ma* means an "interval" between two (or more) spatial and/or temporal things or events. Thus it is not only used in compounds to suggest measurement, but carries meanings such as gap, opening, space between, time between, etc. A room is called *ma*, for example, as it refers to the space between the walls; a rest in music is also *ma* as the pause between the notes or sounds. By the same token it can also mean timing, as in the comic recitation art called *rakugo* where *ma* is quite explicitly a part of the craft and skill.

By extension, *ma* also means "among". In the compound *ningen* ("human being"), for example, *ma* (read *gen* here) implies that persons (*nin, hito*) stand within, between, among, or in relationship to others. As such, the word *ma* clearly begins to take on a relational meaning — a dynamic sense of standing in, with, among or between. Beyond (or with) this, it also carries an experiential connotation in the fact that to be among humans is to experience each other in some dynamic way. Thus, for example in the phrase *ma ga warui* ("the *ma* is bad"), there resides the notion of being embarrassed.

The word, therefore, carries both objective and subjective meaning, that is, it can be discovered in the objective, descriptive world but also can quickly refer to particular modes of human experience. The former element is important for this paper but the latter is the point at which *ma* becomes a religio-aesthetic paradigm and brings about a collapse of distinctive (objective) worlds, and even of time and space itself (as the contemporary architect Arata Isozaki says):

> While in the West the space-time concept gave rise to absolutely fixed images of homogenous and infinite continuum, as presented in Descartes, in Japan space and time were never fully separated but were conceived as correlative and omnipresent ... Space could not be perceived independently of the element of time (and) time was not abstracted as a regulated, homogenous flow, but rather was believed to exist only in relation to movements or space ... Thus, space was perceived as identical with the events or phenomena occurring in it; that is, space was recognized only in its relation to time-flow.[2]

The collapse of space and time as two distinct and abstract "objects" can only take place in a particular mode of experience which "empties" the objective/subjective world(s); only in an "aesthetic", immediate, relational experience can space be "perceived as identical with the events or phenomena occurring in it." Therefore, although *ma* may be objectively located as intervals in space and time, ultimately its meaning presses beyond that to a deeper, poetic level.

THE ARTS OF *MA*

One *locus classicus* for *ma* in the traditional arts of Japan is the *nō* drama. Specifically and relatively explicitly it is referred to by the great founder and theoretician of *nō*, Zeami Motokiyo (1363-1443) who says the following in his writing called *Kakyō* ("The Mirror of the Flower"):

> Sometimes spectators of the No say, "the moments of 'no-action' (*senu tokoro*) are the most enjoyable". This is an art which the actor keeps secret. Dancing and singing, movements and the different types of miming are all acts performed by the body. Moments of "no-action" occur in between (*hima*). When we examine why such moments without action are enjoyable, we find that it is due to the underlying spiritual (*kokoro*) strength of the actor which unremittingly holds the attention. He does not relax the tension when the dancing or singing come to an end or at intervals between (*hima*) the dialogue and different types of miming. [Not abandoning this mind/heart (*kokoro*) in the various intervals (*himajima*)] he maintains an unwavering inner strength (*naishin*). This feeling of inner strength will faintly reveal itself and bring enjoyment. However, it is undesirable for the actor to permit this inner strength to become obvious to the audience. If it is obvious, it becomes an act and is no longer "no-action". The actions before and after an interval (*hima*) of "no-action" must be linked by entering the state of mindlessness (*mushin*) in which one conceals even from oneself one's intent.[3]

Komparu says concerning this teaching by Zeami that "Zeami is suggesting implicitly the existence of *ma*. He is saying that Noh acting is a matter of doing just enough to create the *ma* that is a blank space-time where nothing is done, and that *ma* is the core of the expression, where the true interest lies."[4]

This "no-action" or moment "between", this empty interval (*ma*) in visual/oral space/time, is therefore a still or empty center around, within, or out of which the deepest meaning, enjoyment, and interest arises. This empty moment, or "negative space" as Komparu calls it,[5] has aesthetic/artistic power for it "unremittingly holds the attention" of the audience and yet presents or communicates no specific, descriptive content. It is a gap in time which is neither a contrived and self-conscious "act" of no-action nor a meaningless pause in the otherwise eventful sounds and sights on stage. Rather, it is significant and powerful (religiously *and* aesthetically) for faintly revealing the actor's "inner strength" — an inner strength which, in turn, is grounded in the (Buddhist) Mind of no-mind (*mushin*) as the ultimate basis of artistic creativity here. The *ma*, or empty moments between the actions, are thus windows into or gates out from which the "light" of this art might shine. They are pregnant moments of religio-aesthetic power.

These intervals of no-action do not, of course, happen in a vacuum. They are created, in part, by the forms of action which come before and after them — actions which themselves are based in no-mind and actions which are thereby "linked by entering the state of no-mind". The pregnant negative space/time thus works in concert with the figures and forms of the art both to "link" those forms and yet to break through their sequencing and their beauty of appearance into a deeper level beyond appearances.

It is precisely in this latter context that Zeami makes an important distinction in another writing (the *Shikadō-sho* or "Book on Attaining the Way of the Flower") between the essence (*tai*) and the performance (*yo*) in *nō* or, in a more appropriate poetic image, the flower and its fragrance:

> We must distinguish in the art of the No between essence and performance. If the essence is the flower, the performance is its fragrance. Or they may be compared to the moon and the light which it sheds. When the essence has been thoroughly understood, the performance develops of itself. Among those

who witness No plays, the connoisseurs see with their minds, while the untutored see with their eyes. What the mind sees is the essence; what the eyes see is the performance.[6]

The true power or essence of *nō* is a mind/heart/spirit (*Shin, kokoro*)-power which lies, as it were, beyond the more superficial appearances. The audience is being asked to see with their own mind/heart/spirit beyond the appearances, breaking through those appearances, however beautiful and interesting they may be. The intervals of no-action therefore both link the appearances yet help one "see" at a different level or in a different way.

All of this is, of course, based primarily in particular modes of experience, whether the no-mind and inner strength of the actor or the "mind's eye" of the connoisseur in the audience. *Ma* does not exist, or at least does not function or "work", without a certain kind of experiential sensitivity — one which, certainly in this case, is both religious and aesthetic.

In fact, the Buddhist influence here is both clear and crucial. The "essence" of *nō*, like the moon in Japanese and Buddhist symbolism, is enlightenment, "middle-way", or no-mind experience. The externals of performance are, like the moonlight, the appearances of things as they arise on the grounds of that experience. Thus in *nō*, as in *ma*, we have both gates and gaps functioning to let the moonlight shine through, both the forms and non-forms (or intervals) of the art "faintly revealing" the depths.

While *nō* might provide one *locus classicus* for the appearance of *ma*, others[7] have pointed to *ma* in painting, tea and calligraphy, and have described it as "imaginary space" (*yohaku, kuhaku*) filled more by one's own mind than by an objective content. Komparu, in fact, relates *ma* to the pervasive stylistic distinction (based in calligraphy but not limited thereto) between *shin* ("correct" or formal), *gyō* ("going" or relaxed) and *sō* ("grass" or informal). In each of these artistic styles the intervals or gaps serve as an empty "ground" or basis against or within which the forms or "figures" of the art function. Although present in the *shin* and *gyō* styles, one best sees this in the *sō* style which tends to feature this emptiness.[8] Especially in the latter "grass" style, the visual forms of the art tend to deconstruct or become dislocated from their normal, more descriptive, "correctness". This style leaves more space or "ground" for the imagination to enter, and for the viewer to be taken beyond mere appearances or "figures". Such an art is less representational and symbolic of some specific content or meaning than it is presentational of an immediate experience or atmosphere. *Ma*, too, functions this way in the arts (as the *nō* example indicates).

Another traditional art form with suggestive ties to the idea of *ma* is poetry. Much of Japanese poetry has avoided a "filled-up", three-dimensional, narrative/descriptive style. Rather, it has tended to crystallize or freeze a specific experiential moment — one with clear overtones of an imaginative, unarticulated reality as importantly present. The resultant poetic forms have often manifested gaps, holes, or intervals in the flow of words and images which have broken or dislocated a narrative, descriptive theme. A classic example can be found in Basho's (1644-94) frog *haiku*:

Furuike ya	Old pond!
Kawazu tobikomu	Frog jumps in;
Mizu no oto	Sound of water.

While the images cohere around a particular situation which could be more narratively described, the terse and grammatically unjoined phrases create gaps or breaks in a merely descriptive or narrative reading (such as 'There was an old pond into which a frog jumped, making a splashing sound'). If sensitively read or "heard" the poem pulls one out of such a narrative reality and into the rich negative or imaginative spaces in between.

In light of this it is interesting to note that the great *waka* poet, Fukiwara Teika (1162-1241), once said that "excellent poetry is not found among the 'related verses' (*shinku*) . . . It is precisely because these verses are all too predictable, each phrase taking up so surely after the previous one . . . In "unrelated verses" (*soku*), however, each phrase stands apart from the next, better for the unexpected to come about."[9] The *waka* scholars Brower and Miner point out the effect of Teika's use of the uncommon, broken, or unrelated images when they say: "His unexpected rearrangement of nouns and verbs works with the allusions (to more ancient literature) to create a world of imaginative, mysterious beauty out of the natural order of time and place.[10]

Such a poetic process deconstructs or dislocates a descriptive or "natural" order of things; it breaks, cracks, and otherwise creates holes in the mundane flow of time and space. As Kurokawa goes on to say of such non-linked poetic images, "the space between the images gives the impression of non-sensual ambiguity and multiple images . . . The gap left unfilled and undone becomes a transitional, complex, silent, multivalent space."[11]

Another poetic example of this same affirmation of spaces between can be found in linked verse (*renga*). Writing of the Buddhist influence on this poetry, Gary Ebersole says that the "Buddhist essence of *renga*, then, is not to be located in the (literary) universes or scenes . . . created by the semantic relations posited between two links by the poets and the listener/reader, but in the space between the linked poems — that is, in the dissolution of the literary universe."[12] The same could be said for the *nō* drama example already given. In both, narrative story and action give way to a deeper message which shines through the cracks and gaps in those forms.

The Buddhist point, here, is important to underline for it affirms again one religious grounding for much of this affirmation of spaces in between. The "Buddhist essence" in this case is the direct realization of the impermanence (*mujō*) of things. Just as the descriptive/literal world is in constant flux, and the experiential awakening to that fact "empties" one into another perspective, so also the poetry is "linked" precisely through unlinking or "gaping" so that no *thing* and no narrative sequence abides. In Buddhism, the radical realization of *mujō* is synonymous with emptiness experience (*sunyata, kū*). Emptiness experience, in turn, is "middle way" or "betweenness" experience which abides nowhere and constantly deconstructs/reconstructs the world. The *renga* poet Shinkei (1406-75) has said: "The mind of the true poet is not caught upon existence or nothingness, upon *shinku* or *soku*, but is like the mind-field of the Buddha."[13]

The theme of impermanence and non-abiding, with the resultant poetry of dislocation, finds expression in the poetic life-style as well as in poetry itself. Basho, like many before him, saw the poetic life as one of wandering dislocation without fixed abode, quite literally casting himself to the wind to let it blow him where it would. In fact, Basho referred to himself as a *fūrabō* or "wind-blown hermit," and his life exemplified the detached awareness of the immediately passing, impermanent world grounded in the no-thingness of *mu* or the emptiness of *ku*. The poetic art arising on this ground is dislocated as well; that is, it cannot be "located" in a literal, descriptive, narrative world — the "literary universes" referred to by Ebersole above. The poetry, as in the following example, breaks, cracks, and opens that world to another perspective — a perspective of direct, non-dual experience.

shizukasa ya	quiet!
iwa ni shimiiru	into rock absorbing
simi no koe	cicada sounds

A very different, and very contemporary, place where we can find a rather explicit affirmation of *ma* is in the film art of Yasujiro Ozu (d.1962). As a series of recent articles has made clear, fundamentally Ozu "directs silences and voids".[15] These analyses point out that empty shots (or "codas"), which contribute nothing to the narrative line or character development, are prominent in Ozu's work.

Ozu's films diverge from the Hollywood paradigm in that they generate spatial structures which are not motivated by the cause/effect chain of the narrative ... The motivation (for their use) is purely "artistic." Space, constructed alongside and sometimes against the cause/effect sequence, becomes "foregrounded" to a degree that renders it at times the primary structural level of the film ... At times spaces with only the most tenuous narrative associations (and *no* place in the cause/effect chain) are dominant; narrative elements may enter these spaces as overtones.[16]

At least one of these commentators on Ozu's work directly links this to *ma*,[17] but the likeness, here, to what we've already seen is obvious. Particularly suggestive in the quote immediately above is the relationship to the *shin, gyō, sō* structure; it is precisely an art in the *sō* style that "foregrounds" the empty spaces/times and uses the narrative actions, events, or forms of the art as "overtones." The light that thus shines through is the meaning and power of such imaginative or emotional "negative spaces" that dissolve the narrative, cause/effect world being presented.

The realization that Ozu's gravestone carries the single word *mu* on it only adds an exclamation point to the connections of much of this to what we've seen for *nō* and poetry above. The film critic Paul Schrader, in fact, discusses Ozu's work as a clear example of Zen art in which the "codas" (the "emptyshots" referred to above) cut away from the action to moments of unrelated, non-active, and usually natural scenes to invoke *mu* more explicitly (just as Zeami's moments of no-action). Schrader calls Ozu's films "rituals which create the eternal present (*ekaksana*), give weight to the emptiness (*mu*), and make it possible to evoke the *fūryū* (or artistic/ aesthetic effect)."[18]

This is not to say, of course, that the action, themes and existent narrative or "message" of the films are unimportant. However, the codas or empty shots function to break, dislocate, deconstruct that world of meaning and action — emptying yet opening it to another, deeper, level of experience and reality.

Schrader goes on to say that, while the codas express *mu*, Ozu's "films are structured (finally) between action and emptiness, between indoors and outdoors, between scene and coda."[19] Although Schrader does not go on to do so, I would emphasize the word "between" in this comment. The *ma* of an art is not merely the pregnant intervals in space or time, although those are an important ingredient. *Ma* resides in that form/non-form dynamic or betweenness which is continually breaking open the literal, linear, descriptive world and inviting direct experience of the inarticulate, deconstructed, "empty" reality of immediate (nondual) experience, something I believe F.S.C. Northrop meant by the "immediately experienced, undifferentiated, aesthetic continuum."[20] As such, *ma* as a gap and window also functions to link or bridge the forms and figures of an art; to stand between and thus not opt for either form or non-form.

To shift to yet a fourth and final art form, we are now in a position to better understand what certain contemporary architects mean by *ma* — especially those architects represented by Isozaki and groups responsible for the exhibit referred to earlier. Most generally speaking, *ma* is understood by these people to effect architectural design in a number of ways: the importance of opening, bridging spaces; form defining space rather than space serving form; simplicity, asymmetry, flowing/changing forms, etc. All such characteristics are, Isozaki says, true of all the "arts of MA." All suggest the results of affirming time/space intervals as crucial. This architectural discussion of *ma* takes something of the following form.

A particularly interesting and useful discussion of *ma* (in the context of architecture and city planning) can be found in an article by Gunter Nitschke which is, in turn, based in large part on the work of Isozaki and others. Among other things, Nitschke describes the various meanings of *ma* as: 1) having objectively to do with the four dimensions of length, length/width, area/volume, and time; and 2) having subjectively to do with human experience. This latter element, in particular, brings us face to face with *ma* as a particular way of seeing, experiencing, or being aware of the world. Nitschke suggests that this aspect of *ma* has to do with the "quality of an event . . . as perceived by an individual."[21]

In fact, for Nitschke *ma* is ultimately "place" or "place-making" in that it includes not only form and non-form but form/non-form as imaginatively created or perceived in immediate experience. Such place-making is not merely the apprehending subject's awareness of an objective three dimensional space continuum comprised of an arrangement of *things*, rather, it is "the simultaneous awareness of the intellectual concepts *form* and *non-form, object* and *space*, coupled with subjective experience, . . . it is the thing that takes place in the imagination of the human who experiences these elements. Therefore one could define *ma* as *'experiential' place*, being nearer to *mysterious atmosphere* caused by the external distribution of symbols."[22]

Such experiential "places" are, by their very nature, characterized by a dynamic, active, changing, processual immediacy; it is a reality-sense or paradigm better characterized as poetic immediacy than merely objective or subjective. It is in keeping with what Joseph Kitagawa has described for Japan as a "unitary meaning structure" characterized by "poetic, immediate, and simultaneous awareness" within which past and future, time and space, are collapsed into the present, and "time (is) not perceived as an independent reality from nature (or space)."[23] It is an opening or emptying of oneself into the immediacy of the ever-changing moment beyond distinctions and *in between* the 'this and that' world. It is a third world between subject and object, or subjectivism and objectivism. It is as Isozaki has said above: a place in which space is "perceived as identical with the events or phenomena occurring in it; that is, space (as) recognized only in its relation to time flow."

Another contemporary architect interested in *ma* is Kisho Kurokawa. Emphasizing a "third world between," he discusses the *engawa*, or veranda, of a typical Japanese home as exemplifying the betweenness by which outside and inside, nature and human, etc., is merged to blur boundaries, distinctions, and oppositions. Generalizing upon this example and idea, he talks about Japanese culture as a "culture of grays", or a culture of "Rikyu gray."

En, kū and *ma* are all key words which express the intervening territory between spaces — temporal, physical or spiritual — and thus they all share the 'gray' quality of Japanese culture . . . In design (*ma-dori*, "to grasp the *ma*"), *ke* (*ki*) represents the intermediary spaces; the sense of suspension between interpenetrating spaces is the feeling described by *ke*. In design, then, *ke* is the 'gray zone' of sensation.[24]

This comment stresses the processual, unfixed, dislocated sense of space or place, as well as the importance of experiential immediacy (*ki*). As Kurokawa elsewhere suggests, this grayness arises out of an "open-ended aesthetic" which refuses clear boundaries and fixed viewpoints but rather affirms the fluid, moving, processual viewpoint of direct experience — one which allows infinite variation, interchangeability, and the blurring of separate or distinctive things. As above, he relates this to both *ma* and *kū* as the affirmation of a process of emptying while yet within the world of forms and objects: "If the concept of *sunyata* (*kū*) had a color, it would surely have to be Rikyu gray ... *Sunyata* is not the opposite of matter or being; rather it signifies a non-discriminative and non-perceptual concept of existence that signifies neither being nor nothingness. Hence, it is possible to say that it suggests the spatial dimension of the twilight color of Rikyu gray."[25]

This, however, is the same as to say "betweenness experience" or a "middle way experience" between the this/that world of descriptive, "discriminated" reality. Architectually speaking it expresses itself in shifting planes, open but pregnant spaces, blurred boundaries, and ambiguity. The *ma* of architecture provides a shifting, transient experience of living spaces and forms. It leads to asymmetry and non-fixed "centers" where "place-making" takes place.

One specific architectural form seems important in this regard, and that is the *kekkai* or boundary marker of any sort (especially movable partitions, fences, ropes, etc). The historian of architecture, Teiji Itoh, suggests that these *kekkai* are an important key to understanding and expressing a Japanese aesthetic of transient, changing, processual, and unfixed spacing and spaces. Tying this particularly to ancient Buddhist architecture, but implicating Shinto as well, Itoh says that the fragile, movable partition — now suggesting one boundary and now another but all in a rather subtle and veiled way — links things and spaces in their very flexibility. "In *kekkai* (he says) one finds a fluid concept of space that goes beyond fixed boundaries, and it is a concept of space that ultimately reflects the impermanence not only of space, but of all that is within it."[26]

The Buddhist influence is here again invoked in the sense of impermanence which breaks down the static, objective, three-dimensional, descriptive world into an immediately experienced dynamic process of form and emptiness. As we have seen above, this is central to a *ma* aesthetic (or *ma* perspective) that simultaneously locates and dislocates the world of form and order, and creates a ritual, actional, experiential, between, wandering aesthetic and perspective punctuated by pregnant gaps and veiled, changing forms — a "gray" art which is the "color of emptiness".

While such Buddhist influences have been rather clear and explicit all along, this paper would be incomplete if it did not at least suggest some possible Shinto influences on the meaning and function of *ma*. Though I have spoken at greater length on these influences or potential connections elsewhere, and do not wish to repeat myself here, these connections are important if for no other reason than that the exhibit which inspires this paper features them, suggesting as it does so that we have all perhaps given too much emphasis to Buddhist influences on Japanese culture.

The potential connections between Shinto and *ma* as a religio-aesthetic value or paradigm lie in three interrelated areas: shrines and their nature, the nature of *kami*, and the nature of Shinto ritual. The connection to shrines lies in the idea that shrines were originally little more than rather temporary open, stone-covered, sacred places (*shiki*) marked off by sacred rope (*shimenawa*[27]) and containing a simple pillar, rock or temporary abode (*himorogi*) for the god. The key here is both the pregnant, open, cleaned out spaces as sacred *ma*, and the idea of a temporary, impermanent, even rather fragile shrine form.

Closely related, however, is the idea of *kami* (or *tama*) as formless spiritual energies which can only be temporarily and vaguely experienced as they come into the sacred presence of the shrine and leave again. Seigow Matsuoka, in writing about Shinto and *ma* in the exhibit catalogue, stresses this factor as the "*kehai* (spiritual atmosphere) of *kami*" as it comes into the empty (open) spaces of the shrine and is vaguely experienced by the worshipper. He thus says:

> *Kami* does not abide: its nature is to arrive and then depart. The Japanese word *otozureru*, meaning to visit, is a compound of *oto* (sound) and *tsure* (bring). The ancient Japanese may truly have perceived the sound of *yūgen*, utmost mystery and elegance, accompanying the visitations of *kami*. No doubt this was what is today perceived as *ch'i* by those involved in martial arts and meditation. This "*kehai* of *kami*" has set the basic tone of Japanese culture.
>
> The *kehai* of *kami*'s coming and going was to pervade the structure of homes, the structure of tea houses, literature, arts, and entertainment, and it has developed into the characteristic Japanese "aesthetic of stillness and motion." This is what we call *MA*: the magnetic field from which the *ch'i* of *kami* subtly emanates . . . Space, or *MA*, is the very foundation of Japanese aesthetics. Minute particles of *kami*, as it were, fill that *MA*.[28]

This leads, so Matsuoka claims, to an aesthetic and art built on a "morphology of clouds"[29] — an ever-changing, impermanent, fluid, processual, veiled and ambiguous aesthetic or art in which a spiritual atmosphere (*kehai*, or simply *ki*) is as important as the forms depicted, and the negative, imaginative, open spaces/times are as important as what *is* objectively there.

A third and related idea has to do with the process of Shinto ritual as primarily a stance of waiting in expectant openness and stillness. As private interviews with Shinto priests have suggested,[30] Shinto worship is precisely a matter of waiting for, receiving, and attending to the presence of *kami* rather than an active seeking or petitioning that presence and its benefits. Others have emphasized this same kind of experience through the metaphor of a host awaiting and attending to a guest, but all of it suggests a mode of sensitivity which opens the self to the depth of the moment through a discipline of open receptivity and sensual sensitivity.

Such experience tends to emphasize the fullness of the present moment in its intuitive, aesthetic immediacy as the locus of living reality. As we have already noted from Kitagawa, the ancient Japanese emphasized the immediate, poetic awareness of time/space collapsed into the present moment. In Isozaki we have noted that space and time were experienced as simultaneous, and space was a function of time-events which filled it. On a similar theme, Gary Ebersole has said that *manyō* poetry reflects a non-linear and a historical sense of time in which the past is brought into the present and time is experienced as an "eternal now (*ima*)."[31] Jean Herbert seems to be indicating the same thing when he reports that, "Shinto insistently claims to be a religion of the 'middle-now,' the 'eternal present,' *naka ima* . . . (and reflect an interest in) the domain of immediate experience."[32]

Such forms and modes of experience seem very parallel to what we have already described as *ma* aesthetic. They affirm not only the idea of pregnant intervals in space and time, but also a quality of awareness which seeks to penetrate into the depths of a sacred reality and experience its immediate presentness within or in between the flow or process of space/time.

CONCLUSION

It would seem that the *ma* of art begins — rather literally and descriptively — in the affirmation of pregnant holes or gaps (negative or imaginary space/time) in the sequence of images or events, intervals which function in part to both deconstruct that flow or "narrative" of sequential appearances, and yet to enliven and link those very appearances so dislocated. Hence the moments of no-action in *nō*, the gaps or cracks in poetry, the "empty" codas in Ozu's film, or the empty/filled "places" of architecture all are "centres" and windows — of sorts — around and through which "interest" is aroused, an inarticulated reality is "faintly revealed", and the very forms and sequences of images standing on either side are linked.

The net result is an aesthetic (and art) which somehow stands (but not firmly) *between* the appearances of artistic form and the pregnant gaps, opting for neither one nor the other but granting both — in dynamic togetherness — as signs of the immediately experienced religio-aesthetic, both self-awareness — *jikaku* — and the conjunction of time. "Place" is a continuum, emptied of self/other, past/present/ future, time/space, this/that/ inside/outside, etc. Such a descriptive, "real", three-dimensional world as described by these distinctions is collapsed, deconstructed, or dislocated, allowing another kind of light to shine through — however vaguely in shades of gray, or "through a glass darkly", as in an aesthetic of *yūgen*. In such immediate experience the boundaried, distinguished, descriptive, "objective" world begins to blur, fold together, destabilize and wander creating a "poetic" art of profound ambiguity and impersonal, non-metaphysical (but "spiritual") depth.

Most important, here, is the point about *ma* as a mode of awareness or experience, as a perspective or way of seeing and not merely as an objective criteria or feature of the art forms themselves. *Ma* is finally grounded in a particular kind of awareness and sensitivity in which the self or subject is emptied into the immediacy of each passing moment, a moment including both the passing forms of things and the inarticulate "depth" perceived in, through, and in between them. The self thus discovers the self in direct relationship with the other and not as set-off against it; space and time are not distinct things either from each other or from the human participant but are closely related to the events and experience taking place in them. (The philosopher Nishida Kitaro, in fact, closely relates the idea of place — basho — with both self-awareness — *jikaku* — and the conjunction of time. "Place" is a space/ time continuum as immediately — relationally, dialectually, betweenly — experienced.[33])

The understanding of self as "in relationship" can be extended to relationship to other people as well. On this point it is interesting to note that William LaFleur, in discussing the ethics of Watsuji Tetsuro, refers to *ningen* (human being) as importantly carrying the word *ma* (gen) in it: To be human is to be in relationship or betweenness. LaFleur argues that behind this notion of mutuality and relational existence, at least in Watsuji, is the idea of *kū*. Watsuji, he says, "uses *kū* as a basic term in his system. That is, the very reason why man is both individual and social is because, according to Watsuji, the individual dimension of existence 'empties' the social dimension and, conversely, the social dimension 'empties' the individual one . . . (Existence) is a finely balanced mutuality of dependence."[34]

Watsuji's aesthetics, says LaFleur, are based on the same idea. For Watsuji, he says, each of the arts (under Zen Buddhist influence) has "a common point that the moment of negation lies at its core . . . This moment of negation is not merely a nothing, but the notion of emptiness as co-dependent origination."[35] In painting, for example, "there is a relationship between the void on the canvas where nothing is painted — a wide and deep space — and the dark silhouette of the sparrow."[36]

This mode of experience deconstructs any objective, descriptive, three-dimensional, outer world set over against the inner world of the subjective self. It creates a kind of fluid, two-dimensional, flowing world which is transparent — like the gate of *ma* — to another kind of depth, a depth which is neither beyond this world nor deep in the self/soul of the human as psychological agent. It is a depth of *oku* — a sacred, invisible "center" where the gods dwell; a place (or process) or unfolding to nothing, but a place of rich being; a place (both literally and metaphorically) of "the still heart where nothing happens."[37] This depth dismisses, as Roland Barthes has pointed out, the hidden inwardness of "soul" animating the inanimate, hidden meaning expressed in symbolic gesture. Rather, it reveals an "empire of signs" in which the "signs are empty and rituals have no gods," and "there is nothing to *grasp*."[38]

Such a religio-aesthetic mode of awareness expresses itself not only in the arts, but in the culture of Japan generally. The arts, however, are its clearest expression and they reveal a remarkable similarity across genre lines as they do so. In fact, to the degree that the Japanese arts have reflected *ma* they have reflected a cultural paradigm and helped establish a cultural identity in Japan. Insofar as *ma*, or *ma*-like elements, are paradigmatic for Japanese culture, they issue in common cultural (especially artistic) forms with common aesthetic criteria and common spiritual groundings; they all reveal the shady gray moonlight shining between the cracks and gaps in the gate.

ENDNOTES

1. Kunio Komparu, *The Noh Theatre: Principles and Perspectives* (New York/Tokyo: Weatherhill/Tankosha, 1983), pp.70f.

2. Arata Isozaki, et al., *MA: Space-Time in Japan* (New York: Cooper Hewitt Museum, n.d.), p. 13.

3. Nose Asaji, ed. *Zeami jūrokubu shū hyōshaku*, Vol. I (Tokyo: Iwanami Shoten, 1949), pp.375f. As translated in W.T. DeBary, ed., *Sources of Japanese Tradition*, Vol. I (New York: Columbia University Press, 1964), p.285. Words in parentheses and brackets added by author from original text. The word *hima* is an alternate word for *ma* here.

4. Komparu, p.73.

5. Komparu, pp.xx-xxi.

6. Nose, p.471; DeBary, p.296. Nose makes it clear, here, that words such as mind and essence must be understood Buddhistically and spiritually.

7. See especially Itoh Teiji, *Nihon design ron* (Tokyo: Kashima Kenkyu Shupan Kai, 1974), pp.112-119; and Yoshimura Teiji, *Nihonbi no tokushitsu* (Tokyo: Kashima Kenkyu Shuppan Kai, 1980), pp.178-199.)

8. Komparu, pp.71ff (cf. Itoh, *Nihon.*, pp.120-134.)

9. As quoted in Kisho Kurokawa, "Rikyu Gray: An Open-ended Aesthetic" *Chanoyu Quarterly* 36 (1983), p.428.

10. Robert Brower and Earl Miner, *Japanese Court Poetry* (Stanford: Stanford University Press, 1961), p.277.

11. Kurokawa, "Rikyu . . ."

12. Gary Ebersole, "The Buddhist Ritual Use of Linked Poetry in Medieval Japan" *Eastern Buddhist* XVI/ 2 (Autumn 1983), p.55.

13. Ebersole, "Buddhist Ritual Use . . .," pp.65f.

14. From Basho's *Oku-no-hosomichi* as translated by Cid Corman and Kamaike Susumu, *Back Roads to Far Towns* (New York: Grossman Publishers, 1968), p.99.

15. Kathy Geist, "West Looks East: The Influence of Yasujiro Ozu on Wim Wenders and Peter Handke" *Art Journal* (Fall 1983), p.234.

16. Kristin Thompson and Bordwell Smith, "Space and Narrative in the Films of Ozu" *Screen* 17/2 (1976), p.45.

17. Geist, pp.234f. (Cf. Ochiai Kiyohiko, "Eizō geijutsu no ma" in Minami Hiroshi (ed), *Ma no kenkyu: nihonjin no biteki hyogen* (Tokyo: Kodansha, 1983) pp. 226f.

18. Paul Schrader, *The Transcendental Style in Film* (Berkeley: University of California, 1972), pp.33f.

19. Schrader, p.29.

20. F.S.C. Northrop, *The Meeting of East and West* (New York: Macmillan Company, 1946) chpt. IX.

21. Gunter Nitschke, "'*Ma*': The Japanese Sense of 'Place' in Old and New Architecture and Planning" *Architectural Design* 36/3 (March 1966), p.152.

22. Nitschke, p.117.

23. Joseph Kitagawa, "A Past of Things Present: Notes on Major Motifs in Early Japanese Religions" *History of Religion* 10/1-2 (Aug.-Nov. 1980), p.40.

24. Kisho Kurokawa, "A Culture of Grays" in Tsune Sesoka, ed. *The I-Ro-Ha of Japan* (Tokyo: Cosmo Public Relations Corp., 1979), pp.9, 17. (Cf. his "Rikyu Gray and the Art of Ambiguity" in *Japan Architect* 266 (June, 1979), pp. 26-56; and Itoh, pp.32-51. See also "Rikyu Gray . . ." above.)

25. Kurokawa, "Rikyu Gray . . . Open-ended Aesthetic," pp.38, 41f.

26. Keiji Itoh, "Kekkai: The Aesthetic of Partitions" *Chanoyu Quarterly* 32 (1982), p.57.

27. Itoh, in "Kekkai . . ." p.47, suggests that the origin of *kekkai* may go back to the idea of the *shimenawa* as a sacred movable boundary marker.

28. Seigow Matsuoka, "Aspects of *Kami*" in Isozaki, *MA*. . . , pp.47, 56.

29. Matsuoka, p.56.

30. Particularly interviews with Okamoto Kenji, Assistant Chief Priest at Atsuta Shrine in Nagoya (Fall, 1983).

31. Gary Ebersole, "The Religio-Aesthetic Complex in Manyōshu Poetry With Special Reference to Hitomaro's *Aki no No* Sequence" *History of Religions* 23/1 (1983), pp.34f.

32. Jean Herbert, *Shinto: At the Fountain-Head of Japan* (London: George Allen & Unwin Ltd., 1967) pp.32f.

33. Nishida Kitaro, *Nishida Kitarō Zenshu* (Tokyo: Iwanami Shoten, 1978-79); Vol. XII, p.66; XIV, p.353.

34. William LaFleur, "Buddhist Emptiness in the Ethics and Aesthetics of Watsuji Tetsuro" *Religious Studies* (14, June 1978), p.244.

35. LaFleur, p.246.

36. LaFleur, p.247.

37. Peter Popham, "God is in the Gaps: Tradition and the Architecture of Arata Isozaki and Fumihiko Maki," *Japan Society Newsletter* (April 1985), p.9. Cf. Fumihiko Maki, "Japanese City Spaces and the Concept of Oku" *Japan Architect* 263 (March 1979), pp.51-62; and Maki (et al.) *Miegakure suru toshi* (Tokyo: Kashima Shuppan Kai, 1983), pp.167-223.

38. Roland Barthes, *Empire of Signs* (New York: Hill and Wang, 1982), pp.108f and *passim*.

Relevant Kanji

(arranged alphabetically)

1. basho	9. kami	17. ma no torikata	25. otozureru	33. sukibito
2. en	10. kehai	18. mu	26. shiki	34. tama
3. furabo	11. kekkai	19. mujo	27. shin (kokoro)	35. yohaku
4. furyu	12. ki (ke, ch'i)	20. mushin	28. shin	36. yugen
5. gyo	13. ku	21. naishin	29. shinku	
6. hima	14. kuhaku	22. naka ima	30. senu tokoro	
7. himorogi	15. ma	23. ningen	31. so	
8. jikaku	16. ma dori	24. oku	32. soku	

Related works by the author of this paper

1. "Intervals (*Ma*) in Space and Time: Foundations for a Religio-Aesthetic Paradigm in Japan", *History of Religions*, Feb. 1986.

2. "Foundations for a Religio-aesthetic Tradition in Japan", in D. Apostolos-Cappadona (ed.) *Art, Creativity, and the Sacred*, New York: Crossroad, 1984.

3. *Buddhism and the Arts of Japan*, Chambersburg, PA: Anima, 1981.

MIPELA SIMBU!
THE PIG-FESTIVAL AND SIMBU IDENTITY

Ennio Mantovani

The Melanesian Institute, Papua New Guinea

1. INTRODUCTION

In tribal societies a group finds and expresses its identity in and through culture. In turn, culture finds its deepest meaning in religion. As Paul Tillich writes: "Religion as ultimate concern is the meaning-giving substance of culture, and culture is the totality of forms in which the basic concern of religion expresses itself. In abbreviation: religion is the substance of culture, culture is the form of religion."[1] By studying the religion of a group one has the possibility of discovering the roots of the identity of that group.

In this paper I shall be analysing the Pig-Festival to come to an understanding of the meaning, the substance, of Simbu culture and consequently of the roots of Simbu's identity.

Simbus had their first contact with Europeans in the early thirties. Roman Catholic and Lutheran missionaries settled among them in 1933. The churches reacted differently towards the pig-festival. The Lutherans and later the SDA forbad the festival as expression of pagan faith. The Roman Catholics allowed the festival to continue once the so called pagan aspects were omitted. The communities were to decide on what to keep and what to omit.[2]

The festival was interpreted by the missionaries to be a sacrifice to the ancestors. It aimed at propitiating the spirits and the ancestors through the killing of pigs. Humans gave pork to the ancestors and spirits and the ancestors returned the favour by giving good life to the humans.

It is the contention of this paper that missionaries came to such an opinion of Simbu religious beliefs because the Simbu expressions of religion, especially the Pig-festival, have been interpreted from a wrong symbolic system.

The pig-festival has to be interpreted from the religious experience of the Melanesian tubers cultivators, which finds its oral expression in the *dema* mythology. From such a perspective the pig-festival becomes an impressive and authentic Melanesian religious expression, different from but not inferior to any other religious expression. To recognize this is to give identity and status to the people who have created and who celebrate this festival.

2. THE PIG-FESTIVAL

General Observations

The Pig-Festival expresses all the key values of Simbu society. These key values are 'life', and in the light of 'life', community, relationships, and exchange.[3] In the case of the pig festival, 'life' is expressed through the long rows of pigs, the heaps of food, the abundance of shells etc. That wealth is the proof of the presence of 'life' for everyone to see. Relationships are at the centre of the celebration, with the exchange aiming to strengthen old relationships, create new ones, and restore the broken. The community emerges strengthened in its identity, cemented by the experience of the co-operation, and with renewed consciousness of the meaning of its life.

The one element which is not so visible is the religious one. One may see the relationships to the ancestors expressed in the ritual, but that is not what is meant by religion. Relationship to the ancestors is a relationship to some very important members of the community; it is part of the social relations which are strengthened. But by religion we do not mean such a relationship. There is a relationship to the Ultimate, to the Source of everything. This relationship we shall call religion within the context of this article. The expression of this relationship to the Ultimate is not immediately obvious. One must understand the symbolic system to be able to see this religious dimension. The element I intend to highlight in the case study of the pig festival is the religious one: the concern with the Ultimate as experienced and expressed in what I call the biocosmic religion.

Biocosmic Religion

Let me explain what I mean by biocosmic religion.

At the base of any religion, taken as a public system of beliefs, rituals, behaviour, there is a religious experience. Within the context of Melanesia it is very important to realize that there are different types of religious experiences. There are experiences which can be grouped under the term theistic and there are other experiences which are as real and religious and which can be grouped under the term biocosmic.[4] Let us explain the two categories. Characteristic of the theistic pattern is an Ultimate who is called God. Such a God is personal, both far and near, totally other. Everything utterly depends on God for its existence. Yahwism is a good example of theism.

The biocosmic religious experience is not characterized by an Ultimate called God, theos, but by an Ultimate experience as bios — the Greek word for life. It is characterized by the experience of 'something' which is absolutely necessary for existence, of 'something', in which everything participates. I call this 'something', 'life'. The more a reality participates in that 'life', the stronger, healthier, richer, more important that reality becomes. If 'life' ebbs away, then sickness and eventually death follow. 'Life' is more than biological life, or material existence, it is material, biological and spiritual. In a sentence: everything which is experienced as positive has its source in that 'life'; anything negative is experienced as a loss of that 'life'.

There is another essential element in this biocosmic experience. That 'life' is not experienced as personal either in itself (ontologically) or existentially. It is cosmic: everything participates in it in various degrees and everything is bound together into a unity by it. Animals and plants are different from humans, but are still linked together into a cosmos, an ordered whole, by that 'life' without which nothing could exist. Everything which exists shares in the same 'life'. I call this experience biocosmic from the two main elements in the word: the bios, Greek for life, and the cosmic from the Greek word for 'ordered universe' which means universality and interrelatedness. The symbolism of the biocosmic experience is horizontal, with a stress on the blood, the womb, the tomb, the phallus.

Religious Aspect of the Pig Festival

As Eliade observes: 'It is enough to say that all responsible activities (puberty ceremonies, *animal* or *human sacrifices* [my emphasis], cannibalism, funerary ceremonies, etc.) properly speaking constitute a recalling, a "remembrance", of the primordial murder.'[5] The celebrations become memorials, i.e. the making present of that event that initiated the flow of the true 'life'. By making present that life-giving event the participants are immersed into that true 'life' and come to participate in that 'life'.

The Changing Aspect of Traditional Religions

Having observed pig festivals for more than twenty years and listened to the discussions prior to and during the festivals, I have come to the conclusion that there seems to be a general outline of the celebration which is commonly known and followed but the details are very much a topic for heated arguments even within the same lineage.

The younger generation which blames the mission for the present-day changes misses the whole point.[6] The reason for those changes is, and was, that rituals have to prove themselves efficacious. An efficacious ritual provides 'life'. One that fails to do so is changed. The fact that there are changes in ritual today, in favour of Christian symbols and rituals, is not a discarding of the way of the ancestors but a very traditional way of increasing the efficacy of the rituals. It is a pity that today's elite has been taught to understand the pig-kill only in theistic terms and not in Melanesian biocosmic terms. The irony is, that by wanting to freeze the rituals according to a certain tradition, the elite works towards the killing of traditional religious celebrations: they prevent them from being a living, changing religion and force them to become museum pieces or a mere folkloristic show.

3. DESCRIPTION OF THE FESTIVAL

The Myth

Often the same theme is expressed in story-form as well as in drama. When I first observed the pig festival I was quite aware of the possibility of a myth rendering the theme of the pig-festival but I did not find such a myth. My article in "Christ in Melanesia"[7] was written prior to the discovery of the myth.

The only myth I could find in the Gumine area of the Simbu goes as follows:

"Once upon a time some poeple were hunting frogs and followed the Kingaima creek to its source. When near its source they saw two beings who were dancing and wearing the decoration people today use to wear when they celebrate the pig-festival. Up to that moment people did not know how to celebrate the pig-festival. The frog-hunters tried to come closer to the two decorated beings but the two took off. One, though, had a bad leg and could not run. The frog-hunters grabbed him. He told them: 'When you kill pigs you should put on these ornaments and use the items you see. Do not forget: if men eat the liver of the pig, women should abstain from eating it; if women eat the liver of the pigs men should abstain.' That's how we learned to dance, how to put on our decorations, how to use the wig (gibilinkobe), the geruas, the flutes (nebare) and how to kill the pigs."

The myth gives the origin of the festival but not the nature of the festival. It was only later that I discovered a myth that seemed to give the meaning of the festival.

I found the myth reported by William Bergmann among the Kamanuku further to the north. The Sina-Sina, Gumine and Salt Nomane areas do not seem to know such a myth. The myth is of the dema type and goes like this:

Once upon a time there were two brothers who lived in heaven. One day they appeared like a flash of lightning through the sky and descended to the ground, touching the tip of the Kama shrub on their way. The elder brother's name was Mondo and the younger's name was Gande. They came and lived at Wonkama. Mondo made an *arigl* head-gear, went to the bush, and stayed there until night. Then he came home and slept. Gande wondered what the elder brother was doing in the bush all day long. Next morning Gande followed his older brother to the bush without being seen. As soon as Mondo arrived he took off the *arigl* head-gear, drove a stick into the ground which had a fork on top of it and hung his *arigl* on it. He then bent down and started digging as pigs do. He kept digging until night. At dusk he took his *arigl* and put it on, but the *arigl* kept slipping off his head. So he said 'Did Gande come that you act this way? Stay put!' He then went home wearing his *arigl*. When he came home he asked Gande, 'Did you follow me to the bush and see me?' 'Yes, I came and saw you.' Mondo continued, 'You saw where I hung my *arigl*. You must kill me and bury me there and put a fence around the place. Kungi grass will soon grow on the spot and when this happens, go and look.' So Gande took his brother to that place, killed him, buried him there and put a fence around the place. Then he went home. He kept an eye on the place and watched the Kungi grass grow. Within the fence there appeared several pigs of different colours — brown, yellow, white, black, and some with black spots and some with stripes. He returned with his parents and brothers and put ropes around their legs and took them home. Since that time we have bred pigs and eaten them, and we have made *arigl* head-gear and other decorations.

If the man Mondo had not done this for us how could we have obtained the pigs, how could we have bred them? Gande saw them first where he killed and buried his brother and therefore we have pigs now.[8]

This myth does not talk directly about the origin of the pig-festival but about the origin of everything of value. Those values are symbolized by the pig which becomes the symbol for "life". Mondo is both brother (human) and pig. His/its killing by Gande brings about all the values that were lacking before. The myth refers to the origin not of human existence but of "life".

It is in the light of this dema-myth that I intend to interpret the pig-festival. The pig-festival is the making present of the event that originated 'life'. By celebrating the pig-festival the whole clanic cosmos participates in the fullness of "life".

The Preparation
Once it has been decided to hold a pig festival, one can hear the flutes[9] being blown in pairs at night by initiated males. Meanwhile new gardens are being prepared to have sufficient food for the celebrations: there will be many visitors to be fed. Eventually the long houses around the dancing ground are erected which will serve as shelter during the festival. Immediately before the slaughtering of the pigs, a post [10] is erected at the side of the ground where the pigs will be killed. In modern times this post can have a cross nailed on it or it can be simply an iron cross. It is usually a short post of about two feet, driven into the ground, so that most of the post protrudes. Around this post, the people who are holding the festival build a little fence and next to it place their digging-sticks, spades, axes, sweet potato runners, sugar cane and ropes which are used to tie the domesticated pigs. In at least one instance I witnessed, money boxes were laid around the enclosure too.

The Dance
A few months before the actual pig-kill the people who celebrate the festival put on their finery and start dancing. The first few weeks are reserved for the dance

of the children. The parents put all their finery on their children, mostly girls,[11] and the children dance on their home ground. Some of the children wear a special wig called *arigl* in the Kuman language of the Simbu and *gibilinkobe* in the Golin dialect of Gumine.[12] After two or three weeks the men take over the dance and a few of the marriageable girls dance with them. They dance first on their home ground and then visit other dancing grounds to perform there. Some of the men wear the *arigl* wig.

The Killing

The pigs are staked on the dancing ground. Early in the morning the pigs are killed by clubbing them on the head. While clubbing them, the people who do this move their lips. They told me that they invite the spirit (*iban*) of the slaughtered pig to go to the place where the piglets used to feed. When the slaughtered pigs are lined up in rows, the men extol the achievements of the holder of the festival. Sometimes the pigs are given away at this time but sometimes they are cooked first. The owners singe away the hair of the pigs and then proceed to cut them up. Meanwhile other men dig the pits where the pork and tubers are going to be steam-cooked. In the past, before the coming of Christianity, people used to hold or carry the so-called *gerua* boards during the killing.[13]

The Distribution

The following day the guests come in their finery and perform a dance. The dancing group is composed of two lines of dancers facing each other, with a group of dancers in the middle who move up and down between them. While the side rows are stationary, the inside groups advance towards the end of the two rows but then turn their backs and go back. Then, still with their backs turned, they come back once more. In front of the guests' dancing group there is a line of hosts brandishing spears and axes and, in dance form, obstructing the progress of the guests' group. At a certain moment, the hosts move to the side and the guests' group pours into the centre of the dancing ground. Now the distribution of pork takes place. I have seen distribution of money on poles as well to pay for marriages and births. After receiving the gifts the guests leave the ground.

4. TENTATIVE ANALYSIS OF THE MAIN SYMBOLS

The Flutes

I wrote in "Christ in Melanesia".

No real myth is remembered about the flutes. The old men no longer know the meaning of the flutes. They only know that they (the flutes) are 'strong' in the sense that they can make the boys strong and therefore are shown to them at initiation to change them from boys into men. They also make pigs grow. Because of this belief among the Yui people of the Salt region I saw the flutes being blown outside the pig festival during a girls' initiation before the pigs were slaughtered.[14]

In the Gumine myth the flutes are shown to the people by the two mythical beings.

The men told me that they played the flutes for the pigs so that they would grow and fill the eyes of the beholder and the bellies of the guests.[15]

There is also another fact to be considered. The flutes, said to be as male and female, are played only in pairs and, male and female together, symbolize fertility, life, and new life.

Linguistically, according to John Nilles, there is a link between the flutes and female menstruation and genitals, which also indicates that the flutes are symbolic of fertility.[16]

According to K.E. Reed, the flutes symbolize *nama*: 'To the Gahuku-Gama the sacred flutes are a manifestation of the external supernatural force which watches over their well-being and destiny.'[17] Read further explains that the force which is symbolized by *nama* is the power of society itself.

Both Read and Nilles take this power to be personal. Read says it 'watches over their well-being ...' and Nilles calls it 'a real animated personal being'.[18] Nilles says 'personal', though his informants never went beyond a 'something that exists'.[19] I agree with Nilles that it is something very 'hard to define'.[20] The question is: is that 'something that exists' a survival from theistic past when the ancestors of the Simbus were collectors — Read and Nilles can be read in that sense — or is it the experience of the cultivators, of that Ultimate as 'life' on which the whole cosmos depends? 'Life' seems to be the function about which present Simbus are concerned.

The flutes' function, as 'sanction of men's influence over women', seems to have been accidental. Recent events have shown it to be an effect rather than the cause of the practice. My experience is mostly in the time when the flutes were public, although in 1963 I visited an area where the flutes were still secret. In all the other cases and places the flutes were not secret anymore. The fact that they were still blown after they had been made public indicates that the purpose of the exercise was not primarily to deceive and dominate the women but, as my informants told me, to make the pigs grow, and to make things grow.

According to R. Johnson the power of the flutes comes from their secret use, from the secrecy which surrounds them. The secrecy gives meaning to them as tools to keep male superiority as a means of social oppression.[21] In my opinion there is more to it than only secrecy. Johnson reports that the flutes were used first by the mythical ancestors to initiate their sons,[22] implying that the flutes are powerful in themselves and that is the reason why the ancestors handed them down to their descendants. Secondly the flutes used to belong to the women and the men stole the flutes from them.[23] Women are symbols of 'life' and fertility. Is the myth saying that, even if the flutes are handled by men today, they are nevertheless powerful and loaded with 'life' like a woman? An explanation why the myth of the theft is not part of the instruction at the boys' initiation could be that recounting the myth would only prove to the boys that women are fundamentally more powerful than men — an idea that the initiation intends to undermine in favour of male superiority.

The Post

The phallic nature of the post does not have to be proved to anyone who has seen it. Even for those clans who do not perform the symbolic coitus as described by Louis Luzbetak and Nilles[24], the phallic symbolism seems fairly obvious. That the post must be planted into the tomb of the ancestor seems to be symbolic too. The link, tomb/womb, is rather common in mythological narration. The grave of Mondo is the womb giving birth to 'life'. The planting of the phallic symbol into the tomb/womb, analogous to the sexual union, could be a symbol for 'life'. What Luzbetak and Nilles describe is an alternative, more explicit form, though Luzbetak mentions the 'burial' of the post as well.[25]

'Life', symbolized by the phallic object, is proclaimed to be based, not on any ancestor, but on the original ancestor. From all reports, and from my observations, the post is never planted on a grave in the cemetery (historical ancestors), but on a special grave elsewhere: the grave of a non-historical, mythical, ancestor. Could the symbolic message be saying that 'life' is coming from the tomb/womb of the mythical ancestor? Is that mythical ancestor the dema of which we heard in the Kamanuku myth?

The substitution of the cross for the post,[26] or the imposition of the cross on the original post, would be a Christian statement that the cross is the true symbol of 'life', which symbol was prefigured by the post in the past.

The argument about the tomb of the mythical ancestor is not as stringent as it might sound. As a matter of fact, though the dead are buried in individual cemeteries, at least among the Golin of the Gumine area, the soul of the deceased (iban) in times of crises e.g. sickness in the family, is lead to the burial ground of the mythical ancestors where eventually the pig festival is going to take place. (This ritual raises interesting questions: why are the historical ancestors placated by being led to the mythical ancestors grave? Does it express a need of the historical ancestors for something they do not have but which can be found with the mythical ancestor?) In spite of this fact in time of family crisis pigs still seem to be slaughtered in the individual cemeteries while the big slaughtering which climaxes the pig-festival is held at the mythical ancestral grave. It remains true that the post is never planted in an individual cemetery or on an historical grave, no matter how famous the historical ancestor may be. It seems to say that 'life', as symbolized by the phallic object, at least does not come directly from the historical ancestors.

The Killing

Whether one fully agrees with Eliade or not, that all sacrificial killings in this type of religion are memorials of the original killing, the theistic symbolic system does not explain the facts I saw or heard described. Even if we admit, that some inconsistency is a characteristic of human behaviour, one must still assume a basic consistency in any cultural system.

Why do those who kill the pits send the 'spirit' of the pigs away to the place where pigs used to feed? In the mortuary feasts the spirits of the pigs are not sent away but presented to the dead. In this killing just described however, the spirits of the pigs are not given to the ancestors. What then is given to the ancestors?

The explanation given by the performer of that ritual, and also accepted by the missionaries, is that the sprinkling of the blood which pours from the noses of the pigs, gives growth to the sweet potatoes, to the pigs which will subsequently be tied with ropes sprinkled with it, and to the gardens which will be prepared and cultivated with tools also sprinkled with blood. So it seems then that it is the blood which gives growth not the ancestors.

The Blood

From my observation at the various pig-festivals and pig-kills for rites of passage it seems that the blood of the pigs is not "sacred" and powerful in itself but only when and if it is used as symbol of the violent death of the pig.

There is no pouring out of blood in the sense of a blood offering. The blood seems to be only an occasional by-product. Not all the pigs bleed that much. If blood would be the main thing then people would make sure that blood pours out of the pig. It is not done. The blood which falls on the ground is left there and I saw people stepping on it and dogs licking it. The idea never comes to people of carrying and sprinkling it in the gardens.[27] It seems that it is not the blood in itself which is sacred and powerful but its symbolism, its symbolic relation to the actual killing. The blood is not sacred in itself. It is mainly used to make sausages!

A totally different picture is given when we consider the menstrual blood. Menstrual blood is powerful in itself and people are in fear of it. A man can get sick and die because of contact with it whether accidental or not. Not so with the blood of the pigs. People step on it, make sausages out of it, they put seasoning in it; they cook and eat it. Such food is far from being special in any way. It is special because seldom not because of other properties. The blood of the pigs is valid only when used as a symbol. The traditional ritual of sprinkling of blood on the sweet potato runners, the sugar cane, the digging-sticks and other gardening tools, signifies that, for Simbus, 'life' and growth come from the killing of the pig of which the blood is the symbol. If this be so, then the theory that the ancestors are 'givers of "life" ' is a misinterpretation. The interpreters are using criteria from their own religious system to evaluate another. That many Melanesians will agree with the missionaries' interpretation is more indicative, I believe, of the strength of the churches' teaching on this matter, than on any weakness in the argument.

Because the post is a phallic symbol, it seems to imply that human sexuality receives vitality from the same source as the gardens and the ancestors: the ritual killing of the pig of which the grave of the mythical ancestor is a symbol. In the ritual, human sexuality is brought into contact with the source of 'life'. In the mythical perspective, the source of 'life' is the killing of the pig which makes present, or reactualizes, the original killing of Mondo or of the dema on whose tomb the post is planted.

If, within the context of the symbolic system of the digging-stick cultivators, we take the ritual killing to be 'the making present of the original killing' which initiated the flow of true 'life', then everything else seems to follow logically. The killing is the actual event which gives 'life', and the whole cosmos participates in the abundance of 'life'. That participation of the cosmos in 'life' is symbolized and dramatized by the smearing of the blood, or the painting with red colour, of whatever participates in that growth or flow of 'life'. The whole cosmos is symbolized by the sweet potato runners, the working tools, the graves of the historical ancestors, and the post.

The Dance

It took me a long time to work out the symbolism of the dance because I did not try to understand it within the context of the biocosmic religious system, where community symbolizes 'life', where sex and marriage serve the community. The link with the birds of paradise, expressed beautifully in the documentary film, 'The Voices in the Forest',[28] further helps us understand the meaning of the dance. As the male bird through its sound and display attracts the female, so the group of dancers entice female spectators to join them and become their wives.

Another symbolism which seems to be represented by at least some groups and their dances is the ambivalence of relationships. It symbolizes the enmity which is eventually overcome and the friendly relationships which triumph and are expressed and cemented through the pork exchange.

The Arigl

People use a wig called *arigl*. Not everybody wears such a wig. It is worn by some dancers whether children or adults. I saw it being worn by women the day of the actual killing of the pigs. I sometimes saw the *arigl* lying on the bodies of the dead pigs when they were lined up before distribution. The myth says that Mondo was wearing an *arigl*. I was unable to find out many details about the *arigl* wig, although I was told that it is a sign that a man has many pigs and hence a sign of abundance of wealth, of 'life'. The myth links the *arigl* wig with Mondo himself. In the Gumine myth the wig is given by the two mythical beings. The wig is one of the symbols which have been retained by Christian Simbus when performing the pig-kill.

The Gerua Boards

In the past there was another important symbol which today has been discarded because, in the eyes of the Simbus, it was incompatible with Christianity: the *gerua* boards. However, it seems that in the eyes of the people this omission has not compromised the success of the pig-kill. Does it mean that the *gerua* boards are not essential? Or have the Simbus found a functional substitute? Who told the Simbus that the *gerua* boards were anti-Christian? The missionary of the time did not know what the *geruas* were, and he did not take part in the people's discussions.[29] What perception did the Simbus have of Christianity at that time? What did they see in the *geruas* that made them think they were incompatible with Christianity?

The *geruas* have been discarded, the flutes have been made public, and the *arigl* continues. Why the difference? Do the *geruas*, beside their overt function, have another function which is thought to be incompatible with Christianity? These are pertinent questions for any analysis of the *gerua* board. Joachim Sterly writes: 'They (the *gerua* boards) are sacred objects of cult, which make it possible to preserve the spiritual breath of the pigs which, as they come from the body of Mondo, are as siblings of the human beings.'[30] This 'spiritual breath' is like a fluid emanating from the pigs.[31] I agree that one has a problem in expressing the reality the Simbus perceive in the *gerua* complex, but I doubt whether a term like 'fluid' is ever going to bring us near to a formulation of the reality behind *gerua*. We seem to be dealing with symbols of realities which are perceived but escape description. I suggest that *gerua* symbolizes, or is linked closely with 'life' of which the killings of the pigs is an efficacious sign. That 'life', as Sterly rightly says, is cosmic.[32] It is more than fertility: it is growth, well-being, health, wealth, and good relationships. It is not only limited to the human sphere; the whole cosmos represented by children, pigs, gardens, environment, shares in it.

If the *geruas* had another symbolic function in the past, at least when I was collecting my information they had been interpreted to fit the biocosmic religious system. This interpretation is indicated by the painting of the rhombus on the *gerua* boards. In Kuman, the rhombus is called *Mondo numbuno*.[33] Both the fertility sign of the rhombus and the name given to it indicate the boards are now understood in terms of the Mondo myth and belong to the complex of the symbols of 'life'.

Summarizing

All the symbols seem to point to growth and 'life'. They can be grouped into two categories: one centering around sex, the other around violent death.

Tentative results of this analysis

The pig festival is first of all not an offering to the historical ancestors, to the dead. It is not an offering to the mythical ancestors either. It is the repetition of the original killing which brought 'life' to the Simbus. It is not a repetition in the sense of a new distinct act in linear history. What is done now is what has been done in the past. The two cannot be separated. The whole power of the original act is present now.

The ancestors and spirits, symbolized by the graves, *geruas*, flutes, wig, participate with humans and the rest of the cultural cosmos symbolized by the pig, the potato runners, the instruments of work, the money boxes, in this event. By participating they share in the 'life' that flows from the primordial killing of which the pig festival is an efficacious symbol.

From a theological point of view the pig festival can be understood as a statement of faith that the whole cosmos utterly depends on something which is not of the cosmos, but without which the cosmos cannot exist. That something I call 'life', a life that is not only biological but spiritual as well, a 'life' which is health, wealth, well-being, good relationships, good name, prestige, meaning etc.

Further, that 'life' is mediated through the death of the dema, a death which was the genesis of this historical time. That 'life' is a gift that the cosmos could not obtain by itself. The ritual is fundamentally not a human initiative but obedience to a non-human command. The ritual must follow the tradition: what the dema commanded. It is an act of active obedience.

The blood and the colour red symbolize this original life-giving-death. To smear with blood or red is a symbol of the necessity of 'life' and the desire for the flow of 'life'. It is further a symbol of the certain hope to be able to participate in that flow of 'life'. That 'life' does not come from the symbol but from the symbolized i.e. the original killing.

Sex, sexual organs, the male-female pair, symbolize the 'life' which comes from the death of the dema. While blood symbolizes more the origin, the efficacious killing, sex symbolizes more the result, 'life' itself. In this sense blood and sex are religious symbols and can become religious rituals when they are acted out.

This is a possible interpretation of the pig festival according to the biocosmic religious symbolic system. It opens up great possibilities for dialogue. The theistic religious symbolic system explains the killing in terms of sacrifices to ancestors and so in terms of idolatry. In the theistic system, sex outside marriage is a simple aberration based on human sinfulness. Ritual is human manipulation of the divine. I have my doubts whether the latter is a more accurate explanation.

5. CONCLUSION

The first step towards recognising the identity of the Simbus is for outsiders to recognize the different symbolic system through which Simbus life must be interpreted. It would be more sensible to call the type of primal religion I just described by its proper name i.e. biocosmic instead of animistic, which latter term defines more our ignorance than the nature of that religion. This would be the first step towards recognising the identity of all those who profess that religion. Once we start using the right name and the right symbolic system then we become aware that we deal with equal partners in a dialogue. Christianity is now part of the Simbu culture and religion. It can be a foreign element rejected by a healthy body like a survival from colonial time or it can be a deepening in dialogue of the Mondo myth and its re-enactment. When fifty years ago the Simbus substituted the cross for the post on the tomb of the mythical ancestor they entered into a dialogue with Christianity using the language of visible symbols in an effort to safeguard their own specific identity. May this paper show the way for a new appreciation of the Simbu religion and so of the Simbu identity so that what has been done in a more intuitive way fifty years ago can be continued in a reasoned way today.

END NOTES

Simbu is the present official spelling used when referring to the Province which used to be called Chimbu.

1. Tillich (1972:42).
2. Schafer (1981:216-218).
3. Mantovani (1984a:195-212).
4. Mantovani (1984b:31:33), (1977:156).
5. Eliade (1978:38).
6. *Niugini Nius*, Tuesday, January 3, 1984.
7. Mantovani (1977:154-165).
8. Bergmann (1970, III:32-34).
9. The flutes are made of bamboo. They are about 60cm long and 5cm thick, One end is closed and 10cm from that end there is a hole through which the player blows adjusting the opening at the other end of the flute with the palm of his hand. The flutes are always played in pairs by males. Cf. Johnson (1982), Lutkehasu (1982), Nilles (1950, 1969, 1982), Read (1952), Sterly (1977) and Wedgwood (1937).

10. Post: it can be a pole of between 4 and 5 metres protruding about 50 cm from the roof of the *Bolin* house. It can be a short post of 60cm, 10cm in diameter, which is driven into the ground and protrudes about 40cm Cf. Luzbetak (1954), Nilles (1982).

11. As I was told the boys will have many opportunities to dance when they grow up, while their sisters will not have any opportunity once they are married. Lately though, I saw married women dancing with the young girls prior to the pig-kill.

12. The *arigl* or *aregl* is a stiff wig covering the back and sides of the head and neck and reaching to the shoulders. Cf. Sterly (1977:135), Nilles (1969, 1982).

13. The *gerua* board is a piece of flat, cut wood, with geometrical designs. It can be small, about 20cm by 8cm, or large, over 150cm by 50cm. Cf. Luzbetak (1954:106ff), Knight (1979:181-182), Mantovani (1977:158), Nilles (1950:59-60, 1969:69, 1982:253-254), Sterly (1977:18ff).

14. Mantovani (1977:159)

15. Cf. Sterly (1977:46)

16. Nilles (1960:61, 1969:135;136, 1982:255). Lutkehaus says the same about the flutes on Manam Island (1982).

17. Read (1952:24).

18. Read (1952), Nilles (1950:60).

19. Nilles (1950:60).

20. Nilles (1950:60).

21. Johnson (1982:417, 422).

22. Johnson (1982:421).

23. Johnson (1982:418). Cf. Lutkehaus (1982).

24. Luzbetak (1954:109), Nilles (1982:251), A *gerua* board of diamond shape with a perforation in the middle was slipped over the *Bolin* pole.

25. Luzbetak (1954).

26. Knight (1979:188-189), Mantovani (1977:157), Schafer (1981:219).

27. The idea is known in the North Coast's Mythology. Z'graggen (1983:276)

28. 'Voices in the Forest', from the series: *Edge of Survival*, ABC. Written and narrated by David Attenborough.

29. Schafer (19081:216-218).

30. Sterly (1977:73).

31. Sterly (1977:21,25).

32. Sterly (1977:21).

33. Nilles (1969:164) translates it simply: 'diamond-shaped sign'.

REFERENCES

Bergmann, W
1969-70 *Die Kamanuka*, 4 Vols. (Manuscript). Mutdapilly M/S 121 Harrisville, Qld., Australia.

Eliade, Mircea
1978 *A history of Religious Ideas*, Vol. 1, Chicago & London: Chicago University Press.

Johnson, Ragnar
1982 'A Re-Examination of the New Guinea Sacred Flute Complex: The Spirit Cries Played During Ommura Male Initiations'. Mankind 13(5):416-423.

Knight, James
1975 'Interpreting the Pig-kill', in Norman Habel (ed.), *Powers, Plumes and Piglets*, Adelaide: AASR, Sturt College of Advanced Education.

Lukehaus, Nancy
1954 'Ambivalance, Ambiguity and the Reproduction of Gender Hierarchy in Manam Society: 1933-1979', *Social Analysis*, 12.

Luzbetak, Louis
1954 'The Socio-Religious Significance of a New Guinea Pig Festival', *Anthropological Quarterly* 27:59-80; 102-128.

Mantovani, Ennio
1977 'A Fundamental Melanesian Religion', in *Point* 1977: Christ in Melanesia.
1984a 'Traditional Values and Ethics' in Darrell Whiteman (ed.) *An Introduction to Melanesian Cultures*, Goroka: The Melanesian Institute
1984b 'What is Religion' in Ennio Mantovani (ed.) *An Introduction to Melanesian Religions* Goroka: The Melanesian Institute.

Nilles, John
1950 'The Kuman of the Chimbu Region, Central Highlands, New Guinea', *Oceania* 21(1):25-65.
1982 'Zu einigen Glaubensvorstellungen and Kulthandlungen der Simbu im Zentralen Hochland von Neuguinea', *Jahrbuch des Museums für Völkerkunde zu Leipzig*, Bd.XXXIV, Berlin: Akademie Verlag.

Read, Kenneth
1952 'Nama Cult of the Central Highlands, New Guinea', *Oceania* 23(1):1-25.

Schäfer, Alfons
1981 'Christianized Ritual Pig-Killing', *Catalyst* 11(4):213-223

Sterly, Joachim
1977 'Über ein gerua-Kult im Zentralen Hochland von Neuguinea', *Baessler Archiv*, Neue Folge, Bd.XXV, 1-82.

Tillich, Paul
Theology of culture. London Oxford; 1959/1972
1959/1972 NY: Oxford University Press.

Z'graggen, John
1983 "Topics of New Guinea Legends" in *Asian Folklore Studies*, Vol 42, 2: 263-288.

AUSTRALIAN LITERATURE, RELIGION AND CULTURE:

The Question of Identity

James Tulip

The University of Sydney, Australia.

It was thirty years ago, in 1955, that Australian literature took a decisive step towards achieving what many now consider its modern cultural maturity. Three books were published in that year which, broadly speaking, released Australian literature and culture from its past and the status Australia had as a dependent nation. These books were A.D. Hope's poems *The Wandering Islands*, Patrick White's novel *The Tree of Man* and Ray Lawler's play *The Summer of the Seventeenth Doll*. Along with other texts from around that time — and here I think particularly of the poetry of Judith Wright — these books brought literature into relation with Australian culture in terms of a recognisable, general and modern way of life. They expressed an energy and intelligence which was urgent, often abrasive and subversive, and especially in the theatre usually profane. They were self-critical, self-accepting, and to a certain extent self-transcending. A shock of recognition, or self-recognition, was felt at their disclosure of Australian identity. It was a shock of recognition which painters, playwrights, filmmakers, actors and dance groups have all made their own, and in a way that has won world attention.

These three writers have a normative position in modern Australian literature. Yet the fact remains that they share little common ground with one another. Hope's review of White's novel was a matter of controversy at the time. And since then Hope has gone on to develop a deeply conservative stance while White has moved into radicalism of a cultural and political kind such that for all his winning the Nobel Prize in Literature he now gives the impression of being a man without a country. Personal as the differences between Hope and White may have been, the divergence in their ways also says something about Australian culture. It is a deeply divided society. And the difficulties in finding and establishing identity in such a culture are acute.

Religion in Australia has not helped. It was in 1955 that the Catholic Church — or part of it at least — entered the political sphere with a strongly anti-communist stance which had the effect of splitting the Labour Party and giving control of the country to conservative forces. The role of the Church — despite the many liberal, ecumenical and progressive voices within it — has been to enforce a broad, formal and ideological commitment to conservatism in Australian culture, a position which admittedly has always been latent in the Australian tradition but which since 1955 has become clearer as a major structural principle and option in Australian society and culture.

How poets respond in such a situation is the subject of my paper. For while proceeding from a heavily conservative cultural base Australian poets have been making moves to redefine identity and relationships between literature, religion and culture.

It was A.D. Hope himself who wrote in his poem "Australia" the line "if still from the deserts the prophets come", and in doing so has touched on the role which poets have come to play in what some commentators have called the most secular society in the world today.

I wish briefly to outline four aspects or images of Australian writing in order to illustrate the complex nature of identity as defined between literature, religion and culture. First, the change in conservatism itself; second, the opposite experience of aboriginal culture and the change that has taken place there; third, the central reworking by certain poets of images of identity drawn from religious sources; and fourth the image of the artist as seen by the artist and in relation to Australian society.

Let me begin, then, with the conservative figure par excellence of James McAuley. Following on his conversion to Roman Catholicism in 1952, McAuley adopted what might be called an ideologically fundamentalist stance on all matters to do with literature, religion, politics, education and culture. Prior to this time he had played a part through his contribution to the Ern Malley hoax of 1944 in effectively scuttling the modernist boat for Australian poetry. He had also resisted what he thought to be the simplistic efforts of the Jindyworobak school of Australian poets who were opening themselves up to the native culture of aboriginal Australia. Yet McAuley's stance has never been merely a negative one. His poem 'Envoi' defines a serious and original relation for himself with the Australian land and the life of Australian society. It expresses the once-European mind that now knows it belongs to a new land and culture. It is a kind of love-hate relationship, and he puts it in terms that are plain and prosaic but telling:

There the blue-green gums are a fringe of remote disorder
And the brown sheep poke at my dreams along the hillsides;
And there in the soil, in the season, in the shifting airs,
Comes the faint sterility that disheartens and derides.

Where once was a sea is now a salty sunken desert,
A futile heart within a fair periphery;

It is almost a cliché of European-Australian experience, but true nonetheless. McAuley states the way 'the reluctant and uneasy land resents / The gush of waters, the lean plough, the fretful seed'. Australia is a profound disappointment in this regard, and McAuley carries it over to the people. They are 'hard-eyed, kindly, with nothing inside them'. Yet clearly he wants to affirm his own attachment to Australia. 'I am fitted to that land as the soul is to the body'. These are abstract and conceptual terms to use for such a relationship. They do not balance out the weight of his critical feelings. Something self-conscious, unstable and willed stands as the image of his identity in this poem.

The uncertainty of values which marks the poem — for all its striking clarities — also marks the course of McAuley's later career. More Catholic than the Catholics, he felt betrayed by Vatican II. His book *The End of Modernity* (1959) reads today like a purely abstract schema, an Antipodean Jacques Maritain denouncing virtually everything modern, including Jacques Maritain. But a change came for McAuley in the late 1960s, when along with Vincent Buckley and others he stepped beyond his ideological style of the 1950s to rediscover the personal element in his own writing and that of other Australians. The autobiographical poems of his book *Surprises of the Sun* (1969) had a profound impact on his Australian public. The world of childhood, family and suburban existence was a new subject for him, a new way of addressing reality. And while McAuley did not persist in this style of dramatising his own life for long, his change reflected a deep transformation in cultural values which for his part enabled him to find in his late poetry a renewed and delicate lyricism of a kind close to religious meditation and prayer. He has contributed many of the finest hymns to the *Australian Hymn Book*.

'In the Huon Valley' is one such poem from the later McAuley. It is about the Tasmanian autumn and is autumnal in mood. The essential thing to note in this poem, however, is the primacy and initiative given to the natural world. Nature is alive here. It is the subject.

> Propped boughs are heavy with apples,
> Springtime quite forgotten.
> Pears ripen yellow. The wasp
> Know where windfalls lie rotten.
>
> Juices grow rich with sun.

There is here a reverence before nature, a receptivity towards what is given, and a humbling of the self. The human identity is not lost; the old McAuley is still there looking for and finding rational order and beauty. But now it is a shared total ritual: the human and the life outside the human belong together in the one ceremonious cycle and process.

The move from distance to closeness which we see here is characteristic of much white Australian experience in this generation. It has been matched, unfortunately, by an equal and opposite move in black Australian experience. Only recently has the general reader had access to the traditional poetry of aboriginal Australians. Anthropologists have known of it, and there has been a broad understanding in white society of the aboriginal Dreaming and the unselfconscious intimacy which native people have with the land. Song cycles such as the Moon Bone cycle of Arnhem Land have slowly revealed themselves as part of the Australian heritage; and while it is still too soon to claim to have responded properly to poetry of this kind, there is in the great catalogues, the process of naming, the repetitions, and what seems to white readers as the non-reasonings a remarkable demonstration of identity of a different kind. It is a poetry that celebrates being.

Yet this story changes, too. Instead of this traditional intimacy and oneness with the land, alienation, anger and irony are now felt in the voices of black writers. Jack Davis, Kath Walker and Kevin Gilbert are among those writing in English of their loss of identity. As Kevin Gilbert says in his poem "Earth" from his book *End of Dreamtime* (1971):

> I am earth:
> earth has its own high God, Ba'aime.
> I dreamed that there was nothing
> that could part me from my God
> and his many spirits.
>
> I am earth:
> my God spoke to me as friend,
> as he breathed, so I; on the hunt
> together walked we two on earth,
> and sometimes in the sky.

I am earth:
from earth I did arise,
to earth I shall return. And now
across the empty earth I go,
saddened and alone.

These lines speak for themselves. The dispossession of a heritage and the loss of identity match those of white society in coming into possession of the land and finding identity there.

I wish to turn now from extremes to the centre, from oppositions to what I see as a sharing of identity among poets. Here I will take three poets — Judith Wright, Les Murray and Fay Zwicky — who locate their poems close to religious experience but not explicitly so. Theirs is more the implicit prophetic role which writers in a secular culture are called upon to play, or are drawn towards playing. Judith Wright, over forty years, has come to be a central spiritual and imaginative resource for her readers, and, as I wish to suggest here, for other writers. Her meditative and philosophical stance touches on matters from the simplest to the most profound, from such things as a totemic sense of Australian birds to a fiercely committed sense of the destruction of the Australian environment. Les Murray shares Judith Wright's background in the Australian bush, but has more sharply experienced the urban take-over of Australian culture in the past twenty years, which he resists trenchantly. Fay Zwicky speaks from a Jewish vantage point, and has had to confront the inertia and apparent formlessness of white-anglo-saxon-protestant-catholic culture in Australia in order to ask many of the central critical questions of today, especially to do with the place of women in Australian society.

Let me begin by comparing Judith Wright's poem 'Night Herons' with Les Murray's 'An Absolutely Ordinary Rainbow'. A visitation occurs in both poems. Two birds suddenly appear in a small-town street in the Wright poem, while in the Murray poem a man is discovered in Martin Place in the centre of Sydney, weeping. Some pattern or parable is being felt for by both poets. Are the birds a kind of angelic annunciation and is the weeping man a kind of Christ figure? The poems do not say so, but use the confrontation of these randomly experienced phenomena with the people of each poem as an intimation of a possible transcendence occurring in the midst of ordinary living.

The Judith Wright poem has a simple tone and manner of narration which is in keeping with her meaning and her feeling both for the birds and the Australian people. Let me read it now:

Night Herons

It was after a day's rain:
the street facing the west
was lit with growing yellow;
the black road gleamed.

First one child looked and saw
and told another.
Face after face, the windows
flowered with eyes.

It was like a long fuse lighted,
the news travelling.

No one called out loudly;
everyone said 'Hush'.

The light deepened; the wet road
answered in daffodil colours,
and down its centre
walked the two tall herons.

Stranger than wild birds, even
what happened on those faces:
suddenly believing in something,
they smiled and opened.

Children thought of fountains,
circuses, swans feeding;
women remembered words
spoken when they were young.

Everyone said 'Hush';
no one spoke loudly;
but suddenly the herons
rose and were gone. The light faded.

Compare this poem now with the Les Murray poem. There are obvious similarities. Yet Murray locates his poem in the centre of Sydney, at the heart of secular society, at the shrine of Australian natural or civic religion, a place given over to the prevailing modern gods of western society — commerce, war, entertainment and politics. Provocatively, Murray projects his kind of Christ figure into this scene. He confronts the sterotype of the unfeeling Australian male:

There's a fellow crying in Martin Place. They can't stop him.
...
There's a fellow weeping down there. No one can stop him.

Murray shares many of the qualities he seems to be resisting in this poem. He uses a laconic, homespun humour to create a disbelieving aura around the man. His poem holds itself back from commitment, even from response to the man. But this kind of tension in the intelligence works to release the phenomenon of the weeping man purely and starkly as phenomenon.

The man we surround, the man no one approaches
simply weeps, and does not cover it, weeps
not like a child, not like the wind, like a man
and does not declaim it, nor beat his breast, nor even
sob very loudly —— yet the dignity of his weeping

holds us back from his space, the hollow he makes about him

in the midday light, in his pentagram of sorrow,
and uniforms back in the crowd who tried to seize him
stare out at him, and feel, with amazement, their minds
longing for tears as children for a rainbow.

It has to be on Murray's terms an absolutely ordinary rainbow, however. There is to be no overt religious meaning or intent to the poem. That is part of its truth. It sidles up to its centre or climax intimately, even inconsequentially.

and I see a woman, shining, stretch her hand
and shake as she receives the gift of weeping;
as many as follow her also receive it
and many weep for sheer acceptance, and more
refuse to weep for fear of all acceptance

'But the weeping man', as Murray goes on, 'requires nothing'. Like the poem itself he refuses to engage and resolve the issue. 'Evading believers, he hurries off down Pitt Street'.

Murray's poem has become something of a *locus classicus* of modern Australian spirituality. Teasing, annoying, yet knowing — it marshalls Australian negativities or resistances into a position where only a parable can work. As indeed it does. Murray — himself a convert from a strict Presbyterian background to Catholicism — uses a strange kind of wit here both to propound and to deny. He has an instinctive sense of an Australian style.

The two poems — 'Night Herons' and 'An Absolutely Ordinary Rainbow' — may be said to share an identity of a modern quasi-religious kind in treating what could have been the symbolic term or object as purely phenomenological. It is the response of the people in each poem to the phenomenon of the birds and the weeping man respectively that generates the vitality, tension and meaning of the poems. The religious dimension is contained within, confined within, the human existential situation.

But Judith Wright can also work in an opposite way. By beginning with a figure or situation which is recognisably religious or scriptural, she shows how to advance towards a revelation of the human situation. One famous instance of this is her poem 'Eli, Eli' where she takes Jesus' suffering on the Cross and appropriates it into more broadly human, even mystical, terms. But a more pertinent instance is where she takes the figure of Eve as her starting point and offers a critique of modern male-female relations. Written in the mid 1960s, 'Eve to her Daughters' anticipates the feminist thrust of the past twenty years.

Eve allows Judith Wright to adopt a voice, a character, an identity which is playful, highly intelligent, and alive with barely suppressed anger and scorn. Eve begins by seeming to accept the punishment of God in being banished from the Garden of Eden:

But Adam, you know . . .!
He kept on brooding over the insult,
over the trick They had played on us, over the scolding.
He had discovered a flaw in himself
and he had to make up for it.

Outside Eden the earth was imperfect,
the seasons changed, the game was fleet-footed,
he had to work for our living, and he didn't like it.
He even complained of my cooking
(it was hard to compete with Heaven).

So he set to work.
The earth must be a new Eden
with central heating, domesticated animals,

mechanical harvesters, combustion engines,
escalators, refrigerators,
and modern means of communication
and multiplied opportunities for safe investment
and higher education for Abel and Cain
and the rest of the family.
You can see how his pride had been hurt.

In the process he had to unravel everything,
because he believed that mechanism
was the whole secret — he was always mechanical minded.

He got to the very inside of the whole machine
exclaiming as he went, So this is how it works!
And now that I know how it works, why I must have invented it.
As for God and the Other, they cannot be demonstrated,
and what cannot be demonstrated
doesn't exist.
You see, he had always been jealous.

Judith Wright's critique of modern society ranges wide around her central focus on the sexist question. The poem is mainly directed at the male, and the female world is present mainly in terms of the author's felt presence and tone of voice. Where the female world enters the poem explicitly, it is presented with a mock irony:

But you are my daughters,
you inherit my own faults of character
you are submissive.

Judith Wright confines her female identity in this poem to this mock *persona*, and the irony of this role is something of limitation on the poem's achievement. Yet it is tellingly comic and satiric:

... nothing exists but our faults.
At least they can be demonstrated.

But it's useless to make
such a suggestion to Adam.
He has turned himself into God,
who is faultless, and doesn't exist.

Another poem which works in a similar way — and indeed may have been inspired by the Judith Wright poem — is Fay Zwicky's 'Mrs Noah Speaks' from her sequence 'Ark Voices'. Again, a biblical subject is taken over and appropriated to a modern experience. Fay Zwicky's approach derives partly from her Jewish background and partly from her more modern feminist feeling. She is more inside the character of her speaker than Judith Wright was. Mrs Noah is a broader, rounder, more humorous presence. She presumes to be in a kind of conversation with God or Yahweh, complaining about life on the Ark:

Lord, the cleaning's nothing.
What's a pen or two?

Even if tapir's urine
Takes the paint clean off
There's nothing easier.

But sir, the care!

I used dream perpetually
About a boat I had to push
(yes, *push*) through a stony town
without water
There was no river and no sea and yet
I pushed a boat against a tide.
It wouldn't float although I pulled and
hauled, my flesh eddying,
drifting with the strain of it.
Is *this* a dream?

Fibre my blood, sir.

The new strength of comic tone here helps Zwicky to be generous in understanding the larger human situation. She has Mrs Noah look at her husband and say: 'Noah is incorruptible and good, a large / sweet soul'. Irony is never absent, but the game is played in such a way as to allow Mrs Noah's deep pain to emerge alongside her poised judgement of her husband's greatness. She sees them held together finally:

Strangers in this ark, this one small 'Yes'
afloat on a vast 'No', your watery negative.

Fay Zwicky's sense of the Flood, Les Murray's Rainbow and Judith Wright's understanding of Creation — all reveal how in a central way religion has bearing on literature's power to identify and make real the life of our times. I wish to conclude now with a final image of the artist as a selfconscious figure, concerned in the case of David Malouf with defining an identity for himself in a society and culture such as Australia. Over the past fifteen years David Malouf has opened up the discussion of identity perhaps more than any other Australian author, and specifically at a level where the planes of literature, religion and culture seem to intersect in what is apparently a secular society. Malouf has created for himself the voice of the tribal talker, part reflective, part fictional, part conversational, a voice of ironic wisdom that gives Australians and — increasingly — readers around the world real pleasure and delight. His award (1985) of the Vance Palmer Prize for Fiction for his short stories *Antipodes* is a sign that the way he is addressing reality in terms highly relevant to this paper is meaningful today.

His finest novel, *An Imaginary Life*, which deals with the Roman poet Ovid, is full of dramatic insight into religious and cultural matters. It tells of the discovery and creation of identity between two opposite kinds of life and existence, that of the cosmopolitan Ovid in exile and that of a wolf child. It is a kind of love poem in prose, with the subtlest awareness of discrete identities. It brings love, hate and fear into dynamic relationship in the experiencing of identity.

I wish, however, to point to his most recent novel *Harland's Half-Acre* as having more application to Australian culture. It is the story of an Australian painter growing up through the years of the Great Depression, World War II and the affluence of the Fifties and early Sixties. The novel has some connection with the life of a famous artist, Ian Fairweather, who became a hermit on an island off the Queensland coast. But Malouf uses the story to range further afield — to look at Australian sexuality, Australian-European relations, and finally to consider the place of the artist in such a world.

This last concern emerges best in the middle of the novel when Harland shows the narrator three of his paintings. One is of a half-caste aboriginal boxer at practice with his punching bag. It presents an image of real pathos — the outsider in Australian society fighting against a non-feeling, but heavily resistant, force or object.

> ...he was hugging the punching bag as if he were hanging on hard against forces that might tear him away ... despairingly baffled but not defeated, he was shadow-boxing with it, lunging wildly at the shadow while the bag itself, slack and puffy with evil, solidly passive, simply hung there and half-obscured him, pushed him out to a corner of the frame. There was a naked globe. And all around stood the silent watchers, tree-trunks or house-stumps or transmogrified elders or wooden gods.

The second painting is of two women, their abstract but entwined figures offering as allegory an image of new female affirmation of identity. Significantly, the painting is called 'Two Fates', as if waiting for a third female presence to appear to regain the ancient mythic status of the Three Fates as the spinners and weavers and controllers of the human life span.

But it is the third painting that finally concerns us here. It is a self-portrait of the artist, but not in a literal or biographical sense.

> ...It was a self-portrait, the face all fragments. A force from 'out there' that was irresistible but might not, in the end, be destructive had struck it to splinters that met the flat board at every angle, so that the figure emerged simultaneously in many planes.

The artist, Malouf is saying, lives on many levels and feels many pressures. He highlights this phenomenon of the artist's existence by titling the painting 'The Iceman as Heavenly Bridegroom'.

There are some local allusions within the book which add meaning to the playful, bantering tone of this title. But generally Malouf is suggesting the artist as a Christ figure bringing a kind of love to the world. Yet it is cold and it melts. Malouf offers an ironic image of the identity of the artist, a point he underlines when he writes of Harland:

> He saw himself in that comic light: as an imminent but un-annunciating angel

The artist is always on the point of telling the truth but can never — in the terms of this novel — pop the question or demand belief in an ultimate reality. Fiction is an as-if reality, ultimately itself un-annunciating for all its torrent of words. Yet while provisional and playful, literature — as Malouf understands it here — is reaching out in a central modern way to touch and tap the profound sources of traditional religion and human culture.

"Night Herons" © Judith Wright 1971.
Quoted from Judith Wright Collected Poems (Angus and Robertson) and by permission of the publishers.

GENERATIONAL IDENTITY AND RELIGIOUS CHANGE IN AMERICA SINCE WORLD WAR II

Dale R. Bengtson

Southern Illinois University at Carbondale, U.S.A.

The question of identity, personal and cultural, coalesces in the question of generations. The generation whose inception followed the close of the Second World War brought about protean changes in all aspects of American life. In religion, Americans shifted from a traditional Judeo-Christian mode of expression to consumers of new religious movements and trans-cultic phenomena. Prior to the late Sixties, personal experience was mediated through the Protestant, Catholic, and Jewish traditions, and the slogan, "One Nation Under God", summarized civil religion. Since then, a radical turn in American religious expression yielded an outpouring of extra-ecclesiastical religion.

A number of perspectives emerge to contribute to our understanding of the revolution in religion.[1] Sociological explanations include the influences of secularization, the need for community, the emergence of value crises, and the desire for a holistic self-definition in a differentiated society. Psychological perspectives focus primarily on the conversion process and indoctrination techniques. These sufficient explanations suffer, on the other hand, from a functional fallacy. "If the function of the phenomenon to be explained is an unintended consequence, it is a logical fallacy to explain the phenomenon by reference to its function."[2] Functional explanations tell us something important about the socio-cultural revolution; they say something less about the revolution of the American religious experience. Indeed, the devotee of Krishna may sense a loss and re-gaining of community, or a disintegration and reintegration of the psyche, or have renewed values. Yet these may be interpreted as unintended consequences of the new found faith, not causes. Functional interpretations presuppose that our experience of the phenomenal world is primary and the determining factor for explaining human responses. Causal relationships depend on our sense perception and subsequent stimulus and response. It is just as tenable, however, to begin with internal experience as primary and interpret all other experiences. including those of the phenomenal world, in terms of it.

My purpose is to suggest an alternative model for interpreting the religious changes in America wrought by a generation. It is a model which assumes that a generation is the primary agent of social and religious change, and, secondly, that the generational process is identifiable as a ritual process.

A generation is what happens to people; as is the case with a social class or ethnic group, one is born into it. A generation's self-identity is so powerful and compelling that older and younger generations are drawn into its particular *Weltanschauung*. As an agent of change, the impact of a generation is directly related to its size. During the French Revolution, for example, forty percent of the population were between the ages of 20 and 40; only twenty percent were over 40.

The American Revolution and Protestant Reformation were predominantly youthful. Traditionally totalitarian movements are built on the backs of committed youth. These examples make generations worthy of study[3] even though such a study may be accused of demographic determinism and oversimplification.

My second assumption is that the generational process is identifiable as a ritual process. Religious experience, if not all extra-ordinary experience, partakes of the particular and concrete and, more significantly, of an ever-present pattern. Otto suggests that the pattern is constituted by the *mysterium*, or a sense of the "holy".[4] In contrast to everyday ordinary experience, the sense of mystery is extra-ordinary and modulated according to two modes. One mode is the *tremendum*, or sense of destruction inherent in religious experience, e.g. a devotee is "slain" by the Lord at a nineteenth century camp meeting, St John of the Cross encounters the dark night of the soul, a Hari Krishna devotee may have the felt sense of being destroyed by a prior drug experience. The other mode of experience is the *fascinans*, the affirmation sensed by being touched with the holy, e.g. a renewal through the *imitatio Christi*, the chanting of a *mantra*, the sense of being one of the "elect". Thus, according to Otto, all religious experience partakes of Power, of destruction and affirmation, of engagement, crisis, and renewal.

In addition to the affective dimension, the expressive dimension deserves attention as well. The felt sense of being religious correlates with the inclination to act as if these feelings made a difference. The expressive dimension is acted out in the drama of the ritual process, involving three phases.[5] A pre-liminal (liminal signifying "threshold") phase in which persons and society are structured according to roles and types; in other words, human beings participate fully in maintaining and structuring society. During the second phase, liminality, structure undergoes a process of destruction or *tremendum* and then affirmation, symbolic restoration, and *fascinans*. Liminal entities are neither here nor there; they are "betwixt and between". They constitute both the apex of the structural system and the community as an unstructured unit. In post-liminality, the third phase, a "new" coherent unity, founded on the values gained in liminality, issues in the "new" being or "new" society. In religious terms, the three phases indicate a process whereby we move from the profane into the sacred, with a destruction of the profane, affirmed by a sense of personal renewal, and out into the profane with a new sense of commitment.

Given Otto's understanding of religious experience and Turner's studies in liminality, the last forty years of American religious and cultural history can be interpreted as a ritual process, particular to a generation. Internal experience is the necessary precondition for how we respond to external stimuli. Cultural forms recapitulate that experience in much the same way as the individual life cycle corresponds to what Hannah Arendt calls "the notion of irresistibility."[6] Culture as ritual both constitutes and expresses our humanness.

Destruction becomes the independent variable for assessing each phase of the process. Destruction is integral both to the ritual process and, since Hiroshima, essential for understanding how human beings conceive of themselves and the world in which they live.

> Heretofore, life had been the dominant term, and death had been comprehended by life. Following Hiroshima — that awesome, tragic, and paradoxically catalytic event — a reversal and interchange occurred within the fundamental relationship: death became the commanding term, and life was conceived in terms of death, first, for those directly affected by the war, but gradually for an increasingly larger number of persons.[7]

How the destructive tendencies are characterized and defined by each phase of the ritual process tells us something about ourselves as cultural and religious beings.

Phase I: The pre-liminal phase of the American ritual process, from 1945 to 1963, was a period when destruction was viewed as containment. The destructive tendencies in American culture were pushed into the background of experience, both through historical and personal silence. This is the meaning of the Eisenhower years, in which a general who leads a nation in victory becomes a steadying president. The phase ends with the assassination of John F Kennedy, the last president of such stability. During the eighteen year period, the aggressive tendencies were symbolicly contained on a variety of levels. The Cold War depicted a political tension and military rivalry between nations which stopped short of an actual full-scale war. Even the thirty-seven months of the Korean War, one of the bloodiest in history, were referred to as a "police action". The McCarthy investigations attempted to contain the last vestiges of destruction by ferreting out alleged communist influence and infiltration into government, education, defense industries, and other fields of human endeavour.

The structured aspects of this period were carry-overs from the Second World War. In victory the rightness of the order was exemplified and took on various cultural forms. Barracks became the Levittowns and planned suburbs of America; the familiar K-ration was transformed into the TV dinner and transported to the frozen food sections of grocery stores; authority, whether military or domestic, emphasized its pyramidal structure. It was also a period of an unprecedented birthrate which began in 1946 and peaked in 1957. What was to constitute a significant percentage of the American population during the mid-Sixties was conceived between 1946 and 1948. Manchester calculated[8] that "During those years a wife was being impregnated once every seven seconds, and the U.S. Bureau of Census was blushing." The significance of the so-called "baby boom" will become evident during the liminal phase of the American ritual process.

The predominant religious forms which served to contain destruction at all levels of experience were two: 1) *Traditional religions*, the so-called "mainline churches", whether Protestant, Catholic, or Jew; and 2) *Civil religion*, in which religion, politics, and economics were intertwined and given divine sanction. "The God of the civil religion is not only rather 'unitarian', he is also on the austere side, much more related to order, law, and right than to salvation and love."[9] Eisenhower, in 1954, justified the religious outlook. "Our government makes no sense unless it is founded on a deeply religious faith — and I don't care what it is." Whichever religious affirmation was used to check destruction, the memory of the depression, World War II's destructiveness, and the atom bomb was employed at a distance, not in terms of the immediacy of everyday experience. Hence it was an age of silence, but also a time of existential anxiety. On the popular level, both features were exploited to produce a more generalized religiosity concerned with peace of mind and confident living. It was, what Ahlstrom called[10] "an Indian summer of confident living and renewed religious interest", presided over by Norman Vincent Peale, Fulton J Sheen, Rabbi Joshua Liebman, and Billy Graham.

The general tenor of post-war American sensibilities was reflected in the academic study of religion. The theological musings and exclusiveness of an older generation were challenged by the more urgent need for religious understanding, if not unity. Instructive in this context is the founding, in 1950, of the International Association for the History of Religions. Although its stated purpose was "the promotion of the academic study of the history of religions",[11] by the 1958 Tokyo Congress of the

IAHR, the mood focused on Friedrich Heiler's paper, "The History of Religions as a Way to Unity of Religions". Placed first in the conference report, Heiler's address argues that "scientific insight into this unity calls for a practical realization in friendly exchange and in common ethical endeavour, 'fellowship' and 'cooperation'."[12]

In America, the need for a more comprehensive unity was coeval with a post-war isolationism which affirmed the rightness of the traditional order. The historian of religions, Joachim Wach, can be taken as illustrative. He was one of four American members of the IAHR (along with W.F. Albright, A.D. Nock, and R.H. Lowie), and taught at the University of Chicago from 1945 until his death ten years later. In speaking both as a committed Christian and historian of religions, he laboured enthusiastically to establish a theoretical and practical basis for unity. At the same time, Wach reflects the general attitude of American scholarship which viewed religion as a means to contain conflict. He states in the Preface to his *Sociology of Religion*:[13]

> Personal experience has aided the author in realizing the vital importance and significance of *religion as an integrating factor in human society* and in understanding its function in the contemporary crisis of civilization in East and West. [emphasis added]

The assumption that religion functions primarily to contain conflict and act as "an integrating factor" was not seriously challenged until the late Fifties. As a paradigm, it reflects both the general attitude of scholarship and the republic whose official motto became, in 1956, "In God We Trust".

Phase II: By the time of Kennedy's assassination, the pretensions of the Anglo-Saxon religious "empire" of the 1950's and before are crumbling. The sensibilities of the nation are cued for transformation from a sense of being a domineering empire to a new appreciation for redefining traditional symbols in terms of modern experience. The psychological and historical parameters of the events of the Kennedy-King assassinations, from 1963 through 1968, set the stage for the first phase of liminality in which the religious consciousness of the nation was sharpened by a ritual usurpation of destruction as *tremendum*. The events of the period, too well-known to need elaboration, include Vietnam, the drug culture, political frustrations, and violence towards the self, the universities, and the government.

Why did the radical shift from the relatively placid Fifties to the violent Sixties occur? Although no single cause can be designated, I would suggest a correlation between the internal experience of destruction as *tremendum* during this six year period and the high birthrate of the mid-1940's. By the mid-Sixties, post-war babies had reached the age of social and psychological puberty. The American experience was dominated by a collective rite of initiation. In traditional societies, initiation rites are preceded often by the act of circumcision — a cutting away from the mother; in America, the 1960's indicate a period of a collective cutting away from the Motherland and subsequent loss of identity. An identity crisis issues in what Erikson calls [14] *distantiation*, "the readiness to repudiate, isolate and, if necessary, destroy those forces and people whose essence seems dangerous to one's own"; or it takes on the characteristics of a negative identity, "an identity perversely based on all those identifications and roles which at critical stages of development, had been presented to them as most undesirable or dangerous and yet also as most real." The identity crisis was expressed in the form of a revolution, a revolt against the post-World War II militarization of society.

At the same time, a ritual killing of the absent father eclipsed the study of religion. J.A.T. Robinson's *Honest to God* appeared in 1963. It was preceded in 1960 by H. Richard Niebuhr's *Radical Monotheism* and Gabriel Vahanian's *The Death of God: The Culture of Our Post-Christian Era* (1961), and followed by Pierre

Berton's *The Comfortable Pew* (1965) and Harvey Cox's *The Secular City* (1965). The media popularized the "death of God" movement and gave the names of Altizer and Hamilton, to mention only two, household familiarity. Closely related to radical theology was a "tidal wave of questioning of all the traditional structures of Christendom."[15]

The most critical intensities of destruction during the 1960's — which yielded a correlation between a loss of authority, a loss of identity, and the theological and experiential death of God — were countered by the affirmative usurpation of destructive forces, now turned into religious channels. By 1968, the death of a binding Father allowed the children their freedom to usher in the second phase of liminality.[16] Two other types of religious forms, distinct from the traditional and civil religions of the 1950's turn destruction into an affirmation of broader and more diverse vistas of meaning. 1) *The New Religious Movements* which emphasize personal experience, for example, in the appearance of religious cults, but also in the seemingly cultic bonds among such persons as civil rights workers and anti-war protestors. With the loss of a symbolic center, whether divine or human, destruction was carried over into a destruction of the self. Innumerable examples can be extracted from the time — the Beatles bond with Maharishi, Rennie Davis (of SDS fame) becomes a devotee of Mahara Ji, Richard Alpert metamorphoses into Baba Ram Das, Cassius Clay into Mohammed Ali, and Timothy Leary simply drops out. 2) A second religious form develops during this time into what can be called *symbolic religion*, for example, the new sense of tribalism marked by McLuhan's "global village" and consciousness-raising movements. In this instance, personal experience is either down-played or becomes politicized in the service of cultural experience in which personal appropriations of expanded awareness take place.

Concurrent with the second phase of liminality, the study of religion undergoes a dramatic change. Departments for its study proliferate in universities and colleges. The adjective "religious", as in Religious Studies, is preferred over the noun "religion", as in Department of Religion or Religion Study. Traditional topics such as historical studies and systematic theology are displaced by the history of religions and cross-cultural studies in religion. Eliade and Campbell, Jung and Watts become the "paradigms" for its study, and popular literature includes sacred texts from the Amerindian and Asian traditions. Collectively, the various changes indicate that religious studies shifted to a position of defining the new religious consciousness and providing a context for potential religious experiences. In other words, Religious Studies both forms and is informed by the second phase of liminality.

Further, the study of religion as religious studies became a religion. During the 1960's, a ritual destruction of priestly forms of religious and political leadership occurred, generating a subsequent loss of a sense of the nation as community. The precipitative factor was a collective identity crisis, mediated through *distantiation* and a negative identity, which gave rise to cultic and symbolic forms of religion. The traditional and civil forms did not, indeed could not, serve as affective bonds to incorporate the new sensibility. The collapse of an effective symbolic authority in America created a sense of "cultural failure" and accelerated the search for new "centers". Studies in the history of primitivism have shown that a feeling of cultural failure is accompanied by a sentimentality for that which is believed to be a simpler and more genuine mode of being. Chronologically, Americans turned to their respective historical foundations in order to recreate an early Christian community, Druidic or Celtic traditions; by some, the ecological consciousness of the Hopi and Navajo was idealized; others turned to their African heritage. On the other hand, those exposed to the East, either through Vietnam, the mass media, or other contacts, expressed a "cultural primitivism" in their discovery of Krishna, Meir Baba, Ananda Marga, Tibetan

Buddhism, Zen and Vedanta.[17] Within this cultural and religious milieu, religious studies took on the role of providing alternative modes of being in the world. It was a decentralized religion "with no scripture, but many stories".[18] The architects, whether an Eliade or a Jung, were those who could synthesize an "archaic mentality" with modern experience.

Phase III: The years 1973 and 1974 are crucial for our understanding of current American religious history. They signify a transition from the liminality of the 1960's into a "new" post-liminal mentality. By 1973, Vietnam was over for all intents and purposes. Those born immediately following the Second World War by this time had been ushered through the ritual process of initiation and had reached their late twenties and early thirties, thereby ending the crisis of social and psychological puberty. The events of the two year span establish also the flavor of the new post-liminal consciousness. The proximity of Watergate and the popularity of the film, *The Exorcist*, are illustrative. Both, in their respective ways, were attempts to remove the destructive tendencies from American culture. Watergate exposed them, *The Exorcist* eliminated them. Taking these two events as indicative, the new post-liminal mentality can best be described as effacement, an erasing of both destruction and affirmation, of *tremendum et fascinans*, a flight from feeling to the Apollonian structure of the machine. "What is significant is the replacement of actual emotion by the sensation of the operator who gets things done, who wheels and deals despite all odds."[19]

The image is that of Apollo and not the Dionysius of the new religious movements and symbolic religion. The Apollonian distrusts, as Nietzsche stated in his *Birth of Tragedy*, "the annihilation of the ordinary bounds and limits of existence," required in a commitment to the other; he "knows but one law, measure in the Hellenic sense." But unlike the Apollonian civil religion of the 1950's, in which one became committed to the communal other, the technological religion of the 1970's and 1980's harbors a spiritual and secular narcissism, a concern only with the smooth functioning of the individual isolated machine. The theme for the age is expressed in the title of the feminist book, *Our Bodies, Ourselves.*[20] One has only to examine the intentions behind the ecology movement , the values placed on being female or male, Black or Chicano, the health foods fads, the cult of running, the public outcry over the harmfulness of selected jobs, foods, and smoking, the fantasy of becoming a bionic man or woman, the revival of themes expressed through Country Western music, and the search for family roots. Sensation has replaced emotion or feeling, whether it be destructive or affirmative. It is a cult of psychic and physical self-improvement in which one hungers "not for personal salvation, let alone for the restoration of an earlier golden age, but for the feeling — even if it is only a momentary illusion — of personal well-being, health and psychic security."[21]

In contrast to the secular narcissists are the spiritual narcissists. Although the ways of being religious in the 1970's and 1980's are multiple, two popular, yet diverse, trends can be singled out as representative: 1) *Western fundamentalism*, and 2) the use of *meditational techniques* from religious traditions and therapeutic models. Effacement before destruction and affirmation is most evident in the meaning given by fundamentalists to the person of Jesus. As the multisignative symbol of western consciousness, Jesus appeared during the 1950's as a means of containing destruction. Confronted with indecision and conflict, Christians were admonished with the question, "What would Jesus do?" In the 1960's, with an emphasis on naturalness and usurpation of destruction, Jesus symbolizes the revolutionary heroic figure of pop posters; yet he remained the harbinger of culture for those over thirty. In an age of effacement, however, the question is not what would Jesus do, but what *did* Jesus do? The shift implies that the image of Jesus has collapsed into nature, mediating not between nature and culture, but between the cyclical pattern of life and death. Have we not moved from a death denying age to one that is death obsessed? The conversion experience of increasing numbers often takes them into fundamentalist and evangelical groups where narcissism and the effacement of destruction combine a burial of feeling with an overcoming of the dread of death. Similarly, this type of fundamentalism, in erasing the last barrier of narcissism — death — has spilled over into the non-sectarian world and elevated Kübler-Ross and her colleagues to American sainthood.

Parallel to the fundamentalists are those engaged in self-fulfillment programs which utilize meditational techniques. In fundamentalism the image is that of a Superman who crosses the threshold to eliminate personal destruction, whereas meditational techniques evoke the image of Proteus who could change his own form at will. The theme is self centeredness. Rather than conforming to an Absolute, what is true and good is what helps me out of my suffering; what is false and evil is that which locks me into it.

Complicated by the threat of nuclear annihilation, both fundamentalists and those who rely on meditational techniques, in their emphasis on personal salvation, exhibit a spiritual narcissism combined with the seemingly contradictory eclipse of Man. Studies[22] confirm that narcissism is not exaggerated self-love, but rather its opposite — self-hatred, self-destruction. The self-idolatry of the narcissist becomes a defense mechanism in the face of a feeling of self-worthlessness. Because he is loveless, Narcissus must wrap himself in self-love. The loss of the other as an "object" of love and hate turns the need for affirmation and the defeat of destruction inward, thereby causing the narcissist to flee, to escape the human condition. The type of fundamentalism which gives a literal reading to the Biblical message and the writings of Hal Lindsey,[23] eclipses the self in the denial of a personal death and the hope for the millenium. The means of effacing destruction and affirmation in meditation, on the other hand, is through the elimination of the ego, often without asking the question of the function of the ego and the nature of the self.

Given the cultural tendency towards privateness and the subsequent effacement of human experience, what is the focus of religious studies? In the 1950's, efforts were directed to articulating the functions of religion in containing destruction. The first phase of liminality spelled not only the death of God and the loss of transcendence, but the death of theology as the locus of truth. The affirmative forces of liminality allowed religious studies to center on the relative absoluteness of all religious traditions. In an age of effacement the study of religion again reflects the cultural fashion. It has become a field without a focus, a discipline without a method. "In the absence of a paradigm or some candidate for paradigm, all of the facts that could possibly pertain to the development of a given science are likely to seem equally relevant."[24] Appropriately, the 1985 IAHR Congress is addressing the theme, "religion and identity".

In the absence of a paradigm, investigators of religion are thrown back on their own shadows. Traditional approaches no longer seem appropriate. The phenomenological *epoche*, with its intended separation of the observer's perspective from the analysis of the data, requires heroic measures which are sociologically and psychologically improbable. The religious unmusicality of functionalist approaches has been challenged from within various disciplines. In their place observer-participant studies are prominent. Consider Bennetta Jules-Rosette's *African Apostles*,[25] an observer-participant study of the church of John Maranke by an anthropologist turned convert.

> The loyalty that I had displayed preceded a glimpse of new realities. To resolve the conflict between their formal models of indigenous beliefs and lived experience, researchers often settle for loyalty. The models are presented as detached from

experience and, therefore, can be seen from a relativistic perspective. Through loyalty, researchers appear to provide translations of member's beliefs and categories. These renderings substitute the sympathy of the detached observer for the test of performance and performative description. The turning point in my research, the critical conversion experience, required the step from loyalty to assertion.

Mea culpa. Does the presence of the observer-participant in religious studies represent methodological sophistication, in which the demands for the immediacy of experience dictate the necessity for the experience? Ought we to expect historians of religion to be more "religious" when we do not expect economic historians to be more "economic" or political historians to be more "political"? What ought to be the relationship between the study of religion and its practice? If we attempt the former does that attempt depend on the latter? If "truth" becomes a function of "faith" then all religions are equally valid. Particularly in the light of Jonestown, how are we to distinguish between those religions which suggest a genuine religious experience and those which are merely spurious? The question is one of definition. Yet without a paradigm no definition is possible; without a definition no paradigm is possible.

Cultural, religious, and disciplinary changes are, in part, dependent on a generational ritual process, one that centers on the pivotal rite of initiation. Such a process will focus on movements or phases, not periods. Traditionally, societies have spawned institutions — familial, cultural, educational, religious, and military — in which the initiate is submitted to the authority of the ritual elder, easing the transformation process from childhood to the generative man or woman. Without such ritual elders (or paradigms), the focus will continue to be on a confirmation of "the necessity of feeling young, thinking young, acting young" without asking if there are good or bad ways of expressing it.[26] At the same time, "De-mythologized religion reflects our modern consciousness that has been narrowed to ego identity. To become as a child and to be led by a child means to reverse the process of ego development."[27]

REFERENCES

1. Cf. Thomas Robbins, Dick Anthony, James Richardson, "Theory and Research on Today's 'New Religions'," *Sociological Analysis,* 39/2 (1978), pp.95-122.

2. Melford E. Spiro, *Burmese Supernaturalism, A Study in the Explanation and Reduction of Suffering* (Englewood Cliffs, New Jersey: Prentice-Hall, 1967), p.66.

3. Cf. "Generations," *Daedalus,* 107/4 of the Proceedings of the American Academy of Arts and Sciences (Fall 1978). Landon Y. Jones, *Great Expectations, America and the Baby Boom Generation* (New York: Coward, McCann & Geoghegan, 1980).

4. Rudolf Otto, *The Idea of the Holy,* trans. by J.W. Harvey (London: Oxford University Press, 1923).

5. Victor Turner, *The Ritual Process, Structure and Anti-Structure* (London: Routledge & Kegan Paul, 1969).

6. Hannah Arendt, *On Revolution* (New York: The Viking Press, 1965), p.40.

7. Walter H. Capps, "The War's Transformation", *The Center Magazine* (July/August 1978), p.18.

8. William Manchester, *The Glory and the Dream, A Narrative History of America, 1932-1972,* I (Boston: Little, Brown, 1973-74), p.524.

9. Robert N. Bellah, "Civil Religion in America," *Daedalus* (Winter 1967), p.97.

10. Sydney E. Ahlstrom, *A Religious History of the American People* (New Haven: Yale University Press, 1972), p.1008.

11. Quoted in Eric J. Sharpe, *Comparative Religion, A History* (New York: Charles Scribner's Sons, 1975), p.270.

12. *Ibid.*, p.251.

13. (The University of Chicago Press, 1944), p.iii.

14. Erik H. Erikson, *Identity, Youth and Crisis* (New York: W.W. Norton, 1968), pp.136, 168.

15. Ahlstrom, *op. cit.*, p.1083. In this connection, Peter Berger's *The Noise of Solemn Assemblies* (1961), Gibson Winter's *The Suburban Captivity of the Churches* (1961), and Richard Rubenstein's *After Auschwitz* (1966) come to mind.

16. In traditional societies, following the act of circumcision, the initiate is shown the *sacra* of the people. The rite of initation is, in this sense, a demythologization.

17. On cultural failure and primitivism, see James Baird, *Ishmael* (Baltimore: The Johns Hopkins Press, 1956). For a fuller account of the distinction between chronological and cultural primitivism, see the introductory chapter of *Primitivism and Related Ideas in Antiquity: A Documentary History of Primitivism and Related Ideas*, eds. Arthur O. Lovejoy, Gilbert Chinard, George Boas, and Ronald S. Crane (Baltimore: Johns Hopkins Press, 1935).

18. David Miller, *The New Polytheism: Rebirth of the Gods and Goddesses* (New York: Harper and Row, 1974), p.76.

19. Herbert Hendin, *The Age of Sensation* (New York: W.W. Norton, 1975), p.329.

20. *Our Bodies, Ourselves: A Book by and for Women.* The Boston Women's Health Book Collective (New York: Simon and Schuster, 1973).

21. Christopher Lasch, "The Narcissist Society," *The New York Review of Books*, XXIII/15 (September 30, 1976), p.7.

22. Cf. Shirley Sugerman, *Sin and Madness, Studies in Narcissism* (Philadelphia: Westminster Press, 1976).

23. Notably *The Late Great Planet Earth* (Zondervan, 1976).

24. Thomas S. Kuhn, *The Structure of Scientific Revolutions* (2nd ed., enlarged. Chicago: The University of Chicago Press, 1970), p.15.

25. (Ithaca: Cornell University Press, 1975), p.256.

26. George Boas, *The Cult of Childhood.* Studies of the Warburg Institute, Vol 29, ed. by E.H. Gombrich (London: The Warburg Institute, 1966), p.102 and passim.

27. James Hillman, *Insearch: Psychology and Religion* (New York: Scribner's Sons, 1967), p.115.

CATHOLICITY:
A Threat or Help to Identity?**

Walter H. Principe

Pontifical Institute for Medieval Studies and University of Toronto, Canada.

During Pope John Paul's visit to the East Indies the television broadcast of people dancing for the pope in their traditional dress caused quite a stir in one Toronto rectory. The housekeeper, a devout lady of Spanish origin, after watching the ceremonies on her own set, rushed in and exclaimed to the pastor with shocked look and voice: "Father, did you see those people dancing in front of the pope? They were half naked! And they even went and received Holy Communion dressed that way!" Dancing in the liturgy the Spanish lady might have understood since in Toledo in her native Spain the venerable Mozarabic liturgy incorporates dance into eucharistic worship. But, having seen women barred from Spanish churches because their arms were bare, she found it hard to understand or accept an expression of welcome, reverence, and worship so culturally different from her own.

This little event illustrates the tension between cultural or national diversities and unity in faith that will be examined here in relation to the general theme of our Congress. Have cultural or national identities been threatened or helped by application of the notion of "catholicity"? As I hope to show, catholicity as an ideal — or, if you will, a religious myth — involves a tension between unity in essentials of faith and diversity in the way this faith is expressed and lived in various cultures. To state my thesis briefly: if catholicity, seen as a fundamental trait of the church, is used to insist on a uniformity that overrides differences, it tends to threaten cultural, national, and even personal identity. But if it is used to open a unified but strictly defined faith or belief to all manner of cultural variety, it can be a help to such identity, even the identity of minority groups within a larger national body. I hope to show this by historical examples.

This paper will deal first with how the notion of catholicity developed historically within Roman Catholicism, to which this discussion must be limited (the Orthodox, Anglicans, and different Protestant traditions have concepts of catholicity that in part agree with but in part differ from that in Roman Catholicism). As distinguished from "Roman Catholicism" (i.e., the faith, system, and practice of the Roman Catholic

** Limitations of space have required elimination of the extensive notes and references in the original paper. With two exceptions, only documentary sources and general encyclopedia articles will be indicated within the text, using the following abbreviations:

Abbott — W.M. Abbott, ed., *The Documents of Vatican II* (New York, 1966).
Cath — *Catholicisme*
Congar — Y. Congar, *L'Eglise une, sainte, catholique, apostolique* (Paris, 1970).
DocCath — *La Documentation catholique*
DTC — *Dictionnaire de théologie catholique*
Klauser — T. Klauser, *A Short History of the Western Liturgy* (London, 1969, rpt. 1973).
NCE — *New Catholic Encyclopedia*
Origins — *Origins: National Catholic Documentary Service*
PL — *Patrologia latina*

Church in its concrete historical and cultural life), "catholicity" is a characteristic or "note" of the church. The word "catholic" derives neither from the Septuagint nor the Christian scriptures but rather from secular Greek, *kath' holou*, meaning "on the whole" or "in general". The Fathers of the early church used "catholic" of the church in two distinct but related meanings: first, the catholic church as the universal church distinguished from the particular or local church, i.e., the church spread throughout the world yet maintaining unity of faith, sacramental life, and fellowship or communion despite the variety of peoples embracing Christianity; second, the catholic church as the true, orthodox, authentic church, identified as such because considered as possessing the totality or universality of teachings and gifts coming from Christ — a universality distinguishing it from those called sects, heretics, or schismatics (names implying partiality).

The link between these two meanings is found in many patristic texts, e.g., those of Cyprian (d.258), or in this remarkable text of Cyril of Jerusalem (d.386):

> The church is called "catholic" because it extends through all the world, from one end of the earth to another. Also because it teaches universally (*katholikōs*) and without omission all the doctrines which ought to come to the knowledge of human beings about things both visible and invisible, heavenly and earthly; and because it brings under the sway of true religion all human classes, rulers, and subjects, learned and ignorant, and because it universally (*katholikōs*) treats and cures every type of sin committed by means of soul and body, and possesses in itself every kind of virtue which can be named, in deeds and words, and spiritual gifts of every kind (*Catacheses* 18, 23).

A little further on Cyril draws a practical conclusion for his catechumens:

> When you are staying in any city, do not inquire simply "Where is the Lord's house?" For the sects of the impious attempt to call their dens "houses of the Lord". And do not simply ask where the church is, but say: "Where is the Catholic Church?" For this is the special name of this holy church which is the mother of all (ibid. 26).

Augustine (d.430) developed the theme of the church as the *catholica* in opposition to the North African Donatists. They held they were the only true church because they claimed they had preserved pure faith, holy ministers and hence valid sacraments where others had lost them by apostasy in times of persecution. In relation to our Congress theme, we note that their religious position was linked with an ethnic and social problem since they drew support from the native Berber population, which disliked those who were Romans by origin or who had accepted Roman culture in North Africa (see *NCE* 4, 1001-03). Augustine frequently calls them the *pars Donati*, the "part" or "portion" of Donatus, their leader, and opposes to them the universal church spread through the world — the *catholica*, a name the Donatists cannot claim (see *PL* 43: 81-82, 114, 190, 194; cf. *schisma Donati, PL* 43: 114, 190). He ridicules the Donatists for thinking that the true church could have perished from the entire world and have remained only in Africa (see *PL* 43: 190, 194, 297-300). He opposes to their particularity the certitude of the whole world, which he says, "is secure in judging that they are not good who in any part of the earth cut themselves off from the whole world" (*PL* 43: 101). Although these texts stress geographical extension, Augustine links this closely with the other aspect of catholicity, authenticity or orthodoxy (see *PL* 43: 333-34, and Congar, p. 154).

The Donatists' refusal to engage in discussion together with the violence of some among them led Augustine to abandon his earlier conciliatory attitude and to seek the intervention of the emperor, who sent a tribune, Marcellinus, to preside over a conference or debate at Carthage in 411. Persuaded by Augustine's arguments, Marcellinus required the Donatists to submit or suffer the penalties of civil law. Here one sees an instance of catholicity, supported by the emperor's civil authority, used to work against a particular group whose identity was based not only on theological and religious characteristics but also on ethnic and cultural traits (see *DTC* 1, 2277-80, and *NCE* 4, 1001-02).

In the middle ages, catholicity tended to be described with increasing emphasis on orthodoxy (faith as *fides "catholica"*), this qualitative aspect founding the quantitative or geographical aspect (see Congar, pp. 157-59). A text of Boethius, influential since frequently commented on, went in this direction (*De Trinitate,* 1). For Albert the Great and Thomas Aquinas catholicity was less quantitative and more qualitative, i.e., the fullness of Christ communicated to the church through a faith open to all persons and corresponding to the totality of human aspirations (See Congar, *ibid.*).

The rise of Protestantism shifted emphasis in the concept towards universal geographical (quantitative) extension. Since in its early days Protestantism was restricted to a few countries, Catholic apologists claimed catholicity for their church by reason of its extension to all nations, including the new ones being evangelized by Catholic missionaries (see Congar, p.17). This view, still found in some 20th-century textbooks, lost force as Protestant missions spread worldwide. Emphasis shifted back to the qualitative aspect, interpreted to mean that the church is catholic by possessing all truth, all means of salvation through the working of Christ and the Spirit bringing everything under Christ as Head. This qualitative catholicity is thus seen as the spiritual efficacy of Catholic Christianity to transcend all particularities and to integrate the positive human cultural values of each group or people within catholic unity (see Congar, pp.159-79). That this unity is not the same as uniformity is being brought out increasingly today through the concept of "inculturation", which is being used not only by theologians but by all church officials. Inculturation means that the Christian gospel must be allowed to take root in different cultures, feeding the worship and spiritual life of Christians while remaining as free as possible of cultural importations. The Word of God and church life must incorporate the best elements of each culture even while criticizing any aspects of a culture judged incompatible with the gospel message. Catholicity is thus taken to mean that Christ and his gospel can respect diversities and yet bring them into a harmonious unity without uniformity.

Pope Pius X1 had already expressed this attitude practically by encouraging native priests and bishops and by changing church attitudes towards cultural customs in countries such as China (see *NCE* 1, 120-22; *Catholicisme* 2, 1060-63). The most important endorsement of catholicity and inculturation came in many documents of the Second Vatican Council emphasizing the need for variety within unity for the church itself, for liturgy, ecumenism, the missions, eastern churches, and the church in the modern world (see Abbott, pp. 65-66, 151, 300-301, 347-49, 357-61, 376-77, 595-96). Based on these conciliar teachings the new *Code of Canon Law* (15 Jan. 1983) stated the rights of all church members to their own (approved) liturgical rite and to "their own form of spiritual life" so long as this accords with church teaching (no.214). These provisos and that of canon 216 saying that "no initiative . . . can lay claim to the title 'catholic' without the consent of the competent ecclesiastical authority" suggests a continuing (and perhaps fruitful) tension between the centrifugal push of diverse cultures and the centripetal pull of church leaders to unity.

This new attitude towards variety within unity remarkably reversed a long-standing tendency to stress orthodoxy as a unity often translated into uniformity not only in basic faith but in many details of Roman Catholic life, worship, and practice, a tendency that was already evident in the 4th century (see Congar, p.172). In relation to our

Congress theme, let us look — with some fear of oversimplification — in this second part at some historical examples where, first of all, catholicity viewed as uniformity tended to threaten cultural, national, and even personal identities.

One such example, from the middle ages on, is the relations between the Roman Catholic Church and the Orthodox Churches of the east. Although there was some mutual respect for legitimate varieties between these two great branches of the Christian church (e.g. different liturgies, the role of patriarchs), a number of debated points raised problems, e.g., the use of leavened or un-leavened bread in the Eucharist, the importance of the epiclesis or invocation of the Holy Spirit in the Eucharist, the insertion by the Latin church of the disputed *Filioque* clause into the creed used in the liturgy, and the pope's claim to universal jurisdiction. In the matter of the *Filioque* and in the claim of the pope to universal jurisdiction, the Roman Catholic Church seemed to the Orthodox to be aggressive and to be challenging their doctrines. And since these and the other matters already mentioned were deeply rooted in the cultures and lives of the Orthodox (who always maintained a close link between religion and nation), the Latin church's attitude could seem to threaten as well their national and cultural heritage and identity. Indeed, some scholars hold that these cultural-national issues were often as basic as the theological differences or at least prevented mutual understanding and compromise (see *NCE* 2, 936-50, and 5, 21-25).

One might argue that insistence by the Orthodox on their positions threatened western culture and identity. They, however, at least never made a claim to universal jurisdiction and would have been (and I believe still would be) ready to accept the pope as patriarch of the west provided it did not threaten the authority of their own patriarchs. In this respect, I think we can see today that the newer notion of catholicity is not a threat but a help to affirming the rights and so the identity of the Orthodox. In a strikingly new approach, the Second Vatican Council acknowledged past deficiencies of the Roman Catholic Church towards the Oriental Church and also spoke very positively about the legitimate variety and richness of their traditions not only in liturgy, spirituality, and discipline, but even in expression of doctrine (see Abbott, pp.355-61). More concretely, on December 7, 1965, Pope Paul VI and Patriarch Athenagoras of Istanbul joined in nullifying the mutual excommunications that had been proclaimed centuries earlier, and in 1975 the same pope kissed the feet of Metropolitan Meliton to show his desire to serve humbly to help achieve unity — facts recently recalled by Pope John Paul (see *Origins* 15, p.127).

Another example where catholicity as a drive for uniformity caused tension and a threat to cultural diversity was the western liturgy. The ancient Gallican rites of the northern European peoples, more rhetorical and poetic than the combined Roman-Frankish liturgy that supplanted it, seem to have been the victim of such concerns for uniformity (see Klauser, pp.45-46, 72-76; *NCE* 6, 258-62). A clearer case, because better known historically, was the imposition in 1568 of the *Breviarium ROMANUM* and in 1570 of the *Missale ROMANUM* by Pius V on the western church except in sees having had their own special liturgy for more than two hundred years. A Congregation of Rites was soon set up with authority to rule in all liturgical matters; then came the *Pontificale ROMANUM* and the *Rituale ROMANUM*. The whole process is described by Klauser (p.117) as a "rigid unification in the liturgy and rubricism". Before this, local bishops or groups of bishops had the right to regulate liturgical action more suited to their own cultural or national identities. In France many could claim a "Gallican" tradition of more than two hundred years and the growth of Gallicanism led to French opposition to uniform Roman liturgy; this opposition spread into Tuscany but was headed off by a national synod (*ibid.*, pp.119-20).

Gallicanism itself was one of the most tenacious movements in western Europe seeking to maintain national identity against Roman pressures and the views of French

Ultramontanists. Gallicanism seems to have originated in the 13th century when the arrival of the Franciscan and Dominican Orders introduced in practice the role of papal authority that had formerly be claimed in theory. In both universities and parishes the advent of the well-trained, inspiring friars, backed by the authority of the pope, was seen as a threat by the secular clerics who were professors at the university and by the bishops and local diocesan clergy. At first the secular clerics of the University of Paris had been helped by the pope in the very establishment of the university and its privileges, but at a certain stage the influence of the Mendicant Friars changed their allegiance and they appealed to the bishops to make common cause for the good of the local church; both groups then began to ally themselves with the king in his growing nationalistic policies and struggles against the pope. Much of this was, of course, a matter of power, but the alliance of the friars with the pope to extend his influence seems to have been reenforced by a certain view of catholicity. Gallicanism became an even stronger force at later times in French history (see *NCE* 6, 262-67). Even at the First Vatican Council it played a part in the opposition of a group of French bishops to the definition of papal infallibility, one result of which they saw as the weakening of the local churches.

The great missionary movements of the 16th and 17th centuries and later point up the issue of catholicity in relation to cultural identities. The expansion of a partially homogenous western Catholicism into North and South America, Asia, and eventually Africa and Australasia forced missionaries to ask themselves how they should preach and teach and how they should develop the worship and spirituality of converts from backgrounds so diverse from their own European culture (see *NCE* 1, 120-22). How much uniformity was required?

Coming into contact with an ancient rich civilization in China, the Jesuit Matteo Ricci sought to integrate as much of traditional Chinese religious views and practices into Christianity as he could (see *NCE* 12, 470-72). Rivalries among missionary groups and among European nations seeking control in China added fuel to a controversy about such adaptations. There were serious theological issues involved in the Chinese rites of homage to Confucius and veneration of ancestors as well as in use of certain Chinese terms to speak about God, but at least one element in the opposed views was how much diversity in concrete cultural expression could be allowed by unity in faith (see *DTC* 2, 2364-91; *NCE* 3, 611-15). At the time Ricci's opponents won out and these adaptations were eliminated. Although earlier in this century the policy was changed and use of these rituals was accepted as not being superstitious or opposed to Catholic faith, Roman Catholicism in China kept a very strong European flavor, as I experienced on a visit to China when I observed church decoration, ritual, and spirituality that differed little from that of the European past (see *Cath* 2, 1060-63; *DocCath* 80, no.1843, pp.17-19).

We could ask similar questions about the extensive missionary efforts of the Spanish and Portuguese in South and Central America and in the south and west of what is now the United States (see *NCE* 9, 944-74). The general impression is that the conquerors, colonisers, and missionaries submerged the existing rich cultures of the Indians with European ways; in religion this meant a Christianity of Spanish or Portuguese flavor. Thus the mission churches of the Spanish, beautiful as they are, did little to incorporate the culture of the original peoples. The same is true, with minor exceptions, of the liturgy: I have seen the old Mass books, vestments, altar pieces and statuary in the surviving Spanish missions, and they are straight out of European Spain and are fully conformed to Roman usage. One exception that should be noted was the work of the Jesuits in establishing "reductions": these were attempts to achieve a good measure of inculturation of the gospel (see *NCE* 12, 165-66).

Another interesting exception to the general pattern, and an example of qualitative catholicity respecting cultural identity, is the devotion to Our Lady of Guadalupe among Mexicans and other Hispanic Americans. It is devoutly believed that Mary, the mother of Jesus, impressed an image of herself on the cloak of an Indian peasant. The devotion to Mary and her Son that followed upon this, with the approval and encouragement of the bishops, can be seen as an affirmation of catholicity in its qualitative sense because the image is not that of a Spanish lady but rather of a Mexican Indian madonna, an image that contrasts strikingly with the Spanish features of paintings and statuary in the mission churches. It would be hard to imagine a stronger assertion of the value of the native Indian identity and culture than such a portrait and the ensuing devotion, a devotion that now supports the identity of millions of Hispanics in Mexico and elsewhere, including many in the United States (see NCE 6, 821-22).

North American Indian tribes were so diversified that one would have to study each in detail to form an accurate judgment on how the notion of catholicity was interpreted and put into practice. If one may judge by reactions today that reaffirm the cultural and religious values of past Indian traditions, the native peoples judge that Catholic missionaries by and large threatened their cherished cultural and tribal identity by the way they presented Christianity. There were, however, different approaches and, as in China and South America, the Jesuits, with their traditions of humanism and greater openness to secular culture, seem to have made serious attempts to understand and preserve the best elements of native culture. Nevertheless, they brought with them an intellectual and cultural baggage that Indians and scholars of the Amerindians would consider weighted with European and French Catholic outlooks. There were differences in approach among the Jesuits themselves, and those seeking greater adaptation were, as in China, criticized both by their brethren and by other missionary groups.

On his visit to Canada in the summer of 1984 Pope John Paul in three addresses stressed the importance of the native cultures and the need to integrate them within the gospel teaching (see DocCath 81, no.1881, pp.941-43, 968-70, and 972-74). A very moving occasion was his taking part in a ceremony of purification conducted by the Indian leaders, one of whom waved smoking wands, as a sign of harmony with nature and of purification, not only in the four directions but also about the pope himself. He received the gesture reverently, but I could not help noticing that some of the other church dignitaries on the stand with him seemed somewhat disgruntled and remarkably unenthusiastic!

As with the Spanish missions and the Amerindians, it is impossible to generalize about the missionary movement in Africa. Some attempts have certainly been made to integrate elements of various African cultures into Catholic life and practice, but it seems true that the notion of one true faith and its European inculturation taken as normative have threatened African culture and identity. For example, Catholic teaching and discipline concerning monogamy has disrupted established social and economic structures, especially by rendering the position of widowed women economically difficult through rejection of the leviratic practice that had provided support for these women. Another example: at a conference a few years ago African theologians called for the development of an "African theology", i.e. an understanding of the gospel in relation to the particular culture, history and problems of Africa (see DocCath 75, no.1736, p.196). This initiative, however, received a rather cool response from Rome, and this may have been why Pope John Paul II was somewhat rigid in his reaction to African cultural expression on his first visit to Africa, especially in regard to the liturgy. But it must be added that his world travels seem to have modified his views and he now speaks constantly on these visits about the value of each culture and the need for inculturation (see *DocCath* 82: no.1890, pp.225-26; no.1892, pp.341-44; no.1893, pp.367-69).

The liberation theology of Hispanic America and the reaction to it by some in these lands and by the Roman curia seem to me to be partially a tension between two views of catholicity. In 1970, at a theological conference in Brussels, I heard Gustavo Gutierrez say that although the theology of the conference was undoubtedly interesting for the Europeans present, those from South America would have to develop their own theology in relation to the culture and needs of their own people. In informal gatherings at the same conference theologians from North America were saying the same thing. Gutierrez and others did develop such a theology, working from the praxis or concrete religious life and needs of the people and in turn, by their theology, supporting efforts towards justice and humanity. But their work has become a constant and, I am afraid, almost morbid preoccupation of Roman curialists worried about Marxist elements in some of its exponents (see *DocCath* 81, no.1881, pp.890-900). Gutierrez recently denied the essential role of Marxism in this theology (see *ibid.*, pp.906-909). I have seen this preoccupation and fear — perhaps arising from other sources not always expressed — in Rome at meetings of the International Theological Commission. The conflict seems to be between a view of catholicity that insists on one standard way of presenting the gospel and one which insists on inculturation, taking the official pronouncements in favor of it seriously whereas others become fearful when inculturation or qualitative catholicity begins to happen in concrete reality. To the extent that a rigid, narrow theology of the Roman curia and like-minded South and Central American prelates prevails, there seems to be a threat to cultural and national identity and values.

Looking at the other side of the picture, has the notion of catholicity been a help to the cultural, national, or personal identities of some peoples? Here I am thinking not so much of the simple fact that many groups or nations are mainly Roman Catholic and so have integrated their faith and practice into their cultural and national life, but rather what is the influence on their identity coming from their sense of belonging to a church or communion that transcends the limits of their own culture and nation, a church that is indeed universal both geographically and qualitatively?

Perhaps someone might object that it is paradoxical if not downright contradictory to think that such a notion could help cultural or national identity. On one level one could reply to that objection by saying that because the Christian gospel requires self-reflection and *metanoia* or conversion with respect to selfish or destructive manifestations within one's culture or nation, it helps that identity by making it more authentic and more faithful to its nobler aspects, and this by helping to overcome any narrowness, selfishness, or other weaknesses that could debilitate its better identity. I think this is true, and would point to the example of the bishops of the United States, wrestling, in communion with the pope and bishops of other lands, with questions of nuclear armaments and economic structures and drawing elements of critique from their Catholic communion. Their prophetic challenge to the people of the United States to become the morally dedicated nation it has always thought itself to be is an example of how a more universal communion or catholicity can help to better a national culture or identity.

Here, however, I would like to proceed on another level by suggesting a few concrete examples of instances where I think the sense of belonging to a universal or catholic communion has reenforced national or cultural identity. The simplest case is perhaps that of Poland in many periods of its history. Poland's link with the universal church began with the baptism of Mieszko, Poland's first ruler, in 966; Mieszko's elder son, Bolesaw, secured political and ecclesiastical independence for

Poland. For centuries the Poles defended the Christian west against the east, but it was especially between 1795 and 1918 that the link with the universal church was crucially important for Polish identity as Germany, Russia, and Austria tried to suppress Poland. In this period the church came to be regarded as the one force that could help preserve Polish culture, language, and identity.

Although between the two world wars the church lost the support of many intellectuals, it retained its influence with the peasants and to some extent with the workers. Soviet domination of Poland and the good record of the church during the second world war and afterwards again made the church the rallying point for Poles of every group or class. And, of course, the election of Cardinal Wojtya to be head of the Roman Catholic Church was a most striking symbol as well as a social and political force aiding Polish confidence in its identity against those it considers its oppressors.

Ireland can be examined as another possible example, although, as my Irish friends are the first to point out, its history is too complex and difficult for anyone, especially an outsider, to grasp fully and to summarize. It does seem that when Protestant rulers repressed Catholics during several centuries, it was not only the Catholicism of the Irish that had become part of their culture but also their sense of a link with the universal church that helped unite them in opposing the English restrictions and strengthened their identity. When, however, it came to seeking national independence, the matter was less simple because some of the people and the church's hierarchy rejected and condemned those opposed to the treaty of 6 December 1921 giving complete autonomy to the south; the opponents to the treaty were part of the Sinn Fein movement that refused to negotiate with the British and sought complete independence of all Ireland. They became bitter towards the church, a bitterness that still remains among those seeking full independence of Ireland by taking over the six counties of the north, by force if necessary. They do not, however, represent all Irish people, many of whom agree with the hierarchy in condemning violence as a means of establishing complete national independence (see *NCE* 7, 613-27).

Another complicated example is that of Québec in Canada. Most Québecois consider themselves a nation or at least a people with an identity quite distinct from that of other Canadians, whom they used to call *les maudits anglais* or, if they were English-speaking Catholics of any national origin, *les irlandais*. The basic distinction of the Québecois from other Canadians was rooted in their colonizing history and in the language and religious culture they had brought from France. It is true that their own history in Canada gradually gave them a self-identity distinct from that of France as well as from that of other Canadians, but at the time of the French revolution and afterwards this distinction of identity from France was reenforced by their sense of catholicity. For as the French nation turned away from the church in the late 18th and the 19th centuries, the people of Québec, led by their clergy and by priests from France who came to Québec because they rejected the French revolution, intensified their loyalty to Rome and to the universal church. In the process Québec became increasingly aware of its unique identity. Today, even though Québec society has become very much secularized, the French version of the Canadian national anthem still sings of carrying *la croix* together with *l'épée*, and the most secular and anti-clerical must take account of Québec's traditional sense of catholicity even as they seek to define its national and cultural identity in new ways (see *NCE* 12, 14-17).

Another example, or series of examples, is that of immigrant groups forming minorities within a larger national population. For Roman Catholic immigrants the integration of their native language, customs and religion in their homeland culture undoubtedly helped them to maintain a cultural identity within new lands and differing cultures. But I would suggest that their sense of catholicity, of belonging to a universal church linking them not only to their homeland but to other Catholics in general and to Catholics in their new homeland, helped them to preserve a certain cultural identity within a larger and sometimes hostile majority. In Canada, for example, Irish Immigrants were greatly helped at first by Québec Catholics on their arrival and sometimes afterwards; in turn, the Irish and Scots Catholics in Canada helped the Italian immigrants, and in the west Ukrainian Catholics were aided by German Catholics who had already established themselves there. Similar examples could be given for the United States and undoubtedly for Australia.

Finally, help to cultural and national identities would seem to be forthcoming from the new views of catholicity and inculturation that have already been mentioned. The Second Vatican Council, building on the work of theologians, reflected the new anthropological awareness of the richness of all cultures, including many formerly thought primitive and impoverished. It therefore emphasized catholicity as embracing cultural variety within unity of belief, and this theme has been stressed by church officials and others since the council. There are good examples of its effects. The internationalization of the college of cardinals has already led to the election of a non-Italian pope and serious consideration of a non-European pope. The growth of indigenous clergy and the gradual replacement of foreign-born bishops and other administrators also serve to make the church more truly catholic, especially as these bishops take part in the synods called regularly for discussion of major issues in the church.

Nevertheless, despite these excellent statements by councils, synods, and popes, and despite the real progress that has been made, it would be unrealisatic to ignore that within Roman Catholicism catholicity is still sometimes interpreted as emphasizing a unity that tends towards uniformity and that therefore threatens cultural or national identity. A recent example is the suspension of several Ukrainian priests of the Oriental rite who, being married, were ordained in Canada by their bishop. Ukrainian Eastern-rite Catholics maintain that at the time of their union with Rome they were promised the right to a married clergy, which they have in the Ukraine; in North America, however, perhaps under pressure from other Roman Catholic bishops, this right has been denied them.

Another case is the attitude and practice of the Roman curia manifested in many ways towards the churches of North and South America and towards missionary bishops. At the beginning of this century the so-called "heresy of Americanism" was condemned by Rome even though this "heresy" was later shown to be largely the invention of European theologians (see NCE 1, 443-44). Today it appears that many European members of the curia fail to understand the North American cultural identity and too quickly judge elements within it to be incompatible with Catholic tradition. North Americans played a leading role at the Second Vatican Council in the drive for a document favoring religious liberty and met their greatest opposition from some European bishops. Today, very pessimistic views about North American Catholicism have been issued by leading Roman curialists. Religious orders, especially of women, have been treated in ways that show an ignorance of the place of women in North American society, e.g., by insisting on a style of obedience, dress, apostolate, and way of life that might still be acceptable to Italians, Poles, and Germans but not to most North American religious women. The importance of national episcopal conferences have been downplayed, perhaps, one suspects, because the episcopal conferences of the United States and Canada have adopted an open, democratic method of consulting all Catholics, a method that derives from North American and British cultural traditions but that is literally foreign to the mentality of most European curialists, whether German or Italian or whatever.

In South America pressure has been put on the bishops of some countries to condemn or silence theologians of liberation. When I was in Rome in 1984 the bishops of Peru had been summoned to the Vatican for this purpose, but they refused to go along with the curial pressure. Documents have been produced concerning South America that show little evidence of consultation or concern for local conditions. And throughout the world bishops in missionary lands and others in ministry who have pleaded for new thinking about ordination and ministry in the face of a drastic shortage of priests have been given only minor concessions that do not really meet the problem.

Thus, despite real advances, the tension seems to continue and a remark made by Marshal McLuhan in a lecture he gave in Toronto some years ago seems more pertinent than ever. He spoke about communication now taking place at the speed of light (Marshall never worried about the accuracy in physics of his metaphors!) and said that as this process draws the world together more and more, the crucial question for the Christian churches is whether they can cease to be churches of European and (in some cases) North American culture alone and whether they can open themselves to becoming the church or churches of all cultures and nations. For the Roman Catholic Church this question means which interpretation of catholicity, and of the related concept of inculturation, will prevail, and this not only in theory and pronouncement, but in concrete daily practice. Future historians of religion will, I believe, look on the remaining years of our century as one of the most crucial periods for the resolution of this issue.

NATIONAL AND INTERNATIONAL IDENTITY IN A JAPANESE RELIGION

(Byakkō Shinkōkai)

Michael Pye

Philipps Universität, Marburg, Germany

INTRODUCTION

The first announcement of this conference defined the conference theme as 'intended to emphasize the role of religion in forming and maintaining individual and group (national, ethnic, sectional, tribal, family) identity.' With this phrasing there is omitted one reference point of major importance, namely what may be called world identity.

World identity may be subdivided into two aspects. Firstly there is what may be called a sense of cosmic identity, well known indeed to the phenomenological tradition in the study of religion. This aspect may be readily combined with the particularist forms of religion mentioned in the announcement. That is, a religion directed primarily towards an ethnic identity, such as Shinto, may convey a strong sense of cosmic rootedness through myths of origin, relation to nature, annual recurrence, and so on. Secondly however there is in some religions an evident attempt to seek a group identity which has a world dimension at human level. Nor is it necessarily just a vague sense of universal good-will, though in some cases this may be the residue of ebbing religious influence. Much of the interest in the study of major religious traditions lies in the relationship or tension between universalist claims and local, particularist identity-creating forms. Consider Catholicism in Poland and Buddhism in Thailand. Looking at it the other way round, some religions which are strong in local or ethnic identity, such as the Hindu or even more strikingly the Sikh faith, may easily display a universalising trend when circumstances favour it. Moreover the various forms of identity creation are often closely interwoven. Cosmic, national and individual identity may be successfully fused in one religious conception.

The search for world identity beyond particularist definitions appears most evidently in the context of the major traditions: Buddhism, Christianity and Islam. Yet it is a theme of some importance in a number of new religious movements, overlooked no doubt because these are so interesting in other ways. This paper focuses on one as yet little known modern Japanese movement known in English as the White Light Association. This movement is centred on prayers for world peace in a manner which dramatically emphasises the search for world identity as a function of religion.

The theme of the paper arose out of a fortuitous encounter in Japan, in 1983 (about the time when the conference theme for the IAHR Congress in Sydney was published). On previous occasions I had been intrigued by some vertical stickers seen on doorposts bearing the slogan 'Sekai jinrui ga heiwa de arimasu yō ni' (May peace be with mankind). Coming across this slogan, prominently displayed, in front

234

of a building in Tokyo, apparently open to the public, it became clear to me that this was not a freely floating peace sticker but the mark of an organisation of interest to the student of religion, namely the Byakkō Shinkōkai or, in English, the White Light Association. During the month of August 1983 I was able to visit both the above-mentioned branch and the headquarters of this movement and to make observations to which I will return later. First however some introductory information will be necessary. I am grateful to the Byakkō Shinkōkai for making various materials available for background study.

The Byakkō Shinkōkai arose as the result of the life-work of Masahisa Goi (name given in western order) (1916-1980), known to followers as Goi-Sensei which is rendered by the organisation into English as Master Goi. His biography will no doubt eventually be the subject of detailed study. His life covered the period of strident Japanese nationalism, defeat, and postwar reflection and reconstruction, a period for the whole of which Japan's relations with its neighbours or with 'the world' (as they say in Japan) have been a crucial determinant of daily life. Thus the question of Japanese identity in the world arises naturally in the movement which he founded. Indeed, as will be seen, the Byakkō Shinkōkai may be taken as a paradigm for the structure of this whole problem. My thesis is that the religious dimension provides both a dramatisation and stabilisation of this structure in Japanese consciousness.

THE PRAYER FOR WORLD PEACE

The central activity of the White Light Association is a system of prayer for world peace. It is a system in the sense that it takes various predefined forms for use at various levels. Most widely evident are the stickers, already mentioned, which may be affixed anywhere (see illustration at end of this paper). The standard form is a slim rectangle bearing the phrase 'Sekai jinrui ga heiwa de arimasu yō ni', for which the English equivalent promoted by the White Light Association is 'May peace prevail on earth'. Equivalents are available in several other languages, notably French, German, Bulgarian, Spanish, Portuguese, Russian and Chinese. The phrase used for mankind means literally 'world mankind', thus making this dimension of interest quite explicit.

More substantial is the peace stupa (heiwatō), a two-meter high and ten-centimeter square post which bears exactly the same slogan, without any further indication of the name or the leading ideas of the movement, as is explicitly emphasised in a promotional pamphlet. (These 'stupas', or 'poles' as they are referred to in English-language promotional literature, should not be confused with the much larger 'peace stupas' erected as veritable buildings by a Buddhist movement in the Nichirenite tradition.) The objective is to raise consciousness for peace, starting in Japan, by encouraging people to set up these posts in towns and villages, on mountains, in office and factory grounds, and in shops, temples and shrines.

In a more extended but still general form the 'Prayer for the peace of the world' runs as follows:

> 'May peace prevail on earth.
> May peace be in our homes and countries.
> May our missions[1] be accomplished.
> We thank thee, Guardian Deities and Guardian Spirits.'[2]

The Japanese text of this prayer, formulated by Goi-Sensei, runs as follows:

> 'Sekai jinrui ga heiwa de arimasu yō ni
> Nihon[3] ga heiwa de arimasu yō ni

Watakushitachi no tenmei ga mattōsaremasu yō ni
Shugoreisama arigatō gozaimasu
Shugojinsama arigatō gozaimasu.'[4]

In another Japanese form of the prayer Goi-Sensei's name is added to the last part, thus:

' . . . Shugoreisama, shugojinsama, Goi-Sensei, arigatō gozaimasu'(i.e. 'Guardian Spirits, Guardian Deities, Master Goi, we thank you')[5]

Even in English the prayer may be provided with an interpretative gloss in small print which indicates the spiritual dimension and the mediating function of 'Master Goi' in terms of which the prayer is intended to be understood. This runs:

'Concerning this prayer, an agreement was made between Master Goi and the Divine World. According to this agreement, whenever we pray this prayer, the Great Light of Salvation will definitely shine forth, without fail. Then you yourself will be saved and at the same time an immense power will be manifested, transforming the vibration of world mankind into a Great Harmonious Light Vibration.'[6]

It is clear therefore that prayer in this context is more than the mere expression of a political wish. In Goi-Sensei's own words:

'Prayer means opening up one's original mind or buddha-nature, leading the vibrations of light from the world of deities and spirits (the original mind) into the world of flesh.'[7]

There seems to be no doubt therefore that the prayer for world peace is more than it may appear to be and that it is understood as leading into religious truth.

It may be recognised in passing that Buddhist themes are drawn upon lightly here. These are immediately balanced by the continuation:

"The sentence in the Lord's Prayer in Christianity 'Thy will be done on earth, as it is in heaven' is equivalent to 'May peace prevail on earth' and 'May peace prevail in Japan'."[7]

In fact Buddhist ideas are adduced quite generously by Goi, but usually he draws away again, in a typical syncretist syndrome, from too close an association with them. An investigation of his work *Hannya Shingyō no atarashii kaishaku* ('A New Interpretation of the Heart Sutra')[8] would lead too far afield in this context. It will be noted however that the summary of his teaching entitled 'How man should reveal his inner self' begins with a clear statement running 'Man is originally a spirit from God and not a karmic existence'.[9] A more extensive account of his teaching may be found in the English-language work *God and Man* and here the extensive but un-Buddhist use of the idea of karma and its displacement by the principle of divinity, both within and without man, may be pursued in detail.[10]

The central prayer is also developed into an extended litany which is offered at regular meetings at the headquarters of the movement at Ichikawa near Tokyo.[11] For this a booklet of about 180 pages is used. The litany repeats the second and third lines of the prayer already given, but with the names of as many countries inserted as the Japanese Foreign Ministry lists in its 'table of countries of the world' (Sekai no kuni ichiranhyō). To go through all of these by continent at a ritualised pace takes about thirty minutes. After doing this in Japanese the process is then repeated in English, which takes a little longer, to indicate internationalism, the pronunciation of all the English words and names being given in *katakana* (Japanese phonetic script). Thus, to give one example:

'May peace be in the Democratic Republic of Madagascar,
May the Democratic Republic of Madagascar's missions be accomplished.'[12]

The whole liturgy is concluded with 'We thank thee, Goi-Sensei, Guardian Deities and Guardian Spirits.'[13]

While the litany is being recited, leaders at the front of the hall place a marker at the position of each country, as it is mentioned, on a huge map of the world hung for all to see. Thus this liturgy of word and action cannot be regarded otherwise than as a sustained effort to identify with the peoples of the whole world, recognising their diversity of destiny (for no attempt is made to define their 'missions' for them) while praying for their peace. As a peace-loving and religious person, as well as being a participant observer engaged in the study of religion, I could not fail to be impressed by this sustained world prayer. Interestingly however, as has already been hinted, there is more to the White Light Association than the peace prayer, and this means that the nature of the world identity to which aspiration ascends must be understood in a more complex way, as will become clear.

GOI-SENSEI AND THE BELIEVERS

The 'unity meeting' (tōitsukai) in the context of which the above described prayer is offered takes place at the headquarters of the movement which is named Hijirigaoka Dōjō. Hijiri is an established term in Japanese religion meaning something like 'holy man with supernatural powers', so that the name Hijirigaoka might be explained, without translating, as 'holy man hill'. Dōjō is likewise a standard term meaning 'place of meditation'. The full-length peace prayer in two languages is a central feature of the meeting held here, but it is by no means the only one of interest. For one thing the members enter into a close form of meditative communion while holding up one, two or three fingers, often quivering slightly. Beginners are asked to hold up one finger only because the power of the vibrations would otherwise be too much for them. At another stage in the meeting hands are held firmly against the forehead while communication with Goi-Sensei takes place. Goi-Sensei is present. However he is not just present in a general or theoretical way. He is present because he is drawn down through upraised hands to participate in the meeting. He speaks through the powerful mediumship of Mrs Masami Saionji (name in western order)[14]. Eventually hands are slowly raised towards the ceiling and Goi-Sensei returns to the spirit world. Clearly the hijiri or 'holy man' of 'Hijiri Hill' is none other than Goi-Sensei himself. The dōjō is a place of meditation, but in the sense of meditative unity with the spirit world effected through the link with Goi-Sensei.

The role of Goi-Sensei in the consciousness of believers is central. The literature says almost nothing about his early life, except that he was born in Tokyo. Nothing is of importance, in the religious consciousness, until he experienced in 1949 his own unity with the divine (shingaittai) and become an enlightened person (kakusha). Thereafter he devoted himself to the life of the White Light Association until he "returned to the Divine World" in 1980. Publications since 1980 continue to carry writings from his prolific pen as if he were timelessly present. Individually believers may carry, as a protective device, a small photograph of the white light which Goi-Sensei's mind becomes when he "elevates his consciousness to the Divine Level".[15] Although doctrinal elaboration about his person might be described as not yet far advanced, he is regarded de facto not only as the teacher par excellence, but also as pure and bright in his nature and thus unlike other men however wise and splendid they may be.[16]

The Japanese language magazine *Byakkō* carries regular interviews with believers about their experiences, including how they came to be granted a karmic connection with Goi-Sensei. The November issue for 1984, for example, tells of a man in his sixties who, disappointed with various other religions such as Tenrikyō, Oomotokyō, Tasukaru Michi and Hito no Michi, finally came to a firm faith on reading the autobiography of Goi-Sensei, *Ten to chi o tsungu mono* ('A man linking heaven and earth').[17] Thereupon his son was healed from an illness and his work-situation improved. Thus he felt 'In my case I have received this-worldly benefits (*genzeriyaku*).[18]

The direct relationship to Goi-Sensei is also encouraged by means of a letter-writing programme. Even after his return to the spirit world he is regarded as continuing to broadcast the great light of salvation for the happiness and peace of mankind. In addition, the *Byakkō* reader learns, he turns his ear and extends the hand of salvation to those in need of individual assistance. Thus letters may be addressed to Goi-Sensei with messages of anything to be reported, words of gratitude, subjects of grief or requests of any kind. They should be sent to Goi-Sensei's correspondence secretary (if not delivered in person) and will then be placed before him, after which an answer may be expected at any time. After delivery the letters will be offered up ceremoniously in flames,[19] and as the envelopes will still be unopened no donations of money should be included.[20]

Less directly linked to Goi-Sensei but nevertheless operative within the religious context which he defined is the principle and practice of purification (*kiyome*). The branch building in Tokyo mentioned earlier had two parts, a western-style reception area with a small office and stands for the sale of literature and stickers, and a Japanese-style area consisting of two *tatami* rooms set aside for the practice of o-*kiyome* (the honorific prefix is usually added). The first of the two *tatami* rooms was used as a simple registration and waiting room, and when a small group of four or five had assembled they were ushered into the smaller inner room to be greeted by the officiant (female). After introductory prayer each person was free to state particular needs and was then purified by having a series of about twenty hand-claps addressed to them, first facing and then with back turned. One of those present at the o-*kiyome* which I observed was a teacher who placed before her on the matting photographs of five children who were experiencing particular difficulties at school, thus enabling them to benefit unknowingly from the o-*kiyome*. As far as could be ascertained this practice of o-*kiyome* has no explicit connection (it certainly had none on the occasion observed) with the peace prayer movement. There is an historical question to be explored about the development of the coexistence between these two practices.

INTERPRETATION

As was said at the outset, there is present in much though not all religion a thrust towards universalism which implies a search for identity beyond natural, e.g., clan or national boundaries. This thrust may be regarded as a normal religious motivation which can be observed in Japanese religion just as well as elsewhere. Leaving Buddhism aside, in that its universalising traits may be held to stem originally from outside Japan, one could take as distinct examples Tenrikyō, Oomotokyō, PL Kyōdan, and of course the White Light Association. A transnational or world identity is however not so easily achieved in practice. Much depends on the general level of national consciousness and the extent to which relations beyond the natural group are regarded as a problem in general. The relatively low success rate in universalisation (in spite of the theory circulating within the religions) may be regarded as a function of the high importance assigned to the question of Japanese identity. (Zen Buddhism is an exception with exceptional explanations.)

In this context the presentation of the wish for peace by the White Light Association is of great interest. Arising shortly after the end of the Pacific War it strikes a major chord in the Japanese consciousness of the second half of the twentieth century. The projection of the wish for peace is explicit, sustained and specifically related to all the countries of the world. The message is extremely simple. There is in fact no political peace programme. The definition of the "missions" of each country is left to the countries concerned (as I was assured in an interview at the headquarters office). The question of conflicts arising between these "missions" does not arise. It could only do so on the basis of an inadequate understanding of the "missions" of each country. But there is no political critique of national self-understanding. Instead there is a ritualised incorporation of all identifiable states into the prayer, even though a great many of these states are in no sense a threat to world peace. To point this out is not to deny possible value in praying for each and any country, or other community, but to make clear that the real purpose of the prayer, or at least its religious function, is to establish an identity. The prayer is the expression of a heartfelt wish, a wish for peace, but at the same time it is a quest for identity, namely a world identity. Japan is to be understood as a respected and indeed a leading member of a chain of nations, extending through all humanity, which are not at war.

The position of Japan is of great importance here. Not only does Japan figure prominently in the short form of the prayer (in the Japanese text only, admittedly, but then most of the members *are* Japanese); not only does Japan appear first in the long form of the prayer with all the other countries' names following; the writings of Goi-Sensei actually promote and justify beginning with Japan on the basis that this is an acceptable form of patriotism and that if Japan becomes peaceful the peace consciousness will then spread out to other countries.[21] In explaining this Goi-Sensei does refer to political questions in a general way, especially to the conflict between the superpowers and to fear of communism. Moreover he urges avoidance of political extremes. This general interest in political questions is maintained today by means of the series of foreign visits being undertaken by Mrs. Saionji, as illustrated in the periodical literature and in the brochure *World Peace Through Prayer.*[22] It is clear from all these presentations however that quest for world identity has meaning in relation to the question of Japanese identity, which for the majority of Japanese people is an important consciousness issue. This may also be documented by the essay "Kore kara no Nihon, kore kara no sekai" ("Japan from now on, the world from now on") which is prominently housed in the first volume of Goi-Sensei's collected works.[23] Thus the search for world identity in the form of the prayer for the peace of the world may be understood as a ritualised means of coping with the fact, bitterly experienced, that Japan is not alone in the world.

Naturally this understanding of the matter may be held to be in slight tension with the self-understanding of the believers themselves, of whom at first glance it might simply be said that they are praying for world peace. Of course, so they are. It cannot be overlooked, however, that the prayer for world peace, especially in its longer ritualised form, has deeper functions internal to the White Light Association as a Japanese religion. One major reason for drawing this conclusion has already been made clear above, namely the fact that the peace prayer does not issue in political action of any kind. There is a second reason however, the basis for which has also been laid in the foregoing descriptions, and this is that the White Light Association also solves other religious problems in a manner which may appear to be unrelated to the peace prayer movement (that is, to the casual observer). Thus the branch building had a western room for solving the world identity problem and a Japanese room for solving personal difficulties through purification. At the large-scale "unity meeting" the liturgy for world peace is accompanied by the descent of the spirit of Goi-Sensei, which for people of other faiths or none is irrelevant to the solving of political problems. For the believer, what is actually taking place is that the wish for peace as an expression of the need for world identity is being ritually integrated into a context which provides reassuringly Japanese religious features. Thus for the Japanese participant the various strands do all belong together. They provide identity and succour at family, community, national, and world level. Goi-Sensei has a message for all of these, and hence his presence at the liturgy for world peace is not strange.

One of the basic problems in Japanese consciousness, however articulated, is how to deal with outside, abroad, the world. In a period of growing international interaction, this problem is dealt with in many ways to which a large number of religious organisations contribute. There is a wide spectrum to consider, including straightforward missionary outreach through work in foreign languages, the Esperantism of Oomotokyō, and the public relations for peace carried out by Risshō Kōseikai and Sōka Gakkai leaders. In most cases the function of these activities within Japan, for the benefit of the members of the organisations, is at least as important as any possible effect on the outside world. In this context the *Byakkō Shinkōkai*, because of the prominence given to the peace prayer and the peace liturgy, provides a particularly fine example of the structure of national and international identity in Japanese consciousness as articulated by religion.

NOTES

1. Another text has "our divine missions", seeking a translation element for the *ten* of *tenmei*.

2. Text inside cover of magazine *Heywa (sic)*, No. 18, November 1982.

3. Sometimes *sokoku*, "ancestral country", is added after "Nihon".

4. Text frequently reproduced in Goi-Sensei's handwriting.

5. Text in *Sekaikakkoku no sekaiheiwa no inori*, Ichikawa n.d. but 1983.

6. *Heywa*, No. 18, November 1982, inside cover.

7. Goi, Masahisa, *Sekai heiwa no inori*, Ichikawa 1982, p.10.

8. Goi, Masahisa, *Hannyashingyō no atarashii kaishaku*, Ichikawa n.d. but 1983.

9. *Heywa*, No. 18, November 1982, inside cover, and many other places. The Japanese text of this summary is worth noting, for it tells us that man is a participatory spirit or a sub-spirit (*wakemitama*) of the "original God". The English version is in general rather free, and it should also be noted that in the last sentence we read "enlightenment" where the Japanese has "true salvation" (*makoto no sukui*).

10. Published posthumously by White Light Association, Ichikawa 1983, this work is described as constituting the "liturgical documents of the Master's White Light Association" (page 1, note). As the selections do not appear to be used liturgically or to be at all suitable for such use, the implication is probably that they represent an authorised core of representative extracts from his otherwise voluminous writings.

11. The address of the headquarters is: Byakkō Shinkōkai, 5-26-27 Nakakokubun, Ichikawa-shi, Chiba-ken 272, Japan.

12. *Sekaikakkoku no sekaiheiwa no inori* (c.f. note 5), p.110.

13. *Ibid.*, p.179.

14. Born in 1941 (and a descendant of the Ryukyuan royal family) Mrs. Saionji is the "Chair Person" of the society (*kaichō*). There is also a president (*rijichō*), Mr. Yosuke Seki (name in western order).

15. Goi, Masahisa, *God and Man*, page 56 (explained in translator's note).

16. Thus described in a Japanese-language promotional postcard from headquarters.

17. *Byakkō*, 11, 1984, p.54. The autobiography referred to was first published by the White Light Association at Ichikawa in 1955.

18. *Ibid.*, p.55.

19. This ceremony is thus in principle similar to the *goma* ceremony in Shingon Buddhism, in which simple prayers written by believers on short lengths of wood are burned in the temple by the priests. In the Shingon case the burning symbolises, at least for the priests, the consuming of the this-worldly attachments which are the object of the petitions. It is not clear whether this dialectic is intended in the burning of Goi-Sensei's postbag.

20. *Ibid.*, p. 40.

21. Goi, Masahisa, *Sekaiheiwa no inori*, Ichikawa 1982, pp.8ff.

22. Ichikawa, n.d. but 1985.

23. Goi, Masahisa, *Zenshū* (13 Vols.), Ichikawa 1980.

Appendix 1: Text referred to at note 9

Man is originally a spirit from God, and not a karmic existence.

He lives under the constant guidance and protection provided by his Guardian Deities and Guardian Spirits.

All of man's sufferings are caused when his wrong thoughts conceived during his past lives up to the present manifest in this world in the process of fading away.

Any affliction, once it has taken shape in this phenomenal world, is destined to vanish into nothingness. Therefore, you should be absolutely convinced that your sufferings will fade away and that from now on your life wil be happier. Even in any difficulty, you should forgive yourself and forgive others; love yourself and love others. You should always perform the acts of love, sincerity and forgiveness and thank your Guardian Deities and Guardian Spirits for their protection and pray for the peace of the world. This will enable you as well as mankind to realize enlightenment.

Appendix 2: The peace sticker in Japanese

世界人類が平和でありますように

Related works by the author of this paper:

1. "Religion and reason in the Japanese experience", in *King's Theological Review* 5:1 (Spring 1982), 14-17.

PART B

THE CONGRESS PROCEEDINGS

1. THE CONTEXT
From Paris 1900 to Sydney 1985

An Essay in Retrospect and Prospect

Professor Eric J. Sharpe

University of Sydney

The first international congress of the history of religions took place in Paris in 1900, the last year of the nineteenth century. At that time Australia was still largely a *terra incognita*, still not a unified nation (it was proclaimed a Commonwealth in 1901), and it is safe to say that not a single one of the Paris delegates banqueting in the Eiffel Tower could possibly have anticipated the holding, eighty-five years later, of another congress banquet in another tower close to the point where that reluctant British rabble Australia calls the "First Fleet" had landed in 1788.

In 1900 Australia was not without interest to the world of scholarship. On the contrary, few parts of the world were studied with more energy and enthusiasm. Not, however, for the sake of anything European settlers were able to contribute; rather because Australia contained the widest possible range of "survivals" — geological, biological and (not least) human — in the light of which to reconstruct the earliest history of the world. All the talk was of totemism, the *alcheringa* and evolution. One suspects that of all the well-bred academic participants at the Paris Congress of 1900, not a single one had ever set foot in (or even contemplated setting foot in) Australia. The Eiffel Tower stood secure; Australia, meantime, being a specimen, an assembly of colonies on the rim of the inhabited earth.

Eighty-five years later the International Association for the History of Religions, still reckoning its ancestry from that pioneer congress in Paris, gathered at the University of Sydney — the first such assembly in the Southern Hemisphere and only the second to meet outside the "North Atlantic Axis". The Paris fathers would no doubt have marvelled.

The International Congress (in whatever subject) is of course a phenomenon belonging to the second half of the twentieth century, and to a world made small by jet travel. But the principle was recognized long before it became practicable: that international communities of specialists need to meet regularly to get to know one another, to compare notes and to appropriate the results of one another's labour. Still, it was not easy. When it took up to a fortnight to cross the Atlantic, and several months to get from Europe to Australia, it was inevitable that even "international" gatherings would be largely local. To achieve anything more required vast effort and a good deal of expense — expense very few could afford.

The first international gatherings of scholars in the field of religion all took place in association with much larger, nationally and commercially financed trade exhibitions — those taking their cue from the London "Great Exhibition" of 1851. Arguably the exhibitions provided only the framework and the opportunity. But behind the scenes there was a deeper connection. The World's Parliament of Religions, which met in Chicago in 1893, was motivated by the belief that the emergent modern world should be given the opportunity to find a modern religion, a religion intelligent, progressive and universal, to which to respond. Chicago 1893 was not altogether unscientific; but its science came in fits and starts, and often was subordinated to an apologetical pragmatism owing more to the marketplace than to the professor's lectern. Four years later, in 1897, a much smaller gathering took place in Stockholm. But here again scholarship emerged in a less than dominant position, even though the assembly designated itself a "Congress of the Science of Religion". The trouble in Stockholm was that its chief organizer, Samuel Fries, was engaged in attempting to turn the Lutheran Church of Sweden in a "liberal" direction, and inevitably what took place in 1897 reflected an internal struggle almost as much as the state of scholarship at the time. This Congress began and ended with prayers and sermons; it was presided over by a Lutheran Bishop; and only one non-Christian scholar was present (he was a Jewish Rabbi, incidentally). So while on the level of intentions it might be argued that our modern sequence of international congresses began at this point, what actually took place there has to be seen in the light of an ongoing struggle between liberal and conservative factions within Protestant Christianity.

Secular France was another matter entirely. Thus when in 1900 *Le Premier Congrès International d'Histoire des Religions* was held in Paris, it was possible to argue that the study of religion had finally escaped from pragmatism, apologetics and party warfare, and emerged into the clear light of science. It had not, of course. But the organizers believed that it had, and that scientific work in the area of religion would no longer need to defer to confessional interests. Albert Réville expressed this ideal in his opening address, and pointed a way into the future: "In spite of all that still separates us from the ideal goal which draws us, the nineteenth century will have the honour of bequeathing to the twentieth, in respect of the History of Religions, a capital which cannot but grow."

The Paris Congress did one other thing: it secured its own succession. Not for another half-century was a permanent international organization created to further a broadly-based non-confessional study of religion. But at least it was determined at this point that congresses should continue to be held at four-yearly intervals, and that each congress should appoint a committee to help arrange the next one. And so the pattern continued — to Basel in 1904, Oxford in 1908 and Leiden in 1912. Then came the colossal upheaval of the first world war, and it was not until 1929 that the sequence could be taken up again, this time in Lund, Sweden (where it was not unnaturally claimed that the enterprise had begun in 1897 in Stockholm). Only one other congress was held, in Brussels, between the wars; this was in 1934. Sixteen years were to elapse before a resumption could take place.

Two things need to be said about this chain of congresses, from 1897 and 1900 to the outbreak of the second world war. The first is that they were to all intents and purposes exclusively European, shuttling as they did back and forth between those university centres where one or other form of *Religionswissenschaft* was taught. The second is that they were trying to be non-confessional, certainly; but the confessions from which they were escaping were those of Protestant Christianity, Lutheran on the one hand, Calvinist on the other. Some of those who took part represented a purely secular point of view; but a fair proportion were liberal Christians, some of whom were no less dogmatic in their way than were the conservatives in theirs. In practice this meant that the congresses (or rather, those who took part in them) were using scholarship for different purposes, one of which was certainly to further the cause of liberal religion. There was absolutely nothing dishonourable about this. But motives were not always clearly stated, and the history of religions enterprise could be viewed — not least by outsiders — from either angle, as furthering either the cause of value-free science (if such exists) or of liberal Christianity on the pattern of Söderblom, Otto and van der Leeuw.

This same ambiguity persisted in the post-war years, as the sequence of international congresses was taken up afresh, by now under the canopy of the

International Association for the History of Religions (founded in 1950). Among the founding fathers of the IAHR, some were most certainly liberal Christians on the "phenomenological" pattern; they included from Holland, G. van der Leeuw and C.J. Bleeker, from Britain, E.O. James, and from Germany by way of America, Joachim Wach. Others again were not. An additional factor was provided by scholars coming in from overwhelmingly Catholic countries, notably Italy. What all shared was a deep desire to keep the study of religion as far as possible separate from questions of personal belief on the one hand, and from ecclesiastical control on the other, the latter being far easier to achieve than the former.

In the 1950s and 1960s tentative moves were made outside Europe — first and most excitingly to Japan in 1958, and then to California in 1965. Asian and African scholars began to attend congresses, though still only in small numbers. The Africans generally were Christians; the Asians generally were not. But the tradition of empirical research continued to be maintained, at least on the official level — though at the same time, the members of the growing number of national societies becoming affiliated with the IAHR were not able to be forced into one mould. By the 1970s, fewer and fewer were confident that purely empirical research in the field of religion was even a possibility, let alone an achievable goal. And in any case, religion itself was becoming more and more a "hot issue" in the wake of the febrile experimentation of the 1960s and the changing patterns of international economics and politics. Many concluded that cool scholarship could not be expected to deal with hot issues — at least not without burning its fingers in the process.

At no point during the period between 1950 and 1985 has the IAHR really occupied a strong position in the world of international scholarship. As a federation of (for the most part) small national societies, meeting collectively only at five-yearly intervals, its activities have centred around the person of whoever has happened to be its General Secretary at any given time. In addition, its stated intentions have been of a very general nature, and in a world of mushrooming specialist conferences and colloquia it has found it hard to create a recognizable profile of its own. This has led to at least one interesting consequence: that of the siphoning off of the most dedicated scholars into more neatly defined societies of specialists, thus leaving much of the field of "comparative religion" (or whatever else it may be called) open to a smallish number of those who prefer not to be specialists — or at least to relate their specialisms to larger issues. Congress themes, too, have changed markedly during the last thirty years — from subjects as historically specific as "The Sacral Kingship" (Rome 1955) to the comparatively vague, or at least flexible, themes prescribed for more recent congresses. The specialist colloquia which formerly took place in non-congress years have been discontinued, along with the *International Bibliography of the History of Religions*. The journal *Numen* survives, on the other hand, along with its series of scholarly supplements, though here again, in face of a level of international competition unknown in 1950.

So we see that the sequence of international congresses which began in Paris in 1900, and of which Sydney 1985 was the most recent, reflects far more than simply the developing concerns of a small number of academics working along the North Atlantic axis. It has a place, albeit a modest place, in intellectual history, chiefly (though not exclusively) that of the geographical West, though a West brought more and more inexorably into contact with the remainder of the world. Also it represents at least part of the "religious" (including the anti-religious) face of the West in the twentieth century. Non-Western involvement in the IAHR and its congresses, with the sole exception so far of Tokyo 1958, has been deplorably small — and that too is part of the overall picture. But where precisely does Australia, and the

Pacific region generally, fit into this picture, and what prompted the IAHR to take such a huge geographical leap in 1985.

* * * * *

Often the history of Australia is represented, not least by Australians, as a history of (among other things) anti-intellectualism. Often this aspect has been overdrawn; but hardly in respect of religion. The everpresent danger of sectarian conflict, chiefly between English and Scottish Protestants on the one hand and Irish Catholics on the other, created, together with the third factor of aggressive secularism, a climate of opinion in Australia in which it was assumed that the study of religion could only be carried on safely within denominational confines. Certainly religion would have to be studied in one sense — for how otherwise could the ministry and priesthood be maintained? — but not as part of a secular university curriculum. Tentative steps were taken in the 1930s to introduce the study of theology into at least some of Australia's universities, on the basis of a consensus concerning non-controversial elements in the curriculum (study of the text of the Bible, church history, and so on); but this was at best a half-hearted measure, and in any case proceeded largely at the undergraduate level — even where a Bachelor of Divinity degree was introduced as a second degree, it was still to all intents and purposes a second undergraduate degree, based entirely on the successful completion of prescribed courses. Anything falling outside this pattern of study had to be pursued overseas or (more commonly) not at all. Certainly there were elements within the Christian churches advocating, and to some extent pursuing, something resembling "comparative religion" as early as the 1920s; some individuals were ultimately able to gain a foothold in the universities (of these, the anthropologist A.P. Elkin may serve as the best example); some university departments found ways to introduce "history of religions" material into their course offerings. But what did not happen before the 1970s was the establishment of independent, non-confessional university departments capable of studying religion as a subject in its own right, independently of the needs of the churches. Thus before the mid-1970s there was lacking in Australia the institutional foundation on which the IAHR, and before it, the congresses, had been able to build in Europe and North America.

However, an institutional basis was created ultimately — though only during the very last phase of IAHR development I have attempted to sketch. In 1970 (which year I am tempted to take as marking the end of the "empirical" phase in IAHR history), the history of religions in Australia was still sustained mainly thanks to the non-university agency of the Charles Strong Trust, in one small journal, the Melbourne-based *Milla-wa-Milla*, and through occasional visits by international lecturers. By 1980 things had changed radically.

Writing as I am from Canada, I am not able to describe in detail the developments of the 1970s, and must content myself with the barest outline. Important new initiatives took place in two centres: at the University of Queensland in Brisbane, where a long-established but inadequate Department of Divinity was reshaped into a Department of Studies in Religion, under the initial leadership of Rev. Eric Pyle, formerly of the University of Glasgow; and at a group of Colleges of Advanced Education (which subsequently became the South Australian CAE) in Adelaide, where Religion Studies were established under the energetic leadership of Norman C. Habel and Victor C. Hayes, among others. To bind the emergent discipline together there was created the Australian Association for the Study of Religions, of which Norman Habel was the first President. Its first national conference took place in 1976 in Adelaide, and its second in 1977 in Brisbane. The tenth Conference coincides with this IAHR Congress, and AASR membership has grown to more than 300.

The University of Sydney entered the field only in 1977, when the present writer arrived from Lancaster to set up a Department of Religious Studies more or less on the Lancaster model. In Sydney too there had been since the late 1930s an institute for the teaching of Christian theology, but unlike the University of Queensland, it was not incorporated into the new department, and still exists as an independent entity (though with some overlap of courses).

By the late 1970s, therefore, the study of religion in Australia was being pursued with energy and dedication by small groups of scholars in all of Australia's major cities, and in numerous universities and colleges. The universities were free of confessional attachments, as were all but the Catholic colleges. This was not to say, on the other hand, that those involved in teaching these various programmes were without theological interests. On the whole rather few could be regarded as "secular" scholars, and many held a form of dual citizenship, being "theological" and "scientific" at the same time. Not all were Christians, of course; some were Hindus and others Jewish; others again — notably on the Orientalist side — sought to maintain a secular stance in face of what some clearly regarded as an undue emphasis on questions of Christian theology. All in all, the positions occupied by Australian scholars in the field by the late 1970s mirrored fairly accurately the divisions observable anywhere in the world — albeit on a much smaller scale.

The decision to hold the fifteenth congress of the International Association for the History of Religions in Australia no doubt came as a surprise to those who had grown used to holding their five-yearly congresses on one or other side of the North Atlantic. The proposal was put to the IAHR Executive on August 17, 1980 — at which time the Australian Association was not even officially affiliated to the IAHR (the affiliation was formalized a couple of days later)! Had there been any other offers, then it is doubtful whether the Sydney proposal would have been accepted. But there were not; and it was. Those of us who had gone to Winnipeg from Sydney (Garry Trompf, Arvind Sharma and myself) bearing the offer emerged both dazed and apprehensive.

What factors had influenced the decision? One was certainly the international economic climate, which by 1980 had ruled out the holding of international congresses (particularly those involving the "poorer" academics in the humanities) in many centres. In some countries, security had become a problem. Hence at the time few national societies and associations were willing to commit themselves to the holding of even moderately sized academic gatherings too far in advance, since much might happen in five years. Another factor working in our favour concerned the "image" Australia had acquired since the expansive early 1970s. This was practically impossible to quantify, but at least Australia had been brought to world attention through the film industry, Patrick White's Nobel Prize, the opening of the Sydney Opera House and the vague sense that Australia might yet prove to be a refuge from the ills besetting much of the rest of the world. There was an additional personal factor. I had been Acting General Secretary of the IAHR from 1971 to 1975, and my wife and I had organized the 1975 IAHR Congress at Lancaster. Thus the prospect of Sydney, though geographically remote by North Atlantic standards, was less daunting to the IAHR than it might otherwise have been.

In short, whether or not all these factors actually were in the minds of the IAHR leadership in 1980, there were several reasons why the holding of an international congress of the history of religions in Australia was an attractive prospect. Ten years earlier it could not have been contemplated. At the time of the founding of the IAHR in 1950 it would have seemed on all counts hardly less unrealistic than the holding of a congress in Tashkent or Timbuktu. In 1980 it was both desirable and (on the surface at least) feasible.

* * * * *

The securing of the 1985 congress was one thing. The actual setting in motion of the machinery for its realization was another thing entirely. We in Sydney had not really anticipated that our offer would be accepted, and we had made no preliminary enquiries or costings of any kind. We had no guaranteed finance to cover initial expenses. In 1981 the Vice-Chancellor (Sir Bruce Williams) on whose initiative the Department of Religious Studies in Sydney had been set up, left Australia to take up another post in Britain. Somewhat belatedly, at about the same time the financial troubles that had beset universities elsewhere in the world began to be felt also in Australia. In August 1981 I returned to Australia after a year spent in Sweden, feeling that the offer to host the congress had been a grandiose gesture which ought not to have been made in the first place, and which could never be brought to a successful completion.

That we were able to move ahead at all was due to one totally unexpected stroke of good fortune (or the intervention of Divine Providence), namely, the making over by Sister Judith Hill of the James Macartney Hill Bequest Fund to the Sydney Department of Religious Studies. Without the Bequest, the congress could not have taken place. Dr. Peter Masefield was engaged as Organizing Secretary. The Charles Strong Trust allocated a sum of money toward the publication of this present volume. The University of Sydney granted the use of university facilities practically rent free. The show, as they say, was on the road.

The selection of the theme of the congress, "Religion and Identity", was largely the responsibility of the present writer. It was, as it happens, a second choice. The first, provisional theme had been "Holy Ground", and this would have opened up a discussion of such matters as religion and territory, the promised land, Aboriginal sacred sites, and much else of importance; whether the decision to change the theme was a wise one, I am still not sure. But changed it was. Professor Hans Mol's "Religion and Identity" monographs came into my hands at a moment of indecision. And having in a manner of speaking borrowed the theme from him, it seemed only fitting to ask Professor Mol to deliver a keynote address on the first morning of the congress. Some participants were a little afraid that the theme on which we finally settled would be too "sociological" for a history of religions congress. It could hardly be denied, on the other hand, that the history of religions itself (as a blanket term to cover the study of religion in all its vast variety) had become far more aware of the social sciences since the 1960s. The ghosts of some of the founding fathers of the IAHR might not have approved; but there was little that could be done about that.

In some ways the Congress proved desperately difficult to organize at such a vast distance from the places where most of the participants actually lived. Postal services were slow and sometimes erratic, and sometimes the better part of a month could elapse between the asking of a fairly simple question and the receiving of an answer. There were miscalculations and misunderstandings. Communications occasionally broke down. The back-up organization in Sydney proved inadequate to cope with the last-minute floods of inquiries. And when the week of the Congress itself finally arrived, participants from various parts of the world came bringing their unique problems with them — lost luggage, lost money, inadequate money, ill-health, language difficulties, accommodation wrongly booked or not booked at all, and the like. But of course all these were only to be expected in general, though many could not have been foreseen in detail. Some of the problems were solved, while others were not. Much the same could no doubt have been said about every one of the IAHR's congresses hitherto.

It is practically impossible for any one person to gain an overview of any academic gathering which functions in a number of "sections" simultaneously. The academic standard appears to have been high, with an unusually high proportion of papers delivered on the congress theme. As is usual in IAHR gatherings, the world of religion was covered in all its vastness. More than one visitor, however, remarked on the curious fact that Australian scholars appeared to have little interest in Australian Aboriginal religion. There were the Charles Strong Senior and Junior Lectures delivered in the Great Hall as "plenaries", both of them on Aboriginal themes; but otherwise there was practically nothing. It is hard to explain this in a few words, except to say that Aboriginal studies in Australia have become almost the sole prerogative of anthropologists, historians of religions meantime being too aware of the mistakes of the past to want to perpetuate or repeat them. One group of congress participants was taken by a Sydney anthropologist, Dr. John Clegg, to view Aboriginal rock art north of the city. Those who came to Sydney expecting the Aboriginal theme to stand high on the history of religions agenda, on the other hand, went away disappointed. The omission was not deliberate; rather it reflected the fact that Australian scholars in the religion field have generally approached it from some angle other than that of anthropology. There may however be a lesson here for the future.

At intervals during the past twenty or so years, questions have been asked — or rather, the same question has been asked again and again — "why the history of religions?" Why, among all the names and designations that might be chosen for the non-confessional study of religion, should "the history of religions" have been adopted in the first place, and why, in the light of all that has happened since 1950, does the IAHR still carry it? To this the usual answer given is that since what took place last week can only be recorded and evaluated with the help of some form of historical method, history is the one approach central enough to serve as a counterweight to confessional theology. Historians are historians, certainly; but so too in a sense are sociologists, philologists, anthropologists and even psychologists historians. Without pursuing the argument further, no one could fail to note how much of the Sydney Congress was devoted to themes and discussions which extended the historical approach into areas which certainly were not present in earlier IAHR congresses. The "Women and Religion" symposium organized by Penelope McKibbin was historical and contemporary; so too were the sections on religion and the arts and religion and literature. The sociological and psychological sections involved methods and approaches which once would have been called no more than "sub-disciplines", but which are now entirely autonomous. The anthropologists present maintained their own characteristic identities, as other than historians; while the methodological section devoted itself to the "how to" questions that are so hard to avoid in these days. There was one rather special commemorative symposium, that organized by Arvind Sharma to celebrate the 200th anniversary of the first translation of the *Bhagavadgita* into English — as it turned out, the first of several to take place in different parts of the world. Looking at all this variety, some must have wondered at a historical designation which was often more implicit than explicit. In the event, however, no one at this congress challenged the organization's title — though some had threatened to do. Had they done so, it would have been instructive to see what might have been proposed in its stead, particularly in a country in which four centres of the study of religion have opted for four different labels — comparative religion (Melbourne), studies in religion (Brisbane), religion studies (Adelaide) and religious studies (Sydney).

The Sydney Congress revealed, as have many other such gatherings over the past couple of decades, the almost infinite variety possible in the field of religion and its study. The usual dutiful attempts were made by a proportion of those present to impose system on that variety — though one fears with no more success than normally attends such ventures. Still, perhaps, the crunch comes at the point at which religion in particular meets religion in general, where the devotee meets the investigator and the desire to change the world (always for the better) meets the modest wish to observe and record. Prior to the developments of the last decade or so, Australia has known the former, the latter remaining a *rara avis*. Perhaps then for Australia's part the Sydney Congress might have exhibited to the community at large an assembly of rare birds in concentration — except that, as I have tried to say, the climate of opinion among students of religion is presently moving beyond observation and interpretation into application.

Nevertheless I believe that the XVth Congress of the IAHR will prove to have been of importance. Certainly it was important in placing the Pacific Region on the map, where international scholarship is concerned. Significantly, the Congress was followed by other conferences in the area, in Brisbane and in New Zealand (though the New Zealanders are still pondering whether or not to affiliate with the IAHR), and the cumulative effect of these gatherings certainly has had an impact. Also in a part of the world where physical isolation is still a problem, it helped to create contacts, and turn names into faces. But most of all the bringing together of students of religion belonging to different religious, national and intellectual traditions without trying to pour them all into the same mould or stretch them on the same Procrustean bed may have been significant to our part of the world. All honour to those who during the past decade have been labouring to establish the academic study of religion, free from ecclesiastical control and on a par with other studies in the humanities, in the universities and colleges of the Pacific Region. Their greatest challenge has been to lodge their ideals in the minds of the general public. And their greatest difficulty has been connected with their sense of isolation — physically from the rest of the world, intellectually from the world of "religious" opinion around them. The holding of this congress will have been of value if it has helped to sustain their efforts into another decade.

2. RECORD OF FORMAL EVENTS

Opening Addresses

Sir Hermann Black

Opening Speech by the Chancellor of the University of Sydney, Sir Hermann Black, M.Ec., Hon. D. Litt (Newcastle), F.C.I.S. (Abridged for this volume)

President Schimmel, Distinguished Guests, Ladies and Gentlemen:

It is a pleasure to bid you welcome, and I add my appreciation as Chancellor that you honour The University of Sydney by choosing to inaugurate your Congress here, in this Great Hall.

This Hall is the centre of the academic ceremonies of this university and is a replica, to two-thirds the size, of Westminster Hall in London. You will notice the heavenly host of angels aloft. I hasten to add that in the distant past examinations were conducted in this Hall and many a student, myself included, often looked despairingly aloft to those angels for a little divine inspiration in answering the questions — only to discover that their hearts were made, if not of stone, then at least of first-class Australian hardwood. The students therefore passed on their merit without divine intervention or were damned with failure for their sins, without divine mercy.

Each of you comes to this Congress with what the great Scottish economist, Adam Smith, called an "invisible baggage" — the ideas, conceptions, theories and insights which are the furniture of your minds. This invisible baggage you will all open, mind to mind, in free discussion, and this means that we here in Australia will be especially enriched by your presence and by that discourse ... If I now thank you for that in advance, I do so in complete confidence that so it will transpire.

You will be engaged in what the celebrated philosopher, David Hume, called "fermentations", namely, those intellectual exchanges which bring theory and explanation into assessment by fact, and in which implications are drawn and their logic put under scrutiny. Though it was said long ago of the Oxford Movement in Christian thought, I guess you will all be engaged here in "spiritual mixed bathing".

It is, I believe, one of the never-ending charms of historical study and of the work of the historian, that it is never finally done ... Scientific inquiry is kept alive by continuous questioning ... "All truths wait in all things", wrote Walt Whitman, "They neither hasten their own delivery nor resist it."

This is a secular university, not entitled to preach or require the practice of a particular religion. In the middle of the 19th Century, when the Government of the then colony of New South Wales was moving to establish this, the first and oldest of the nineteen universities of Australia, there was much turbulence of thought about the idea that it should be established without religious tests for students and staff.

One bishop of those times denounced the University as "godless", and another group called the liberalism of the day "intolerant". A Roman Catholic journal forecast that the University would chiefly benefit a personage called "the infidel". Nevertheless, despite all these dire warnings, happily we have instead of our infidel our own Professor Sharpe in the Chair of Religious Studies, and I know with what anticipation and zeal he has worked for the organisation and success of this Congress ...

Some thirty-five years ago, Bertrand Russell passed his judgment on Australia during a visit here, and both parts of what he said are still valid. We were, he said, "a nation of doers", but he hoped for "a little more emphasis on the contemplative virtues". Your assembly here to discuss the history of religions will, I hope, yield a double harvest. First, I hope that it deepens and widens our understanding in this most sensitive area. Second, I hope it will afford this country, by demonstrated example, encouragement to pursue a manner of thought that will help Australians to "know themselves", thereby the better to understand our own historical development, and so promote the contemplative virtues.

Australian scholars are greatly encouraged by this Congress being located here in what was once called "terra incognita" ... That you have come the long journey to these shores to examine the religious dimension of the human story, la condition humaine, means that as I declare again our welcome to you, I also declare our gratitude as I salute the opening of this Congress with every good wish for its success.

Dr Annemarie Schimmel

Opening Address by the President of the International Association for the History of Religions, Dr Annemarie Schimmel, Harvard University/University of Bonn. (Transcribed)

Chancellor, Mr. Vice-Chancellor, Dear Colleagues:

Let me first express my gratitude to the Australian Organizing Committee, to the Australian Association for the Study of Religions and to the authorities of the University of Sydney for kindly inviting us here to Australia — a place which, I am sure, is for many of you as strange and new as it is for me. Only someone who has been involved in the organization of such a conference, embracing more than 400, perhaps 500 people, knows the enormous amount of work involved. Therefore we are grateful to be in the hands of our Australian colleagues who are trying everything to make us feel at home.

For me, if I may say something personal, it is a great experience to attend this conference for a very simple reason: I think I may be the only one in this illustrious gathering who has attended all the conferences from the foundation of the present International Association in Amsterdam in 1950!

Amsterdam had the great personality of Gerardus Van der Leeuw presiding and guiding us in our first steps into the wide world; then Rome, and the name of Professor Perrazzoni is remembered; then Marburg with its very special charm and Professor Heiler's never-ceasing enthusiasm. Then, in 1965, our first steps in a new direction with a conference in Claremont, California. Only those who were at Claremont know of the tensions and friction which evolved between the representatives of the more old-fashioned school of thought and those who wanted a new direction in our field. Then came Stockholm and Lancaster, most lovable memories, followed by another step across the Atlantic to Winnipeg, a conference which, as I may say, turned out to be highly interesting and was graced by the first presence in such a meeting, of scholars from mainland China.

Many of those who participated in these conferences are no longer with us. The great names of the previous years and decades are no longer here. And I may remember now fondly one of our great scholars who had served on the committee from 1950 onwards, namely, Professor Bleeker of Amsterdam, whom we lost two years ago. I'm sure he would have been happy to be here with us.

Seeing the history of these conferences makes one feel how tremendously our field has expanded: from the traditional ways of the history of religion, phenomenology of religion and perhaps a little bit of sociology of religion, completely new areas have been discovered. And when one reads the most recent publications about methodology, which lead us into the fields of biology or modern technology, one sees that our field is apparently endless, and needs many more workers. I am, therefore, particularly happy to see that the Sydney Conference, according to the Program, brings a great number of younger colleagues who will share with us their experiences, and their studies in fields like the Aboriginal Australian religion. I am, as an Islamicist, particularly happy to see that the Islamic section, which was practically non-existent in Amsterdam and grew only slowly over the decades, is well represented here. And, as a woman, I am of course happy to see that we have a good number of women scholars who are going to talk about various aspects of history and psychology and theology of religion, even though we do not have here — although we did have in Winnipeg — a special section on Women and Religion ...[1]

For all of us, with the exception of course of those lucky enough to live here, Sydney has been a very far away place; and I must say that when I woke up this morning and looked out of my window and saw that the sun was rising again in the East, I was consoled because, according to a tradition of the Prophet Muhammad, it is said that the door of repentance is open until the sun rises in the West! So even here, the sun rises in the East. And not only the door of repentance is open, but also the door of hope and the door of work.

It seems to me, then, that this conference in the southern hemisphere will bring — and this is my hope and wish — many new ways to approach the great mystery which we call by the name of religion, a mystery which generations of scholars have tried to understand and which more generations of scholars will be trying to understand in the future.

And now, with best wishes, along with my thanks to our Australian colleagues, I declare this Congress open.

---

1. See, however, pp.275f below [Ed.]

The Congress Program

PLENARY SESSIONS AND SPECIAL EVENTS (1985)

OPENING CEREMONY
Great Hall, Sydney University, Sunday, August 18, 8pm.
(See below for Opening Speeches by the Chancellor of the University and the President of the IAHR)

VICE-CHANCELLOR'S RECEPTION
Great Hall, Sunday, August 18, 9pm.

OPENING ADDRESS BY HANS MOL
Great Hall, Monday, August 19, 9am.
(Included in this volume, above)

CHARLES STRONG SENIOR LECTURE by Peter Willis, "Colonial Australia and Aboriginal Religion"
Great Hall, Monday, August 19, 4pm.
(Printed by the Charles Strong Trust and available from Dr Robert Crotty, South Australian College of Advanced Education — Salisbury, S.A., Australia 5109.

CHARLES STRONG JUNIOR LECTURE by Tony Swain, "On Understanding Australian Aboriginal Religion"
Great Hall, Tuesday, August 20, 4pm.
(Available from Dr Robert Crotty, as above)

WAYANG PURWA PERFORMANCE
The Rite of Rojo Suyo. A Javanese Shadow Play
Great Hall, Monday, August 19, 8pm.
Dalang (Puppeteer): Panut Darmoko of Nganjuk, Java.
Gamelan (Musical) Assistant: Hardjodiroko Soegito
Invocatory Dancer: Yanti Suhartono
Compere: Ratih Hardjono
Supported by a Grant from UNESCO funds.

ALTAR OF FIRE
Great Hall, Tuesday, August 20, 8pm.
A film on the world's oldest surviving ritual, by Frits Staal.

CONGRESS BANQUET
Summit Restaurant, Australia Square
Thursday, August 22, 6-10pm.
(This is the world's largest revolving restaurant, located on the 47th Floor of Sydney's second tallest building)

IAHR GENERAL ASSEMBLY
Great Hall, Friday, August 23, 10am.
At the conclusion of the business of the Assembly, Addresses were given by the outgoing Secretary-General (Professor Zwi Werblowsky), the incoming Secretary-General (Michael Pye) and the President (Annemarie Schimmel).

BUSINESS MEETINGS
IAHR Executive Committee (Out-going) August 18, 11am.
IAHR International Meeting (Out-going) August 18, 2pm.
Sectional Co-ordinators' Meeting, August 18, 4pm.

AUSTRALIAN ASSOCIATION FOR THE STUDY OF RELIGIONS (AASR):
Annual General Meeting, August 22, 1985.
IAHR Executive Committee (In-coming) August 23.
IAHR International Committee (In-coming) August 23.

(It is anticipated that the Executive Officers of these Associations and Committees will circularise all relevant memberships with the Minutes of these meetings, as well as those of the IAHR General Assembly).

SOCIAL PROGRAM
The lively and attractive Social Program associated with the Congress included the following items:
Complimentary Harbour Cruise (Sydney Harbour); Sydney Opera House Performances; Excursions
to The Blue Mountains and Jenolan Caves, Canberra, Hunter Valley Vineyards, Aboriginal Rock Engravings at Devil's Rock, Northern Beaches, Southern Beaches.

OF GENERAL INTEREST
An Exhibition of Michael Onken's Paintings. Wine Tasting. Congress Book Exhibition.

3. THE SECTIONAL PROGRAM
of the 15th IAHR Congress, Sydney, 1985

Section co-ordinators have confirmed that the following program of papers and presentations is the one that actually took place, i.e., programmed papers that were not given have been excluded and late additions to the program have been included.

Section (and Co-ordinator)	*Number of papers read in each section*
1 African Religions (Etherington)	13
2 Anthropology and Sociology of Religion (Mol)	18
3 Art and Religion (Moore)	13
4 Australia, Oceania and Melanesia (Trompf)	8
5 Buddhism (Masefield, Harrison)	18
6 Christianity (Jack and Cahill)	27
7 Comparative and Phenomenological Studies (Wiebe)	16
8 East Asian Religion (Rule)	9
9 Indian Religions (Barz and Bailey)	24
10 Indonesia and South East Asia (Quinn)	4
11 Islam (Shboul)	18
12 Judaism (Crown)	10
13 Literature and Religion (Tulip)	12
14 Methodology and Hermeneutics (Wiebe)	19
15 Near Eastern and Mediterranean Antiquity (Jobling and Sharpe)	17
16 Philosophy of Religion (Dockrill)	12
17 Psychology of Religion (Hutch)	13
18 Religion, Ethics and Society (Coffey)	7
	259
Apauruseya Panel (Bailey, Barz)	6
Bhagavadgita Symposium (Sharma)	7
Symposium on Women and Religion (McKibbin)	6
	278

AFRICAN RELIGIONS

Co-ordinator: Dr N Etherington, University of Adelaide, Australia

Theme: **Religion and Identity (1) — in the multi-ethnic role**

J K Olupona, University of Ife
"Religion and varieties of identity in Nigeria"

J Hodgson, University of Cape Town
"Sacraments, symbols and identity among black people in South Africa"

J P Kiefnan, University of Natal
"The formation of new black religious identity in South Africa"

Theme: **Religion and Identity (2) — fragmenting or binding together new states**

A B Van Fossen, Griffith University
"Ritual murder, polity and identity in Swaziland"

W E van Beek, State University of Utrecht
"Identity management in two African religions: The cases of the Kapsiki and the Dogon"

Theme: **Religion and Identity (3) — the use of symbols in "identity management"**

S P Battestini, Georgetown University
"The sacred ukara cloth as a sign of identity/alterity in South-Eastern Nigeria"

J G Platvoet, Katholieke Theologische Hogeschool, Utrecht
"Cool shade, peace and power: The Akan gyedua (tree of reception) as an instrument of identity management among the Akan peoples of Southern Ghana"

J G Platvoet, Katholieke Theologische Hogeschool, Utrecht
"The Domankoma/Abonsamkomfo (anti-witchcraft) cult in Asante in 1879–1880 as a 'Puritan' movement"

Theme: **Religion in Everyday Life (1) — social control**

A D Rogers, Dorset Institute of Higher Education
"Human prudence and implied divine sanctions in Malagasy proverbial wisdom"

R Hackett, Georgetown University
"Religious encounters of the third kind: Spiritual technology in modern Nigeria"

Theme: **Religion in Everyday Life (2) — health and healing**

J O Awolalu, University of Ibadan
"Scapegoatism in Yoruba traditional religion"

N Etherington, University of Adelaide
"Missionary doctors and African healers in mid-Victorian South Africa"

S Onibere, University of Ife
"The Udiaye ceremony"

ANTHROPOLOGY AND SOCIOLOGY OF RELIGION

Co-ordinator: Professor Hans Mol, McMaster University

Theme: **Australasia**

E Kolig, University of Otago
"Post-contact religious movements in Australian aboriginal society"

K Dempsey, La Trobe University
"Ministers in a country town: Power, ministerial styles and identity"

D Turner, University of Toronto
"Who is fallen now?"

H Loiskandl, University of Queensland
"National clergy, tradition and Melanesian identity"

M Allen, University of Sydney
"Male identity and the power of ritual-boar sacrifices in North Vanuatu"

M Samra, Sydney University
"The development of Sephardi identity in Sydney, Australia"

Theme: **Asia**

S Gopalan, National University of Singapore
"Personal identity and the Indian caste structure"

Theme: **Modernisation and Cults**

R Chagnon, Université du Québec à Montréal
"Religion and Identity: New religious movements in Québec"

I Manukata, Sophia University
*"A paradigm-construction toward a theory of comparative cosmology
— a study based on the world-view of Japanese fishermen"*

Theme: **South America**

R Ireland, La Trobe University
*"Varieties of personal and corporate traditions in Brazil: some
political consequences"*

L Sullivan, University of Missouri-Columbia
"Local theories of the construction of anthropos"

Theme: **U.S.A., Britain and South Africa**

P E Hammond, University of California
*"The fate of religious liberalism: Does liberal American Protestantism
have a future?"*

K Knott, University of Leeds
"Ethnic minority religions in Britain"

G C Oosthuizen, University of Zululand
*"The African independent churches (AIC) in the context of 'becoming
modern'"*

Theme: **U.S.A. and Trinidad**

A Geertz, University of AArhus
"Ritual person among the Hopi Indians of Arizona"

S Vertovec, Oxford University
"Ethnic identity, religious pluralism, and syncretism in rural Trinidad"

Theme: **Indo-Europeans**

P Buchholz, University of South Africa
*"Religious foundations of group identity in prehistoric Europe:
The Germanic peoples"*
A V Williams, University of Sussex
"The real Zoroastrian dilemma"

ART AND RELIGION

Co-ordinator: Professor Albert C Moore, University of Otago

Theme: **History, Comparison and Theory**

J Y Pentikäinen, University of Helsinki
"Myths on rocks — on the religious message of Finnish rock paintings"
G B Samuel, University of Newcastle
"Art and Religion: The dialectic of play and structure"

Theme: **Indian Sub-continent**

H D Smith, Syracuse University
"Popular Hindu poster art"

Theme: **Islam and the Middle East**

G Aidun, Brandon University
"Mishkin-Qalam"

Theme: **Religion and Modern Artists**

D Apostolos-Cappadona, George Washington University
"The artistic language of the sacred in the work of Mircea Eliade"
A C Moore, University of Otago
"Religion, magic and modernity in the art of Klee"

Theme: **India and Africa**

W H McLeod, University of Otago
"Popular Sikh Art"

Theme: **Australia and India**

J Clegg, University of Sydney
"Australian prehistoric pictures as evidence about prehistoric religion"
P Kumar
"Tribal religion and art of South Rajasthan"

Theme: **Religion, space and dance**

R B Pilgrim, Syracuse University
"The arts of Ma: religio-aesthetic values and cultural identity in Japan"
S N Hammond, University of Hawaii
*"Dance in early New England: Religious accommodation and religious
censorship"*

Theme: **Religion and Music, West Africa**

A Adegbite, University of Ife
  "The concept of sound in traditional African religious music"

J Uzoigwe, University of Ife
  "The concept of immortality in Igbo ritual music"

AUSTRALIA, OCEANIA AND MELANESIA

Co-ordinator: Dr Garry W Trompf, University of Sydney

Theme: **Melanesia**

E Mantovani, The Melanesian Institute
  "Mipela Simbu! The pig festival and the Simbu's identity"

J Pouwer, University of Nijmegen
  (Title not supplied)

G W Trompf, University of Sydney
  "Melanesian 'cargo cults' and the quest for identity"

J May, Melanesian Council of Churches
  "Christian Fundamentalism and Melanesian identity"

Theme: **Australasia and Polynesia**

B Elsmore, Victoria University of Wellington
  "The Taiaha and the Testament — Maori religious movements"

J Irwin, Knox College
  "From dependence to autonomy — an outline of the development of the Presbyterian Maori Mission in New Zealand from 1843 to 1955"

J Siikala, University of Helsinki
  "Mythical paths to Christian church"

H V C Harris, McAuley College
  "The Gods of Oz: Ritual in Australian contexts"

BUDDHISM

Co-ordinators: Dr Paul Harrison, University of Canterbury

Dr Peter Masefield, University of Sydney

Theme: **Buddhism in China and Japan**

A Snodgrass, University of Sydney
  "The identity of man, stupa, Buddha and cosmos in Japanese Shingon Buddhism"

J M Kitigawa, University of Chicago
  "Honji suijaku as a religious experience of the Japanese"
  (read in the absence of the author by L Lam-Easton)

T Nagashima, National Diet Library
  "The teaching of the Tsung-men Shih kuei lun (the Treatise of Ten Rules of Zen sect)"

Theme: **Buddhism in Thai Society**

D Gosling, World Council of Churches
*"Thailand's bareheaded doctors — the role of Thai Buddhist monks
in primary health care"*

Theme: **Tantric Buddhism**

D Tempelman
"A study of Buddhist tantric hagiography"

E Stutchbury, Australian National University
"Chopa of Karsha — Drukpa Kargya practitioners in the Western Himalaya"

Theme: **The Buddhism of the Lotus Sutra**

C Naylor, University of Sydney
*"The importance of historical accuracy in assessing the claims of Nichiren;
the silence of the Gods and the confusion of Nichiren"*

T Kubo, International Institute for Buddhist Studies
*"The importance of trust as elucidated in the Lotus Sutra — with
reference to adhimukti and sraddha"*

Theme: **Buddhism in its Encounter with Other Traditions**

H-J Klimkeit, University of Bonn
"Jesus' entry into parinirvana: Manichean identity in Buddhist Central Asia"

P Masefield, University of Sydney
"The Muni and the Moonies"

Theme: **Buddhist Psychology**

R Gross, University of Wisconsin-Eau Claire
"Initiation and oral tradition: Tibetan Vajrayana Buddhism"

P Fenner, Deakin University
"A therapeutic contextualisation of Buddhist consequential analysis"

Theme: **The Historical Development of Buddhism**

A Galla, Australian National University
"Early Buddhism: A regional profile from Amaravati and Nagarjunakonda"

P Harrison, University of Canterbury
*"Who gets a ride in the Great Vehicle? Self-image and identity among the
followers of the early Mahayana"*

Theme: **Buddhist Theories of Personality**

K Werner, University of Durham
"Personal Identity in the Upanisads and Buddhism" .

Theme: **Buddhology and Buddhist Literature**

P Almond, University of Queensland
"The Buddha in the West, 1800–1860"

A Yuyama, International Institute for Buddhist Studies
"An appraisal of the history of Sanskrit studies in Japan"

A Hazelwood, Australian National University
"Late Pali Buddhist Literature"

CHRISTIANITY

Co-ordinators: Professor Ian Jack, University of Sydney

Mr Anthony Cahill, University of Sydney

J Du Preez, University of Stellenbosch
"The significance of John Calvin's 'Institutio' for a biblical theologia religionum"

G Lafleche, Université de Montréal
"La spiritualité des Jesuites de la Nouvelle-France: l'interprétation de visions de Jean de Brebeuf (1640)"

P Bilaniuk, University of Toronto
"Search for religious identity by Eastern Slavs, 9th–12th centuries"

R Chambers, Riverina College of Advanced Education
"Churchmen and nationalism in 19th century Russia"

G Wiessner, Göttingen University
"Religion and identity: A problem of Iranian Christianity"

A Sharf, Bar-Ilan University
"The Armenian agape"

N Kihara, Kinki University
"Some problems of Christianity in Japan"

C Brown, University of Canterbury
"The churches and 'cultural imperialism': The New Zealand experience"

B Thiering, University of Sydney
"The Qumran origins of the Christian church"

P-H Poirier, Université Laval
"Judaisme et christianisme dans la lettre à Diognète"

A Brent, James Cook University
"Towards a concept of an ethnic episcopate"

M Garner and K Luscombe, Newmarket Baptist Church
"The new pluralism and identity formation: An inner-urban case study"

W Campbell, Selly Oak Colleges
"Religious identity and ethnic origin in the earliest Christian communities"

C Manus, University of Ife
"Apostolic suffering (2 Cor. 6:4–10): The sign of Christian existence and identity in Pauline churches"

G Lease, University of California
"Bismark, Hohenlohe and the Vatican: The beginnings of modernism"

M Agnew, Villanova University
"Sacrifice as a mechanism of sacralization: Roman Catholic liturgical reforms since 1925"

P Gifford, University of Zimbabwe
"The almost normative status of a purely contingent theological tradition"

A Wettstein, Rollins College
"Self-knowledge and knowledge of God in Jacob Boehme: The problematic of a Protestant mysticism"

M Lattke, University of Queensland
"Rudolf Bultmann on Rudolf Otto"

D Wetherell, Deakin University
"Oxford defended — Anglican responses to dissenting attacks on church
privileges 1760–1854"

R Hind, University of Sydney
"William Wilberforce, his religion and Britain's national identity"

G Pratt, University of Waikato
"Trinity in history: The Christian identity of God"

U Berner, Göttingen University
"Das Synkretismus-Problem in Christlicher Theologie"

D Dockrill, University of Newcastle
"William Sherlock and English trinitarian theology 1660–1697"

D Crawford, University of Sydney
"Church courts, the parish and the individual in England: 1500–1558"

W Principe, Pontifical Institute of Mediaeval Studies
"Catholicity: A threat or a help to identity?"

P Staples, State University of Utrecht
"Denominational identities versus ecumenical utopias"

COMPARATIVE AND PHENOMENOLOGICAL STUDIES
Co-ordinator: Dr Don Wiebe, University of Toronto

Theme: **Change and Identity in Religion**

P Slater, University of Toronto
"The Buddha and the Christ: Focus of identity and change"

N King, University of California
"Egeria, Fa Hsien and Ibn Battuta: Search for identity through pilgrimage"

Theme: **Religion and Identity**

H Pernet, Switzerland
"Masque rituel et identité"

H Bürkle, University of Munich
"Phänomene Religiöser Inkulturation als Ausdruck der Suche
nach 'Identität'"

Theme: **Self-Identity and Self-Critique:
The Christian Tradition**

P McKenzie, Leicester University
"The phenomenological study of christianity and the problem of
self-identity"

J Ramisch, Carleton University
"Religion and gender identity: The use of contemporary experience to
question the Christian tradition"

Theme: **Comparative Studies**

D Bradley, Duke University
"Prophet, guru, sage; Three paradigms of the hierophant"

U Bianchi
A presentation (Untitled)

L Lam-Easton, St Lawrence University
  "Changing Chinese perspectives on classification systems"
R Crotty, South Australian College of Advanced Education
  "Systems of religious knowledge"

Theme: **Third-World Religions — two studies**

J Roberts, Eastern Baptist Theological Seminary
  "A critical comparison of Afro-American and African Religions/Theologies"

C Starkloff, Regis College
  "Finding out who we are: The recovery of cultural integrity in new tribal religious movements in North America"

Theme: **Values and the Historian of Religions**

H Martin, Graduate Theological Union/Dominican School (Berkeley)
  "A hierarchy of values in Genesis: A problem of interpretation"

S Nigosian, University of Toronto
  "Religion in the global age"

Theme: **Scriptures and Theosophy**

R Fernhout, Free University of Amsterdam
  "Nathan the Unwise: Lessing's view on holy scriptures as a correlate of loss of religious identity"

T Ahlbäck, The Donner Institute for Research in Religious and Cultural History
  "Theosophy and socialism in Finland: An unsuccessful coup d'état at the beginning of the century"

EAST ASIAN RELIGIONS

Co-ordinator: Dr Paul Rule, La Trobe University

Theme: **Japanese Religion**

E Adams, University of Hawaii at Hilo
  "The religious elements of Japanese identity"

Michael Pye
  "National and International Identity in a Japanese religion"

Theme: **Taoism**

Y-H Jan, McMaster University
  "Cultural borrowing and religious identity — case study of the Taoist religious codes"

B Tsui, Chinese University of Hong Kong
  "Descriptions of the immortals and the Taoist identity"

S Mackie, University of Sydney
  "Women in Shangqing Taoism"

Theme: **Popular Religion**

H J Kok, University of Sydney
  "Symbols and rites in relation to the Seven Spirits of the Chinese"

Theme: **(Confucianism and) Neo-Confucianism**

Julia Ching
"Who are the ancient Confucian sages?"

P Jiang, Macquarie University
"Tien-jen ho-yi: The union of Heaven and Man as the goal of self-cultivation in Confucian tradition"

Paul Rule, La Trobe University
"Neo-Confucianism: Theism, atheism or neither?"

INDIAN RELIGIONS

Co-ordinators: Dr G Bailey, La Trobe University

Dr R Barz, Australian National University

Theme: **Ghandi (1)**

J Jordens, Australian National University
"Mahatma Ghandi and religious pluralism"

P D Bishop, Brighton Polytechnic
"The positive achievements and dire consequences of Ghandi's appeal to Hindu India"

J Wilson, University of Canterbury
"Ghandi's God — a substitute for the British Empire?"

Theme: **Indian Religion Outside India**

J Holm, Homerton College
"Hindu children growing up in an alien culture — a study of families in Cambridge, England"

Theme: **Bhakti**

M Thiel-Horstmann, University of Bonn
"In defeat of time: The semantics of vigil in a North Indian sect"

R Barz, Australian National University
"The Nepali Bhanubhak Ramayan and its place in the Ramayan tradition"

S Vertovec, Oxford University
"Trends in the development of Hinduism in Trinidad"

M Klaiman, La Trobe University
"Vaishnavism, Brahmanism, and Hindu identity in medieval Bengal"

K Young, McGill University
"Antal: God's slave as she who rules"

Theme: **The Puranas**

G Bailey, La Trobe University
"The function of the Devasuryayudda theme in the Vamanapurana"

A Couture, Université de Sherbrooke
"Akura et la tradition Bhagavata selon le Harivamsa"

C Hospital, Queen's University
"Ravana and South Indian identity: The mythological background"

Theme: **Sikhism**

W H McLeod, University of Otago
"*The Sikh Rahit — the Khalsa code of conduct*"

R Jayaraman, University of New England
"*Sikhism and caste: A sociologial analysis of Sikh religious ideology
and its relationship to the caste system*"

S Singh, Royal Prince Alfred Hospital
"*Factors responsible for creating a sense of Sikh identity*"

Theme: **Popular Hinduism**

G Oddie, University of Sydney
"*Aspects of hookswinging and firewalking in the Madras Presidency in the
nineteenth century*"

H Oberoi, Australian National University
"*The Sakhi Sarwar cult in the Punjab (1850–1900): Some implications in
the study of popular religion*"

M McLean, University of Otago
"*Ramprasad Sen: Sources for a biography*"

Scialpi, University of Rome
"*Introduced culture and national identity in Hindu religious feasts*"

Theme: **Yoga and Vedanta**

J Bader, University of Melbourne
"*Sankara's Yoga and Sankara's Vedanta: A re-examination*"

P Connolly, West Sussex Institute of Higher Learning
"*Some critical comments on Vyasa's interpretation of selected Yoga Sutras*"

Theme: **Miscellaneous Indian Religion**

M Mehta, University of Windsor
"*Dharma and moksha in Indian religion*"

K Bhattacharya, Centre Nationale de la Recherche Scientifique
"*The heretic's attitude toward the Veda*"

Paul Morris
"*The thought of K C Bhattacharya*"

INDONESIA AND SOUTH-EAST ASIA

Co-ordinator: Dr George Quinn, University of Sydney

Theme: **The Shape of Hinduism in Indonesia and Malaysia**

A Vickers, University of Sydney
"*The Hindu Balinese encounter with Islam*"

Singaravelu, University of Malaya
"*Some aspects of syncretism between Hindu religious belief and
the indigenous Malay folk-belief in peninsular Malaysia*"

Theme: **Politics, Practice and Symbol in Javanese Mysticism**

P Stange, Murdoch University
"*The politics of mysticism in Indonesia*"

J Howell, Griffith University
   *"Shamanism and salvation: Perspectives on religious evolution
   from South-East Asian cases"*

ISLAM

Co-ordinator: Dr Ahmad Shboul, University of Sydney

Theme: **Classical Islamic Thought**

A Hamdani, University of Wisconsin-Milwaukee
   "Theology of the Brethren of Purity and its time"
E Nakamura, University of Tokyo
   "An approach to Ghazali's conversion"

Theme: **Women's Identity in Islamic Society**

M Hermansen, San Diego State University
   "Female identity in Ibn Sa^cd's 'Kitab al-Tabaqat al-Kubra' "
H Begum, University of Dacca
   "Moral code for women: An egalitarian analysis"

Theme: **Islamic and Eastern Christianity**

A Shboul, University of Sydney
   "The religious dimension in the Arab-Byzantine encounter"

Theme: **Islamic Reform and Islamic Identity Today**

J Waardenburg, University of Utrecht
   "Aspects of Islamic identity: Reform movements reconsidered"
W Shepard, University of Canterbury
   "Islamic identity in the modern world: Five ideological orientations"

Theme: **Islam Today**

J Nevo, University of Haifa
   "Religion and national identity in Saudi Arabia"
E Waugh, University of Alberta
   "The Munshidin: The mystical singers of Egypt"

Theme: **Islam Today — India and Pakistan**

M Hedayetullah, Vanier College
   "Role of Islam in the creation of Pakistan and after"
C Ernst, Pomona College
   "Islam in India according to Azad Bilgrami"

Theme: **Islam in the World Today**

Y Jin, Chinese Academy of Social Science
   "Islamic schools in China"
A Nanji, Oklahoma State University
   "The Ismaili Muslim identity and changing contexts"

P Johnstone, Oxford University
   "Millet or minority — Muslims in Britain"
P Antes, University of Hannover
   "Islamic identity and the Turks in West Germany"
Three papers were added to the program.
They were by Drs Oxtoby, Rizvi, Said.

JUDAISM

Co-ordinator: Dr Alan Crown, University of Sydney

J Neusner, Brown University
   "Religious affections in formative Judaism"
E-M Laperrousaz, Ecole Pratique des Hautes-Etudes à la Sorbonne
   "La 'Guerre Sainte' dans les Manuscrits de la mer Morte"
   (read in the absence of the author by Barbara Thiering)
S Schmida, Tel-Aviv University
   *"The role of Judaism in reforming and maintaining Jewish national
   identity during the first decades after 70 CE"*
M Lubetski, City University of New York
   "SM as a deity"
R Pummer, University of Ottawa
   "The Samaritan liturgy today"
A Crown, University of Sydney
   "Samaritan religion in the fourth century"
W Gao, Chinese Academy of Social Science
   "On the history of Judaism in China"
R Ahroni, Ohio State University
   "The concept of sainthood in Yemen"
R Gaffin, University of Natal
   *"The 'Akeda' (binding of Isaac) as reflection of Judeo-Christian religions
   and history"*
M Samra, Syracuse University
   "Naming patterns amongst Jews of Iraqi origin in Sydney"

LITERATURE AND RELIGION

Co-ordinator: Professor James Tulip, University of Sydney

D Pollack, University of Rochester
   *"The religious contexts of language and the problem of self-identity in
   Yukio Mishima's novel 'Kinkakuji'"*
T Tennuissen, University of Manitoba
   "The fiction of Walker Percy: The American version of 'The Man Who Died'"
E Hinz, University of Manitoba
   "The religious roots of the feminine identity issue"
J Tulip, The University of Sydney
   "Australian poetry, religion and culture: The question of identity"

N Chaney, Otterbein College
"Alastair MacIntyre's 'After Virtue': On the quest for personal identity"

R Lacey, Institute of Catholic Education
"Inventing a history: At work with religious 'life narratives' in Australia"

L Robinson, Macquarie University
"Images of Christianity in the fiction of China and Japan"

R Ross, Southern Methodist University
"The emerging myth: Partition in the Indian and Pakistani novel"

C Runcie, University of Sydney
"Matthew Arnold's Christ"

D Atkinson, University of Lethbridge
"Dogmatism, doubt and dialectic: The religious views of Arthur Hugh Clough"

B Colless, Massey University
"The Syriac Song of the Pearl as Christian allegory"

C Kroeger, University of Minnesota
"Antiope as salvation figure, mediatrix and justifier of Zeus"

METHODOLOGY AND HERMENEUTICS
Co-ordinator: Dr Don Wiebe, University of Toronto

Theme: **Sexism, Identity and the Study of Religion**

U King, University of Leeds
"Female identity and the history of religions: a critique of some classical and contemporary approaches to the study of religion"

Theme: **Religiousness, Religious Identity and the Study of Religion**

H Seiwert, University of Hannover
"The identity of a religion"

J Waardenburg, University of Utrecht
"Scholarly hermeneutics in the study of religion: Some observations and proposals"

Theme: **New Directions in Theory and Method**

E Perry, Northwestern University
"The perennial problem of normative religious outlooks and the research of religions"

E Sharpe, University of Sydney
"Dual citizenship: The study of religion and the problem of religious identity"

N Smart, Universities of Lancaster and California
"Identity and a dynamic phenomenology of religion"

H Coward, University of Calgary
"Phenomenology and religious studies: Past experiences and future possibilities"

K Rudolph, University of California
"History of religions (Religionswissenschaft) between philosophy and theology: A challenge of understanding and explanation"

C Vernoff, Cornell College of Iowa
"Worldview: The foundational category of religiology"

M Prozesky, University of Natal
"Explanations of religion as a part of and problem for religious studies"
Under this theme *two panels* were also held.
Discussants included N Smart, H Coward, E Perry, E Sharpe, J Neusner,
D Wiebe and C Vernoff

Theme: **Explanation, the Social Sciences and the Study of Religion**

T Lawson, Western Michigan University
"Explanation and interpretation: Some unfinished business"

R Segal, Louisiana State University
"Have the social sciences been converted to the history of religions?"

Theme: **Sound, Light and Language: Some Methodological Implications
for the Study of Religion**

F Staal, University of California
"The sound of religion"

L Sullivan, University of Missouri-Columbia
"The hermeneutics of performance"

Theme: **The Study of Religion and the Hermeneutic Enterprise**

C Prado, Queen's University
"Analysis, hermeneutics and religiousness"

F Streng, Southern Methodist University
"Understanding religious life as processes of valuation"

L Leertouwer, University of Leyden
A brief report on *"Ritual and Identity"*

Theme: **Religion and Hermeneutics: Habermas and Ricoeur**

D Daye, Bowling Green State University
*"Buddhist hermeneutics and Habermasian rationality: A case study in
cross-cultural philosophy of religion"*

E White, University of Sydney
"Tensions in Paul Ricoeur's hermeneutics of the sacred"

NEAR EASTERN AND MEDITERRANEAN ANTIQUITY

Co-ordinators: Dr W J Jobling, University of Sydney

Professor E J Sharpe, University of Sydney

J Bergman, Uppsala University
*"Evidence of female identity of dead women in Egypt during the
Graeco-Roman period"*

G Tanner, University of Newcastle
"Apollo: past problems and continuing relevance"

G Horsley, Macquarie University
"Name changes as an indication of religious conversion"

R Doran, Amherst College
*"One revolt, two legitimations: A study of the symbolism of I and II
Maccabees"*

R Block, Ecole Practique des Hautes Etudes
  "Le peuple étrusque et sa religion"

E Conrad, University of Queensland
  "The annunciation of birth and the birth of the Messiah"

M H Pope, Yale University
  "Rephaim and Marzeah"

J Leclant, Institut de France
  "Recherches sur les textes des pyramides et les pyramides à textes de Saqarah"

Majella Franzmann, Pius XII Seminary and McAuley College, Brisbane
  "Odes of Solomon"

E Newing, Macquarie University
  "The 'send-up' of Solomon in I Kings 2:12-11:40. An example of ancient rhetorical technique"

I Chirassi-Colombo, University of Trieste
  "Identification and margin: The role of the entheoi, the God-possessed, in the Greek city state. A historico-religious comment to Aristotle's 'Problemata Physica XXX'"

J J Scullion, United Faculty of Theology, Melbourne
  "Can we speak of the (or a) religion of the Patriarchs?"

L H Martin, University of Vermont
  "Technologies of the self and self-knowledge in the Syrian Thomas tradition"

S Pickering, Macquarie University
  "Some papyri preserving liturgical and prayer texts"

W J Jobling, University of Sydney
  "Popular devotion to Dushares: New epigraphic evidence"

F Andersen, University of Queensland
  "Computer-assisted studies in the language of the Hebrew Bible: the vocabulary of the Book of Job"

A B Knapp, University of Sydney
  "Copper production and divine protection on bronze age Cyprus: an archeological analysis"

PHILOSOPHY OF RELIGION

Co-ordinator: Dr David Dockrill, University of Newcastle

R Laura, University of Newcastle
  "Towards a new theology of transcendence"

D Schlitt, Université Saint-Paul
  "Hegel on religion and identity"

A Khan, University of Toronto
  "Kierkegaard's two forms of conscious despair"

K-M Wu, University of Wisconsin-Oshkosh
  "Spontaneity and self-identity — a taoist perspective"

P Donovan, Massey University
  "Do different religions share a moral common ground?"

R Gascoigne, Catholic College of Education
  "God and objective moral values"

P Burke, Temple University
  "*Theism and human values*"

R Franklin, University of New England
  "*Evil and faith*"

D Wiebe, University of Toronto
  "*The prelogical mentality revisited*"

M Leahy, University of Newcastle
  "*Religious education in a democracy*"

N Coleman, University of Newcastle
  "*Preliminary sketch for a theory of universalism*"

N Nielsen, Rice University
  "*Fundamentalism as a crosscultural phenomena*"

PSYCHOLOGY OF RELIGION

Co-ordinator: Dr Richard Hutch, University of Queensland

Theme: **The Psychology of Religious Expression**

C MacLeod-Morgan, University of Adelaide
  "*Quantifying the unspeakable: The incidence of numinous experience in an Australian university sample*"

P Nelson, University of Queensland
  "*Why study religious experience?*"

D Bengtson, Southern Illinois University
  "*Personal and cultural identity: Changing patterns in American religion since World War II*"
  (*Respondent*: Philip Almond, University of Queensland)

Theme: **The Universality of Symbols**

A Cunningham, University of Lancaster
  "*The identity of symbols: Jung's psychology and the history of religions*"
  (*Respondent*: D Bengtson, Southern Illinois University)

Theme: **The Psychology of Religious Leadership**

Richard Hutch, University of Queensland, and
D. Klass, Webster University
  "*Charisma and contemporary culture: Elisabeth Kübler-Ross and popular piety*"

B Hyman, York University
  "*The psychology of messianic allegiance*"

Theme: **Identity, Continuity and Change**

J Szmyd, Cracow School of Education
  "*Attitude towards tradition and religiosity: Some psychological aspects of identity process*"

J Dourley, Carleton University
  "*Personal and collective identity: The religious implications of the self in the psychology of C G Jung*"

Theme: **Cross-Cultural Psychological Methods**

Richard Hutch, University of Queensland
"Comparative biography: A methodological focus for the academic study of religion"
(*Respondent:* B Hyman, York University)

Theme: **Western Psychology Headed Eastward**

Peter Bishop, South Australian College of Advanced Education
"An ecological identity: The life and work of Francis Younghusband, mystic and explorer"
(*Respondent:* S Gopalan, National University of Singapore)

Theme: **Eastern Psychology Headed Westward**

S Gopalan, National University of Singapore
"Yoga theory of personality: An interpretation"
(*Respondent:* Peter Bishop, South Australian College)

Robert Smith, Trenton State College
"Readings of Memories, Dreams, Reflections: Daimons and Creativity in C G Jung" (read by John Noack)
(*Respondent:* John Dourley, Carleton University)

Hetty Zock, University of Leydon
"The role of modern man in Erickson's theory of religion"

RELIGION, ETHICS AND SOCIETY
Co-ordinator: Dr David Coffey, St Patrick's College, Australia

Theme: **Particular Ethical Questions**

D Ardagh
"Aquinas and 'Humanae Vitae'"

G Weckman, Ohio University
"Religious guidance in the allocation of medical resources"

S Sargent, University of Wisconsin-Oshkosh
"Religious books in public libraries: Questions and basic principles"

Theme: **General Ethical Questions**

J Horne, University of Waterloo
"Destiny, morality and identity in the thought of J H Newman"

Sumana Siri, Buddhist Realists' Centre
"Universal ethics in the making: A Buddhist speculation"

Theme: **Australian Questions**

B Kaye, University of New South Wales
"Christianity and multi-culturalism in Australia"

A Gabay, La Trobe University
"Alfred Deakin, God and Federation"

APAURUSEYA PANEL

Co-ordinators: Dr G Bailey, La Trobe University

Dr R Barz, Australian National University

P Bilimoria, Deakin University
"Mimamsa on apauruseya"

G Chemparathy, University of Utrecht
"Three cardinal theses of the Nyaya-Vaisesikas concerning the validity of the Veda"

H Coward, University of Calgary
(Title not supplied)

B Gupta, University of Missouri
"In what sense is scripture preterhuman (apauruseya) in the Samkhya-Yoga tradition"

K Sivaraman, McMaster University
"Theistic re-orientation of the 'trans-personal' nature of revelation (apauruseya) in Saiva thought"

N Smart, Universities of Lancaster and California
"Some remarks on apauruseya sruti"

BHAGAVADGITA SYMPOSIUM

Co-ordinator: Dr Arvind Sharma, University of Sydney

This symposium was co-sponsored by
The Society of Asian and Comparative Philosophy (North America) and
The Asian and Comparative Philosophy Caucus (Australia)

E J Sharpe, University of Sydney
"Western Images of the Bhagavadgita, 1885–1985"

P Bilimoria, Deakin University
"Mohammad Iqbal and the Gita"

S Gopalan, National University of Singapore
"The concept of duty in the Bhagavadgita: An analysis"

P Munschenk, Western illinois University
"The psychology of the Bhagavadgita: Non-attachment in the modern world"

B Miller, Barnard College
"The Bhagavadgita and the Gitagovinda: Textual and contextual parallels"

P Jash, Visva-Bharati University
"The Bhagavadgita in historical perspective"

U King, University of Leeds
"Images of the Bhagavadgita in modern Hinduism"

SYMPOSIUM ON WOMEN AND RELIGION

Co-ordinator: Penny M McKibbin, South Australian College

This Symposium was included in the Congress Section: "Religion, Ethics and Society", and took place on Thursday August 22, 2:00—5:30p.m.

For whatever reason, this Symposium had not been included in the Congress Program Book. It took place in any case and attracted some one hundred persons. It featured four women speakers, each from a different religious tradition: Judaism, Hinduism, Christianity and Islam. These women were:

Peta Jones Palach of the Women's International Zionist Organization;

Jyoti Thaakur, a Gujerati Hindu from the Ethnic Affairs Commission;

Marie Tulip from the Commission on the Status of Women in the Australian Council of Churches and the National Women's Consultative Council; and

Aziza Abdel Haleem, spokesperson for Muslim women on the Executive of the Islamic Council of Southeast Asia and the Pacific.

A Response was given by Dr **Hester Eisenstein** and this was followed by an Open Forum. (Two Aboriginal women, chosen by their Sydney community to speak about women in Aboriginal Christianity, were finally unable to appear.)

4. LIST OF PARTICIPANTS — WITH ADDRESSES

The 15th IAHR Congress, Sydney, 1985

(Addresses are those recorded at the time of Congress)

Adam, Mrs. Enid L., 13 Daniel Street, Attadale, 6156. Australia.

Adams, Dr. Evyn M., Humanities, University of Hawaii, Hilo, H1 96720. U.S.A.

Adegbite, Dr. A., Music, University of Ife, ILE-IFE, Nigeria.

Agnew, Dr. Mary B., St. Francis Xavier Seminary, 101 Morialta Road, Rostrevor, 5073. Australia.

Ahern, Sister Clare, C/- P.O. Box 58, South Perth, 6151. Australia.

Ahlback, Dr. Tore, The Donner Institute, POB 70, SF-20501 ABO, Finland.

Ahroni, Dr. Rueben, 3503 Liv-Moor Drive, Columbus, OH 43227, U.S.A.

Aidid, H., Sydney, Australia.

Aidun, Mrs. Gol, 5 Hemlock Crescent, Brandon, Manitoba, Canada R7B 021.

Allen, Professor Michael R., Anthropology, University of Sydney, N.S.W. 2006. Australia.

Almond, Dr. Philip C., Studies in Religion, University of Queensland, St. Lucia, 4067. Australia.

Althorp, Mr. John A., Kingston College of TAFE, Majors Road, O'Halloran Hill, 5158. Australia.

Alton, Professor Bruce S., Trinity College, Toronto, Ontario, Canada M5S 1H8.

Andersen, Professor Francis I., Studies in Religion, University of Queensland, St. Lucia, 4067. Australia.

Antes, Mrs. Monika, Bismarckstrasse 2, D-3000 Hannover 1, West Germany.

Antes, Professor Dr. Peter, Bismarckstrasse 2, D-3000 Hannover 1, West Germany.

Apostolos-Cappadona, Dr. Diane, Religion, George Washington University, Washington, DC 20052. U.S.A.

Ardagh, Dr. David W., 45 Wilks Avenue, Wagga Wagga, 2650. Australia.

Atkinson, Dr. David W., Religious Studies, The University of Lethbridge, Lethbridge, Alberta, Canada T1K 3M4.

Awolalu, Rev. Canon Prof. J. O., Religious Studies, University of Ibadan, Ibadan, Nigeria.

Babbage, Dr. Stuart B., Australian College of Theology, 6/388 Anzac Parade, Kingsford, 2032, Australia.

Bader, Mr. Jonathan, Indian & Indonesian Studies, University of Melbourne, Parkville, 3052. Australia.

Bailey, Dr. Greg M., History, La Trobe University, Bundoora, 3083. Australia.

Bartley, Dr. Christopher J., Philosophy, La Trobe University, Bundoora, 3083. Australia.

Barz, Dr. Richard K., Asian Studies, A.N.U., GPO Box 4, Canberra A.C.T. 2600. Australia.

Bathgate, Dr. David T., 17 George Street, East Melbourne, 3002. Australia.

Battestini, Dr. Simon P., 1416 Hopkins Street NW 14, Washington, DC 20036, U.S.A.

Bazeley, Miss Joan A., 47 Leura Grove, Hawthorn, Vic. 3122. Australia.

Beach, Ruth, Religious Studies, University of Sydney, N.S.W. 2006. Australia.

Begum, Dr. Hasna, 524 Dhanmondi R/A, Road No. 8 (Old), Dhaka-5, Bangladesh.

Bengtson, Dr. Dale R., Religious Studies, Southern Illinois University, Carbondale, IL 62901. U.S.A.

Bergman, Professor Jan, Pumpg. 2, S-58252 Linkoping, Sweden.

Berner, Dr. Ulrich, In Der Spitze 26, 34 Gottingen, West Germany.

Bianchi, Professor Ugo, Via Principe Amedeo 75, Roma 1-00185, Italy.

Bilaniuk, Professor Dr. Petro, Theology & Religious Studies, University of St. Michael's College, Toronto, Ontario, Canada M5S 1J4.

Bilimoria, Dr. Purusottama, Humanities, Deakin University, Vic. 3217. Australia.

Bishop, Dr. Peter D., Humanities, Brighton Polytechnic, Brighton BN1 9PH, U.K.

Bishop, Mr. Peter R., S.A.C.A.E., Lorne Avenue, Magill, 5072. Australia.

Bloch, Professor Raymond, Rue Emile Faguet 12, 75014 Paris, France.

Booth, Mrs. Mary Lou, Religion, Miami University, Oxford, OH 45056, U.S.A.

Booth, Dr. Newell S., Religion, Miami University, Oxford, OH 45056, U.S.A.

Bouma, Dr. Gary D., Anthropology & Sociology, Monash University, Clayton, 3168. Australia.

Bradley, Professor David G., Religion, Duke University, Durham, NC 27706, U.S.A.

Bradley, Mrs. Lorene G., Religion, Duke University, Durham, NC 27706, U.S.A.

Brent, Dr. Allen, History, James Cook University, Townsville, 4811. Australia.

Brown, Mrs. Anne de Laval, Philosophy & Religious Studies, University of Canterbury, Christchurch, New Zealand.

Brown, Mr. Colin G., Religious Studies, University of Canterbury, Christchurch, New Zealand.

Brown, Miss Wendy E., 2/19 Collins Street, West Preston, 3072. Australia.

Buchholz, Dr. Peter, German, University of South Africa, Box 392, Pretoria 0001, South Africa.

Buchner, Mr. Johannes, 24 Chetwynd Road, Merrylands, 2160. Australia.

Bucknell, Mr. Roderick S., Studies in Religion, University of Queensland, St. Lucia, 4067. Australia.

Burke, Professor T. Patrick, 3246 Pebblewood Drive, Dresher, PA 19025, U.S.A.

Burkle, Professor Dr. Horst W., Institut fur Religionswissenschaft, Schellingstr, 3/IV VG, 0-8000 Munchen 40, West Germany.

Cahill, Mr. Anthony E., History, University of Sydney, N.S.W. 2006. Australia.

Cairns, Dr. Hugh, University of Sydney, N.S.W. 2006. Australia.

Campbell, Dr. E. Kay, Westhill College, Wedley Park Road, Birmingham, B29 6LL. U.K.

Campbell, Dr. William S., Westhill College, Wedley Park Road, Birmingham B29 6LL. U.K.

Carozzi, Dr. Pier A., Via Grassi 1/C9, 20052 Monza (Milano), Italy.

Carrigan, Miss Brigid, 1/252, New South Head Road, Double Bay, 2028. Australia.

Chagnon, Professor Roland, Universite du Quebec a Montreal, CP 8888 SUCC 'A', Montreal, Quebec, Canada, H3C 3P8.

Chambers, Dr. Ross C., Humanities & Social Sciences, R.M.I.H.E., Box 588, Wagga Wagga, 2650. Australia.

Chaney, Dr. Norman R., Otterbein College, Westerville, Ohio, 43081, U.S.A.

Chemparathy, Professor Dr. George, Zevenwouden 88, 3524 CV Utrecht, The Netherlands.

Ching, Professor Julia, Trinity College, Toronto, Ontario, Canada M5S 1A1.

Chirassi-Colombo, Professor Ileana, Via D1, Basovizza 17, (Opicina) Trieste, Italy.

Christmas, Mrs. Rosemary, 46 Gordon Street, Clontarf, 2093. Australia.

Clancy, C. Sydney. Australia.

Clegg, John, Anthropology, University of Sydney, N.S.W. 2006. Australia.

Coffey, Dr. David M., St. Patrick's College, Manly, 2095. Australia.

Coleman, Mr. Nicholas G., 1/147A, Lawson Street, Hamilton, 2303, Australia.

Colless, Dr. Brian E., Religious Studies, Massey University, Palmerston North, New Zealand.

Compton, Margaret, 10 Lilley Street, Hendra, 4011, Australia.

Connolly, Mr. Peter, West Sussex Institute of Higher Education, Chichester, West Sussex P019 4PE, U.K.

Conrad, Dr. Edgar W., Studies in Religion, University of Queensland, St. Lucia, 4067. Australia.

Cooper, Mr. John, 20B Barons Crescent, Gladesville. Australia.

Couture, Professor Andre, 2215 Marie-Victorin, Sillery, Quebec, Canada, G1T 1J6.

Coward, Professor Harold G., Calgary Institute for the Humanities, University of Calgary, Calgary, Alberta, Canada T2N 1N4.

Crawford, Mr. David J., History, University of Sydney, N.S.W. 2006. Australia.

Crotty, Mrs. Marie T., 15 Lloyd Street, Hectorville, 5073. Australia.

Crotty, Dr. Robert B., 15 Lloyd Street, Hectorville, 5073. Australia.

Crown, Dr. Alan, Semitic Studies, University of Sydney, N.S.W. 2006. Australia.

Cunningham, Dr. Adrian, Religious Studies, University of Lancaster, Lancaster, LA1 4YG, England.

Davidson, Dr. John, University of Tasmania, Box 252C, G.P.O., Hobart, 7001. Australia.

Daye, Dr. Douglas D., International Programs, Bowling Green State University, Bowling Green, OH 43403. U.S.A.

Dempsey, Dr. Kenneth C., Sociology, La Trobe University, Bundoora, 3083. Australia.

Denley, Ms. Lucy H., 4 Bayley Street, Narrabundah, A.C.T. 2604. Australia.

Denyer, Rev. Edwin A., 62 Yowie Avenue, Caringbah, 2229. Australia.

Devalle, Susana, Asian History Centre, A.N.U., G.P.O. Box 4, Canberra, 2601. Australia.

Dobbin, Dr. Christine E., 9 Prell Place, Hackett, A.C.T. 2602. Australia.

Dobbin, Miss Linda F., 11 Bellamy Farm Road, West Pennant Hills, 2120. Australia.

Dockrill, Dr. David W., Philosophy, University of Newcastle, N.S.W. 2308. Australia.

Donovan, Dr. Peter J., Religious Studies, Massey University, Palmerston North. New Zealand.

Doran, Professor Robert, 169 Triangle Street, Amherst, MA 01002. U.S.A.

Dourley, Dr. John P., Religion, Carleton University, Ottawa, Ontario, Canada K1S 5B6.

Preez, Professor Jannie du, Theology, University of Stellenbosch, Stellenbosch, 7600. South Africa.

Duncan, Mrs. Betty K., Religious Studies, University of Otago, Dunedin. New Zealand.

Elsmore, Ms. Bronwyn M., 10 Rushton Avenue, Otumoetai, Tauranga. New Zealand.

Engelhart, Mrs. R. Monica, Tryffelgrand 7, S-12233 Enskede, Sweden.

English, Patricia, W.A.C.A.E., Pearson Street, Churchlands, 6018. Australia.

Etherington, Dr. Norman A., History, University of Adelaide, G.P.O. Box 498, Adelaide, 5001. Australia.

Fahey, Mr. Stephen J., 52 Clarendon Road, Stanmore, 2048. Australia.

Fenner, Dr. Peter, Religious Studies, Deakin University, Vic. 3127. Australia.

Fernhout, Dr. Reinder, Handelhof 86, 2402 GX Alphen A/D RIJN, The Netherlands.

Filloux, Miss Arlette, Anthropology, A.N.U., G.P.O. Box 4, Canberra, A.C.T. 2601. Australia.

Filoramo, Professor Giovanni, via Spallanzani 26, 10134 Torino, Italy.

Fitzwalter, Pauline E., St. Francis House, 110 Oxford Street, Darlinghurst, 2010. Australia.

Fletcher, Mrs. Elizabeth, St. Vincent's College, Rockwall Crescent, Potts Point, 2011. Australia.

Franklin, Professor Richard L., Philosophy, University of New England, Armidale, N.S.W. 2351. Australia.

Franzmann, Sister Majella M., Presentation Convent, Nudgee Road, Northgate, 4013. Australia.

Freeman, Mr. James, 66 Dagmar Street, Holland Park, 4121. Australia.

Frerichs, Professor Ernest S., Judaic Studies, Brown University, Providence, R1 02912, U.S.A.

Frerichs, Mrs. Sarah C., Judaic Studies, Brown University, Providence, R1 02912, U.S.A.

Gabay, Mr. Alfred J., Religious Studies, La Trobe University, Bundoora, 3083. Australia.

Gaffin, Mrs. Rina, Hebrew & Jewish Studies, University of Natal, Durban 4001. South Africa.

Galla, Dr. Amareswar, Prehistory & Anthropology, A.N.U., G.P.O. Box 4, Canberra, A.C.T. 2601. Australia.

Wangzhi, Professor Gao, Institute for Research on World Religion, Chinese Academy of Social Sciences, Beijing, China.

Garner, Dr. Mark, 47 Rankins Road, Kensington, 3031. Australia.

Gascoigne, Dr. Robert, 44 Poole Street, Kingsgrove, 2208. Australia.

Geertz, Mr. Armin W., History of Religions, Arhus University, DK-8000 Arhus C., Denmark.

Gesch, Dr. Patrick, Divine Word Institute, P.O. Box 483, Madang, Papua New Guinea.

Geyer, Mr. Peter G., 7/21 Glen Street, Hawthorn, 3122. Australia.

Gianotto, Dr. Claudio, Corso Vercelli 74, 10015 IVREA TO, Italy.

Gifford, Mr. Paul J., Religious Studies, University of Zimbabwe, Box MP167, Harare, Zimbabwe.

Golding, Mr. Bradley B., 645 Canterbury Road, Vermont, 3133. Australia.

Goosen, Dr. Gideon C., Catholic College of Education, 40 Edward Street, North Sydney, 2060. Australia.

Gopalan, Dr. Subramania, Philosophy, National University of Singapore, Kent Ridge, Singapore 0511.

Gosling, Dr. David, World Council of Churches, 150 Route de Ferney, 1211 Geneva 20, Switzerland.

Gotoh, Professor Koichiro, 923 Nishikoiso, OISO, Kanagawa Pref. Japan 255.

Goudswaard, Mrs. Dory, Beacon Hill Books, P.O. Box 163, Mitcham, 3132. Australia.

Goudswaard, Mr. Jos W., Beacon Hill Books, P.O. Box 163, Mitcham, 3132. Australia.

Greschat, Mrs. Elisabeth, Sybelstrasse 12, D-3550 Marburg, West Germany.

Greschat, Professor Dr. Hans-Jurgen, Sybelstrasse 12, D-3550 Marburg, West Germany.

Gross, Dr. Rita M., Philosophy & Religious Studies, UW-EA, Eau Claire, WI 54701, U.S.A.

Hackett, Ms. Rosalind, 1416 Hopkins Street #4, Washington, DC 20036, U.S.A.

Hall, Mr. Gerald, Holy Spirit College, P.O. Box 162, Corrimal, 2518. Australia.

Hallam, Professor Herbert E., History, University of Western Australia, Nedlands, W.A. 6009. Australia.

Hamdani, Professor Dr. Abbas H., History, University of Wisconsin-Milwaukee, P.O.B. Milwaukee, WI 53201. U.S.A.

Hamdani, Mrs. Zubeda, History, University of Wisconsin-Milwaukee, P.O.B. Milwaukee, WI 53201. U.S.A.

Hammond, Professor Phillip E., Religious Studies, University of Cálifornia, Santa Barbara, CA 93106. U.S.A.

Hammond, Professor Sandra N., 3788 Hope Terrace, Santa Barbara, CA 93110. U.S.A.

Hardjono, Miss Ratih, 55 Huntleys Point Road, Huntleys Point, 2111. Australia.

Harris, Dr. Chris, 243 Gladstone Road, Dutton Park, 4102. Australia.

Harrison, Dr. Paul, Philosophy & Religious Studies, University of Canterbury, Christchurch, New Zealand.

Hattori, Professor Sho-on, 43 Kitamachi, Hakari-Cho, Tsushima-Shi, Aichi-Ken 496, Japan.

Hayes, Dr. Victor C., 3 Sturtbrae Crescent, Bellevue Heights, 5050. Australia.

Hazelwood, Mrs. Elizabeth A., 11 Waterhouse Street, Curtin, A.C.T. 2605. Australia.

Hedayetullah, Mrs. Faridunnahar, Vanier College, 5160 Decarie Boulevard, Montreal, Quebec, Canada H3X 2H9.

Hedayetullah, Professor Muhammad, Vanier College, 5160 Decarie Boulevard, Montreal, Quebec, Canada H3X 2H9.

Henderson, Dr. John R., 1647 Bentana Way, Reston, Virginia 22090. U.S.A.

Hepworth, Rev. John A., St. Mark's College, 46 Pennington Terrace, North Adelaide, 5006. Australia.

Hermansen, Dr. Marcia K., 407 Dunvegan Drive, Waterloo, Ontario, Canada N2K 2C6.

Hind, Dr. Robert J., History, University of Sydney, N.S.W. 2006. Australia.

Hinz, Dr. Evelyn J., English, University of Manitoba, Winnipeg, Manitoba, Canada R3T 2N2.

Hodgson, Mrs. Janet, Religious Studies, University of Cape Town, Rondebosch 7700, South Africa.

Holm, Miss Jean, Religious Studies, Homerton College, Cambridge C82 2PH U.K.

Horne, Mrs. Jean G., Philosophy, University of Waterloo, Waterloo, Ontario, Canada N2L 3G1.

Horne, Professor James R., Philosophy, University of Waterloo, Waterloo, Ontario, Canada N2L 3G1.

Horsley, Mr. Gregory H., History, Philosophy & Politics, Macquarie University, North Ryde, 2113. Australia.

Hospital, Professor Clifford G., Religion, Queen's University, Kingston, Ontario, Canada K7L 3N6.

Howell, Dr. Julia D., Modern Asian Studies, Griffith University, Nathan, 4111. Australia.

Hoy, Dr. W. Ivan, Box 8348, Coral Gables, FLA 33124. U.S.A.

Hutch, Mrs. Glenda M., Studies in Religion, University of Queensland, St. Lucia, 4067. Australia.

Hutch, Dr. Richard A., Studies in Religion, University of Queensland, St. Lucia, 4067. Australia.

Hyman, Dr. Bron, 337 Palmerston Blvd., Apt.C, Toronto, Ontario, Canada M6G 2N5.

Ireland, Dr. Rowan H., Sociology, La Trobe University, Bundoora, 3083. Australia.

Irwin, Reverend James, 11A, Hikurangi Street, Whakatane. New Zealand.

Isichei, Elizabeth, Victoria University of Wellington, Wellington. New Zealand.

Jack, Professor Robert Ian, History, University of Sydney, N.S.W. 2006. Australia.

Jain, Professor Vimal P., B-1 University Teachers' Quarters, Saraswati Vihar, Jabalpur, 482001. India.

Jan, Professor Yun-Hua, Religious Studies, McMaster University, Hamilton, Ontario. Canada L85 4K1.

Jash, Dr. Pranabananda, Indology, Vidya-Bhavana, Santiniketan 731235. India.

Jayaraman, Dr. Raja, Sociology, University of New England, Armidale. 2351. Australia.

Jiang, Professor Paul, Chinese, Macquarie University, North Ryde, 2113. Australia.

Yijiu, Professor Jin, Institute for Research on World Religion, Chinese Academy of Social Sciences, Beijing. China.

Jobling, Dr. William J., Religious Studies, University of Sydney, N.S.W. 2006. Australia.

Johnson, Dr. R. Boyd, World Vision/South Pacific, P.O. Box 759, Chatswood. 2067. Australia.

Johnstone, Dr. Penelope, Oriental Institute, Pusey Lane, Oxford. U.K.

Jones, Mr. Simon N., 2/15 Mitchell Street, Hill End. 4101. Australia.

Jordan, Mr. Trevor L., Studies in Religion, University of Queensland, St. Lucia. 4067. Australia.

Jordens, Dr. Joseph, Asian Studies, A.N.U., G.P.O. Box 4, Canberra. A.C.T. 2601. Australia.

Kaldor, P.J., Sydney. Australia.

Kamata, Professor Jun-Ichi, 4-9-2 Koyama, Nerima-Ku, Tokyo. 176. Japan.

Kavumkal, Fr. Jacob, Divine Word Seminary, 22 Vida Street, Essendon. 3040. Australia.

Kawamura, Mr. Choji, 1-7-8 Azabudai, Minato-Ku, Tokyo. 106. Japan.

Kaye, Dr. Bruce N., New College, Anzac Parade, Kensington. 2033. Australia.

Khan, Dr. Abrahim H., 88 Sandown Avenue, Scarborough, Ontario. Canada M1N. 3W4.

Kiefer, Mrs. Maria, Religion, University of Leicester, Leicester LE1 7RH, U.K.

Kiernan, Professor James P., African Studies, University of Natal, Durban, 4001. South Africa.

Kihara, Professor Noriyasu, 1G1SU 53-17, Iizuka, Fukuoka, 820. Japan.

King, Professor Noel Q., Comparative Religion, University of California, Santa Cruz, CA 95064. U.S.A.

King, Dr. Ursula, Theology & Religious Studies, University of Leeds, Leeds LS2 9JT, U.K.

Kitagawa, Professor Joseph M., Divinity School, University of Chicago, Chicago, IL 60637. U.S.A.

Klaiman, Dr. Miriam H., Linguistics, La Trobe University, Bundoora, 3083. Australia.

Klimkeit, Professor Dr. Hans-J., Nelkenweg 23, 5308 Rheinbach, West Germany.

Knapp, Dr. A. Bernard, Archaeology, University of Sydney, N.S.W. 2006. Australia.

Knott, Dr. Kim, Theology & Religious Studies, University of Leeds, Leeds. LS2 9JT. U.K.

Kok, Dr. Hu Jin, 13 Starkey Street, Forestville, 2087. Australia.

Kolig, Dr. Erich, Anthropology, University of Otago, Dunedin, New Zealand.

Kolig, Mrs. Josefa N., Anthropology, University of Otago, Dunedin, New Zealand.

Kondos, Dr. Vivienne, Anthropology, University of Sydney, N.S.W. 2006. Australia.

Kroeger, Mrs. Catherine C., 1073 Stony Brook Road, Brewster, Mass 02631. U.S.A.

Kubo, Dr. Tsugunari, 1-7-8 Azabudai, Minato-Ku, Tokyo 106, Japan.

Kumar, Dr. Pramod, 1/24, Lincoln Street, Kensington Gardens, 5068. Australia.

Lacey, Dr. Roderic J., I.C.E. Ballarat Campus, P.O. Box 650, Ballarat, 3350. Australia.

LaFitte, Mr. Gabriel, 253 Booran Road, Glenhuntly, 3163. Australia.

LaFleche, Professor Guy, 30 Place Giroux, Laval, Quebec, Canada H7N 3J2.

Lam-Easton, Linda, Rel. Studies & Class. Lang., St. Lawrence University, Canton, NY 13617. U.S.A.

Langford, G. Sydney, Australia.

Lattke, Dr. Micahel, Studies in Religion, University of Queensland, St. Lucia, 4067. Australia.

Laura, Professor Ronald S., Education, The University of Newcastle, N.S.W. 2308. Australia.

Law, Sister Diana, St. Francis House, 110 Oxford Street, Darlinghurst, 2010. Australia.

Lawson, Professor E. Thomas, 121 Monroe Street, Kalamazoo, MI 49007. U.S.A.

Leahy, Mr. Michael T., 6 Roper Court, Gladstone Park, 3043. Australia.

Lease, Professor Gary, 333 Alamo Avenue, Santa Cruz, CA 95060, U.S.A.

Leclant, Professor Jean, 77 Rue Georges Lardennois, F-75019 Paris, France.

Leertouwer, Professor Dr. Lammert, 36 Rijnsburgerweg, 2333 AB Leiden, The Netherlands.

Lepper, Mr. Larry J., 9 Wattle Grove, Haungaraki, Wellington, New Zealand.

Loiskandl, Dr. Helmut, Anthropology & Sociology, University of Queensland, St. Lucia, 4067. Australia.

Loy, Dr. Allan W., 39 Finch Avenue, East Ryde, 2113. Australia.

Lubetski, Mrs. Edith, 1219 East 27th Street, Brooklyn, NY 11210. U.S.A.

Lubetski, Professor Meir, 1219 East 27th Street, Brooklyn, NY 11210. U.S.A.

Luscombe, Rev. Kenneth L., 14 Brighton Street, Flemington, 3031. Australia.

MacGinley, Sister Mary M., National Catholic Research Council, P.O. Box 98, Leichhardt, 2040. Australia.

Mackie, Ms. Sue, Box 114 Holme Building, University of Sydney, N.S.W. 2006. Australia.

MacLeod-Morgan, Dr. Crisetta, Psychology, University of Adelaide, G.P.O. Box 498, Adelaide, 5001. Australia.

Malone, Ms. Patricia A., Catholic College of Education, P.O. Box 968, Sydney, 2060. Australia.

Mansfield, Professor Bruce E., Deputy Vice-Chancellor, Macquarie University, North Ryde, 2113. Australia.

Mantovani, Dr. Ennio, The Melanesian Institute, P.O. Box 571, Goroka, EHP, Papua New Guinea.

Manus, Dr. Chris U., Religious Studies, University of Ife, ILE-IFE, Nigeria.

Martin, Professor J. Hilary, Graduate Theological Union, 2401 Ridge Road, Berkeley, CA 94709, U.S.A.

Martin, Professor Luther H., Religion, The University of Vermont, Burlington, VT 05405. U.S.A.

Masefield, Dr. Peter, Religious Studies, University of Sydney, N.S.W. 2006. Australia.

Mason, Dr. Michael C., 10 Majella Ct., Kew, 3101. Australia.

Maxwell, Mr. Patrick S., P.O. Box 10478, Scottsville, Maritzburg, 3209. South Africa.

May, Dr. John D'Arcy, The Melanesian Institute, P.O. Box 571, Goroka E.H.P., Papua New Guinea.

May-Klopp, Margareta, The Melanesian Institute, P.O. Box 571, Goroka E.H.P. Papua New Guinea.

McCairns, Mrs. Marie, Religious Studies, University of Sydney, N.S.W. 2006. Australia.

McCann, Mrs. Marie J., 14 Daymar Place, Castle Cove, 2069. Australia.

McKenzie, Dr. Peter R., Religion, University of Leicester, Leicester LE1 7RH, U.K.

McKenzie, Mrs. Renate, Religion, University of Leicester, Leicester LE1 7RH, U.K.

McKibbin, Penny, S.A.C.A.E., Holbrooks Road, Underdale, 5032. Australia.

McLean, Dr. Malcolm, Religious Studies, University of Otago, Box 56, Dunedin, New Zealand.

McLean, Rev. Peter, 65 Ormond Street, Kensington, 3031. Australia.

McLeod, Professor W. H., History, University of Otago, Dunedin, New Zealand.

Mehta, Professor Mahesh, Religious Studies, University of Windsor, Windsor, Ontario, Canada N9B 3P4.

Mickelsen, Mrs. Alvera, 1798 Venus Avenue, St. Paul, MN 55112. U.S.A.

Mickelsen, Dr. Berkeley, 1798 Venus Avenue, St. Paul, MN 55112. U.S.A.

Miller, Professor Barbara S., 175 Riverside Drive, New York, NY 10024. U.S.A.

Miller, Miss Gwenn A., 175 Riverside Drive, New York, NY 10024. U.S.A.

Mol, Professor Hans, Religious Studies, McMaster University, Hamilton, Ontario, Canada L8S 4K1.

Molesworth, Hugh, Religious Studies, University of Sydney, N.S.W. 2006. Australia.

Moore, Professor Albert C., Religious Studies, University of Otago, Dunedin, New Zealand.

Moore, Mrs. Alexa T., Religious Studies, University of Otago, Dunedin, New Zealand.

Moriarty, Sister Betty, 173 Royal Parade, Parkville, 3052. Australia.

Morris, Mr. Paul M., Religious Studies, University of Lancaster, Lancaster, U.K.

Morrison, Angela, A.T.C.I., P.O. Box 108, Balmain, 2041, Australia.

Munakata, Dr. Iwao, 17 Nakanocho Ichigaya, Shinjuku-Ku, Tokyo 162, Japan.

Munakata, Mrs. Masae, 17 Nakanocho Ichigaya, Shinjuku-Ku, Tokyo 162, Japan.

Mundschenk, Dr. Paul E., NEH Seminar, Pacific School of Religion, 1798 Scenic Avenue, Berkeley, CA 94709, U.S.A.

Nagashima, Dr. Takayuki, 32-11 Kumano-Cho, Itabashi-Ku, Tokyo, Japan.

Nagashima, Mrs. Yoshiko, 32-11 Kumano-Cho, Itabashi-Ku, Tokyo, Japan.

Nakamura, Professor Kojiro, 4-17-11, Shakujii-Mach, Nerima-Ku, Tokyo, Japan 177.

Nakazawa, Professor Hideo, Kokubun 2-4-5, 272 Ichikawa, Japan.

Nanji, Professor Azim A., Religious Studies, Oklahoma State University, Stillwater, OK 74078, U.S.A.

Naulty, Dr. Reginald A., Riverina CAE, P.O. Box 588, Wagga Wagga 2650. Australia.

Naylor, Miss B. Christina, 1 Reid Street, Lindfield 2070, Australia.

Nelson, Mr. Peter, 33 The Drive, Bardon, 4065. Australia.

Neusner, Professor Jacob, Judaic Studies, Brown University, Providence, R1 02912, U.S.A.

Neusner, Mrs. Suzanne, Judaic Studies, Brown University, Providence, R1 02912, U.S.A.

Nevo, Dr. Joseph, Middle East History, University of Haifa, Haifa 31999, Israel.

Newell, Professor William H., Anthropology, University of Sydney, N.S.W. 2006. Australia.

Newing, Dr. Edward G., P.O. Box 176, Roseville, 2069. Australia.

Nielsen, Professor Niels C., Religious Studies, Rice University, Houston, TX 77251, U.S..A

Nigosian, Dr. Solomon A., Religious Studies, University of Toronto, Toronto, Ontario, Canada M5S 1A1.

Noack, John F., 2 Devon Street, Eaglemont, 3084. Australia.

Norman, Mr. Richard D., 50 Rosebery Street, Fisher, A.C.T. 2611. Australia.

O'Donoghue, Mr. Michael T., SACAE, Holbrooks Road, Underdale. 5032. Australia.

O'Shea, Janey, MCauley College, P.O. Box 247, Everton Park, 4053. Australia.

Oakley, G., Sydney, Australia.

Oberoi, Mr. Harjot S., Asian Studies, A.N.U., G.P.O. Box 4, Canberra, A.C.T. 2601. Australia.

Oddie, Dr. Geoff, History, University of Sydney, N.S.W. 2006. Australia.

Oliphant, David G., 16 Newdegate Street, Deakin, A.C.T. 2602. Australia.

Olupona, Dr. Jacob K., Religious Studies, University of IFE, ILE-IFE, Nigeria.

Omond, Rev. Peter, St. Barnabas' Anglican Church, 86A Balwyn Road, Balwyn 3103. Australia.

Onibere, Dr. Simon G.A., Religious Studies, University of IFE, ILE-IFE, Nigeria.

Onken, Professor Michael O., School of Art, Southern Illinois University, Carbondale, IL, U.S.A.

Oosthuizen, Mrs. Connie, 2 Jamieson Drive, Westville, 3630. South Africa.

Oosthuizen, Professor Gerhardus C., 2 Jamieson Drive, Westville 3630. South Africa.

Oxtoby, Professor Willard G., Trinity College, Toronto, Ontario, Canada M5S 1A1.

Pannaci, M. Sydney, Australia.

Penrose, Ms. Lyn, 15 Baden Street, Coogee, 2034. Australia.

Pentikainen, Professor Juha, University of Helsinki, Luotsikatu 4 A 1, 00160 Helsinki 16, Finland.

Pernet, Dr. Henry, Chemin de la Teinture, CH-1141 Yens, Switzerland.

Perry, Professor Edmund, 2036 Ewing Avenue, Evanston, IL 60201, U.S.A.

Peters, Mr. Frederic H., P.O. Box 379, Armidale, 2350. Australia.

Pickering, Mr. Stuart R., History, Philosophy & Politics, MacQuarie University, North Ryde, 2113. Australia.

Pickles, Dr. Margaret, 126 Russell Street, Melbourne, 3000. Australia.

Pilgrim, Mrs. Neva S., Religion, Syracuse University, Syracuse, NY 13210. U.S.A.

Pilgrim, Dr. Richard B., Religion, Syracuse University, Syracuse, NY 13210, U.S.A.

Pillai, Mrs. G.P., Sydney, Australia.

Pillai-McGarry, Usha, Sydney, Australia.

Platt, Mr. Paul J., 16 Morris Street, Highgate Hill, 4101. Australia.

Platvoet, Dr. Jan G., Gildenring 52, 3981 JG Bunnik, The Netherlands.

Poirier, Professor Paul-Hubert, Theology, Universite Laval, Quebec, Canada G1K 7P4.

Pollack, Professor David, Foreign Languages, The University of Rochester, Rochester, NY 14627. U.S.A.

Poole, Angela J., 21 Dalmore Street, Ashgrove, 4060. Australia.

Pope, Mrs. Ingrid B., Graduate School, 1504A Yale Station, New Haven, CT 06520, U.S.A.

Pope, Professor Marvin H., Graduate School, 1504A Yale Station, New Haven, CT 06520 U.S.A.

Pouwer, Professor Jan, Heideparkseweg 402, 6532 Ta Nijmegen, The Netherlands.

Prado, Professor Carlos G., Philosophy, Queen's University, Kingston, Ontario, Canada K7L 3N6.

Pratapana, Hare Krishna Society, 112 Darlinghurst Road, Darlinghurst, 2010. Australia.

Pratt, Dr. G. Douglas, University of Waikato, Private Bag, Hamilton, New Zealand.

Preston, Ms. Carol A., 115 Mt. Keira Road, West Wollongong, 2500. Australia.

Prichard, Mrs. Anne, 10 Daymar Place, Castlecove, 2069. Australia.

Principe, Professor Walter H., University of Toronto, 59 Queen's Park Crescent East, Toronto, Ontario, Canada M5S 2C4.

Prozesky, Professor Martin H., Religious Studies, University of Natal, Box 375, Pietermaritzburg, 3200. South Africa.

Pummer, Mrs. Lucille, Religious Studies, University of Ottawa, Ottawa, Ontario, Canada K1N 6N5.

Pummer, Professor Reinhard, Religious Studies, University of Ottawa, Ottawa, Ontario, Canada K1N 6N5.

Pye, Professor Michael, Zur Hege 11, 3550 Marburg, West Germany.

Quinn, Dr. George, Indonesian & Malayan Studies, University of Sydney, N.S.W. 2006. Australia.

Ragavan, Mr. S., Sydney, Australia.

Ramisch, Professor Joseph G., Continuing Education, Carleton University, Ottawa, Ontario, Canada K1S 5B6.

Reat, Dr. N. Ross, Studies in Religion, University of Queensland, St. Lucia, 4067. Australia.

Reed, Vivien, Religious Studies, University of Sydney, N.S.W. 2006. Australia.

Rizvi, Dr. Saiyid, Asian History & Civilizations, A.N.U., G.P.O. Box 4, Canberra, 2601. Australia.

Robarts, The V. Rev. David O., The Deanery, 38 St. George's Terrace, Perth, 6000. Australia.

Roberts, Professor J. Deotis, 7 Appleby Court, Silver Spring, MD 20904. U.S.A.

Robinson, Dr. Lewis S., Modern Languages, MacQuarie University, North Ryde, 2113. Australia.

Rogers, Rev. Alan D., 4 Fossett Way, Wyke Regis, Weymouth DT4 9HD, U.K.

Rogers, Mrs. Betty A., 4 Fossett Way, Wyke Regis, Weymouth DT4 9HD, U.K.

Ross, Dr. Robert L., English, Southern Methodist University, Dallas, Texas 75275. U.S.A.

Rowe, Mr. Noel M., 137 Harrington Street, Sydney, 2000. Australia.

Rudolph, Mrs. Christa, Religious Studies, University of California, Santa Barbara, CA 93106. U.S.A.

Rudolph, Professor Dr. Kurt, Religious Studies, University of California, Santa Barbara, CA 93106. U.S.A.

Rule, Dr. Paul A., History, La Trobe University, Bundoora, 3083. Australia.

Runcie, Dr. Catherine A., English, University of Sydney, N.S.W. 2006. Australia.

Ryan, Sister Mary, National Catholic Research Council, P.O. Box 98, Leichhardt, 2040. Australia.

Ryanto, Rev. Dr. Paul, St. Paul's Seminary, 1 Roma Avenue, Kensington, 2033. Australia.

Samra, Mr. Myer, 237 Ramsay Street, Haberfield, 2045. Australia.

Samuel, Dr. Geoffrey B., Sociology, University of Newcastle, N.S.W. 2308. Australia.

Sargent, Professor Seymour H., Library Science, UW-Oshkosh, Oshkosh, WI 54901. U.S.A.

Sekar, Sashi, Hare Krishna Society, 112 Darlinghurst Road, Darlinghurst, 2010. Australia.

Sawyer, A., Sydney, Australia.

Sayeed, Professor S.M., Syed Manzil Rasala Road, Hyderabad (Sind), Pakistan.

Schimmel, Professor Annemarie, Lennestr.42, 5300 Bonn-1, West Germany.

Schlang, Mr. Stefan, Religious Studies, University of Otago, Dunedin, New Zealand.

Schlitt, Professor Dale M., Saint Paul University, 223 Main St., Ottawa, Ontario, Canada K1S 1C4.

Schmida, Amalia, 36 Beeri Street, Tel-Aviv 64233, Israel.

Schmida, Mirjam, 36 Beeri Street, Tel-Aviv 64233, Israel.

Schmida, Dr. Shmuel, 36 Beeri Street, Tel-Aviv 64233, Israel.

Schmidt, Julia, Bismarckstrasse 2, D-3000 Hannover 1, West Germany.

Scialpi, Professor Fabio, 3 Via A. Allegre, Rome 00196, Italy.

Scullion, Professor John J., Newman College, 887 Swanston Street, Parkville, 3052, Australia.

See, Jo, 45 Charteris Street, Paddington, 4064. Australia.

Segal, Professor Robert A., Philosophy, Louisiana State University, Baton Rouge, LA 70803. U.S.A.

Seiwert, Dr. Hubert, Kollenrodtstr. 16, D-3000 Hannover 1, West Germany.

Selover, Mr. Thomas W., Center for the Study of World Religions, 42 Francis Street, Cambridge, Mass. U.S.A.

Sharf, Professor Andrew, 68 Rosslyn Hill, London NW3 1ND U.K.

Sharma, Dr. Arvind, Religious Studies, University of Sydney, N.S.W. 2006. Australia.

Sharpe, Mrs. Birgitta, Religious Studies, University of Sydney, N.S.W. 2006. Australia.

Sharpe, Professor Eric J., Religious Studies, University of Sydney, N.S.W. 2006. Australia.

Shboul, Dr. Ahmad, Semitic Studies, University of Sydney, N.S.W. 2006. Australia.

Sheen, Dr. Juliet, N.S.W. Anti-Discrimination Board, 8 Bent Street, Sydney, 2000. Australia.

Shepard, Dr. William, Hartford Seminary, 77 Sherman Street, Hartford, CT 06105. U.S.A.

Siikala, Dr. Jukka, University of Helsinki, Franzeninkatu 13, SF-00500 Helsinki 50, Finland.

Sim, Mr. David C., Religious Studies, La Trobe University, Bundoora, 3083. Australia.

Singaravelu, Professor Dr. S., No. 5, Lorong 17/21G, Petaling Jaya, Malaysia.

Singh, Dr. Sardool, Kanematsu Laboratories, Missenden Road, Camperdown, 2050. Australia.

Sivaraman, Professor Krishna, Religious Studies, McMaster University, Hamilton, Ontario, Canada L8S 4K1.

Skruzny, Lilly, P.W.P.A., G.P.O. Box 195, Canberra, A.C.T. 2601. Australia.

Slater, Dean Peter, University of Toronto, 6 Hoskin Avenue, Toronto, Ontario, Canada M5S 1H8.

Smart, Mrs. Libushka, Religious Studies, University of California, Santa Barbara, CA 93106. U.S.A.

Smart, Professor Ninian, Religious Studies, University of California, Santa Barbara, CA 93106. U.S.A.

Smith, Professor H. Daniel, Religion, Syracuse University, Syracuse, NY 13210. U.S.A.

Snodgrass, Dr. Adrian, Religious Studies, University of Sydney, N.S.W. 2006. Australia.

Snodgrass, Mrs. Judith, Religious Studies, University of Sydney, N.S.W. 2006. Australia.

Soegito, Mr. Hardjodikoro, Area Studies, National Library of Australia, Canberra, 2600. Australia.

Soegito, Mrs. Ilse, Chief Librarian, S. & S.E. Asia National Library of Australia, Canberra, A.C.T. 2600. Australia.

Solomon, Mr. Mark, 4 Wentworth Street, Randwick, Australia.

Somerville, Rev. Ian K., 464 Old South Head Road, Rose Bay, 2029, Australia.

Staal, Professor Frits, 3253 Brunell Drive, Oakland, CA 94602. U.S.A.

Stange, Dr. Paul, Human Communication, Murdoch University, Murdoch, 6150. Australia.

Starkloff, Professor Dr. Carl F., Regis College, 15 St. Mary Street, Toronto, Ontario, Canada M4Y 2R5.

Stone, Mr. Greg, G.P.O. Box 1985R, Melbourne, 3001. Australia.

Streng, Mrs. Bette S., Religious Studies, Southern Methodist University, Dallas, Texas 75275. U.S.A.

Streng, Professor Frederick J., Religious Studies, Southern Methodist University, Dallas, Texas 75275. U.S.A.

Studds, Rev. William J., 38 Eureka Crescent, Sadleir, 2168. Australia.

Stutchbury, Elisabeth, Anthropology RSPACS., A.N.U., Box 4, Canberra, 2601. Australia.

Sullivan, Mrs. Lesley, Religious Studies, University of Missouri-Columbia, Columbia, MO 65211. U.S.A.

Sullivan, Professor Lawrence E., Religious Studies, University of Missouri-Columbia, Columbia, MO 65211. U.S.A.

Siri, Rev. Sumana, Buddhist Realists Centre, 59A, MK 13, Air Itam Road, Air Itam, Penang, Malaysia.

Swain, Tony, Australia.

Szmyd, Professor Dr. Jan S., ul. Majora 3m7, 31-422 Krakow, Poland.

Tamaru, Professor Noriyoshi, 5-3-4 Den-en-chofu, Otaku, 145 Tokyo, Japan.

Tanner, Professor Ronald G., Classics, University of Newcastle, N.S.W. 2308. Australia.

Templeman, Mr. David R., 145 The Boulevard, Ivanhoe 3079. Australia.

Teunissen, Professor John J., English, University of Manitoba, Winnipeg, Manitoba, Canada R3T 2N2.

Thiel-Horstmann, Professor Dr. Monika, Indologisches Seminar, Regina-Pacis-Weg 7, D-5300 Bonn, West Germany.

Thiering, Dr. Barbara E., School of Divinity, University of Sydney, N.S.W. 2006. Australia.

Thom, Catherine, Catholic College of Education, 179 Albert Road, Strathfield, 2135. Australia.

Titaley, Mr. John, Satya Wacana Christian University, JL. Diponegoro 54-58, Salatiga, Indonesia.

Tomlinson, Sister Margaret M., Catholic College of Education, 40 Edward Street, North Sydney, 2060. Australia.

Trompf, Professor Garry W., History, P.O. Box 320, The University, Papua New Guinea.

Tsui, Dr. Bartholomew, Religion, Chung Chi College, Shatin, N.T., Hong Kong.

Tulip, Professor James, English, University of Sydney, N.S.W. 2006. Australia.

Turner, Professor David H., Anthropology, University of Toronto, Toronto, Ontario, Canada M5S 1A1.

Usher, Rev. Geoffrey, 15 Francis Street, East Sydney, 2010. Australia.

Uzoigwe, Dr. Joshua, Music, University of IFE, ILE-IFE, Nigeria.

Van Beek, Dr. Walter E.A., Pr. Beatrixstraat 38, 3981 BK Bunnik, The Netherlands.

Van Fossen, Dr. Anthony B., Humanities, Griffith University, Nathan, 4111. Australia.

Van Lier, Mr. Henk, C/- Amro Bank, P.O. Box 2059, 3500 GB Utrecht, The Netherlands.

Vernoff, Professor Charles E., Cornell College of Iowa, Mt. Vernon, Iowa 52314, U.S.A.

Vertovec, Mr. Steven A., Penal Rock Road P.O., via San Fernando, Trinidad, W.I.

Vickers, Mr. Adrian H., Indonesian & Malayan Studies, University of Sydney, N.S.W. 2006. Australia.

Waardenburg, Professor Jacques, 375 Utrechtse WEG, 3818 NL EL Amersfoort, The Netherlands.

Waugh, Dr. Earle H., Religious Studies, University of Alberta, Edmonton, Alberta, Canada T6G 2E5.

Webber, Mr. Andrew J., 393 Liverpool Street, West Hobart, 7000. Australia.

Webber, Mr. Ian J., World Vision of Australia, G.P.O. Box 399C, Melbourne, 3001. Australia.

Weckman, Professor George, Gordy Hall, Ohio University, Athens, OH 45701. U.S.A.

Werblowsky, Professor R. J. Zwi, Comparative Religion, The Hebrew University, Jerusalem 91904, Israel.

Werblowsky-Wirz, Mrs. Alisa, Comparative Religion, The Hebrew University, Jerusalem 91904. Israel.

Werner, Dr. Karel, 32 Etchingham Park Road, London N3 2DT, U.K.

Wetherell, Dr. David F., Social Sciences, Deakin University, Vic. 3217. Australia.

Wettstein, Dr. A. Arnold, Religion, Rollins College, Winter Park, FL 32789. U.S.A.

White, Ms. Erin G., 9 Third Avenue, Eastwood, 2122. Australia.

Wiebe, Dr. Donald, Trinity College, Toronto, Ontario, Canada M5S 1H8.

Wiessner, Professor Dr. Gernot, Universitat Gottingen, Nikolausberger Weg 5B, D-3400 Gottingen, West Germany.

Williams, Dr. Alan V., 36 East Way, Lewes BN7 1NG, U.K.

Williams, Franci A., 29/10 Gow Street, Balmain, 2041. Australia.

Willis, Mr. Peter, Institute for Aboriginal Development, P.O. Box 1238, Alice Springs, N.T. 5750. Australia.

Wilson, Dr. Jim, Philosophy & Religious Studies, University of Canterbury, Christchurch, New Zealand.

Wright, Dr. John, St. John's College, Morpeth, 2321. Australia.

Wu, Professor Kuang-Ming, Philosophy, University of Wisconsin, Oshkosh, WI 54901. U.S.A.

Wu, Mrs. Wen-Yen, Philosophy, University of Wisconsin, Oshkosh, WI 54901. U.S.A.

Young, Dr. Katherine K., McGill University, 3520 University Street, Montreal, Quebec, Canada H3A 2A7.

Yuyama, Professor Dr. Akira, Hansastrasse 22, D-2000 Hamburg-13, West Germany.

Yuyama, Mrs. Hiroko, Hansastrasse 22, D-2000 Hamburg-13, West Germany.

Zipporah, Jenni-Bop, 45 Jones Street, Auchenflower, 4066. Australia.

Zock, Dr. Hetty, University of Leiden, Postbus 9515, 2300 Ra Leiden, The Netherlands.

5. IAHR (AND AASR) INFORMATION

The International Association for the History of Religions
Executive Board 1985-1990

Annemarie Schimmel Harvard University, USA *President*
E.M. Pye Marburg, West Germany Secretary-General
H.J. van Lier Utrecht, Netherlands *Hon. Treasurer*
Ugo Bianchi Rome, Italy *Vice-President*
R.J. Zwi Werblowsky Jerusalem, Israel *Vice-President*
J.O. Awolalu Ibadan, Nigeria
N. Tamaru Tokyo, Japan
Wytold Tyloch Warszawa, Poland
D. Wiebe Toronto, Canada
Peter Antes Hannover, West Germany

The Outgoing Executive Board (1980-1985)

Annemarie Schimmel *(President)*
U. Bianci *(Vice-President)*
J.M. Kitagawa *(Vice-President)*
R.J.Z. Werblowsky *(Secretary General)*
M. Pye *(Deputy Secretary General)*
H.J. Van Lier *(Honorary Treasurer)*
J.O. Awolalu
A. Hultkrantz
J. Ries
N. Tamaru
W. Tyloch

The Australian Association For The Study Of Religions

	Members of Executive Committee	
	1984-85	*1985-86*
President	Eric J. Sharpe	Robert C. Crotty
Vice-President	Richard Hutch	Ed Conrad
Secretary-Treasurer	Penelope McKibbin	Penelope McKibbin
Publications Editor	Victor C. Hayes	Victor C. Hayes
	A.H. Johns	E.J. Sharpe
	Ian Gillman	

(Note: Officers of the AASR may be contacted as follows:
Robert Crotty, South Australian College of Advanced Education (SACAE)—Salisbury Campus,
S.A.Australia 5109; Penny McKibbin, SACAE — Underdale Campus, S.A., Australia 5032; Victor Hayes,
SACAE — Sturt Campus, Bedford Pk., S.A., Australia 5042.)

The 1985 IAHR Congress Australian Planning Committee

Eric J. Sharpe   *Assistants:*
Peter Masefield   N. Hayes (Catering)
Rati Hardjono   H. Molesworth (Book Exhibition)
                        B. Marsden-Smedley (Accommodation)
                        M. Bolan (of Bolan Consulting)
                             (Special Computing Adviser)

The Constitution Of The International Association For The History Of Religions

As accepted and confirmed by the General Assembly of the IAHR at its XIIthInternational Congress held in Stockholm on August 22nd 1970 and amended by the General Assembly at the XIIIth International Congress held in Lancaster on August 22nd 1975.

ARTICLE 1

The International Association for the History of Religions (abbreviated, from its English title, to IAHR), founded in September 1950 on the occasion of the VIIth International History of Religions Congress, is a worldwide organization which has as its object the promotion of the academic study of the history of religions through the international collaboration of all scholars whose research has a bearing on the subject.

ARTICLE 2

The IAHR seeks to achieve this object:
(a) by holding regular international congresses and occasional symposia and colloquia;
(b) by publishing the proceedings of such congresses and meetings;
(c) by assisting the formation of national and regional associations of historians of religions;
(d) by encouraging and sponsoring publications of general interest to the study of the history of religions: e.g. an international review, bibliographical bulletins, monograph series;
(e) by taking all appropriate steps to encourage and further the academic study of the history of religions.

ARTICLE 3A

The IAHR is constituted by national or multi-national (regional) societies for the academic study of religions. These are such societies as are now members and such societies as apply for membership and, on recommendation of the Executive and International Committees (see below), may be admitted by the General Assembly at future International Congresses.

ARTICLE 3B

To the IAHR may be affiliated.
(a) International associations for the academic study of particular areas within the history of religions;
(b) Individual scholars for whom there is no appropriate national or regional society.
Affiliation is effected by the application to the Executive and International Committees and by approval of the General Assembly.

ARTICLE 4

The work of the IAHR is carried out through (a) the General Assembly; (b) the International Committee; and (c) the Executive Committee.

(a) The General Assembly of the Association meets at each international congress and is composed of all members of constituent societies of the association present at that congress. The General Assembly may take action only on matters referred to it from the International Committee, and it may refer any matter to the International or Executive Committees for consideration and report.

(b) The International Committee is composed of:
  (i)   Two representatives each of the constituent national and regional societies, except that there shall not be more than two representatives from any one country;
  (ii) The Executive Committee (see below);
  (iii) Up to four individual members co-opted by the International Committee on the recommendation of the Executive Committee;

(c) The Executive Committee is composed of a President, two Vice-Presidents, a General Secretary, a Treasurer, and five other members. The officers in particular, and the members of the Executive Committee in general, shall be chosen in such a way as reasonably to reflect various parts of the world where academic study of religion is pursued in its various disciplines. A Nominating Committee, appointed by the Executive Committee, shall submit nominations for the next Executive Committee to the members of the International Committee by mail not more than twelve months and not less than nine months prior to each international congress. Members of the International Committee may propose alternate nominations not less than one month prior to each international congress. The International Committee, at its meeting just preceding the General Assembly, shall elect the Executive Committee and shall report this to the General Assembly for endorsement. The members of the Executive Committee shall hold office for one quinquennial term each and be subject to re-election, but not more than two-thirds of the Committee shall be carried on from one term to the next, and no one member shall serve in the same office more than two terms. In the event of the death or resignation of any serving officer of the Association, a suitable replacement may be nominated after consultation among the remaining officials, and shall serve, subject to the written approval of a majority of members of the Executive Committee, until the next quinquennial congress.

ARTICLE 5

The Executive Committee, or at least the President, General Secretary and Treasurer of the Association shall, if possible, meet at least once a year for the transaction of such necessary business as may arise between congresses. The General Secretary shall circulate the minutes of such meetings to all members of the Executive Committee.

ARTICLE 6

The International Committee shall meet on the occasion of each congress, between the meeting of the Executive Committee and that of the General Assembly, and more often if necessary. It reports to the General Assembly.

ARTICLE 7

The resources of the IAHR consist of:
(a) annual contributions paid by the constituent societies, affiliated societies and individual members, the amount of which is assessed by the Executive Committee; and
(b) grants, donations and other sources of revenue.
An audited report will be submitted to the International Committee at every international congress.

ARTICLE 8
The Constitution may be modified only by the General Assembly on the recommendation of the International Committee.

NOTE ON MEMBERSHIP
A person is automatically a member of the International Association if that person belongs to one or another of the national organizations that constitute the International Association or, where no such national organization exists, that person has been awarded individual membership.

PREVIOUS CONGRESSES AND THEIR PROCEEDINGS
I. Paris 1900
Actes du premier Congrès international d'histoire des religions tenu à Paris du 3 au 8 Septembre 1900; procès-verbaux sommaires, par M. Jean Reville ... Paris, Imprimerie nationali, 1901, 02. 2pt.
pt. 1 Séances générales
pt. 2 Séances des sections, 3 fasc.
II. Basel 1904
Verhandlungen des II, Internationalen Kongresses für allgemeine Religionsgeschichte in Basel, 30, August bis 2, September 1904. Basel, Helbing and Lichtenhahn; (etc...) 1905, viii 382 p.
III. Oxford 1908
Transactions of the Third International Congress for the History of Religions, Oxford, The Clarendon Press, 1908, 2 vols.
IV. Leiden 1912
Actes du IVᵉ Congrès International d'Histoire des Religions tenu à Leide du 9-13 Septembre 1912, Leide, E.J. Brill, 1913, 172 p.
V. Lund 1929
Actes du Vᵉ Congrès International d'Histoire des Religions à Lund, 27-29 Août 1929. Lund, C.W.K. Gleerup (1930), 346 p.
VI. Brussels 1935
Mélanges, Franz Cumont, Université libre de Bruxelles, Annuaire de l'institut de philologie et d'histoire orientale et slaves, 1936, 2 vols. 2 vols. plates, etc.
VII. Amsterdam 1950
Proceedings of the VIIth International Congress for the History of Religions, Amsterdam, 4th-9th September 1950, Edited by C.J. Bleeker, G.W.J. Drewes (and) K.A.H. Hidding. Amsterdam, North-Holland Pub. Co., 1952, 193 p. (At this Congress the I.A.S.H.R., later I.A.H.R., was founded.)
VIII. Rome 1955
Atti dell'VIII Congresso Internazionale di Stori della Religioni, Roma, 17-23 aprile 1955, etc. Firenze, 1956, viii plus 499 p.
     The sacral Kingship; Contributions to the central theme of the VIIIth International Congress for the History of Religions. (Rome, April 1955) Leiden, Brill, 1959, (Studies in the history of religions, 4.), xv plus 748 p.
IX. Tokyo 1958
Proceedings of the IXth International Congress for the History of Religions, Tokyo and Kyoto, 1958. August 27th-September 9th, etc. Compiled by the Japanese Organising Committee for the IX I.C.H.R., Science Council of Japan (for the) International Association for the History of Religions, Tokyo, Maruzen, 1960, xiv plus 914 p.
X. Marburg 1960
X. Internationaler Kongress für Religionsgeschichte, 11-17 September 1960 in

Marburg/Lahn Herausgegeben vom Organisationsausschuss, Marburg, Kommissions-
verlag N.G. Elwert, 1961, 241 p.

XI. Claremont 1965
Proceedings of the XIth International Congress of the International Association for
the History of Religions held with the support of UNESCO and under the auspices
of the International Council for Philosophy and Humanistic Studies at Claremont,
California, September 6-11, 1965, Leiden, 1968, 3 vols.
Vol.I The Impact of Modern Culture on Traditional Religions
Vol.II Guilt or Pollution and Rites of Purification
Vol.III The Role of Historical Scholarship in changing the Relations among Religions

XII. Stockholm 1970
Proceedings of the XIIth International Congress of the International Association for
the History of Religions. Edited by C.J. Bleeker, G. Widengren (and) E.J. Sharpe,
Leiden, E.J. Brill, 1975, vii plus 350 p.

XIII. Lancaster 1975
History of Religions. Proceedings of the Thirteenth Congress of the International
Association for the History of Religions. Edited by Michael Pye and Peter McKenzie.
Leicester Studies in Religion II. Published by the Department of Religion, University
of Leicester. 188 p. (no date)

XIV. Winnipeg 1980
Traditions in Contact and Change. Selected Proceedings of the Fourteenth Congress
of the International Association for the History of Religions. Edited by Peter Slater
and Donald Wiebe. Waterloo, Canada: Wilfrid Laurier University Press, 1983. ix plus
788 p.

AASR BOOKS IN PRINT

Selected Papers:
Religious Experience in World Religions, Victor C. Hayes (ed.) 176p
Ways of Transcendence, Edwin Dowdy (ed.) 172p.

Special Studies in Religions:
Let Sleeping Snakes Lie: Central Enga Traditional Belief and Ritual, Paul Brennan.
64p.
Central Australian Religion: Personal Monototemism in a Polytotemic Community,
T.G.H. Strehlow. 64p.
Powers, Plumes and Piglets; Phenomena of Melanesian Religion, Norman C. Habel
(ed.) 234p.
An Introduction to Maori Religion: its character before European Contact and its
survival in contemporary Maori and New Zealand Culture, James Irwin. 86p.
Interpreting Aboriginal Religion (Investigating the Investigators), Tony Swain. 156p.

Major Bibliographies:
Religion in Australian Life: A Bibliography of Social Research, Michael Mason (ed.),
G. Fitzpatrick (compiler). 254p.
High Calling, High Stress: The Vocational Needs of Ministers, An Overview and
Bibliography, Robin J. Pryor. 126p.
All **Orders to Wakefield Press**, 282 Richmond Rd., Netley, S.A., Australia 5037.